WELSH TRADITIONAL MUSIC

Aberystwyth Market Day 1797

WELSH TRADITIONAL MUSIC

Phyllis Kinney

UNIVERSITY OF WALES PRESS
in association with
CYMDEITHAS ALAWON GWERIN CYMRU

© Phyllis Kinney, 2011
Reprinted (paperback), 2015

All rights reserved. No part of this book may be reproduced in any material form (including photocopying or storing it in any medium by electronic means and whether or not transiently or incidentally to some other use of this publication) without the written permission of the copyright owner except in accordance with the provisions of the Copyright, Designs and Patents Act 1988. Applications for the copyright owner's written permission to reproduce any part of this publication should be addressed to The University of Wales Press, 10 Columbus Walk, Brigantine Place, Cardiff, CF10 4UP.

www.uwp.co.uk

British Library Cataloguing-in-Publication Data
A catalogue record for this book is available from the British Library.

ISBN   978-1-78316-857-6
e-ISBN   978-1-78316-858-3

The right of Phyllis Kinney to be identified as author of this work has been asserted by her in accordance with sections 77, 78 and 79 of the Copyright, Designs and Patents Act 1988.

This book has been published with the assistance of Cymdeithas Alawon Gwerin Cymru.

Designed and typeset by Chris Bell, cbdesign

Printed by CPI Antony Rowe, Chippenham, Wiltshire

Foreword

*I*N A MODEL NATION, Phyllis Kinney, under the auspices of an enlightened foundation, would have spent much of the past forty years editing from manuscripts and from recordings the wealth of unpublished traditional music of her adopted country. Wales would have had available to all, with appropriate editorial apparatus, a worthy published corpus of her traditional music. That ideal remains a distant one. Instead, we can only be grateful that a long personal commitment on her part has led to a valuable range of publications – some by herself alone, some in collaboration with Meredydd Evans – which has made public part at least of the heritage of our traditional song and music, and which has greatly advanced our understanding of that tradition.

Phyllis Kinney came to Welsh music, as a trained musician, from the outside. Her knowledge of the sources – printed, manuscript and recorded – is unsurpassed. This book, the first comprehensive survey of the field since W. S. Gwynn Williams's *Welsh National Song and Dance* in 1932, presents a completely fresh appraisal of the material, from the end of the Middle Ages to the present day. In it we learn, for instance, of the few medieval tunes that survived into later instrumental tradition; of the songs in popular medieval metres that survived into the twentieth century in seasonal ritual songs; of the flood of new tunes in the sixteenth and seventeenth centuries that came in from England and elsewhere, entering the Welsh carol and ballad traditions, and how some of these survived in Wales, notably in association with the *plygain*, long after their disappearance from popular use in England (and we learn too of the extraordinary transmutation of some of the English titles into Welsh forms).

This is a work that distils the conclusions drawn by the author from her profound knowledge and long study of the music, and illuminates them with a selection of songs and tunes that is of unprecedented range and richness. It offers not only an authoritative survey of the subject but also a musical anthology that will provide pleasure as well as instruction to many of its readers.

Daniel Huws, May 2009

Acknowledgements

My first knowledge of Welsh folk-song came when I was a college student in Michigan many years ago. One of my lecturers was a Welshman, Gomer Ll. Jones, who taught me some Welsh songs, almost all from Brinley Richards's *The Songs of Wales* (London, 1873). That awakened my interest, and when I came to Britain some years later I was eager to find out more about Wales and its traditional music. I soon discovered that *Songs of Wales* was largely a selection of harp airs with English and Welsh words, and that the true nature of Welsh traditional music lay elsewhere.

As I began to search for books in English on this subject it became obvious that, until recently, musicologists (with the exception of Peter Crossley-Holland and Joan Rimmer) have paid only cursory attention to Welsh traditional music. They have to a great extent ignored the music, in most cases because they do not know the Welsh language, which is an important part of the song tradition. In 1932, W. S. Gwynn Williams published a general survey of the field in English, but much more research has been done since then. Although Welsh universities in general have shown little interest in the subject, some members of the School of Music at Bangor University, especially Sally Harper, Wyn Thomas and Stephen Rees, have written about aspects of Welsh traditional music that have become part of the university curriculum.

This book has been written in the hope that I can pass on to others my enthusiasm for these songs. I am deeply indebted to a number of people who have generously given of their time and effort to help me in the work. First and foremost is my husband, Meredydd Evans, a fine singer with a deep knowledge of Welsh folk-songs and the generosity to pass it on to others. Together, we have read and discussed every aspect of this book. My second reader was Daniel Huws, whose thoughtful advice has been of immense value. Both have saved me from numerous errors. I am especially grateful to D. Roy Saer, formerly of the National History Museum in St Fagans, who enabled me to listen to numerous field recordings of Welsh folk singers and patiently discussed singing styles.

Over the years, many people have contributed generously of their time and knowledge to the development of this book and I would like to thank, in particular, Robin Huw Bowen, Bethan Bryn, Aled Lloyd Davies, the late Hywel Teifi Edwards,

Acknowledgements

Rhidian Griffiths, Robin Gwyndaf, Rhiannon Ifans, Cass Meurig, Huw Walters and members of The Welsh Folk-Song Society and *Cymdeithas Cerdd Dant Cymru*. I also wish to thank Richard Lloyd for preparing the musical examples for publication. In addition, thanks must also go to the staff of the National Library of Wales, St Fagans: National History Museum, and the University of Wales Press. I am particularly indebted to the Welsh Folk-Song Society for their generous financial assistance in the production of this book. I am also deeply indebted to Dafydd Ifans for his meticulous work in compiling the indices. Finally, a very special 'thank you' to my daughter Eluned, who played an important part in the editing of the chapters and was instrumental in getting the book to the press.

Contents

Foreword		v
Acknowledgements		vii
List of illustrations		xi
Abbreviations		xiii
A note on the translation of Welsh terms and transcription of the musical examples		xv
Introduction: What is Traditional Music?		xvii
1	The Oral Tradition	1
2	The Watershed	17
3	Manuscript to Print	35
4	Edward Jones and Traditional Airs	57
5	Seasonal Festivities	71
6	Carols, Ballads and the *Anterliwt*	105
7	The Early Collectors: Iolo Morganwg and Ifor Ceri	127
8	The Great Change	157
9	The Momentum Continues	181
10	J. Lloyd Williams and the Welsh Folk-Song Society	203
Notes		229
Appendix 1	Cerdd Dant	241
Appendix 2	Printed Music Collections	247
Bibliography		251
Index		261
Index of Music		287

List of illustrations

Plate 1   An illustration of tablature taken from the Robert ap Huw MS (BL Add. MS 14905, *Musica*, p. 62). By permission of the British Library.

Plate 2   Psalm II, *Edmwnd Prys, Llyfr y Psalmau wedi eu cyfieithu a'i cyfansoddi ar fesur cerdd yn Gymraeg Drwy waith Edmwnd Prys Archdiacon Meirionnydd* (London, 1621). By permission of Llyfrgell Genedlaethol Cymru/The National Library of Wales.

Plate 3   Portrait of William Williams, 'Wil Penmorfa' (1759–1828). By permission of Amgueddfa Cymru/National Museum Wales.

Plate 4   The title page of *Antient British Music* with an inscription possibly in the hand of Richard Morris. BL Add. MS 14939. By permission of the British Library.

Plate 5   'Calon Drom' from *Antient British Music*, Part II, unpublished specimen (RCM MS 4681). By permission of the Royal College of Music, London.

Plate 6   'Triban Morganwg', an extract from the letter from William Jones, Llangadfan, to Edward Jones. NLW Add. MS 171E. By permission of Llyfrgell Genedlaethol Cymru/The National Library of Wales.

Plate 7   Illustration of the Llangynwyd *calennig* from the archive of St Fagans: National History Museum. The photograph was taken by Mr Frederick Evans. By permission of Amgueddfa Cymru/National Museum Wales.

Plate 8   The Holywell *Cadi* from the archive of St Fagans: National History Museum. The photograph was taken in 1939 by Mr T. P. Hayden. By permission of Amgueddfa Cymru/National Museum Wales.

Plate 9   Photograph of J. Lloyd Williams. By permission of *Cymdeithas Alawon Gwerin Cymru*/The Welsh Folk-Song Society.

List of illustrations

Example 2.2 'Cywydd deuair: Morganwg' as noted by Iolo Morganwg, NLW, Iolo A. Williams MSS, uncatalogued. By permission of Llyfrgell Genedlaethol Cymru/The National Library of Wales.

frontispiece: 'Aberystwyth Market Day 1797'. National Library of Wales Acc. No. MD8520. By permission of Llyfrgell Genedlaethol Cymru/The National Library of Wales.

Abbreviations

ABM	John Parry and Evan Williams, *Antient British Music* (London, 1742).
Airs	John Parry, *A Collection of Welsh, English and Scotch Airs* (London, 1761).
ANAGM	Maria Jane Williams, *Ancient National Airs of Gwent and Morganwg* (Llandovery, 1844). Reprinted by the Welsh Folk-Song Society with introduction and notes by Daniel Huws (1988).
Bardic Museum	Edward Jones, *The Bardic Museum* (London, 1802).
BBCS	*Bulletin of the Board of Celtic Studies*, 1921–93
Blodeu-gerdd Cymry	Dafydd Jones, *Blodeu-gerdd Cymry: Y Trydydd Argraffiad* (Treffynnon, 1823). First edition 1759.
BH	John Parry, *British Harmony* (Ruabon and London, 1781).
Cambrian Minstrel	John Thomas ('Ieuan Ddu'), *Y Caniedydd Cymreig/The Cambrian Minstrel* (Merthyr Tydfil, 1845).
CG	*Canu Gwerin/Folk Song*, 1978–
Gems	John Owen, *Gems of Welsh Melody* (London and Wrexham, 1873).
HGC	Edward Jones, *Hen Ganiadau Cymru* (London, 1820).
John Thomas MS	NLW, J. Lloyd Williams MS AH1/36. Edited in Cass Meurig, *Alawon John Thomas: a fiddler's tune book from eighteenth-century Wales* (Aberystwyth, 2004).
JWFSS	*Cylchgrawn Cymdeithas Alawon Gwerin Cymru/Journal of the Welsh Folk-song Society*, 1909–77.
Llawysgrif Richard Morris	T. H. Parry Williams (ed.), *Llawysgrif Richard Morris o Gerddi, &c [BL Add. MS 14992]* (Cardiff, 1931).

Abbreviations

Melus-geingciau	NLW, J. Lloyd Williams MS AH1/34 (formerly MS 36). 'Melus-geingciau Deheubarth Cymru', a collection made by John Jenkins ('Ifor Ceri') c.1815.
Melus-seiniau	NLW MS 1940Ai. 'Melus-seiniau Cymru', a collection made by John Jenkins ('Ifor Ceri') in 1817–25.
Orpheus MS	NLW Minor Deposit 150. A collection of songs submitted to the Llangollen Eisteddfod of 1858.
Per-seiniau	NLW MS 1940Aii. 'Per-seiniau Cymru', a collection made by John Jenkins ('Ifor Ceri') in 1824–5.
Relicks (1784, 1794)	Edward Jones, *Musical and Poetical Relicks of the Welsh Bards* (London, 1784, with later enlarged editions in 1794, etc.).
Specimens	William Crotch, *Specimens of Various Styles of Music* (London, 1806–7).
WMH	*Welsh Music History/Hanes Cerddoriaeth Cymru*, 1996–

A note on the translation of Welsh terms and transcription of the musical examples

Welsh terms and titles

Where possible, Welsh terms and book titles have been translated into English; however, in some cases (for example, the names of Welsh poetical metres) there is no accepted translation and to attempt one would be either meaningless or misleading. Welsh tune names and song titles have not, generally, been translated into English unless it is essential to the text.

Musical transcriptions

I have generally applied the principle of reproducing the airs and songs as they appear in the original sources. The transcriptions from the original documents have, for the most part, made no attempt to correct inconsistencies but rather to reproduce the music as far as possible as it was in the original. Where examples have been edited, this has been noted in the text or in the references. Square brackets around words in the examples indicate where they have been added to the tune from another source.

The following musical examples have been reproduced by permission of:

Bethan Bryn: Example A.3

Dr Aled Lloyd Davies: Example A.2

Cymdeithas Alawon Gwerin Cymru/The Welsh Folk-Song Society: Examples 2.7, 2.8, 2.10, 5.2, 5.15, 5.36, 5.38, 5.41, 5.42, 5.44, 5.45, 5.46, 5.59, 7.10, 10.2, 10.10, 10.27, 10.28, 10.29, 10.30, 10.31, 10.32, 10.33 and 10.34.

St Fagans: National History Museum: Examples 2.4, 5.13, 5.18, 5.25, 5.28 and 5.40.

Introduction: What is Traditional Music?

DEFINING 'TRADITIONAL MUSIC' can be as elusive as nailing a jelly. Though for many the term conjures up immediate associations with 'folk-songs' and 'folk tunes', 'traditional' and 'folk' are no longer musical synonyms. The International Folk Music Council had good reason to adopt 'traditional music' as its official term in 1981, for the designation 'folk music' has now become a notorious shape-shifter. Increasingly it evokes popular 'fusion' repertories that may indeed draw on 'traditional' tunes and instruments, but also rely on professional performers and commercial studio production.

So what do we mean by traditional music? Four features should perhaps be regarded as essential. First, this is a music that is (or was originally) passed on predominantly by oral (and aural) transmission rather than by written notation. Second, it is generally associated with a distinct people or region, sometimes defined by their own language, and in many cases integral to some aspect of traditional culture (including rural customs). Third, it is a music where variation is often an intrinsic feature. Oral transmission and the practice of variation often lead to varied forms of a single melody: 'tune families' are common, and a single tune may appear in several guises according to region or genre. Fourth, this is a *living* musical tradition. 'Traditional' does not mean 'old', but rather 'handed over', and can include new invention. So, traditional music is still being composed in Wales today, and can be heard sung or played on harp, *crwth*, bagpipes, *pibgorn* and fiddle in the pub, in clubs and societies, or on the *eisteddfod* field. Nevertheless, some of the Welsh antiquarian collectors described in chapter 5 of this book did their best to prove that the ancient roots of certain Welsh tunes lay with their Druid ancestors.

Phyllis Kinney expounds all of these features, revealing Welsh traditional music to be a uniquely indigenous phenomenon. She shows that 'tradition' in Wales, though inextricably linked with the Welsh people and their culture, is by no means invariably defined by uneducated 'folk'. For instance, the first chapter explores the music of the medieval bardic order – highly sophisticated, yet still transmitted by oral means. She demonstrates the delight of discovering far earlier tunes in notated collections copied out during the mid-eighteenth century. She shows the intertwining of so much of the musical repertory with the Welsh language, and our tremendous debt to generations of scholars, antiquarians and collectors, motivated by love for the customs of their own people. Most of all she lays out before us Welsh traditional music in all its glorious variety – love songs, elegies, carols, *penillion* tunes, dances, instrumental tunes – many of them passed down from harper to harper or itinerant fiddler to fiddler. For many this book will reach to the very heart of music in Wales; and the joy is that this Welsh tradition is vibrant and alive today.

Sally Harper, August 2010

I Merêd

1
The Oral Tradition

NO MANUSCRIPTS of secular music have survived from Wales, if indeed there were any, before the end of the sixteenth century. Although music was an important part of Welsh life, the secular tradition was an oral one. The music of ordinary people, the songs and dances of ploughmen, nursemaids, blacksmiths and itinerant fiddlers were not noted down before the eighteenth century, whereas music favoured by cultivated Welsh gentry from later medieval times until the seventeenth century was sophisticated, complex, bound by strict rules and passed on orally from teacher to pupil. Knowledge of music from an earlier period depends upon literary references, passages from the Welsh Laws and comparison with other Celtic societies such as Ireland.

One of the earliest references to music in Wales was made by the sixth-century monk Gildas in *De Excidio et Conquestu Britanniae* where his caustic indictment of Maelgwn Gwynedd, lord of Anglesey and Gwynedd, gives a picture of praise-singing in early Welsh courts. The monk berates the ruler for not listening to the 'tuneful voice' of Christians singing the praises of God with sweet rhythm and melodious church song, instead of his own bards, a rascally crew who yell forth his praises like Bacchanalian revellers. This earliest reference to bards in Wales gives an interesting picture of two styles of singing: the ecclesiastical style, pleasing and harmonious; and the bardic style, strongly declamatory. Some half-century later the churchman Venantius Fortunatus mentions the instruments used:

Romanusque lyra, plaudat tibi barbarus harpa,
Graecus Achilliaca, crotta Brittanna canat.
[Let the Roman praise you with the *lyra*, the barbarian with the *harpa*,
the Greek with the lyre of Achilles, the Briton with the *crotta*][1]

Although Venantius calls these instruments by different names, *lyra, harpa, crotta*, it appears that they were all species of lyre, the 'crotta' of the Britons being the vernacular name for an early unbowed ancestor of the *crwth* (crowd).

The close connection of music and poetry in this period, and for many centuries to follow, is evident in Welsh terminology: a *cerdd* can be either a song or poem and *caniad* can mean poetry or music. However, information about music and poetry in early Wales is extremely scarce. The Roman occupation, which lasted some four hundred years until the end of the fourth century, affected the nature of Celtic society in the conquered areas; for clues to bardic tradition in this period it is necessary to turn to Ireland, which the Romans never conquered.

When St Patrick arrived there in the fifth century, Celtic culture was still similar to that described by Caesar in Gaul. Poets held an important position at Celtic courts and their influence was powerful; in addition to singing praises, elegies and satires, they were prophets, story-tellers, genealogists and historians. In time, court poets formed a professional hierarchy in which each class had its own rank and dignity. The chief poet had a special chair in the court and his status was equal to that of the king. Bardic training was long and demanding; it took twelve years for the chief poet to complete his education and seven for an ordinary bard. Because the appeal of the poetry was first and foremost to the ear, music was an essential part of the bardic performance, sustaining the rhythm of the words.

The Marquis of Clanricarde, in describing the performance of a poem in the presence of a wealthy patron in early seventeenth-century Ireland noted that it was accomplished:

> with a great deal of Ceremony, in a Consort of Vocal and Instrumental Musick. The Poet himself said nothing, but directed and took care, that everybody else did his Part right. The Bards having first had the Composition from him, got it well by Heart, and now pronounc'd it orderly, keeping even Pace with a Harp[2]

Sometimes the harp was joined by the *tiompán*, a kind of lyre, and at a later period the poet sang to his own accompaniment. Although the Marquis was writing in the eighteenth century, the tradition was a conservative one and his description represents a very much older custom.

Welsh society in the period after the Romans left seems to have been much like that of Ireland in terms of bardic duties and status, but references to musicians in early Welsh poetry are vague. Interpretation of the place of music in Wales before the English conquest in 1282 depends upon literary and legal references and the writings of the ecclesiastic, Giraldus Cambrensis (Gerald of Wales). The Laws of Hywel Dda (Hywel the Good) derived their name from the tenth-century king Hywel and represent a native legal tradition which was predominantly oral and which had evolved over a long period, though the earliest extant written manuscripts come from the thirteenth century. Because of this, the Laws incorporate much material which refers to earlier times and many references that suggest the warrior aristocracy of a heroic age.

These Laws describe three kinds of poet. Lowest in stature was the *cerddor*, a bardic apprentice being trained in the craft of poetry and whose status was defined by the fact that no serf or villein's son could practise the bardic craft without the king's permission. Above him came the *bardd teulu*, a court officer and bard of the war-band. At the top was the *pencerdd*, a master-poet who had the privilege of sitting at court in a chair which symbolised his authority and had to be won in poetic competition. In the heroic age, court poets would be expected to perform their songs before battle and at the victory feast after a successful battle where they would sing the praises of the king and his war-band. Although the word 'sing' is used, it would probably be a mistake to think in modern terms since the style was almost certainly declamatory rather than melodic.

By the time the Laws were written down the harp was the supreme instrument of the Welsh; in addition to the performances of professional harpers, harp-playing was part of the education of a noble. However, according to one version of the Laws, two other instruments, the *crwth* and the pipes, had high if not equal status. At a twelfth-century feast held by the Lord Rhys in Cardigan Castle, a chair was awarded to the winner of a competition between harpers, crouthers and pipers.[3]

The inherent conservatism of the bardic order meant that, even after the passing of the heroic age with its warrior aristocracy, poets retained much of their status and influence. Apprentices had to pass through various stages of instruction, which might take as many as nine years before attaining the rank of *pencerdd*, and only a *pencerdd* could assume the right to be a bardic teacher, demanding many years of study through predominantly oral instruction. Although the poetry created was essentially aristocratic and had little or no place in the lives of ordinary members of the community, the bardic order continued to train poets in this style and to hold degree examinations to the end of the sixteenth century.

There is no detailed description of musical styles until the end of the twelfth century when the Norman-Welsh ecclesiastic, Giraldus de Barri, known as Giraldus Cambrensis, accompanied Archbishop Baldwin on a tour through Wales to preach the Third Crusade. The Archbishop, impressed by *Topographica Hibernica* (The Topography of Ireland), an early work by Giraldus, suggested that he should write the history of the tour and it is from his copious notes on the places they visited and the customs of the people, published in his *Itinerarium Kambriae* (The Journey through Wales) and *Descriptio Kambriae* (The Description of Wales), that we have our first significant description of music in Wales. These reports include the music-making of ordinary people for the first time.

The second chapter of the *Itinerarium Kambriae* contains a description of the feast-day of St Eluned in Breconshire, where sick people would come together from far and wide in the hope of being cured. Giraldus describes men and women, in the church or the churchyard, sometimes dancing, sometimes as if in a peaceful trance, then suddenly jumping up in a frenzy and indicating with gestures the work they had been doing unlawfully on holy days. One would appear to put his hand to the plough, another seemed to urge on the oxen with a goad, both singing crude rustic songs as if to ease their work. This first report to give any detail of folk singing in Wales is significant in that the writer mentions oxen songs, a type which continued in use in Glamorganshire until the end of the nineteenth century, some eight hundred years later.[4]

The tenth chapter of the *Descriptio Kambriae* confirms the importance of the harp, with Giraldus remarking that Welsh courtiers consider the ability to play the harp greater than all other accomplishments, while in every house there would be harps and, if guests should arrive early in the day, the young women of the household would play for them on the harp. In the twelfth chapter, Giraldus corroborates the references in the Laws that the Welsh play three instruments – harp, pipes and *crwth.*

It also contains what he said about Irish instrumental performers in the *Topographica Hibernica,* showing how close the two cultures were in his day. He describes them as playing with fingers moving so swiftly that they seem to be disputing with each other, yet preserving harmonic consistency while performing with unfailing artistry a variety of music on diverse instruments with sweet rapidity, unequal equality and discordant concord finishing in tonal unity. Whether the strings sound in fourths or in fifths, the performers always begin with B flat and return to it at the end so as to finish with a pleasing sound. The treble strings are played rapidly above the deeper tones of the lower strings giving particular enjoyment to the listener while concealing their artistry. Those who have studied and who understand the mysteries of this art would get great pleasure from it, but for those who listen without comprehension it would be like a disorderly tumult, producing exhaustion and boredom in unwilling listeners.

Here it is obvious that Giraldus is not discussing the songs of ordinary people but professional instrumentalists performing elaborate music for an aristocratic audience. He seems to be describing music that differs from the general trend of European music of that period but his words are open to more than one interpretation. The final sentences imply that this is sophisticated instrumental music for the educated ear.

In the thirteenth chapter Giraldus describes Welsh singing:

> When they come together to make music, the Welsh sing their traditional songs, not in unison, as is done elsewhere, but in parts, in many modes and modulations. When a choir gathers to sing, which happens often in this country, you will hear as many different parts and voices as there are performers, all joining together in the end to produce a single organic harmony and melody in the soft sweetness of B-flat.
>
> In the northern parts of Great Britain, across the Humber and in Yorkshire, the English who live there produce the same symphonic harmony when they sing. They do this in two parts only, with two modulations of the voice, one group humming the bass and the others singing the treble most sweetly. The two peoples must have developed this habit not by any special training but by age-old custom, by long usage which has made it second nature. It is now become so common with them both and so firmly established that you never hear a simple melody sweetly sung, for it is always in many parts, as with the Welsh, or in two, as with the English of the north. What is even more remarkable, small children sing in parts, and tiny babies do so, too, from the moment they stop screaming and first begin to sing.

> As the English in general do not adopt this way of singing, but only those who live in the north, I think that these latter must have taken their part-singing, as they did their speech, from the Danes and Norwegians, who so often invaded those parts of the island and held them longer under their dominion.[5]

Understandably, Giraldus' description of singing in this chapter has given rise to considerable dissension. As an educated ecclesiastic of the twelfth century who had travelled abroad he would have been familiar with the polyphonic church music of his day and obviously he considered the part-singing in Wales and the north of England to be of a different order. Many suggestions have been offered including the surmise that Giraldus was guilty of immense exaggeration. However, two proposed solutions deserve more serious attention, though they appear to be mutually exclusive. The first is the conjecture by Lloyd Hibberd that what Giraldus heard was heterophony,[6] that is music in which two or more musicians perform variations on a tune simultaneously. Heterophony can still be heard in Britain among the Gaelic hymn-singers of the Hebrides, where each member of the congregation decorates the basic melody line with grace notes according to individual inclination, but the result is a harmonious unity. There is some evidence that Welsh congregations used to do the same thing. The great hymn reformer John Roberts ('Ieuan Gwyllt', 1822–77) wrote in 1859 that singers must be careful to stick to the melody and not sing something they have made up themselves, those homespun parts improvised by people who are too lazy to learn the appropriate parts.[7] Later, in 1863, he chastises singers for their untidy performances – some rushing ahead, some lingering too long on the notes and some overloading each note with three or four or half a dozen grace notes.[8] It is possible that this nineteenth-century description is a distant echo of what Giraldus heard in the twelfth.

On the other hand Ernest Sanders suggests that Giraldus' reference to singing in many parts fits the description of the *rondellus*,[9] a polyphonic technique in which two or three voices exchange phrases at regular intervals. It was normally written in three parts but when sung by a group of men, women and children, it would have been heard at different octaves. The well-known part song, 'Sumer is icumen in' can be sung as a *rondellus* by as many as twelve parts over a two-part ostinato. Giraldus' description of singing as developed 'not by any special training but by age-old custom, by long usage which has made it second nature', suggests improvisation. Certainly there is evidence of improvisation in medieval church music. Early in the twelfth century, John of Affligem described improvised organum as the harmonious combining of different notes, as produced by at least two singers; while one sings the plainsong, the second voice moves around it at different pitches, coming together at the cadence in unison or at the octave. In the *rondellus*, however, the voices exchanged parts and, according to Walter Odington, an Englishman writing about 1300, 'what is sung by one may be sung by everybody in turn ... Each thus sings the other's part'.[10] The *rondellus* and related techniques were well known in areas close to the Welsh border and may perhaps have been influenced by Celtic traditions. Was the singing that Giraldus heard a form of the *rondellus*? It is impossible to be certain, but he was, after all, at pains to make clear that this was a company of many singers, including small children, and that they sang in this manner through long custom rather than training. It is possible that the decorated psalm-singing heard in the Western Isles of Scotland and in nineteenth-century Wales fits that description more closely.

Less than a century after Giraldus died Wales was conquered by Edward I of England and lost its independence, but although Wales was now counted among the lands of the English crown it was not part of England. The princely courts no longer existed, but poets and musicians retained much of their importance through the patronage of the clergy and the *uchelwyr* (influential landed gentry). Many of these new leaders of Welsh society were men of considerable culture, patrons of the arts of prose and poetry, and many poets themselves came from this class. The period between the Conquest at the end of the thirteenth century and the Acts of Union (1536–43), by which Wales became part of England, has been called the most brilliant age of Welsh literature. Music and poetry were still sister arts and much of the poetry was declaimed or sung to instrumental accompaniment, appealing to the ear rather than the eye. Bardic training continued to be lengthy, highly regulated and predominantly oral, and bards were still expected to be learned in the intricacies of the Welsh language, the genealogies of their patrons and in prophetic poetry, praise-singing and elegies.

The other notable area where music was a potent force was the Church and more than one Welsh abbey, especially in the Cistercian order, gave patronage to the bards. Because of the lack of music manuscripts from an earlier period there is no direct evidence of the kind of music used in the Celtic Church before the Normans took control. There are, however, two Welsh manuscripts extant from a later period; the Bangor Pontifical, a manuscript of English origin which throws no light on Welsh music, and the Penpont Antiphonal from the Brecon area, a fourteenth-century antiphonal of Sarum Use which includes matins, lauds and vespers for St David's Day, commemorating the patron saint of Wales. The Sarum Rite was established at St David's cathedral in the thirteenth century to bring it into line with English practice, and the Penpont Antiphonal is important as 'the earliest surviving monument known of the cultivation of music in Wales by Welshmen'.[11]

The poetry of the period is full of terms relating to the music of the church and there is speculation that Dafydd ap Gwilym, generally considered Wales's greatest poet and one of the great poets of medieval Europe, may have been educated in a fourteenth-century *scola cantorum*, perhaps at Strata Florida abbey, for the abundance of musical terminology in his poetry shows his familiarity with church music. Dafydd was also sufficiently accomplished to be able to accompany himself on the harp when declaiming his compositions, as attested by many technical references to the harp in his poetry.

Political developments from outside as well as within combined to bring an end to the hierarchical bardic system. In 1485 the Tudors, a Welsh dynasty, came to the English throne. As a result many Welsh-speaking gentry, who had been patrons of the bards, turned their eyes toward England where they hoped for preferment at court. Opportunities for Welshmen in England multiplied and the English language began to be more important than Welsh, especially after the Act of Union proclaimed that monoglot Welsh-speakers could not hold public office in the king's territories and that English was to be the only language of the law courts. Sons of the gentry were often sent to school in England where they learned the music of English composers like Thomas Morley and William Byrd, while young ladies might be taught by a music tutor such as the one from Salisbury who travelled around the country houses of the north Wales gentry.[12] This was culture of a different kind from the traditional music and poetry of the native Welsh bards, and the increasing anglicisation of their patrons as well as the conservatism of the poets had by 1700 doomed the bardic order and the music associated with it.

Efforts were made to preserve the knowledge of bardic art through writing down what had previously been passed on orally. As early as the fourteenth century a Bardic Grammar was compiled and a few works passed on the teaching of the bardic schools. From time to time an *eisteddfod* (a competitive session of poetry and music) would be held to award degrees to poets who had passed the bardic examinations. Two such were held at Caerwys in north-east Wales for the purpose of reasserting the professional authority of the bards in the face of increasing competition from minstrels and mere rhymesters. English law in the sixteenth century designated musical entertainers, whether singers, fiddlers or pipers, by the name of 'minstrels' and those without licences were classed as beggars and vagabonds. The bardic order in Wales was anxious to confirm its high status in the community, and *eisteddfod* competitions under the patronage of the gentry were a way of establishing the masters in poetic art and weeding out undesirables. In order to emphasise the antiquity of the bardic tradition, the 1523 *eisteddfod* was preceded by a proclamation stating that its purpose was to regulate bardic practices in accordance with the Statute of Gruffudd ap Cynan (c.1055–1137) who was said to have brought bards and musicians with him from Ireland when he came to claim the kingdom of Gwynedd in north Wales. According to tradition, their function was to reform the bardic system in Wales along the lines of Irish practice. Although it is no longer thought that the Statute was the work of Gruffudd ap Cynan – indeed it probably dates from the early sixteenth century – it gave the stamp of historical authority to the *eisteddfod*.

The Statute refers to three classes: *cerdd dafod* (the craft of poetry); *cerdd dant* (the craft of music – literally, the craft of the string); and *atgeiniaid/datgeiniaid* (declaimers). Both poets and musicians had to go through four grades of apprenticeship and only the select few reached the supreme degree of *pencerdd*. The declaimers were not awarded degrees; they were considered inferior because they did not create art themselves but only performed what had been created by others. Nevertheless, they too underwent rigorous training in poetry and music and were expected to be able to play the harp and the *crwth*.

Although the Statute asserted that an *eisteddfod* should be held every three years, it was not until 1567 that the next one was held in an attempt to confirm the decisions of the 1523 sessions. About this time some of the secrets of *cerdd dant* began to be noted down. These treatises are valuable for their information about aspects of *cerdd dant* which had previously been passed on orally but they do not contain any music. For the earliest extant notation of secular music in medieval Wales we must turn to the manuscript of one Robert ap Huw, harper (1580–1665). He came from a well-known gentry family on Anglesey in north Wales and was a poet, like others of his family. But Robert ap Huw was primarily a musician, and his manuscript dated 1613 is the only one extant of Welsh music of the bardic order.[13] There are references to other manuscripts; for instance John Owen, nephew of the scholar, antiquary, poet and map-maker Lewis Morris, wrote to Ieuan Brydydd Hir in November 1758:

> My uncle Lewis has got a curious manuscript wrote in Charles 1st time by one Robt ap Huw of Bodwigen in Anglesey which contains a valuable collection of old Music … I am told there are more of the sort in Bodorgan Library which phaps you may see one time or other.[14]

In the *Myvyrian Archaiology* there is a transcription made by Iolo Morganwg of a manuscript (possibly also by Robert ap Huw) belonging to Rhys Jones of Blaenau, and William Jones of Llangadfan mentions that he had seen still another manuscript:

> I am of opinion that the antient M^s. of British music which you have in London is not the same that I saw in possession of the late M^r. E. Evans in Llanfair Dolhaiarn, & belonged to Mr Davies of Llanerch near S^t. Asaph. That was a folio & contain'd about 50 pieces with an Index of their names, & an introduction prefixt. I imagined that it might be written about the time of Queen Elisabeth. It contains two parts, each prick'd on a scale of six lines, not with such notes as now in use, but with letters or some marks resembling letters. That M^r. Davies had a large collection of Welsh M^{ss}…[15]

The originals all seem to have disappeared, however, leaving Robert ap Huw's 1613 manuscript as the only remaining first-hand source. According to Sally Harper, 'By comparison with the contents and ordering of many contemporary British lute, keyboard and ensemble sources, Robert ap Huw seems to have drawn on a repertory which is unique and very different in both aesthetic and technique.'[16]

There is considerable controversy regarding the interpretation of the tablature of Robert ap Huw's manuscript in which the first seven letters of the alphabet represent the notes of the scale.[17]

Tablature was a reasonably common instrumental notation from about the middle of the fifteenth century to the eighteenth, but the Welsh example presents some atypical problems. It has elements of other European musical tablatures, but the total effect is of a notation devised for the purpose of setting down a particular type of music as performed in Wales. In contrast to modern musical notation, there are no key signatures, time signatures or accidentals.

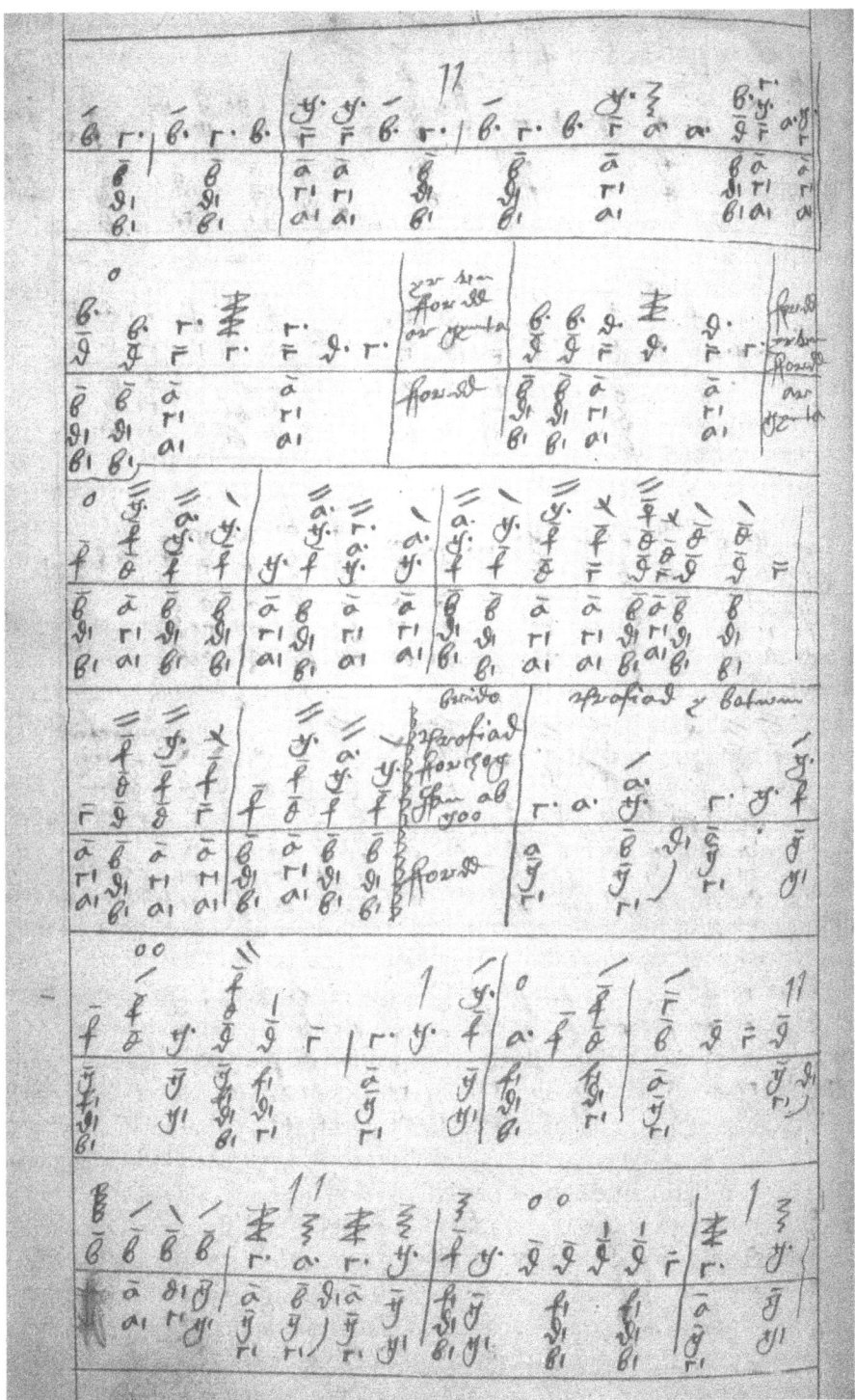

PLATE 1: *An illustration of tablature taken from the Robert ap Huw manuscript.*
By permission of the British Library.

There is no stave either, so a system of doubling letters, adding subscripts, horizontal dashes, or dots is used to indicate the appropriate octave. There are no rhythmic indications in the first third of the manuscript, but in the last two-thirds 'fencing' appears from time to time.

The manuscript does not indicate which instrument was intended, and some early attempts at decipherment such as that of the nineteenth-century harpist John Thomas ('Pencerdd Gwalia', 1826–1913) claimed that it was music for the *crwth*. But, apart from the fact that Robert ap Huw was a notable harper, the range of the tablature is outside that of the *crwth* without considerable retuning, and a contemporary reference to one of the tunings mentions seven strings, unplayable on either the three-stringed or the six-stringed *crwth*. By now it is accepted that the instrument intended in the manuscript was the harp, probably a Renaissance harp with about thirty gut, or possibly horsehair, strings.

According to Peter Crossley-Holland, this manuscript demonstrates 'the existence of an advanced system of homophony during the Middle Ages, unconnected with any known polyphonic origin'.[18] The music is based on a highly systematised treatment of two chords called *cyweirdant* and *tyniad*, which in various combinations make up twenty-four different patterns called *mesurau* (measures). There is little variation in the chords of the lower hand, but the notes in the upper hand could be varied in order and in length. On page 35 of the manuscript Robert ap Huw shows how this was done in the *Gogwyddor i ddysgu y prikiad* (principle for learning the notation) where he lists seventeen different ways of playing the notes in the upper hand, using terms now obsolete such as *plethiad y pedwarbys* (four-finger plait), *kefn ewin* (the back of the nail) or *takiad y fawd* (thumb stop). It is now generally agreed that these are not ornaments to the basic notes, but integral elements of the melodic line.

The musical terminology of the bardic period is of very little help to our understanding, as many of the terms are obsolete and others may have changed their meaning since Robert ap Huw's time. In addition to the names of the chords, which make up the pattern of the measure, the twenty-four measures themselves have curious titles such as 'Mak y mwn hir', 'Fflamgwr gwrgan', 'Trwsgwl mawr' or 'Mak y delgi', and many of the titles appear to be Irish in origin. Each measure has its own particular pattern of chords indicated by the numbers 1 (*tyniad*) and 0 (*cyweirdant*). For example the chordal pattern for 'Mak y mwn hir' was notated 1111 0000 1010 1111 0000 1011, whereas the pattern for the measure called 'Korffiniwr' was 1100 1011 . 1100 1011. The chosen pattern became the basis of a more extended treatment of the music involving repetition of sections and shorter motifs, variation of the melody line and occasionally the interpolation of short passages called *diwedd*. In addition to a section on the twenty-four measures copied from an earlier *pencerdd*, which may have had a pedagogical purpose, the manuscript contains a number of more extended pieces of music called *Gosteg, Cwlwm, Caniad* and *Profiad*, technical terms whose meaning in Welsh is highly debatable.

Further variety was given to this music by the use of different tunings. At the end of 'Caniad San Silin' Robert ap Huw notes that it is best on 'Tro Tant or Is gower', implying that there is more than one choice of tuning for a particular piece. But the tunings mentioned in this manuscript and in Welsh musical treatises of the period bear names that are quite unrelated to those of other known scales or modes, and there are very few guides as to the technique. According to the treatises there are five accredited tunings for the harp: *bragod gywair, is gywair, cras gywair, go gywair* and *lleddf gywair*, and from these basic tunings other tunings can be made. Toward the end of the manuscript, Robert ap Huw gives a diagram for tuning the *cras gywair* as well as diagrams for six others not listed among the accredited tunings.

However, even with these diagrams, there is considerable disagreement as to how the instrument was tuned. Among the various tunings suggested for the *cras gywair* by musicologists are: (a) a pentatonic scale lacking 3 and 7; (b) a scale with notes 2, 3, 5 and 6 all flattened; (c) a major scale. There is a similar lack of unanimity with regard to the other tunings. In 1942, Crossley-Holland concluded that the tunings appeared to correspond to major and minor keys, whereas in 1968 Thurston Dart suggested that Robert ap Huw re-tuned some of the harp strings to sound at different intervals (*scordatura*) producing one pentatonic scale and other scales similar to the old modes.

It is possible that some of this music may have been performed in conjunction with the declamation of Welsh strict-metre poetry such as the *awdl, englyn* or *cywydd*. All of the *gostegion* and some of the *caniadau* have recurrent refrain sections called *diwedd*, which could function as instrumental interludes between extended sections of poetry. Many, perhaps most, medieval Welsh poets could accompany themselves on the harp and a device like the *diwedd* would enable the performer to rest the voice or take time to prepare the next stanza. Robert ap Huw himself gives no clues as to the use of the music in this manuscript unless his note at the end of 'Gosteg yr Halen', stating that this *gosteg* was played before Arthur's knights when the salt (*halen*) was brought to the table, might possibly refer to a musical accompaniment to a tale. In *The Complaynt of Scotland* (1549), a list of names of popular tales current in Scotland, which may have been said or sung, includes tales of Scottish heroes, translations from Ovid's *Metamorphoses* and the Charlemagne cycle, and several tales from the Arthurian romances.[19] These form part of a section on the entertainment of the period that also includes songs and dances. References in various sixteenth-century Welsh musical treatises note the names of music which may be connected with stories, lives and prophecies. These include traditional Welsh tales such as *Caniad y Twrch Trwyth* (The *Twrch Trwyth* Saga), *Yr Ychen Bannog* (The Horned Oxen) and other medieval tales, as well as lives of saints such as *Caniad Beuno*.

After Robert ap Huw's manuscript came into the hands of the antiquarian Lewis Morris in the late 1720s, it was passed around to musicians and musical historians to attempt a solution to its problems. The first to publish was Dr Charles Burney, who thought the tablature was music for the lute and found it difficult to believe 'that a rude, and uncivilized people, driven into a mountainous and barren country without commerce or communication with the rest of Europe, should *invent counterpoint*, and cultivate harmony, at a period when it was unknown to the most polished and refined inhabitants of the earth'.[20] Toward the end of the century, the

French violinist François Hippolyte Barthélemon announced that he had transcribed all of the manuscript but, if so, nothing is left of his work apart from 'Caingc Dafydd Brophwyd', printed in *The Bardic Museum* (1802),[21] said to be by Barthélemon. As mentioned earlier, in 1870 the first Welsh interpreter of the manuscript to publish his findings, John Thomas, ('Pencerdd Gwalia'), one of the most famous harpists of his day, did not recognise it as a harp manuscript and transcribed it for the six-string *crwth*.[22] According to Thurston Dart, his transcriptions are valueless.

Interest increased during the last century, beginning in the 1930s with the early music enthusiast Arnold Dolmetsch, who saw that the tablature was meant for the harp and built himself one to tackle the problems. In 1936, a facsimile of the manuscript was published and another facsimile brought out in 1987. These have facilitated study of the work, and since that time musicologists in Britain, Europe and the United States have postulated theories, scholarly dissertations have been published and transcriptions for the harp have been recorded. Even more importantly, a book of Robert ap Huw studies has appeared recently as a result of a symposium held at Bangor University's Centre for Advanced Welsh Music Studies in 1995, specifically to examine this manuscript and its author in the light of contemporary harp technique and the oral tradition.[23] A few years previously, Osian Ellis discussed the music in some detail in *The Story of the Harp in Wales*. Ellis, a professional harpist steeped in Welsh literature and knowledge of the culture in which the music was performed, maintains that Robert ap Huw did not fully understand the music and that undoubtedly 'he was the last of the harpers to have played this ancient harp music of medieval times, for there is no trace of this style in later Welsh music'.[24] This conclusion is open to argument, for the tradition was an oral one and there are no other Welsh music manuscripts extant before the eighteenth century.

Without more evidence, it is impossible to know with any certainty to what extent the style of bardic music might have influenced the later development of Welsh music but there are a few clues. A ballad, 'Myfyrdod neu Ddeusyfiad Cantores', printed in *Blodeu-gerdd Cymry*,[25] has as its theme a young woman who wishes to be dressed in the popular tunes of the day:

I mae hi'n wyliau oerllid ddigon,
A minnau a'm dillad yn deneuon;
Myfi a ymwisgaf bodwy'n gronyn,
O'r mwyn geinciau sy ar y delyn.
[The holidays are quite cold,
And I with my thin clothes;
I will dress every bit of myself,
With the sweet tunes on the harp.]

In this ballad the names of sixteenth- and seventeenth-century English dance tunes such as 'Crimson Velvet', 'Mall Sims' and 'Greensleeves' are intermixed with contemporary Welsh tune-names, musical terms such as *gosteg* and *profiad*, an accredited harp tuning known to Robert ap Huw (*is gower*) and names mentioned in

Robert ap Huw's manuscript (*Cwlwm mawr, Caniad Beuno, Ystwffl, Tro'r Tant*). The ballad is valuable as a description of the way in which the new dance tunes from England and the continent mingled with Welsh music of the period, but it also indicates that at the time when the ballad was written, probably mid-seventeenth century, medieval Welsh musical terms were still familiar enough to be used in a popular ballad.

There is a further clue. Among the tune-names mentioned in the ballad are 'Tro'r Tant' and 'Ffarwel Twm Bach'. Two versions of 'Erddigan Tro'r Tant' were printed in the eighteenth century, one in *British Harmony* (1781)[26] and another in *Musical and Poetical Relicks of the Welsh Bards* (1784 and 1794),[27] but the musical style is obviously earlier than the eighteenth century. Both of these airs are extended pieces without a balanced formal structure, made up of a series of sequences and the repetition of shorter motifs. The two related pieces differ in detail, suggesting that they were noted from oral tradition. Example 1.1 shows how it appears in *British Harmony*:[28]

Example 1.1: 'Erddigan Tro'r Tant'

continued

Equally striking are the versions of the tune called 'Ffarwel Twm Bach' in the ballad. It was noted under the name of 'Ffarwel Dwm Bâch' by the Anglesey fiddler Maurice or Morris Edwards in an eighteenth-century manuscript. Another version was set down in the 1820s by the harpist Ifan y Gorlan as 'Farwel Dwm Bach or Coeti', and Edward Jones printed a third version called 'Canu yn Iâch i Dwm Bâch' in *Hen Ganiadau Cymru* (1825),[29] all probably noted from oral tradition. The fact that Morris Edwards and Ifan y Gorlan, both working musicians, took the trouble to copy it suggests that the music was still of interest. Thomas Prichard ('Twm bach') of Coety in Glamorganshire, south Wales, who died in 1597, was one of the best known harpers of the sixteenth century. The piece that bears his name is an extended work in three irregular sections, with no strict formal pattern and much repetition of motifs. The contrast between these pieces and the music of the eighteenth century is striking.[30]

Example 1.2: 'Ffarwel Dwm Bach'

2

The Watershed

*I*N THE COURSE of Robert ap Huw's long life Welsh culture underwent a profound change. It was this period that saw the final decline of the bardic order as an institution and English become the preferred language of the more influential of the Welsh gentry. It is true that bards continued to be welcomed into gentry homes at the traditional festivals of Christmas, Easter and Whitsun, and a few continued as patrons of domestic poets. But inflation between 1550 and 1650 caused a serious decline in living standards so that many families could no longer afford to keep a household bard, and the Acts of Union of 1536–43 made the speaking of English a necessity for anyone who wanted to hold public office in Wales. Inevitably the gentry gradually became anglicised.

The situation was less critical for musicians than for poets. Welsh gentry who had lost the language could still enjoy music and dancing, whereas classical poetry of the bardic order had become a closed book to them. But musicians too saw changes in repertoire, style and patronage as the seventeenth century unfolded and more tunes came in from England. A manuscript from Lleweni, a north Wales mansion, notes that in the 1590s a festival was held there during the Christmas holidays and among those who took part were thirteen *gwyr wrth gerdd*, that is poets, harpers and *crwth*-players.[1] They would have been there, of course, to provide traditional entertainment, the declamation of classical Welsh poetry that would have included praise of the head of the house and a recitation of his exalted lineage. But the same manuscript includes a page in a different hand, badly written and worse spelt, which contains the names of seventy-nine tunes, mostly dances, and only one of them Welsh ('Sidanen'). There is no title on the page or explanation of why the names are there but most, if not all, are names of dances and ballads popular in the sixteenth century. A good half dozen of these, including 'Greensleeves' and 'Lusty Gallant' can be found in *A Handefull of pleasant delites* printed in London in 1584 by Richard Jones (who apparently was a Welshman – the motto on his book is 'Heb Dduw, heb ddim' (Without God, nothing)).[2] Others were names of dance tunes, such as 'Pepper is Black' and 'Peg a Ramsey', mentioned in Nashe's *Have With You to Saffron-Walden*, 1596.[3] It would not be surprising if, along with the traditional forms of Welsh culture, an anglicised house like Lleweni included in its Christmas celebrations the newer and more fashionable entertainment from London.

Education too played its part in these musical changes; the sons of the gentry who were sent to school in England learned madrigals, rounds and catches, while their sisters were taught at home to play musical instruments and read music. A list of tunes for lute lessons in the manuscript of one Phillip Powell of Brecon, c.1635, contains thirty-seven tune names, of which only two, 'farwell Ieauan glyn Tivy' and 'Skower [*isgywair*] Sydanen' appear to be of Welsh origin.[4] Ten are of grounds, including some which continued to be popular in Wales, such as 'Rogero' and 'The Hunt's Up'. Some of the tunes he names can be found in music books of the period such as *New Citharen Lessons* (1609–29).[5] The harpers of the gentry might also be exposed to wider musical influences. Sir John Stradling's harper was invited to play before Sir Philip Sidney, and the poet-harper Robert ap Huw was said to have performed at the court of James I.

Welsh poets did not cease writing poetry, but the changing social situation called for a simpler type of poetry with a wider appeal. Those who sang poetry of a more popular nature had probably always coexisted with acknowledged professional bards who sang in classical metres to the princes and the gentry. A fifteenth-century poem describes a patron welcoming not only accredited poets but also performers on the harp, *crwth*, pipes, trumpet, fiddle, drum and psaltery, as well as conjurers and tumblers.[6] Classical bards with their long training and upper-class connections considered popular poets to be mere rhymesters and looked on them with contempt, referring to them as 'poets of the dung-hill' or 'poets who sing at fairs'. Some did not even sing to the harp. The sixteenth-century grammarian, Siôn Dafydd Rhys, described the '*Datgeiniad Pen Pastwn*' as one who couldn't play the harp but had to declaim the poetry, thumping with his staff to mark the accents while standing in the middle of the patron's hall, and some of these *datgeiniaid* were also to be heard declaiming poetry at the fairs of the period.

Popular poets adapted ancient metres scorned by the professional bards, ones that were simple and could be fitted to simple tunes. These metres did not require declamation and could be sung with or without an instrument by ordinary people in a tavern or sitting around a fire. A sixteenth-century poem, 'Ymddiddan rhwng yr Wtreswr a'r Dylluan' (A Dialogue between the Rake and the Owl) describes the scene:

> ...*a chyn y bod hi/n/ hanner dydd*
> *kael kymdeithion yn ddyribydd*
> *gwledd fwyn a gloddaist ddibrydd*
> *a gwyr o gerdd yn gelfydd*
> *a ddoe yno yn ddigon vffydd*
> *y chwanegi fy llawenydd*
> *a chwedi darfod yr dydd passio*
> *a than a chanwill i oleuo*
> *kael telyn rawn a[i] chweirio*
> *a phawb ar hwyl pennhyllio*
> *nid oed rhaid fynd yr yscol*

> *kyn kael dyry a charol*
> *o law y law y rhay yr delyn*
> *y gael ysgower ag englyn…*
> [...and before mid-day
> to have unexpected companions
> a fine feast and happy carousing
> and clever musicians
> to come there quite obediently
> to add to my enjoyment
> and after the day has passed
> with a fire and a candle to give light
> to have a horsehair harp and tune it
> and everybody having fun singing verses
> there was no need to go to school
> before having a light song and a carol
> from hand to hand went the harp
> to have is gywair and englyn…][7]

It is quite clear from this that popular culture had its place in the tavern at the same time that the bards were singing in the halls of the gentry. But because the tradition was still largely an oral one it was the works of acknowledged classical bards that were written down in manuscripts, which were retained in the houses of their patrons. Not until the seventeenth century were the unaffected, pithy verses of popular culture written down, often scribbled in the margins of manuscripts of more profound works.

Another manuscript describes keeping vigil in the Chapel of Mary of Poulton, between Wrexham and Chester, when accredited bards and musicians would perform classical poetry, probably declaiming it to instrumental accompaniment. Young women would also sing carols and light songs. Occasions such as night vigils gave people the opportunity to gather together for entertainment as well as for worship, amusing themselves by singing, reciting tales, dancing and acting. Certainly, some of the singing in the vigil at Mary of Poulton's chapel was unmistakably secular. One of the young women present sang a punning verse with erotic implications about the holly, and the metre and rhyme scheme are very different from the poetry of the classical tradition:

> *A ddoi di, a ddoi di oddyna*
> *I goed y glyn i gylyna?*
> *Lle kair kelyn, a moel gelyn,*
> *A phob amryw gyfryw gelyn.*
> [Will you come, will you come away
> To the valley wood to gather holly?
> Where there is holly, and thornless holly,
> And every kind of holly.][8]

It would not be difficult to sing those words to one of the simple four-phrase tunes that have survived to this century in oral tradition. They are commonly referred to as *penillion* tunes, that is tunes used to sing the kind of verses referred to in the poem about the rake and the owl, and they are also called *penillion telyn* (harp verses), implying that they were sung to the harp. Some of these tunes, such as 'Y Dôn Fechan', will fit the 'holly' words quite easily:[9]

Example 2.1: 'Y Dôn Fechan'

One of the oldest of these metres associated with the folk rather than the classical bards is called *cywydd deuair fyrion*, in which the line consists of a rhymed couplet, usually of four or five syllables each with two accents. Examples of the metre can be found as far back as the poetry of the heroic age,[10] and there can be no doubt that it was sung because the antiquarian Edward Williams, better known as Iolo Morganwg (1747–1826), noted a number of tunes to which *cywydd deuair fyrion* were sung. These tunes tend to be motival in character. Like many amateur notators of music, Iolo writes the tune without time or key signatures and without musical barlines:[11]

Example 2.2: 'Cywydd deuair: Morganwg' as noted by Iolo Morganwg. *By permission of Llyfrgell Genedlaethol Cymru/The National Library of Wales.*

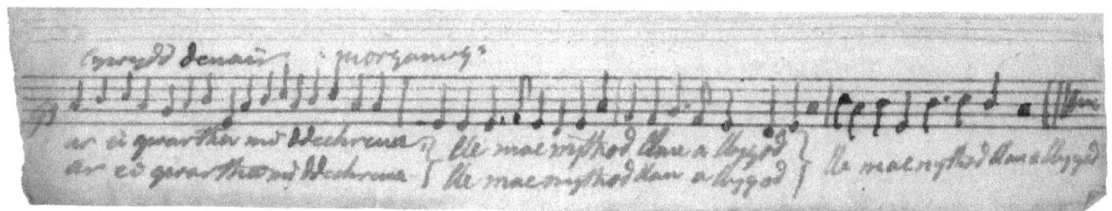

Example 2.3: 'Cywydd deuair fyrion'

The *cywydd deuair fyrion* metre had lost most of its popularity by the eighteenth century, but it is possible that some of the tunes connected with it survived to be used with simpler and more popular quatrains in trochaic tetrameter. There are traces of the motival style occasionally in tunes where each musical line is broken into equal sections of four syllables with two accents, as in the Christmas carol 'Dyma Wyliau Hyfryd Llawen', noted from oral tradition in 1960. Although the metre of the carol words is not *cywydd deuair fyrion*, the style of the tune fits that metre perfectly.[12]

Example 2.4: 'Dyma Wyliau Hyfryd Llawen'

In addition to singing in the tavern and at night vigils people would gather together out of doors for entertainment. According to an account of the late sixteenth century:

> Vpon the sondaies and hollidaies the multitude of all sortes of men woomen and Childerne of everie parishe doe vse to meete in sondrie

> places either one some hill or one the side of some mountaine where theire harpers and Crowthers singe them song*es* of the doeing*es* of theire Auncestors namelie of theire warrs againste the king*es* of this realme and the English nac*i*on ... Here alsoe doe they spende theire time in hearinge some parte of the lives of Thalaassyn [Taliessin], Marlin Beno Kybbye [Merddyn pen beirdd], Iernin [?Iorwerth], and suche other the intended Prophett*es* and Sainct*es* of that cuntrie.[13]

In the last years of the seventeenth century one of the antiquarian Edward Lhuyd's correspondents from the parish of Llandrillo in north Wales wrote that the old *crwth*-player, Dafydd Rowland, 'used every Easter Sunday in the afternoon to go with the parish youngsters to the top of Craig Ddinan to share out the white oxen. Then he would play the tune called *Ychen Bannog* (Horned Oxen) and all the other old tunes, which died with him'.[14] It is possible that not only was the tune played, but that perhaps one of the old Welsh tales about the horned oxen may have been recited as part of the entertainment.

With the decline of the bardic order poets looked for the challenge of new metres and one of the first to combine these new metres with the assonance and rhyme scheme of traditional *cynghanedd* was Edmwnd Prys, a humanist educated at St John's College, Cambridge, who was steeped in the classical Welsh tradition.[15] His verses, adapted to the tune of 'About the Banks of Helicon', may date from the 1570s when he was rector at Ludlow. Prys's ballad, 'Balett gymraeg ar fesvr aboute the banck of Elicon', is not a direct translation of English words and has a freshness which contrasts with the stateliness of much bardic poetry.[16] The poem mingles bardic musical terminology with the names of Welsh tunes, two of which were published by Edward Jones some two centuries later – 'Mwynen Gwynedd' and 'Cainck yr Arglwydd'. The latter is probably the tune referred to in a sixteenth-century poem as 'kaingk yr arglwydd lywelyn' and printed as 'Caingc Llywelyn' in *Bardic Museum*.[17]

Although Prys set his words to a non-Welsh air, the tunes that he names in the course of his ballad are all Welsh. Nevertheless, foreign tunes – predominantly English, but some from Scotland and the Continent – were beginning to be used by other poets too. Welsh words were written to such popular airs of the period as 'Rogero', 'Crimson Velvet', 'The Parson of the Parish', 'Whoop! Do me no Harm, Good Man' and 'Walsingham'. The popularity of most of these was ephemeral but Welsh carols and ballads were still being sung to 'Crimson Velvet' and 'The Parson of the Parish' well into the eighteenth century.

Some Welsh tunes were derived from the harmonic patterns known as ground basses so popular in Renaissance Europe. The sixteenth-century ground 'Dargeson' gave birth to a tune called 'Sedany, or Dargason', which appeared in *The English Dancing Master* (1651).[18] A ballad about Queen Elizabeth I, which appears in *Blodeu-gerdd Cymry* 1759 but was written during her reign, is noted as 'I'w channu ar fesur a elwir Sidannen' ('To be sung on the measure called Sidannen'). At least two other sixteenth-century Welsh ballads praising Elizabeth also fit the tune. The name 'Sidanen' appears to have been used in Wales to designate a beautiful woman and it would have been natural to transfer the compliment to Queen Elizabeth. A few years later, a song in praise of 'Welsh Sydanen' was sung in Anthony Munday's play, *John a Kent and John a Cumber*, in which 'fayre Sydanen' was said to be the daughter of Llywelyn ap Gruffudd, Prince of Wales. 'Sidanen' appears on the list of tunes found in the Lleweni manuscript, and tunes called 'Sidanen' are printed in eighteenth-century Welsh collections, but the latter are quite clearly instrumental display pieces unrelated to the 'Dargeson' ground and unsuitable for ballad words. However, a variant of the 'Sedany' tune can be found in *Relicks* 1794, under the name of 'Mwynen Cynwyd' (first strain only). At some point the tune became part of Welsh folk tradition, becoming attached to a wren-hunt song.[19]

'John Come Kiss Me Now', a tune-family associated with the 'Buffons' ground and a favourite subject for variations or 'divisions' throughout the seventeenth century, was popular as a vehicle for instrumental display and for dancing. In its long life it has given birth to numerous songs in Britain and America but it would seem that its popularity in Wales was due mainly to its use as a tune for singing *penillion*. Eighteenth-century Welsh sources sometimes refer to it by its English name, but more often by its Welsh name, 'Pen Rhaw', and the air continues to be used in Wales to the present day. Another sixteenth-century ground which was a favourite among Welsh harpers was 'The Hunt's Up'. The Welsh versions may have been related to an English tune based on the 'Hunt's Up' ground which was called 'Chow Bente', perhaps from a seventeenth-century theatre piece, *The Variety*, in which one of the characters sings 'The great Choe bent / The little Choe bent ...'. In Wales there are very few references to 'The Hunt's Up', but several to 'Shoe Bend' which in time became translated into 'Plygiad y Bedol Fach' (The Bend of the Little Horseshoe). Although these came to be known by their Welsh names, other ground/tune families popular in Wales such as 'Greensleeves' and 'Rogero' retained their English titles. All these were well-known instrumental tunes in Wales throughout the eighteenth century and in some cases beyond, but the airs were not often used for songs. The tune-family most often connected with words was 'John Come Kiss Me Now / Pen Rhaw', to which a series of disconnected *penillion* would be sung rather than formal songs.

The earliest mention of 'The Welsh Ground' comes in a commonplace book kept by an Anglesey youth, Richard Morris, in the early years of the eighteenth century.[20] He lists the name 'Wales Ground' and notes that he can play it on the viol. It seems to have been quite popular: it is listed twice in the notebook of the fiddler John Thomas, c.1752,[21] and noted at least three times by the nineteenth-century harpist, Thomas David Llewelyn ('Llewelyn Alaw'; 1828–79). In 1761, 'The Welsh Ground' appeared in *The Harpsichord or Spinet Miscellany* and Edward Jones printed it in *Relicks* (1784) with the following note: 'The famous Purcell admired this Welsh ground so much, that he imitated it in a Catch.' There is, however, nothing particularly Welsh about the ground which is in the style of Italian grounds of the seventeenth and eighteenth centuries.

Many ballad airs were as well known in England for dancing or instrumental variations as they were for singing, and that may have been true of Wales too. The difficulty is lack of evidence. Without music books or manuscripts for seventeenth-century Wales (apart from the Robert ap Huw manuscript – which in any case represents an earlier period), it is necessary to depend upon tune-names connected with Welsh poetry or descriptions of the customs of the period. Some of the tunes, which were printed in the country dance books that began to be published in London about the middle of the century, would have been known to the anglicised gentry and to the harpers and fiddlers who played for them. At least half a dozen tunes on the Lleweni list can be found in *The English Dancing Master* 1651, and over forty of the tunes printed in the various seventeenth-century editions of *The Dancing Master* were known in Wales. Tunes such as 'Newcastle', 'Soldier's Life', 'Spanish Gipsy' and 'Lilliburlero' were popular with Welsh harpers and fiddlers, and some became Welsh in both name and style: 'Chestnut or Dove's Vagary' was printed in *British Harmony* as 'Hyd y Frwynen', 'Tros y Garreg' in *Relicks* (1784) is loosely related to 'The Gun', and 'Dadl Dau' in *Relicks* (1794) is a version of 'The Hemp Dresser'. Perhaps the most extraordinary transformation was that of the dance 'Vienna' which took its name from a D'Urfey ballad about the lifting of the siege of Vienna in 1683. The air was popular in Wales as 'Consêt Gruffydd ap Cynan' (Gruffydd ap Cynan's Conceit), thus connecting the tune to the Welsh king who died in 1137.

The evidence with regard to dancing in Wales is patchy. The antiquarian William Jones (1726–95), of Llangadfan in north-east Wales, wrote at the end of the eighteenth century in a letter to the harpist and collector Edward Jones:

> I suppose our Ancestors had no Dances but what they borrowed from the English together with the Terms of the Art; we have not a word in our Language which properly signifies a Dance ... I am inclined to believe that Parties of six were once in general use throughout England & Wales; my Father (as he informed me) lived with a Relation at High Arcal in Shropshire abt. 1686 being 19 years old, and frequented a Green there, and I imagine by his appearance when I first remember him (being above 60 when he married my mother) that he might be at that time a jolly Lad; and as he knew very little or nothing of dancing longways, I suppose (but am not positive) that Parties of six were there in Use ... They formerly here had Dances to Ffarwel Ned Puw, Y Fedle Fawr, Neithiwr ac Echnos, Crimson Velvet & such like, but these were left off before my Time. However Morfa Rhuddlan is a very pleasant Dance if all the party perform their parts well.[22]

The Welsh word for dance in William Jones's time – 'dawns' – comes from Middle English and is ultimately derived from the French. Occasional references to dancing in classical Welsh poetry show that the use of the term in Wales goes back at least to the fourteenth century. Some of these references mention instruments used to accompany the dance, such as harp, pipes or the bagpipe, and one interesting reference from a sixteenth-century *cywydd* describes the dancer as stamping, strutting, bowing, crossing his feet and turning like a whirligig.[23] Earlier words in Welsh for dancing also have European roots. In describing the dancing and singing on the feast day of St Eluned in the twelfth century, Giraldus Cambrensis uses the Latin word *chorea*, a classical term that in time became identified with the *carole*, and a fourteenth-century Welsh religious manuscript counsels the worshipper to sing a particular hymn, meanwhile carolling or hopping to it inwardly. The association of the carol with dancing is well-known but a fifteenth-century Welsh source condemns the sin of *looking* upon a carol being performed.[24] The word 'hop' from the Old English 'hoppian', which signified a playful dance, was still being used in Wales in the twentieth century to mean an informal dance. These terms do not appear to carry the connotation of formal dancing to figures that William Jones describes in his letter, and it may be that the word 'dawns' came into use with a new style of dancing.

The *gwylmabsant*, or Welsh patronal festival described by Giraldus, was a social festival as well as a religious one, and was for many centuries a most important occasion for community celebration in which traditional dancing played its part. An eighteenth-century traveller described dancing in the churchyard at a *gwylmabsant*, or wake, with six couples dancing on one side of the church to the music of a fiddle, while nearby several couples danced to the music of three fiddlers who were seated on a tombstone. These celebrations sometimes lasted several days and nights and could include morris dancing, singing with the harp, fiddle playing, interludes (rustic dramas), sports, football contests, cockfighting, excessive drinking and the inevitable fist fights. One writer born in the early years of the nineteenth century noted that he had a vague memory of seeing men in shirtsleeves adorned with ribbons of different colours and roses from their knees to their hats on a field near Talygarth Isa. They wore slippers and had two or three fiddlers with them. These morris dancers would go from house to house, wherever they would be welcomed, to sing and dance and to solicit beer money.

According to the musicologist John Ward, morris tunes can be divided into 'those belonging to the ritual morris, those belonging to a fashionable, country-dance form of the morris, and those belonging to ... a combination of ritual and social morris dancing, devised as much for exhibition as recreation'.[25] The country-dance type was certainly known in Wales. 'Staines Morris' appeared on the Lleweni list and was also one of the airs named in 'Myfyrdod neu Ddeusyfiad Cantores'. It is quite different from the ritual morris, as are the 'North Welch Morris' in *Aria di Camera*, c.1730,[26] and the 'Welsh Morris Dance' in *The Third Book of the Compleat Country Dancing-Master* of 1735. An example of the ritual morris tune was noted in Wales from oral tradition and can be found among the papers of Iolo Morganwg where it is called 'Morganwg. Morris Dance Tune'. His notation of the rhythm is eccentric but comparison with other morris dance tunes shows that it is a Glamorganshire version of the Helston Furry Dance tune.[27]

Example 2.5: Iolo Morganwg: Morris Dance Tune

With the growth of Protestantism in the seventeenth century, Welsh parishioners had their first opportunity to participate in congregational singing in church. Although music had a prominent part in Roman Catholic services, there was no place for congregational singing. Few if any parish churches in Wales could afford a choir and such music as took place at all was carried out by the chanting of the clergy.[28] But Protestant refugees who fled to Europe to escape persecution in the reign of Mary Tudor took part in congregational singing in churches there, and when they returned to Britain after Elizabeth I came to the throne they brought with them the custom of singing metrical psalms.

Protestantism brought two great benefits to the Welsh. The change from Latin to vernacular languages in the Church saw the appearance in 1588 of the first complete Bible in the Welsh language, an event that established a standard for written Welsh for the next 400 years. And thirty-three years later in 1621 Edmwnd Prys's setting of the psalms into rhymed, metrical poetry gave an impetus to religious singing in Wales that has continued into this century. The tunes to which Prys set his versions of twelve psalms were not Welsh, but were psalm tunes from Protestant sources such as the *Strasburg Psalter* or the *Knox Psalter*. However, these tunes, in which almost every phrase ended on a strong beat, were adapted, probably in the singing, to the Welsh language (the Welsh language has a higher proportion of words ending on the weak beat). The metre Prys chose for the majority of his settings, *Mesur Salm*, was based on the *awdl-gywydd* metre and would have been very familiar to the parishioners who sang it.

A near-contemporary of Edmwnd Prys was Rhys Prichard, born in the last quarter of the sixteenth century and, like Prys, a Churchman. After his ordination he became Vicar of Llandovery and, although he went on to hold more important ecclesiastical offices, he was known to the end of his days as 'Yr Hen Ficer' (The Old Vicar) – testimony to the respect and affection in which he was held. In contrast

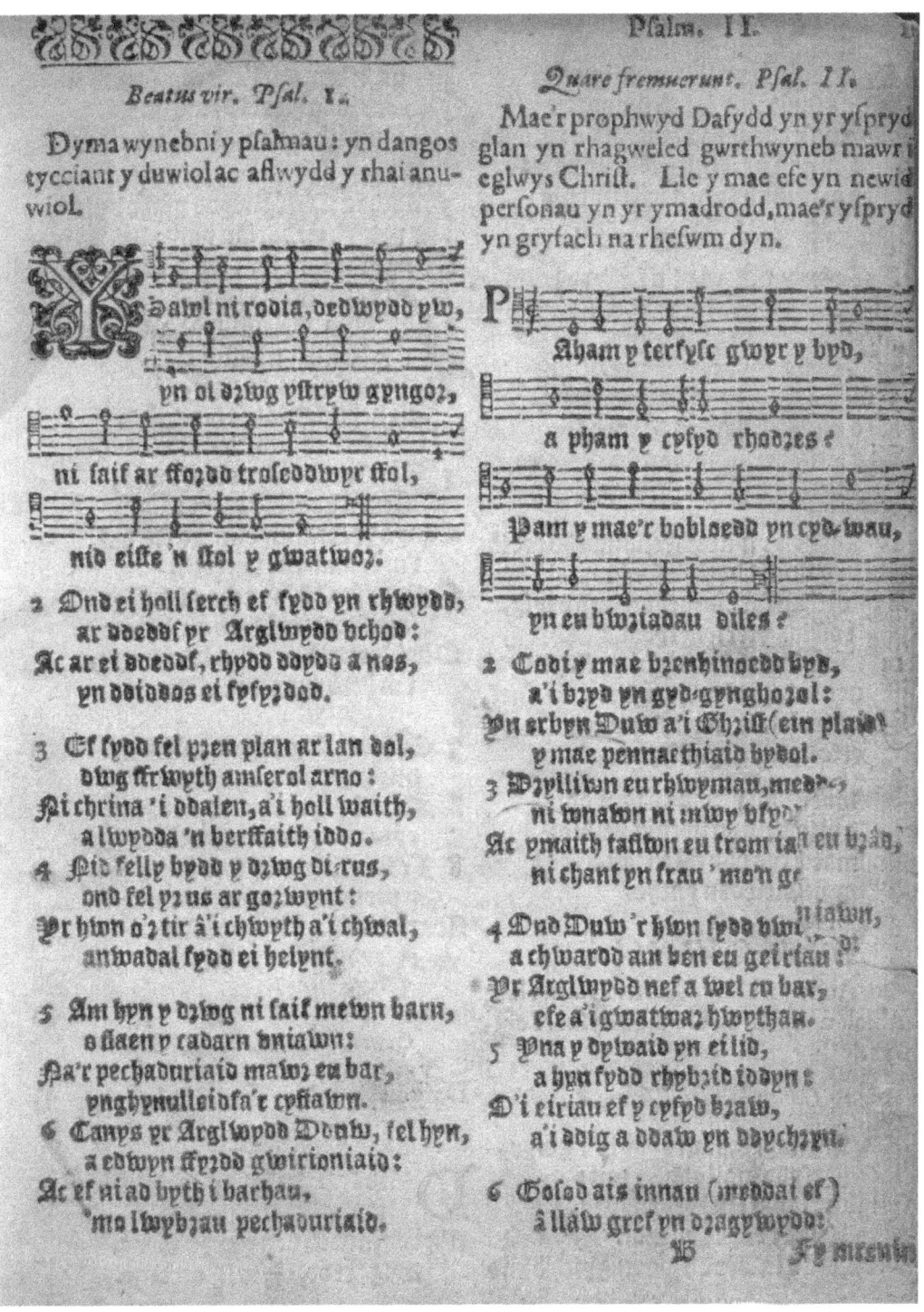

PLATE 2: *Psalm II taken from* Llyfr y Psalmau *Edmwnd Prys (1621).*
By permission of Llyfrgell Genedlaethol Cymru/The National Library of Wales.

to the north-Walian archdeacon Edmwnd Prys, who was adept at writing classical poetry in the bardic style, the south-Walian vicar restricted himself to short, homely verses in simple metres that were easy to learn. The one he used most often was a metre which was also popular in secular *penillion*: trochaic tetrameter quatrains in rhymed couplets. There is no doubt that his poems were popular, for in a period between 1658 and 1730, when many were illiterate and few could afford books, fourteen editions were published of the vicar's verses, *Canwyll y Cymry/The Welshman's Candle*.[29] Vicar Prichard was concerned to present the doctrinal teaching of salvation to illiterate Welsh congregations and, although the message was complex, the language in which he presented it was simple and straightforward, full of dialect and everyday terms. The poems told the story of the Garden of Eden and the Fall of Man, the life and death of Jesus, and the doctrine of the Incarnation in such a way that all could follow and grasp the message. Many learned great chunks of his catchy, pithy verses by heart, and in so doing imbibed Protestant doctrine. The verses might be read, recited or sung. Although no tune-names were suggested above the verses, Prichard sometimes refers to singing them and a few tunes have survived in oral tradition to the present day, together with the vicar's words, as in 'Awn i Fethlem' and 'Clychau Rhiwabon'.[30]

Example 2.6: 'Awn i Fethlem'

Example 2.7: 'Clychau Rhiwabon'

The middle of the seventeenth century was a time of great turbulence in Britain. The year 1642, two years before the death of Vicar Prichard, saw the outbreak of Civil War ending with the defeat of King Charles I and his execution in 1649. Wales, when war broke out, is described by the historian Geraint H. Jenkins as 'an impoverished, downtrodden, and sleepy nation on the outer fringes of Europe ...'.[31] Towns were small and communications poor, the mountainous nature of much of the country meant that a good deal of agriculture was confined to isolated upland farms and transport was difficult. Scarcity of capital contributed to sluggish economic growth and a series of bad harvests could prove disastrous. This period, which saw the final demise of the bardic order, is notable for a form of religious singing called *canu halsingod*, which was popular in the Teifi valley of south-west Wales during the years between the Civil War and the Methodist Revival that began in Wales in 1735. Erasmus Saunders, in the second chapter of his book *A View of the State of Religion in the Diocese of St David's*, described it thus:

> to make their private Instructions more agreeable and effectual, as they are naturally addicted to Poetry, so some of the more skilful and knowing among them frequently compose a kind of Divine Hymns, or Songs, which they call Halsingod or Carolion, which generally consist either of the Doctrinal, or Historical parts of scripture, or of the Lives, and worthy Acts of some eminent Saints ... It is not to be express'd what a particular Delight and Pleasure the young People take to get these Hymns by heart, and to sing them with a great deal of Emulation of excelling each other. And this is a Religious Exercise they are us'd to, as well at home in their own Houses, as upon some Publick Occasions; such as at their Wakes and solemn Festivals, and Funerals, and very frequently in their Churches in the Winter Season, between *All Saints* and *Candlemass*; at which Times, before and after Divine Service, upon *Sundays*, or Holy-days, Eight or Ten will commonly divide themselves to Four or Five of a side, and so forming themselves, as it were into an Imitation of our Cathedral, or Collegiate Choirs, one Party first begins, and then by way of Alternate Responses, the other repeats the same *Stanza*, and so proceed till they have finish'd their *Halsing*, and then conclude with a *Chorus*.[32]

Like the verses of Vicar Prichard, the purpose of the poems sung by these young people was didactic, presenting Biblical stories and Protestant doctrine in a form that made it easy to learn for those who could not read. The tunes they used were not written down and it is impossible to be sure what they were although the metres of the verses were those used in secular folk poetry of the time and it is possible that some tavern tunes found their way into church, as they have done throughout the history of religious singing. There is, however, one mention of a tune in a collection of *halsingod* that refers to singing about Christ's miracles on the customary tune in Churches. Meredydd Evans has suggested that the tune in question was probably a melody that was popular in Europe and America for psalm singing: 'Yr Hen Ganfed' (Old Hundredth). It was one of the tunes used by Edmwnd Prys for his settings of the metrical psalms and would have been very familiar to Welsh churchgoers. The *halsingod* verses can be sung on 'Yr Hen Ganfed' if accented cadences are changed to unaccented.[33]

Example 2.8: 'Yr Hen Ganfed'

In the last half of the seventeenth century, as the call for bardic poetry dwindled to almost nothing, a new type of lighter and more lyrical songs took its place. These songs were being written by a different class of poet, not professional bards who sang the praises of their patrons, but farmers and craftsmen and men of the church. The greatest of these was Huw Morys (1622–1709), a literate farmer's son who was a warden of the Anglican church at Llansilin and a fervent Royalist throughout the Civil War and after. Although he had the patronage of some local gentry families and could write classical poetry in the strict bardic metres, Morys's great contribution was to write love songs, elegies and carols to popular tunes of the day, many of them from England and the Continent. The metres of these tunes with their regular accentuation provided an impetus for a new kind of poetry, and Huw Morys's finely crafted verses that made use of the bardic devices of assonance and internal rhyme gave it real prestige. Lewis Morris, writing in 1762, recognised Huw Morys's achievement in this letter:

> I am still of opinion as far as I can trust my memory that Hugh Morris is the first song-writer in our language that copied Nature or that wrote anything tollerable ... And I don't remember to have seen anything in the shape of a song till the merry reign of Charles 2nd about which time song-writing began to sprout in imitation of the English and French, and all good substantial Cywydds and Awdlau (Odes) about that time hid their heads...[34]

In a later letter on the same subject, he noted that 'song writing is a modern thing in imitation of the English and the French, and Hugh Morris is the only writer of ours that ever shone in it'. Here, Lewis Morris is obviously distinguishing between three types of poetry: bardic declamation, disconnected *penillion* sung to the harp, and accompanied song of thematically linked verses – and it is clear that, in his opinion, Huw Morys was the first to make the 'song' popular in Wales.

The setting of ballad words to well-known tunes had been popular in England since the latter half of the sixteenth century when *A Handefull of pleasant delites* printed ballads to specified tunes such as 'Greensleeves', 'Lusty Gallant' and 'Labandala Shot'. About a quarter of the twenty-seven tunes it names can be traced to continental sources such as Italy, France and the Low Countries. According to John Ward:

> the early Tudor broadside ballads were rarely if ever sung to migrant tunes ... the tunes named in the *Handful*, and others contemporary with them, belong to the second generation, still responsive to cross-Channel influences but fast acquiring an English character.[35]

By the Restoration of Charles Stuart to the throne in 1660, this trend had become a flood in England, especially in the area of topical broadside ballads. Huw Morys, who lived on the Welsh-English border, would undoubtedly have been familiar with many English ballads and the tunes that went with them. Among the tunes, both English and Welsh, to which he set his ballads were some popular in the sixteenth century such as 'Crimson Velvet', 'London Apprentice' and 'Spanish Pavan'; others such as 'King's Round', 'Charity Mistress' and 'Armeinda' were tunes to contemporary seventeenth-century ballads. The oral nature of much of their transmission is apparent in some of the tune-names. 'King's Round' was another name for 'The King's Health', a tune that acquired its name from Thomas D'Urfey's verses praising Charles II. 'Armeinda' appears to be derived from a tune called 'Digby's Farewell' (or 'Lord Sandwich's Farewell'), with words beginning 'Oh pitty Arminda those passions I bear'. Two tune-names popular in Wales result from a mishearing of English titles. 'Charity Mistress' comes from a seventeenth-century ballad tune called 'Gerard's Mistress' and the title 'Sunselia' is derived from 'Since Celia's my Foe'.

Because of the numbers of tunes coming in from England and abroad, it is sometimes stated that English tunes took over completely in Wales and drove out Welsh traditional tunes. A close look at Huw Morys's collection, however, shows that was not the case in his time. Although he relished the challenge of writing words to the unfamiliar metres of new tunes, Morys continued to set songs on such Welsh tunes as 'Neithiwr ac Echnos', 'Cil y Fwyalch' and 'Hun Gwenllian'. Furthermore, a look at his poetry shows that the metres he used most frequently were Welsh, especially the ones called 'Gadael Tir or Leave Land' and 'Calon Drom or Heavy Heart'. The earliest references to these tunes give both Welsh and English names, but there can be no doubt that the tunes were Welsh. Apart from the fact that the English names appear nowhere in English collections, the poetic metres sung to them are indubitably Welsh. The metre of 'Gadael Tir/Leave Land' is the *tri-thrawiad*, an extremely popular metre of the period that gave poets a chance to display their grasp of the intricacies of *cynghanedd*, using consonantal assonance and internal rhyme to bind the phrases together. In a poetic tradition such as this, the music is in the words; a shapely, artistic tune is not only unnecessary, it may also be a distraction. What is needed is a background against which the words can be appreciated and admired, and it is probably this aspect that accounts for the fact that many *tri-thrawiad* tunes are rather monotonous. Stepwise motion is prominent, the rhythm follows the rhythm of the words, and ornamentation is rare.[36]

Example 2.9: 'Tri Tharawiad Gwynedd'

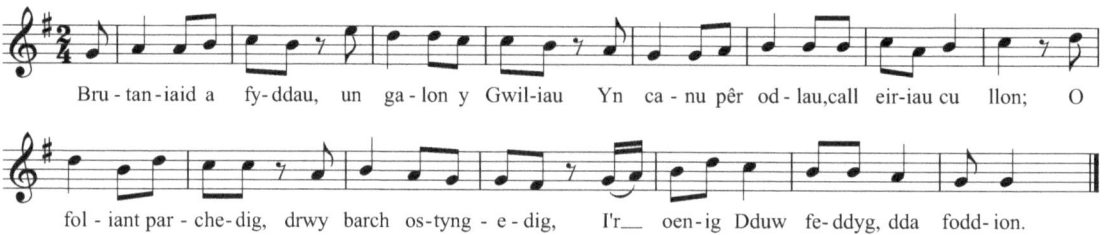

The other Welsh metre used extensively by Huw Morys was 'Calon Drom/Heavy Heart'. It is puzzling that tunes for such distinctively Welsh metres should have been called by both Welsh and English names, but serious poems such as elegies were often in the 'Calon Drom/Heavy Heart' metre and perhaps the English title was used if anglicised patrons inquired as to the name of the tune.[37]

Example 2.10: 'Y Galon Drom' (tune adapted)

Because Huw Morys's poetry was written to be sung, there has been considerable debate regarding the number of English tunes to which he set his poetry. Some, like 'About the Bank of Helicon' and 'Crimson Velvet', had attracted earlier Welsh poets, but Huw Morys was the first to use foreign tunes in such profusion. Although he obviously enjoyed writing in these new metres, and perhaps enjoyed as well the new tunes that went with them, it seems to have been the novelty that caught his interest. He wrote only a few poems to each of these new tunes whereas he wrote over seventy poems in the 'Gadael Tir' metre and forty in the 'Calon Drom' metre, as well as numerous summer carols and poems on Welsh folk metres. Taken as a whole, about two-thirds of Huw Morys's poetry in the 'free' metres (that is metres not constrained by the rules of classical Welsh poetry) was written in traditional Welsh metres to be sung to native tunes. It was the eighteenth century that brought the flood of tunes from the other side of Offa's Dyke.

3
Manuscript to Print

ONLY ABOUT a dozen of Huw Morys's more than five hundred poems were printed during his lifetime. Immensely popular, they circulated in manuscript in the houses of the gentry and middling sorts, and in oral tradition in the mouths of the illiterate. English law licensed publishing only in London and the university towns of Oxford and Cambridge, but in 1695 the law was relaxed and publishing was allowed in other parts of England and Wales. The first Welsh publisher to take advantage of this was Thomas Jones, then working in London, and he immediately moved to Shrewsbury, an important commercial town in Shropshire standing on a highway connecting London and Wales and close to Welsh booksellers.

Jones, a Churchman and Royalist, wanted to raise the religious consciousness of his fellow countrymen by the publication of religious books. The first Welsh publication to contain poetry to named tunes was a short book of anti-Papist verses, *Y Gwir er Gwaethed Yw* (The Truth in Spite of Everything), printed in London by Thomas Jones in 1684. Two of the three named tunes are in traditional Welsh metres: 'Trwm Galon neu (or) Heavy Heart' and 'Gadael y Tir neu (or) Leave Land'; the third is 'Hey, Boys, Up Go We', named on an English broadside ballad sheet of 1681. Two years later in Oxford, a much longer collection of Welsh poetry was printed with tune-names attached to them: *Cerdd Lyfr* (Song Book), by one Ffoulke Owens. The only extant copy is incomplete but it appears to have contained 54 poems, most of which are in traditional Welsh metres such as *tri thrawiad* and *awdl-gywydd*. Only a handful are to specified tunes, including 'Ffarwel Ned Puw', 'Love's a Sweet Passion' and 'Spanish Pavan'. In 1696, after moving to Shrewsbury, Thomas Jones published his most important collection of poetry, *Carolau a Dyrïau Duwiol* (Carols and Godly Songs), which reprinted forty-five poems from Ffoulke Owens's book and added others. Increasing interest in English tunes is shown by the addition of poems in later editions directed to be sung to 'Crimson Velvet' or 'Digby's Farewell'.

Thomas Jones was best known as a publisher of almanacs, bringing them out yearly between 1680 and 1712. The almanac was extremely popular in seventeenth-century England as a calendar listing months and days of the week, times of sunrise and sunset, the date of Easter and other church festivals, dates of fairs, weather predictions, prophecies, advice on the treatment of ailments and the dissemination of all sorts of knowledge. This pattern was followed by Thomas Jones, who also occasionally included poems, some to named tunes. In addition to the tunes named in *Y Gwir er Gwaethed Yw*, he printed verses to be sung to 'Diniweidrwydd', 'Love's a Sweet Passion', 'Greece and Troy' and 'Prince Rupert's Conceit'. In spite of the increasing interest in foreign tunes and metres it is notable that by the time Thomas Jones died in 1712, the *tri thrawiad* metre was still the most popular with Welsh poets. The majority of poems in *Carolau a Dyriau Duwiol* and almanacs from 1681 and 1712 are in the *tri thrawiad* metre, but by the middle of the eighteenth century the metre's popularity had been superseded by named tunes, many from England.

Tune-names printed in books of poetry and almanacs do not necessarily reflect the taste of ordinary people, many of whom were illiterate. Fortunately Richard Morris on Anglesey kept a kind of commonplace book from 1716 to 1718, in which he noted the words of wassail carols, songs, riddles, tongue-twisters and verses in English and Welsh, as well as the names of about 375 tunes of the period – but no music.[1] As might be expected, the majority of the wassail carols are in traditional Welsh metres – *triban*, *tri thrawiad*, *awdl-gywydd* or *cywydd deuair fyrion* – and where no tune-name is given it can be assumed that traditional tunes were used, simple in style and suitable for general singing. However, about half the sets of verses in this manuscript were written to be sung to named tunes, many with Welsh names such as 'Conseat y Ddafad Ddu', 'Ffarwel Trefaldwyn' or 'Triban Morgannwg'. The most interesting of these is a series of verses to be sung to the tune 'Arglwudd Llewelun' ('Arglwydd Llywelyn', or Prince Llewelyn). Some of these are verses beginning with the words 'Eira Mynydd' (Mountain Snow), which may go back as far as the fifteenth century, though in this carol they are mixed in with verses which appear to be much later.[2] But the tune 'Arglwydd Llywelyn' is also old – it is mentioned in 'Englynion y misoedd' possibly as early as the fifteenth century:[3]

gorav kaingk ar y delyn
kaingk yr arglwydd lywelyn.
[the best tune on the harp
the tune of Lord Llywelyn.]

The manuscript also contains twenty-one *dyriau* (songs) that served a number of purposes, be they satirical, religious or amatory. They include ballads in Welsh like the story of William Crismond and a Welsh version of the well-known 'riddle song' in 'Captain Wedderburn's Courtship', but it should be noted that these are versions in Welsh and not translations from English. Most of the tune-names connected with these songs are Welsh, but it is risky to depend on a name as a guide to national origin. 'Leave Land' and 'Heavy Heart' are tunes that call for characteristically Welsh poetic metres, and the names are not to be found in English collections; 'King's Farewell', named three times in the manuscript, has not been found outside Wales. On the other hand, 'Pen Rhaw', equally popular in Wales, is a variant, as noted earlier, of 'John Come Kiss Me Now', which originated in Tudor England.

There remain four lists of tune-names written down at various points in the manuscript: (a) 'Enwa Mesura' (Names of measures); (b) 'The names of the tunes that I can sing on the viol'; (c) 'Henwau mesurau fel y canlun (*mwyn iawn*)' (Names of measures as follows (*very sweet*)); (d) 'Names of tunes as foloweth'. Because of the large number of English tune-names in these lists, it is fair to ask how many of them were actually known to the young Richard Morris. Undoubtedly, he knew the tunes that he could 'sing on the viol' and those he describes as 'very sweet'. He probably also knew the tunes on his list of 'measures'. But what of the 355 tunes on his final list? The lack of music books or manuscripts in Wales during this period makes it necessary to depend largely on non-musical sources including the names of tunes connected with poetry, lists such as the catalogue of sixteenth-century dance tunes bound in with the Lleweni papers or the tunes mentioned in 'Myfyrdod neu Ddeusyfiad Cantores'. Many of these names appear in Richard Morris's manuscript, but where did he get the others? The Welsh tradition was still an oral one, but books of dance tunes were published in England and Scotland as well as on the continent, and Richard Morris notes that he learned to play the fiddle and had lessons in singing and playing the harp. It is probable that he would have learned some tunes from English music books. The majority of the tunes that he could play on the viol have English names and most of them are to be found in country dance books such as Playford's *The English Dancing Master*,[4] or in D'Urfey's *Pills to Purge Melancholy*,[5] or on broadside ballad sheets. However, about a third have Welsh names, including well-known tunes such as 'Morfa Rhuddlan' and 'Sidanen', and others like 'Bwrn o Wellt Haidd' and 'Ffarwel Trefaldwyn', which seem not to have survived. There can be little doubt that many instrumental tunes came from harpers and itinerant fiddlers who may have learned them orally – the spelling of some of the English tune-names suggests such a conclusion. It would account for 'Male Sums' ('Mall Sims'), 'Contraboncin' ('Country Bumpkin') and 'Boni Dawn Di' ('Bonny Dundee') amid a host of others. It would also account for the fact that some tunes appear more than once under different names. Richard Morris noted on his list of measures the name 'Scotch Haymakers', which was used both as a dance tune and for singing ballads. The first verse of the ballad contains four phrases that became separate song titles in Wales:

'Twas within a mile of Edinborough town
In the rosy time of the year
When the flowers were bloom'd and grass was down
And each shepherd woo'd his dear.
Bonny Jocky blithe and gay,
Kiss'd sweet Jenny making hay
The lassie blush'd and frowning said
No no it wonna do
I cannot, cannot, wonnot wonnot, maunot buckle to.

As well as noting the name, 'Scotch Haymakers', Richard Morris also included the names 'Gini Making Hea' and 'Edinburgh Town'. Later, at the end of his life, he included 'Bonny Jockey' in a list of Welsh harpers' tunes, and in the next century the Reverend John Jenkins ('Ifor Ceri'; 1770–1829) noted a variant of the 'Scotch Haymakers' tune under the name 'Dal Atto or Buckle To'. These were probably variant names for the same ballad tune. Other tunes on Richard Morris's list appear under more than one title. The seventeenth-century ballad 'Since Celia's My Foe' was also known as 'The Irish Tune' and both those names as well as a corrupt form, 'Sel Imi Ffo', appear in the manuscript as if they were individual tunes.

Among the names on the long list of 355 tunes, there are 137 that are undoubtedly English, many to be found in issues of *The Dancing Master*, and it is possible that some at least of the names were copied into the manuscript from published country dance books rather than from hearing them played. At the end of the list are the names of twenty-four tunes as they appeared in *24 New Country Dances for the Year 1716*, 'Humbly dedicated to Watkin Williams Esqr by his most humble servant Nat^l Kynaston'. The dedicatee later became Sir Watkin Williams Wynn, the most powerful of the north Wales gentry and patron of the famous harpist John Parry of Ruabon. Whether Richard Morris actually knew these tunes or merely copied the names, they seem to have had little or no currency in Wales because neither he nor any other Welsh sources mention them again.

There is, however, a way of confirming which tunes Richard Morris himself considered to be Welsh. In 1779, the year he died, he sent a list of 'Henwau Mesurau Cerdd Dafod a Thant a arferir yn gyffredinol gan y Prydyddion a'r Telynorion yng Nghymru' (The names of poetic and musical measures generally used by the poets and harpists in Wales) to the harpist Edward Jones who was collecting materials for a book of Welsh music.[6] About 120 of the names on the 1779 list came from his earlier manuscript, with considerable revision of the spelling, and included names of English tunes which had settled in Wales long since, such as 'Greece and Troy' and 'Crimson Velvet'. A few names he changed from English into Welsh – not, perhaps, because he wanted to deceive people, but because he believed that they were originally Welsh tunes that had acquired English names. In an effort to redress the balance, Richard Morris laboured to construct Welsh names from some of the English ones, and the results are often comical: 'Rogero' became 'Rhaid Sirio' (Must Cheer Up), 'Monsieur's Almain' turned into 'Yr Hen Syr Salmon' (Old Sir Salmon) and 'Grymanders Galliard' was changed to 'Goreuman Drws Galia' (The Best Place is the Door to Wales). It must be remembered, however, that these tunes had disappeared from English collections by this time, and there was no reason to feel that they were English. Indeed, in 1742 the three tunes named here appeared untitled in *Antient British Music* as the productions of ancient Welsh bards and musicians. The editors, John Parry of Ruabon and Evan Williams, undoubtedly believed that these were melodies which had been performed in Wales since time immemorial – John Parry even claiming that the English, of all the inhabitants of Britain, had no music of their own.[7]

The provenance of the tunes named in Richard Morris's manuscript spans over two centuries in Wales. As suggested earlier, 'Arglwudd Llewelun' may go back to the fifteenth century; other names, including 'Cainc Stwffw[l]' and 'Dugan y Crythor

Du' can be found in Welsh music treatises of the Tudor period and the Robert ap Huw manuscript. Two tune-names in *A Handefull of pleasant delites* appear in Richard Morris's manuscript along with eight on the 1590s Lleweni list of tunes. Some airs from the Tudor and Stuart periods had been popular over such a long period in Wales that they had acquired Welsh names and were considered to be Welsh. 'Pegi Hath Lost Hur Garter' became 'Megen a Gollodd ei Gardas' when it appeared in print in 1781, and the sixteenth-century Scottish tune 'About the Banks of Helicon' became immensely popular in Wales under the name 'Y Fedle Fawr' as a tune for singing *plygain* (Christmas) carols and ballads until the end of the nineteenth century. The same was true of 'See the Building', an early seventeenth-century tune later called 'Gwêl yr Adeilad' in Wales where it was sung to a variety of words, into the twentieth century. An English Civil War tune, 'Prince Rupert's Conceit', was well known in Wales from the mid-seventeenth century through the nineteenth and even formed the basis for a concert song in the twentieth. On the other hand, tune-names like 'Bohemia of the Queen', 'Irish Bataroo' or 'Poginili Pigynelo' are found nowhere else in Wales apart from Richard Morris's manuscript.

When Wales, a small country on the western fringe of Britain, was unified with England in the sixteenth century, London became its capital. Means of transport were limited and Wales possessed no large cities or towns, and no great educational and cultural institutions such as universities, scientific academies or literary clubs. In addition, apart from illicit recusant printing presses during the Elizabethan period, there was no printing press on Welsh soil until 1718. It was natural in these circumstances that aspiring young men like Richard Morris, literate and with some education, should flock to London to seek their fortune. Richard was the second son in a remarkable family that contributed much to Welsh culture in Wales and in London. The father had been taught to read from seventeenth-century almanacs by a cooper who was the only literate person in his parish, and the father in turn saw to it that his sons could read and write Welsh and English as well as some Latin. Richard was also a competent accountant, and with these assets he left for London where, in time, he became a prominent member of the Welsh community and an assiduous promoter of Welsh culture. His elder brother Lewis, poet, scholar and critic, remained in Wales apart from occasional visits to the capital and the correspondence of Lewis, Richard and William Morris combined presents a lively picture of Welsh life in the eighteenth century.

It was in this period that books containing 'Welsh' music began to be published in London. From time to time tunes bearing names with Welsh connotations like 'Evan's Jig', 'The Welch Whim' or 'Morgan's Thoughts' would appear in country dance books. Apart from 'St David's Day', which is on one of Richard Morris's tune-lists, none of these tunes seems to have created any lasting interest in Wales; but around 1726 a printed book appeared containing 75 secular tunes, of which five were claimed as Welsh. This was *Arla di Camera* and the Welsh airs were 'Welch Morgan', 'North Welch Morris', 'Meillionen o Feirionydd', 'Welch Richard' (usually known as 'Sweet Richard') and 'Morva Ryddlan'. The latter three were popular Welsh dance tunes and poetry was written to be sung to 'Sweet Richard' and

'Morfa Rhuddlan'. The melody of 'Sweet Richard' is related to a tune called 'Wood Waltham Green' in the third volume of *The Dancing Master* (c.1726–8) and William Crotch has three versions of 'Sweet Richard' in the section called 'Welch Tunes' in his *Specimens of Various Styles of Music*,[8] one of which is described 'as played in England 1796 &c'. However, Huw Morys wrote more than one set of words to it, showing that the tune was popular in Wales at least a hundred years earlier.

Of course, London had already become a magnet for Welsh people after 1485, with the accession of Henry Tudor, crowned as Henry VII. The gentry came to attend Parliament or enjoy the social 'Season' and brought their servants; drovers came to London regularly with cattle and sheep; professional men, such as lawyers and bankers as well as craftsmen of all kinds, found the city a good place to ply their trade, and there was a steady supply of Welsh musicians, especially harpers.[9] But by the eighteenth century, so many Welsh natives had settled in the capital that they began to form Welsh clubs meeting regularly for socialising, and some of these clubs included music-making.

PLATE 3: *William Williams ('Wil Penmorfa')*. By permission of Amgueddfa Cymru/National Museum Wales.

The most famous of the Welsh musicians was John Parry (later known as John Parry, Ruabon), a blind harper born c.1710 in Caernarfonshire, in north-west Wales. Blind children were frequently put to sing or play a musical instrument as a means of earning a living, but few can have been as naturally talented as Parry. According to one source, Parry was taught to play the harp by a relative who had himself learned his art from old traditional harpers, and he became so proficient that when he was a young man he entered a competition with the domestic harper to the Earl of Powis to determine who was the better performer. Parry was declared the winner, and it may have been this that provided the necessary start to an illustrious career; Parry became domestic harper to Sir Watkin Williams Wynn and later to his son, a connection with the family that remained until his death. As a member of Parliament, Sir Watkin would naturally spend a good deal of time in London, and thus Parry was introduced to a very different society and culture.

The musical atmosphere of London was lively with functions of all kinds designed to appeal to the aristocracy and to the bourgeoisie. Concert life, which had begun to develop there in the late seventeenth century, played a very important role in ensuring that musicians were heard beyond the circle of their patrons and many musicians considered the concert to be a prime source of attracting pupils to add to their income. Among those who sponsored concerts was Sir Watkin Williams Wynn, but private concerts were also provided by musicians such as Charles Burney. John Parry played concerts in London, Oxford, Cambridge, Leeds and Dublin. The poet Thomas Gray, who was also a good musician, heard Parry in Cambridge and wrote in a letter of May 1757:

> Mr Parry has been here, & scratch'd out such ravishing blind Harmony, such tunes of a thousand year old with names enough to choak you, as have set all this learned body a'dancing, & inspired them with due reverence for *Odikle*, whenever it shall appear. Mr Parry (you must know) it was, that has put Odikle in motion again ...[10]

The life of musicians in this period was precarious and even those who had wealthy patrons needed to make money in a variety of ways, which included performing, teaching and publishing. It is clear that, in spite of his blindness, John Parry participated in all of these. The benefit concert was one way of earning money, and it is known that he had more than one benefit. He also had a number of pupils. A school of harpers in the nineteenth century was known as 'Blind Parry's School', and his influence was so great that it is possible for at least a century after his death to trace the musical descent of most of the famous Welsh harpers to John Parry.

It was the publication in London, in 1742, of the first book claiming to consist entirely of traditional Welsh melodies that caused John Parry's fame to outlive his gifts as a performer. This book of twenty-four airs without words, each titled simply Aria, was published in 1742 by John Parry and his co-editor, Evan Williams, as *Antient British Music*.[11]

The anonymous introduction to the publication is said, by Richard Morris, to be the work of his erudite elder brother, Lewis. It states that 'The most antient Account we find of our *British* Music, is in the Time of the *Druids*', and goes on to speculate that the Druids escaped to Ireland at the time of the Roman conquest and that what remained in Britain of their music and culture was driven into hiding in the mountains of Wales: 'The peculiar Air of their Music, and Method of Singing, plainly shews it, even at this distance of Time.' This is followed by a mention of the music in the Robert ap Huw manuscript (in Lewis's possession at the time), and the Irish nature of some names of measures. He ends by quoting Latin passages from Giraldus Cambrensis that deal with music in Wales and Ireland, and concludes that 'the *British* Music (which hence may be taken for granted to be a Remains of *Druidism*) had then arrived at a very great Perfection'.

Lewis Morris's claims were not as ludicrous then as they have since been shown to be. Interest in the history of the Druids was awakened by the availability of classical texts in the Renaissance and given status in the seventeenth century by Milton's reference in 'Lycidas' to the Druid bards of Anglesey. In the eighteenth century, the antiquarian William Stukeley popularised the idea that Stonehenge and Avebury were built by the Druids. Welsh poets in Wales and London were proud of their bardic descent from such progenitors and this pride pervades *Antient British Music*. The collection contains twenty-four melodies, a number which had considerable resonance in the Welsh culture of earlier ages and may have been chosen deliberately to reinforce the connection with antiquity.

According to a variety of early sources there were twenty-four officers of the king's court, twenty-four pence to be paid to the *pencerdd* by each minstrel upon finishing instruction in the twenty-four acknowledged poetic measures (*cerdd dafod*) or the twenty-four musical measures (*cerdd dant*), twenty-four *clymmau cytgerdd,* twenty-four feats a gentleman was expected to be able to accomplish, and so on.

Although the tunes were not as 'antient' as the title implies, more than half of the pieces go back to the sixteenth and seventeenth centuries. Here is the list of the untitled airs in *Antient British Music* with names as they were noted in the manuscripts of harpers, collectors and other musicians.[12]

Aria I   (Sidanen): An instrumental tune, irregular in form with repetition of phrases and sequential treatment of broken chords. The name goes back at least to the sixteenth century although it is worth noting that the tune in *Antient British Music* bears no relationship to the 'Sedany, or Dargason' tune mentioned in chapter 2.

Example 3.1: Aria I (Sidanen)

Aria II (Bro Gwalia/Bro Galia/Fro Golier): A highly ornamented version of John Dowland's late sixteenth-century tune 'Frog Galliard'

Aria III (Blodeu'r Dyffryn/Dewis Meinwen/My Lady Byram/Biron/Bryan): Some of the names given to this tune connect it with a Lady Byron. The first Lord Byron, created Baron of Rochdale in 1643, was Field Marshall of the King's forces in north Wales during the Civil War, and held Caernarfon Castle for a time. Perhaps this graceful tune was a favourite with his wife.

Example 3.2: Aria III (Blodeu'r Dyffryn/Dewis Meinwen/My Lady Byram/Biron/Bryan)

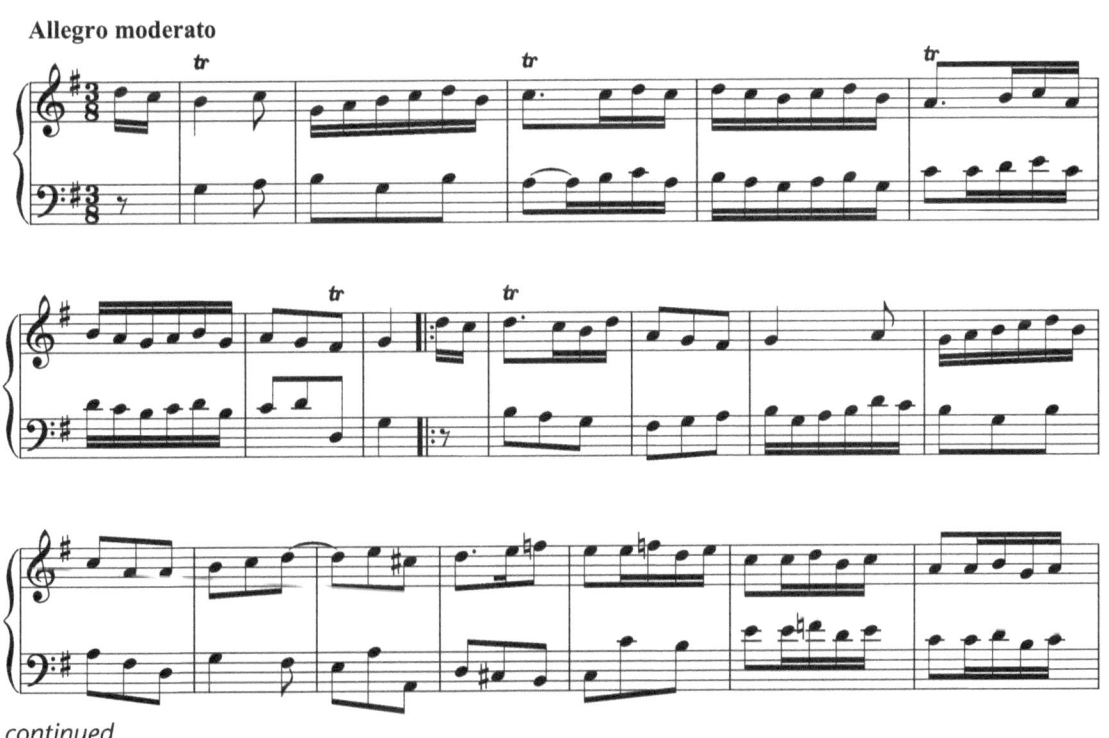

continued

Aria IV   (Consêt Arglwydd Strain/Lord Strain's Fancy/Arglwyddes Druan): The title of Lord Strange of Knockin in Shropshire, not far from the Welsh border, was created in the fourteenth century; this tune, which may have been a favourite with a member of the family, probably dates from the seventeenth century.

Aria V   (Margaret Fwyn ach Evan/Mwynder Meirionydd): It has been suggested that the redoubtable Margaret Evans of Caernarfonshire who lived in the eighteenth century was the 'Fair Margaret daughter of Evan' of Welsh poetry. She was reputed to be a blacksmith and carpenter who could make shoes, build boats and make fiddles and harps as well as play them, and her fame was celebrated by the poets of the area. However, the tune with its ambiguous tonality, limited compass and a somewhat meandering melodic line, may in fact be a good deal older than the eighteenth century.

Example 3.3: Aria V (Margaret Fwyn ach Evan/Mwynder Meirionydd)

Aria VI (Dynwared yr Eos/Gwatwariad yr Eos): This tune appeared earlier in *24 Country Dances for the Year 1711* as 'Mock Nightingale'.

Aria VII (Twll yn ei Boch): A graceful minuet simple in style.

Aria VIII (Ffarwel Abel Salmon/Mwynen Môn): An early seventeenth-century-style almain.

Aria IX (Burstoy/E Fu Ers Doe/First Day): Almost nothing is known of this tune, in three equal sections, which may have been a dance.

Aria X (Mounsier Salmon/Moses Solomon/Moes Hen Salmon): A florid version of the sixteenth-century dance tune 'Monsieur's Almain', a name which seems to have baffled Welsh harpers who called it by a variety of titles.

Aria XI (Triban/Triban Lewis Llwyd): The triban was a very popular Welsh poetic metre, especially among folk poets, and two triban verses will fit easily on this tune.

Aria XII (Sweet Richard/Per Alaw/Per Oslef/Os Wyt Richard): The tune called 'Welch Richard' in *Aria di Camera* has been popular in Wales since the seventeenth century giving rise to numerous variants as instrumental pieces, dances or settings for words

Aria XIII (Cow Heel/Sawdl y Fuwch/Cainc y Wraig o Faes-y-Neuadd): The title 'Cow Heel' may derive from a broadside ballad in the Pepys collection, 'An Oxford Scholar and his Penny Cow-Heel'. The name 'Sawdl y Fuwch' is a Welsh translation of 'Cow Heel', but the third title suggests that this sprightly tune was a favourite with a lady of the Wynne family who lived at Maesyneuadd, Meirionethshire.

Aria XIV (Breuddwyd Dafydd Rhys/Ffarwel Dai Llwyd/King's Farewell/Ymadawiad y Brenin): 'Breuddwyd Dafydd Rhys' is the correct name for this triple-time tune. The other titles refer to a related tune, usually called 'King's Farewell', in duple time and four bars longer.

Aria XV (Difyrrwch yr Arglwyddes Owen/Lady Owen's Delight): This appears to be a variant of a seventeenth-century English ballad tune 'Methinks the Poor Town Has Been Troubled Too Long' and the name 'Lady Owen's Delight' indicates that it was a favourite with a titled lady.

Aria XVI (Rogero/Yr Hen Rogero Bengoch/Rhaid Sirio): Although in one copy of *Antient British Music* the name 'Rogero' has been written above this tune any relationship to sixteenth-century tunes based on the well-known ground is very doubtful since this highly ornamented piece is unrelated to 'Rogero' in melody, harmony and form.

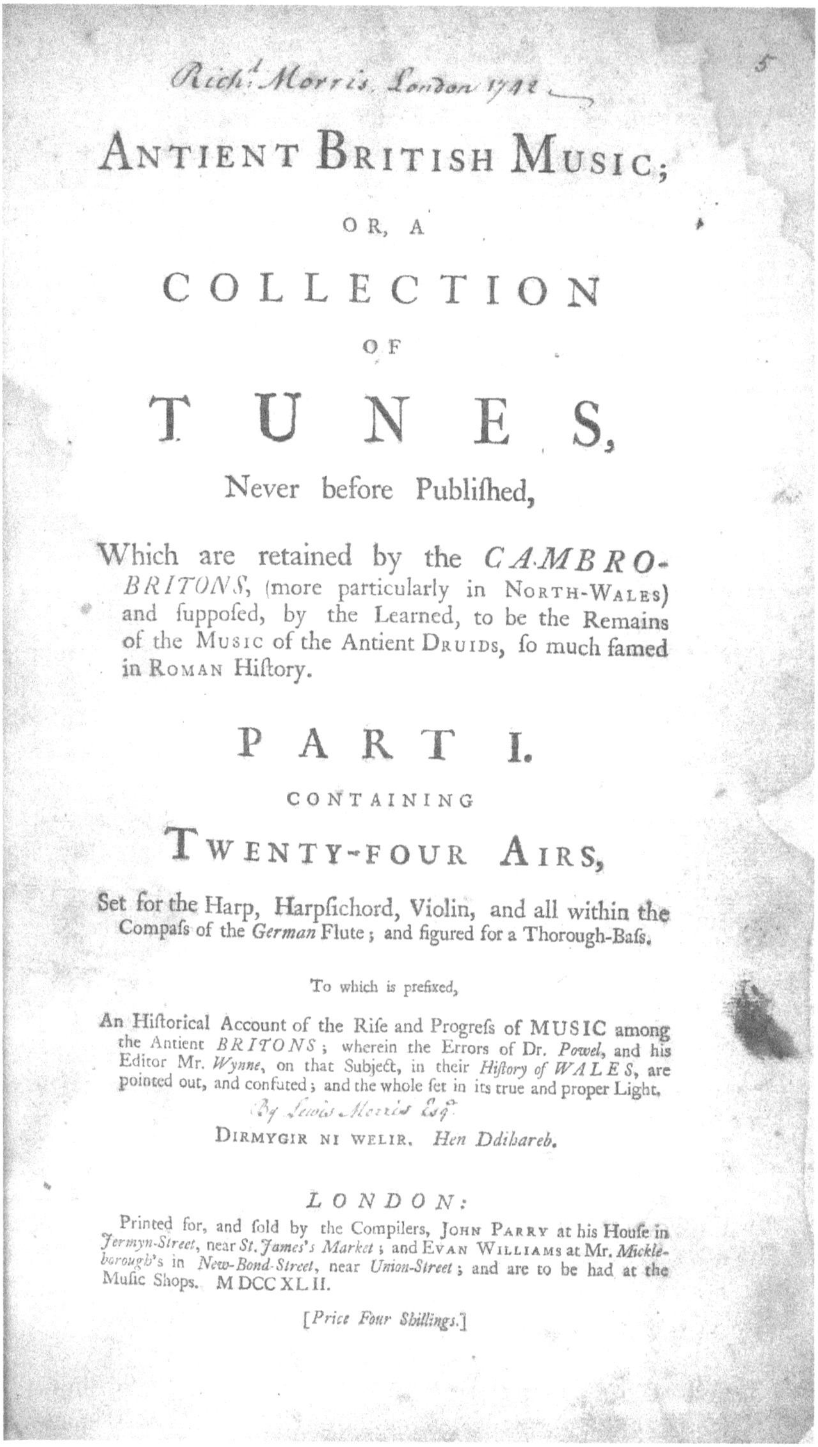

Richd: Morris. London 1742

ANTIENT BRITISH MUSIC;

OR, A

COLLECTION

OF

TUNES,

Never before Publiſhed,

Which are retained by the *CAMBRO-BRITONS*, (more particularly in NORTH-WALES) and ſuppoſed, by the Learned, to be the Remains of the MUSIC of the Antient DRUIDS, ſo much famed in ROMAN Hiſtory.

PART I.

CONTAINING

TWENTY-FOUR AIRS,

Set for the Harp, Harpſichord, Violin, and all within the Compaſs of the *German* Flute; and figured for a Thorough-Baſs.

To which is prefixed,

An Hiſtorical Account of the Riſe and Progreſs of MUSIC among the Antient *BRITONS*; wherein the Errors of Dr. *Powel*, and his Editor Mr. *Wynne*, on that Subject, in their *Hiſtory of WALES*, are pointed out, and confuted; and the whole ſet in its true and proper Light.

By Lewis Morris Esqr.

DIRMYGIR NI WELIR. *Hen Ddihareb.*

LONDON:

Printed for, and ſold by the Compilers, JOHN PARRY at his Houſe in *Jermyn-Street*, near *St. James's Market*; and EVAN WILLIAMS at Mr. *Mickleborough*'s in *New-Bond-Street*, near *Union-Street*; and are to be had at the Muſic Shops. M DCC XL II.

[*Price Four Shillings.*]

PLATE 4: *The title page of* Antient British Music *with an inscription, possibly in the hand of Richard Morris. By permission of the British Library.*

Aria XVII   (Shoe Bend/Plygiad y Bedol): The name 'Shoe Bend' may be connected with a sixteenth-century lute piece called 'Chow Bente' based on the Tudor ground, 'The Hunt's Up', as discussed earlier in chapter 2. However, the two versions of the tune given in *Antient British Music* do not fit the ground, although they are the same length and have some of the same harmonies.

Aria XVIII   (Gorddinam/Garddinen/Y Gerddinen): There is some dispute about the titles of this instrumental melody. 'Gorddinam' appears to derive from the name of a small hill-fort near Dolwyddelan in north-west Wales, but 'Y Gerddinen' is the rowan tree, or mountain ash.

Aria XIX   (Grymanders Galliard/Gray Mundus/Gramwndws Galia/Goreu Man Drws Galia): The popularity of the galliard, a sixteenth-century dance form, faded about the middle of the seventeenth century and this galliard is noted only once after its appearance in *Antient British Music*.

Aria XX   (Ffarwel Philip Ystwyth/Digan Philip Ystwyth): This typical eighteenth-century harp piece first appeared in *Antient British Music* and later versions appear to be copied from it.

Aria XXI   (Erddigan Hun Gwenllian/Digan Wil Bifan Bennoeth/Rhyfelgan ap Ifan Bennaeth): The strong dotted rhythm of this tune gives it a quasi-military air that matches one of its titles: 'Rhyfelgan ap Ifan Bennaeth' (The War-song of the son of Ifan the Chief). The alternative title, 'Erddigan Hun Gwenllian', suggests a connection with 'Hun Gwenllian' in the Robert ap Huw manuscript, but the *Antient British Music* tune is not related in style or musical content.

Example 3.4: Aria XXI, (Erddigan Hun Gwenllian/Digan Wil Bifan Bennoeth/Rhyfelgan ap Ifan Bennaeth)

Aria XXII (Meillionen/Consêt Syr Watkin/Sir Watkin's Delight): Versions of this well-known Welsh dance tune were printed in *Aria di Camera* and in Walsh's *Caledonian Country Dances, Book I* of 1733. It was a favourite of John Parry's patron, Sir Watkin Williams Wynn.

Aria XXIII (Mael Syms/Mael Swm/Symlen Ben Bys): The two versions of the tune printed in *Antient British Music* are distantly related to the Elizabethan dance tune 'Mall Sims' but the differences are great.

Aria XXIV (Morfa Rhuddlan): This popular Welsh tune has been used as a theme for variations on the harp, as a dance and as the setting for at least a dozen poems. It appeared first in *Aria di Camera*.

The *Antient British Music* airs are an interesting mixture of dances, instrumental compositions and tunes to which poetry might be set. The dances include sixteenth-century *galliards* and *almains* as well as eighteenth-century minuets and country dance tunes. But although the collection appears to be purely instrumental, words were written to be sung to at least fifteen of the twenty-four tunes, usually in the eighteenth-century style that combined *cynghanedd* with regularly accented metres. (One of the poems in *Blodeu-gerdd Cymry* is set to be sung to 'Blodeu'r Dyffryn'. This, as already indicated, is one of the names given to Aria III. The poem in question can easily be adapted to it.)[13]

Example 3.5: 'Blodeu'r Dyffryn' with words from *Blodeu-gerdd Cymry*

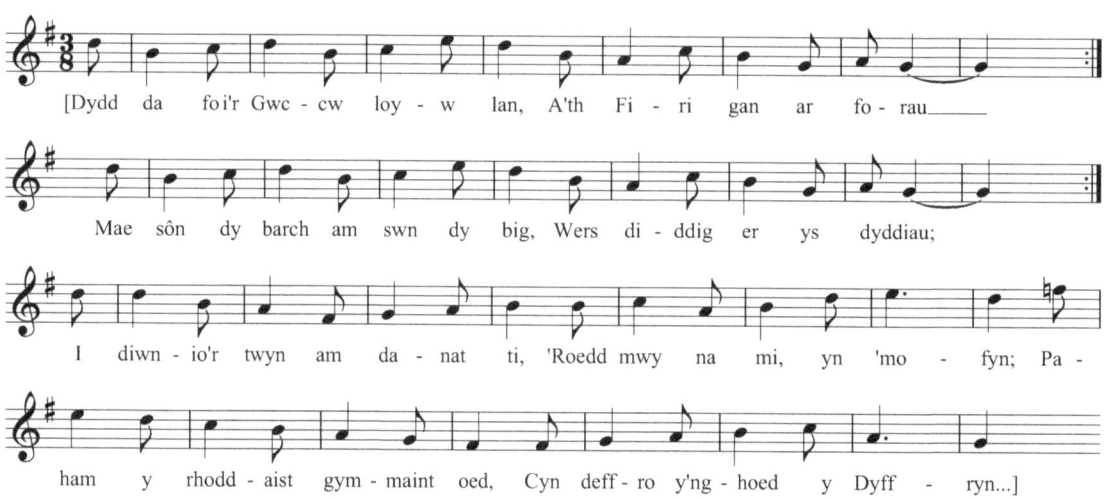

There can be no doubt that most of the *Antient British Music* tunes were well-known in Wales since all but five of the names appear in Richard Morris's early eighteenth-century manuscript. The statement that the tunes were 'never before published' is of course misleading, since arrangements of three of them had appeared about fifteen years earlier in *Aria di Camera*. But the publication of *Antient British Music* did break new ground by presenting tunes played by Welsh musicians to a sophisticated English public. According to Simon McVeigh in *Concert Life in London from Mozart to Haydn*:

> Perhaps the only nation to maintain a distinctive voice was Wales. London audiences heard a number of Welsh harpers, notably John Parry (who retained the traditional triple harp) and Edward Jones. Their product was both unusual and fashionable.[14]

Certainly, the 201 names on the *Antient British Music* subscription list testify to the willingness of London society to support the publication of such music. About half these names appear to be of members of the Welsh gentry or connected with Wales, but the rest include such figures as the Duke of Devonshire, the Duchess of Newcastle and the Earl of Halifax as well as members of the musical bourgeoisie.

In view of the success of the 1742 volume, the editors embarked upon the publication of an edition more specifically Welsh in content. Certainly, the most characteristically Welsh music was to be found in the setting of Welsh verses to harp tunes, and it was decided to publish some of these. In April 1745, a proposal for printing part II of *Antient British Music* was circulated:

> PART II I containing Thirty Tunes set for the Harp, Harpsichord, Violin, and all within the compass of the German Flute; and figured for a thorough Bass; ... And to render the work more agreeable the Songs in the *Antient British* will be set to them, also attempted in *English* verse as the Language will admit of: which will show the Nature of singing with the Harp, Violin, &c. at this time by the *Welsh* at their *Musical Meetings*.[15]

Subscriptions were invited and a specimen was to be prepared for prospective customers, but nothing more seems to have been heard of the project. It was assumed that the work was never undertaken until in the 1970s the harpist Osian Ellis discovered the manuscript of what appears to be the unfinished specimen of part II bound in with a copy of *Antient British Music* in the Royal College of Music in London. It includes seven traditional Welsh songs set to the harp with words in Welsh and English, and gives a picture of a different kind of music-making from that of the earlier publication, showing the interaction of voice and harp in the Welsh style sometimes called *canu penillion* (singing verses) or *canu gyda'r tannau* (singing with the strings). Edward Jones writing later in the century described it in *Relicks* (1794):

> There are several kinds of *Pennill* metres, that may be adapted and sung to most of the following tunes; and some part of a tune being

occasionally converted into a symphony [that is a section for instrument only]. One set of words is not, like an English song, confined to one tune, but commonly sung to several.

The skill of the *pennill*-singers in this is admirable. According to the metres of their *penillion*, they strike into the tune in the proper place, and conduct it with wonderful exactness to the symphony, or the close. While the Harp to which they sing is perhaps wandering in little variations and embellishments, their singing is not embarrassed, but true to the fundamental tune.[16]

This style of singing verses with harp interpolations was considered in London to be distinctively Welsh as is shown by Thomas D'Urfey's song 'Of Noble Race Was Shenkin' in the 1693 play *The Richmond Heiress*. The song, which satirises a Welshman, was written to be sung to the harp and includes a phrase for solo harp. In 1709, D'Urfey used the tune again, describing the song as 'set to a famous Tune on the Welch Harp', this time with two harp 'symphonies'.

In order to show how poetry and music interact in this distinctive style six examples were arranged in the *Antient British Music* Part II specimen, each in a different poetic metre and with harp symphonies at various points in the song: (a) 'Pencraig'; (b) 'Gadel Tir'; (c) 'A Phrŷnn Sy' Ar'; (d) Sr Harri Ddû; (e) 'Gwên Dando'; (f) 'Calon Drom'. A seventh song with words, 'Malldod Dolgellau', was included as a song with harp accompaniment but no symphonies.

Undoubtedly, Evan Williams was responsible for making the music ready for publication, since John Parry himself was blind. Judging by the settings in *Antient British Music,* which include imitative passages and figured bass, Williams was a competent musician who was in contact with the art music of his time. The settings for harp and voice in the specimen are much simpler than those for solo harp in the earlier volume and there is considerable evidence that the melodies in the specimen were edited to conform to the taste of a mid-eighteenth-century urban public.

The nature of the editing becomes clear when these settings are compared with other variants of the same tunes to be found in native Welsh harp and fiddle manuscripts. The melodic line and implied harmony of 'Pencraig', for example, differs in important ways from the same tune that John Parry published, untitled and arranged for guitar, in *A Collection of Welsh, English and Scotch Airs*. 'Calon Drom' was a tune popular with seventeenth and eighteenth-century Welsh poets who always wrote eight-line verses to it in a distinctive metre. The example in the manuscript, however, gives six-line verses in a different metre (which may have been written especially for the specimen by Evan Williams himself) and omits two bars from the B section.

Another aspect of the editing to have caused controversy is what appears to be the use of melisma in three of the songs: 'Pencraig', 'Calon Drom' and 'Gadael Tir'. Melisma is very rare in Welsh traditional song because elongation of the vowel distorts the word, and the close connection between music and poetry in Wales

PLATE 5: *'Calon Drom' from* Antient British Music, *Part II, unpublished specimen.*
By permission of the Royal College of Music, London.

means that the words must always be clear. Did Evan Williams intend the singer to treat these phrases as extended slurs? They come in places that might easily be harp symphonies, and Williams does not always place a slur over these phrases as might be expected.

There is no other indication of extended slurring in Welsh music of the period and if the editors did intend these phrases to be treated as melismas it may have been because they felt the style would appeal to a London public admiring of the vocal music of Handel.

Two tune-names were changed. 'A Phrŷnn Sy' Ar' seems to be an attempt to cymricise the name 'France Air', and 'Gwên Dando' is a variant of 'Queen Dido', a sixteenth-century English tune, perhaps because the editors thought that London antiquarians would scoff at these tunes as examples of genuine Welsh music if they were printed with English names, even though they had long since been part of the repertoire of Welsh musicians. Attached to the manuscript is a list of thirty-one names of tunes presumably meant to be included in the finished book. Over half of these are undoubtedly Welsh – some from the Robert ap Huw period or earlier, others more recent – but some tunes known to young Richard Morris by English names had by the mid-eighteenth century acquired Welsh ones; 'Loath to Depart' had become 'Anhawdd Ymadel', 'Soldier's Life' was changed to 'Bywyd y Milwr' and 'Queen's Dream' became 'Breuddwyd y Frenhines'.

After 1745, nothing more was heard of the musical partnership between John Parry and Evan Williams, and it was not until 1761 that Parry's next book appeared, *A Collection of Welsh, English and Scotch Airs*.[17] Although the only name connected with the book is that of Parry, the blind harper must have had an amanuensis. It has been suggested that Evan Williams's name does not appear as co-editor because he and Parry had quarrelled over Williams's arrangements, but no sound evidence has been produced to support this and it may have been John Parry's son, David, who took Williams's place and transcribed his father's arrangements for *Airs* and *British Harmony*. According to another John Parry ('Bardd Alaw'; 1776–1851) the father and son 'used to perform Handel's Choruses on two Welsh Harps, at the Court of George III, some seventy years ago' (that is in about 1778).[18]

From the standpoint of traditional Welsh music, *Airs* is the least interesting of Parry's publications. Three of the named tunes, 'Sweet Richard', 'Rhydlan Marsh' and 'Meillionen', had previously been published in *Aria di Camera* and *Antient British Music* in different arrangements. 'Of Noble Race Was Shenkin' and 'Can Love Be Controul'd By Advice' were popular theatre tunes, 'Highland Laddie', 'Gin Thou Wert Mine Ain Thing' and 'The Lass of Patie's Mill' were well-known Scots airs, and a sprinkling of pieces by Handel included 'Gavot in Otho' and 'Minuet in Ariadne'. Parry also included four harp sonatas of his own composition, which he called 'Lessons'. Musically the arrangements in *Airs* are more graceful than those in *Antient British Music*, possibly reflecting more closely John Parry's own style, but also perhaps reflecting changing musical taste in the years between 1742 and 1761. Most interesting from the traditional point of view are twelve untitled pieces for the guitar. The first eight of these melodies, noted without words, harmony or variations, are tunes familiar in Wales. 'Mwynen Môn' (1) and 'Difyrrwch Arglwyddes Owen' (2) had already appeared in *Antient British Music* in quite closely related versions, but 'Pencraig' (4) differs considerably from the version in the 1745 manuscript. 'Glan Meddwdod Mwyn' (3), 'Cwympiad y Dail' (5) 'Pigau'r Dur' (6), 'Nos Galan' (7) and 'Megan a Gollodd ei Gardas' (8) appear for the first time in *Airs*.

It is not known when John Parry finally left London and returned to Ruabon in north Wales, but it was there in 1781 that he published his last book, *British Harmony*. From the standpoint of traditional music, this is by far the most interesting of John Parry's publications with a mixture of ballad and carol tunes, popular Welsh melodies and harp airs. *British Harmony* contains forty-two items, of which thirty-three appear for the first time. Although no words are ever given with Parry's tunes, three of the pieces in this volume appear to be connected with Welsh traditional practices. 'Calenig' may derive from a New Year *quête* song, since the name is suggestive and traditional *calennig* verses will fit the air:[19]

Example 3.6: 'Calenig'

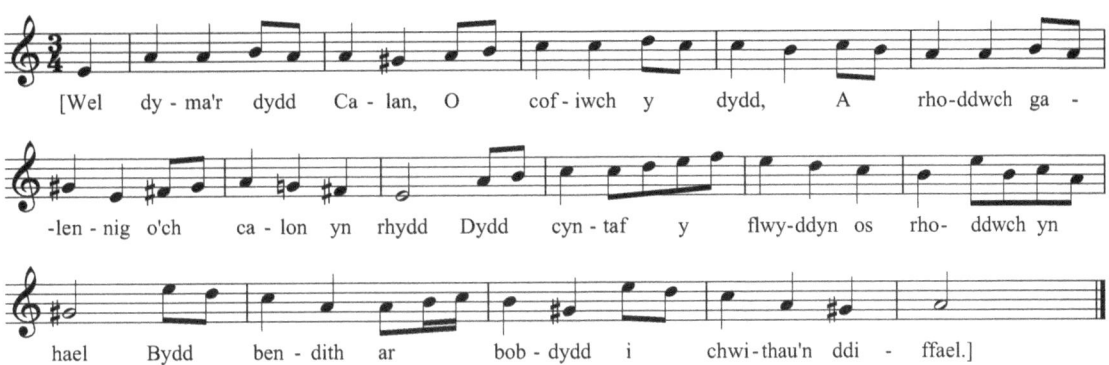

[Wel dy-ma'r dydd Ca-lan, O cof-iwch y dydd, A rho-ddwch ga--len-nig o'ch ca-lon yn rhydd Dydd cyn-taf y flwy-ddyn os rho-ddwch yn hael Bydd ben-dith ar bob-dydd i chwi-thau'n ddi-ffael.]

Some eighteenth-century May Day carols were sung to 'Mwynen Mai'. The example in *British Harmony* is a highly ornamented May Day carol tune, probably meant to be performed by voice with instrumental symphonies.[20]

Example 3.7: 'Mwynen Mai'

'Nos galan' is a typical *penillion* tune used extensively in New Year's Eve gatherings. Traditional verses and harp interpolations or nonsense syllables could be interwoven in the air.[21]

Example 3.8: 'Nôs Calan'

Several tunes used for singing Welsh ballads and carols also appear here for the first time; 'Ffarwel Ned Pugh', 'Mentra Gwen', 'Susannah' and 'Y Fedle Fawr' (slightly adapted here to set a verse from a wassail song):[22]

Example 3.9: 'Y Fedle Fawr'

These were all popular tunes for secular ballads and songs as well as for *plygain* carols.[23] In contrast to them are instrumental items like 'Dynwared yr Eos', a display piece for the harp, or 'Dyferiad y Gerwyn', made up of running figures and typical harp sequences; both are followed by sets of variations. Two airs from *Antient British Music*, 'Dynwared yr Eos' and 'Difyrwch yr Arglwyddes Owen' reappear in *British Harmony* in new arrangements followed by variations.

4
Edward Jones and Traditional Airs

IN 1784, three years after the publication of *British Harmony*, came the first book of Welsh tunes to include words to some of the airs. This was *Musical and Poetical Relicks of the Welsh Bards;* an enlarged edition appeared in 1794. It is obvious that this work was much more ambitious than any of John Parry's publications. Edward Jones, its author, was not only a notable harpist but an antiquarian with a wide-ranging interest in old Welsh music. He was born in 1752 to a cultured, well-to-do farming family in Llandderfel, Merionethshire, an area abounding with harpers where *penillion* singing was popular, and Edward grew up to the sound of the old traditional tunes.[1] In the introduction to *The Bardic Museum*, he wrote:

> The greatest part of these melodies I have committed to writing from hearing them sung by the old people, and from their being played by the most venerable Harpers, in North Wales; and it is very fortunate that I did so, because most of them are since dead. Being a native of Meirionydd, where our national customs are best retained, and where I generally used to pass my summers; being also well acquainted with most of the popular Welsh airs from my infancy, from having been brought up in the musical profession, and having always had a predilection for native customs; I may perhaps, have the advantage of my contemporaries on this subject ...[2]

In addition to being a good musician Edward Jones was well-read in both English and Welsh, which stood him in good stead when he left Wales in 1774–5 to pursue a professional career in London with the support of prominent Welsh gentry families. In May 1775 the young harper played at a concert held in the house of Dr Charles Burney, an occasion recorded by Burney's daughter, Fanny, who described Edward Jones in her diary as 'a silly young man'. Judging from the description of those who knew him well, Edward Jones was reserved in character and rather taciturn, and it seems likely that Fanny Burney described him as 'silly' to mean 'countrified' or 'unsophisticated'. She went on to note that he played with great neatness and delicacy, but little expression. Edward Jones never married and, although he became one of the foremost harpers of his age, his playing may not have held the charisma of his great predecessor, John Parry, Ruabon, perhaps due to Jones's naturally reserved nature. However, he moved in fashionable circles and at some point, probably in the mid-1780s, he was appointed 'Harper to the Prince of Wales', though he preferred to call himself 'Bard to the Prince'. In 1820, when the king died and the prince became King George IV, Edward Jones styled himself 'Bard to the King' and was from then on known in Wales as 'Bardd y Brenin'. Acceptance in the higher levels of English society undoubtedly helped the young harper in his career; he acquired pupils from among the gentry, gave concerts, played for dancing and at private parties, and composed salon pieces, drawing-room ballads and lessons for his pupils, in addition to publishing numerous arrangements of national airs from Europe and the East. But his lasting contribution to music is the collection of over 200 Welsh airs published in several volumes between 1784 and 1825.

Although these publications are usually referred to as collections of harp tunes, twenty-six airs were printed with words. The 1784 volume of *Relicks* contains three *penillion* tunes arranged in different styles for voice and harp: 'Gadael Tir' with instrumental introduction, 'Ar Hyd y Nos' with occasional verbal refrains, and 'Nos Galan' with interlaced 'fa la la' refrains. The other three songs in this volume have English verses on Welsh themes. The 1794 volume retained the above songs and added another ten, six with Welsh words (four *penillion* tunes of various types,[3] an old ballad and a lullaby) and four with verses in English on Welsh themes. However, the Welsh-language songs in *Relicks* (1794) were the last ones Edward Jones published. When *Bardic Museum* appeared in 1802, all five songs were in English. The only one with a possible Welsh connection, 'A Druidical Song' with three English verses and chorus 'in imitation of the ancient', is almost certainly a composed song, possibly by Edward Jones himself and perhaps written for one of the Welsh clubs in London that he frequented from time to time. The five songs in his last publication, *Hen Ganiadau Cymru* (1820), all have English words. Only two songs in *Hen Ganiadau Cymru* have any connection with Welsh themes, indicating that the interest of the London public in Celtic airs had long since passed its peak.

The first edition of *Relicks*, dedicated to the Prince of Wales, is the most Welsh of Edward Jones's publications. Of the fifty-nine tunes in this volume, fifty-six were well-known in Wales. It is possible to trace most of them through names on tune-lists of the period, such as those made by Richard Morris in 1717 and 1779; through words sung to them, especially poetry noted in manuscripts, published in almanacs and in books such as *Blodeu-gerdd Cymry*; through use in the *anterliwt* (interlude), a popular rural entertainment; and through comparison with other music collections of the period. The latter include the two manuscripts of fiddle tunes (those of John Thomas and Morris Edwards) mentioned in previous chapters; three harp manuscripts chiefly of non-Welsh airs, and the sixty-seven Welsh airs in John Parry's publications. Although Edward Jones claimed that the music had never before been published, a few of the airs in *Relicks* (1784) are close variants of Parry's melodies and some are more distantly related, though the settings are usually different.

According to Edward Jones's antiquarian notes:

> The most ancient style of Welsh music is the *grave*, and *solemn*, which was consecrated to religious purposes. The next, distinct from the former, is strikingly *martial* and *magnificent*. Another is *plaintive*, and *expressive of sorrow*, being appropriated to elegies, and the celebration of the dead. Another is of the *pastoral* kind, and of all, perhaps, the most agreeable; coming nearest to nature, and possessing a pleasing melancholy and soothing tranquillity, suitable to genial love. There are also, dancing Tunes, or jigs, which are extremely gay and inspiring.[4]

The twenty airs that he lists as 'pastoral' are simple folk-like melodies such as 'Ar Hyd y Nos' and 'Nos Galan' – *penillion* tunes that have remained popular to this day. Fourteen airs, including some marches, are classified as 'martial and magnificent'; and nine tunes, all but one in the minor, are listed as 'plaintive and expressive of sorrow'. At least ten airs in *Relicks* (1784) are tunes to which *penillion* were known to be sung in the style illustrated by the Parry and Williams specimen manuscript, and described in the introduction to *Relicks* (1784), but the author himself gives no musical examples showing how singers might fit verses to these tunes. One of his antiquarian correspondents, William Jones, a Llangadfan farmer and antiquary, sent him a copy of 'Triban Morganwg' with the sections for the voice marked 'So' (solo) and the sections for harp alone marked 'Sy' (symphony) (see Plate 6).[5]

However the version printed in *Relicks* (1784) gave no hint that words were sung, and when the tune reappeared in the 1794 volume it was set, without symphonies, as a poem by Sir Walter Scott with English words in a different metre.

In *Relicks*, the *penillion* tunes 'Ar Hyd y Nos' and 'Nos Galan' have verbal refrains instead of instrumental symphonies, and although 'Gadael Tir' starts with a harp symphony, the voice then enters and continues without a break to the end of the verse in the manner of a song. However, the various ways of using symphonies depending upon the metre of the verse added to the competitive element that figured so prominently in the art. In *Journey to Snowdon* (1781), Thomas Pennant describes *penillion*-singing on social occasions:

> Some vein of the antient minstrelsie is still to be met with in these mountainous countries. Numbers of persons, of both sexes, assemble, and sit around the harp, singing alternately *pennylls*, or stanzas of antient or modern poetry. The young people usually begin the night with dancing, and when they are tired, sit down, and assume this species of relaxation. Oftentimes, like the modern *Improvisitore* of *Italy*, they will sing extempore verses. A person conversant in this art, will produce a *pennyll* apposite to the last which was sung: the subjects produce a great deal of mirth; for they are sometimes jocular, at others satyrical, and many amorous. They will continue singing without intermission,

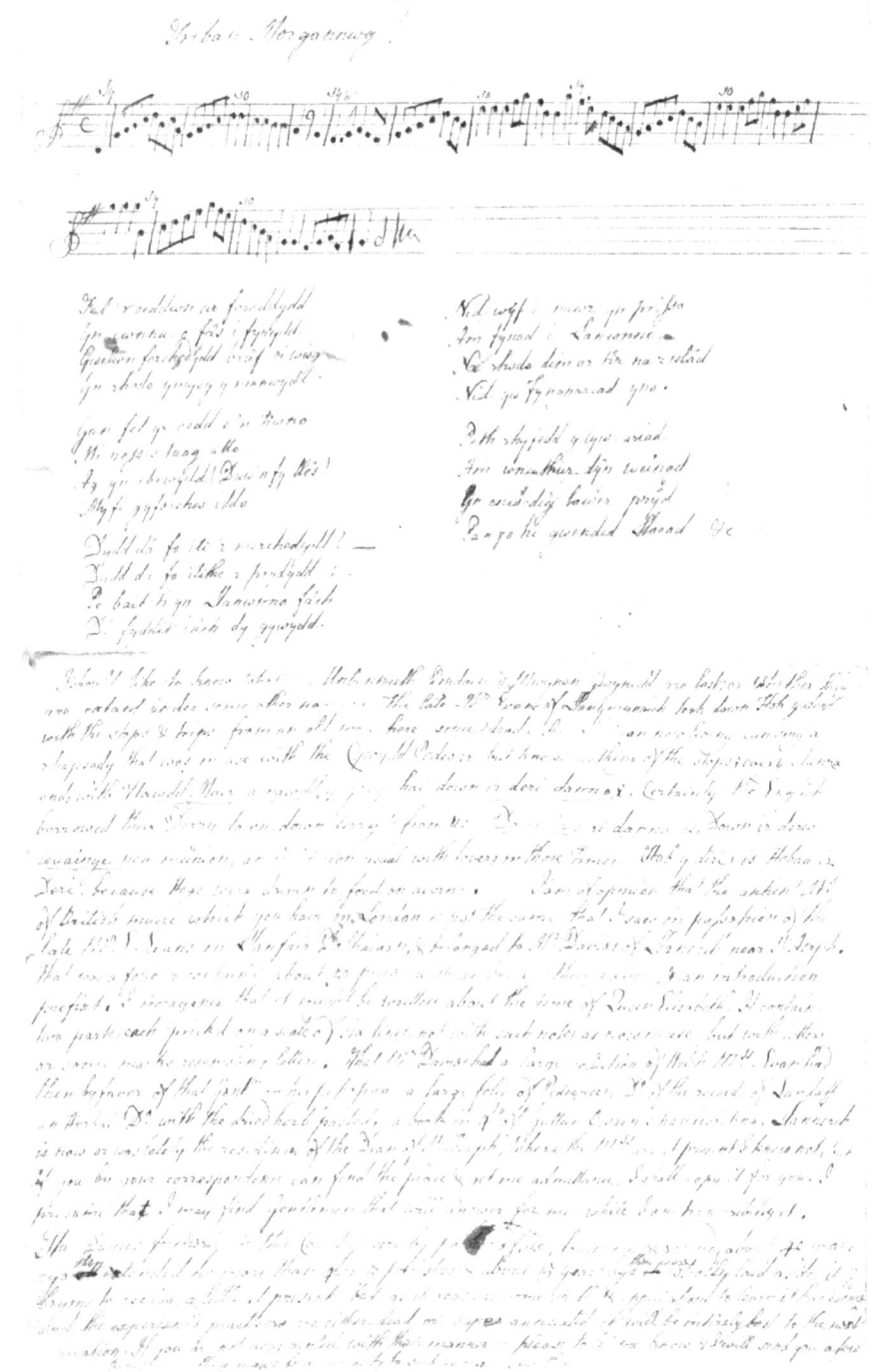

PLATE 6: 'Triban Morganwg' (showing the 'So' and 'Sy' sections), an extract from the letter from William Jones, Llangadfan, to Edward Jones.
By permission of Llyfrgell Genedlaethol Cymru/The National Library of Wales.

and never repeat the same stanza; for that would occasion the loss of the honor of being held first of the song. Like nightingales, they support the contest throughout the night ... The audience usually call for the tune: sometimes only a few can sing to it; and in many cases the whole company: but when a party of capital singers assemble, they rarely call for a tune; for it is indifferent to them, what tune the harper plays. Parishes often contend against parishes; and every hill is vocal with the chorus.[6]

Penillion singing continued to be popular and tunes such as 'Breuddwyd y Frenhines', 'Wyres Megan', 'Llwyn Onn', 'Pen Rhaw' or 'Codiad yr Ehedydd', which appeared in print for the first time in Edward Jones's volumes, were still used by *penillion* singers well into the twentieth century.[7]

Some sixty per cent of the airs in *Relicks* (1784) were in use by Welsh bards as settings for poetry – probably not to such stylish arrangements as those made for London patrons, but to the tunes as they were played in Wales. An analysis based on the collection of *cerddi* in the National Library of Wales[8] shows that all but three of the airs most often called for by poets were to be found in *Relicks* (1794) and the rest in later volumes;[9] at least three of these, 'Gadael Tir', 'Y Galon Drom' and 'Breuddwyd y Frenhines', could be sung either in *penillion* style or as songs. Irregularity in an air was not necessarily a drawback, for it provided an opportunity to display poetic invention in word-setting. 'Erddigan Tro'r Tant', a tune-name found in the Robert ap Huw manuscript, is an extended motivally-based piece with a change of rhythm from 4/4 to 6/8 in the last section. A poem 'I'w ganu ar fesur, "Erddigan Tro'r Tant"' (To be sung on the measure 'Erddigan Tro'r Tant'),[10] in two contrasting poetic metres, fits the air well enough. On the other hand, 'Erddigan Caer Waun' in four equal sections (4/4, 4/4, 6/8 and 4/4) is a shorter example of the same kind of adaptation of words to air.[11]

Example 4.1: 'Erddigan Caer Waun'

continued

According to John Parry ('Bardd Alaw'), writing in the journal *The Cambro-Briton* in 1820, 'The *datgeiniaid*, or singers with the harp, are very fond of this tune, because it affords them an opportunity of displaying their ingenuity, in adapting *Pennillion* of the same metre, to music of two measures'.[12]

Apart from their use with words, most of Edward Jones's tunes were dances, show-pieces for the harp with variations, or shorter pieces that could be used as harp lessons. Almost half the airs in the 1784 volume appear to be dances, some of which go back to the seventeenth century or earlier, such as 'Symlen Ben Bŷs', a distant variant of the sixteenth-century dance 'Mall Sims'; two *almains*, 'Alaw Salmon' and 'Mwynen Môn' and a *galliard*, 'Megen a Gollodd ei Gardas'. 'Cudyn Gwyn' is loosely based on 'Whitelocke's Coranto', written for a masque in 1633, and at least four airs are derived from seventeenth-century country dance tunes.[13] Of the native Welsh dances, perhaps the oldest is 'Ffarwel Ned Puw' with its three self-repeating sections, a dance that William Jones of Llangadfan, born in 1726, described as 'left off before my time'. He also stated that 'Morfa Rhuddlan is a very pleasant Dance if all the party perform their parts well'.[14] Two airs are described in *Relicks* (1784) as minuets, another as a jig, and there are several binary tunes, almost all with parallel cadences, which may have served as dances.

Eight airs in *Relicks* (1784) were published with variations ranging from 'Shenkin', with one variation, to the Welsh ground 'Cynghansail Cymru', with twenty-four. Although the title page of the volume states 'To the tunes are added Variations for the Harp, Harpsichord, Violin, or Flute', most of these variations are meant for the harp and some specifically for the triple harp. In his 'Dissertation on the Musical Instruments of the Welsh', the author says that 'I am rather an advocate for the

Triple Harp, because I admire its venerable and stately appearance; and particularly the sweet re-echoing effect of its unisons, which are played with both hands, and are peculiar to that instrument'.[15] That effect can be found in several of his variations and in some of John Parry's.

In *Relicks* (1794), some of the most popular Welsh airs to be found there for the first time include 'Gorhoffedd Gwŷr Harlech' (The March of the Men of Harlech), 'Dadl Dau' and 'Hob y Deri Dando'. The number of airs almost doubled and more tunes were printed with words. Essays were edited and augmented; the 'Historical Account of the Welsh Bards and Their Music and Poetry' doubled in size and many more examples of Welsh poetry were included. To these were added a section on the function of medieval Welsh poets and the above 'Dissertation on the Musical Instruments of the Welsh' – 123 pages in all, compared to forty-one in the 1784 edition. The fifty-nine airs from the earlier volume were retained in 1794, but almost every one was changed in some way, perhaps to enable the author to declare that they were 'never before published'. Sometimes the change was as simple as adding an English translation to a Welsh tune-name or changing a title ('Gorddinam' became 'Y Gerddinen' and 'Tôn y Fammaeth' became 'Difyrrwch Gwŷr Dyfi' among others). Some antiquarian footnotes were extended and new ones added, while two Welsh airs previously included without words were printed with English words in a different metre, altering the melodies. The anglicisation of the 1794 volume may have been because many of the subscribers to these expensive books, particularly the English nobility, did not speak Welsh and wanted a book they could understand.

Airs were also altered. Rhythmic changes were usually basic and most melodic alterations were also insignificant – indeed, six tunes were printed unchanged – but there were substantial changes in about a quarter of the airs as in 'Mentra Gwen', where English words were added, one bar omitted and a four-bar coda tacked on the end. Alterations in 'Y Fwyna'n Fyw' were even more considerable; in addition to a change of key, the two versions differ considerably in ornamental detail and the implied harmony of the middle section. Bass lines too were altered by variations in rhythmic patterns, changes of register and fuller chords; and occasionally, as in 'Ffarwel Ednyfed Fychan', much of the bass line was rewritten.

Bardic Museum, containing sixty-one airs, appeared in 1802. Several well-known airs, such as 'Llwyn-Onn' (The Ash Grove), 'Pant Corlan yr Ŵyn', 'Hafod y Wraig Lawen' and 'Codiad yr Haul', were published here for the first time, but this volume contains fewer popular airs than *Relicks*. About ninety per cent of the 102 airs in *Relicks* (1794) were noted or mentioned in other Welsh sources, compared to only sixty-four per cent in *Bardic Museum*.

Edward Jones the antiquarian appears to be more to the fore in this volume, not just in the footnotes but also in the choice of airs, such as 'Caingc Dafydd Brophwyd', 'Orddigan Hun Gwenllian' and 'Caniad Pibau Morfydd', all of which are titles found in the Robert ap Huw manuscript; 'Gorhoffedd Owain Cyfeiliog' and 'Hoffedd Hywel ab Owen Gwynedd' are names connected with twelfth-century poet-princes; 'Mwynen Gwynedd' and 'Caingc Llywelyn' are tune-names that occur in medieval poetry. It is difficult to know to what extent these airs, as printed, reflect the period of their titles since musical evidence is extremely sparse. 'Caingc Dafydd Brophwyd' in *Bardic Museum* is Barthélemon's late eighteenth-century transcription of a *cainc* in Robert ap Huw's manuscript, but 'Orddigan Hun Gwenllian' is unrelated to 'Caniad Hun Wen Llian' in the same manuscript, and some versions of the tune in other Welsh sources call it 'Erddigan William Befan Benouth'.[16] However, 'Caniad Pibau Morfydd', although not apparently related to the *cainc* bearing that name, is quite different from the usual eighteenth-century tunes; it is strongly motival in structure and the opening and closing sections of the work are based on two chords only, like many pieces in Robert ap Huw's manuscript.

In an oral tradition that lasted until almost the middle of the eighteenth century, airs which passed from one harper to another might well have been altered to adapt them to changing tastes, or a familiar name attached to a new air. There were almost two hundred years between the date on Robert ap Huw's manuscript and the publication of *Bardic Museum*, with Edward Jones's emphasis in the introduction that he noted most of his tunes from Welsh country harpers. In *Bardic Museum* he printed another tune with an old pedigree, 'Caingc Llywelyn', apparently without noticing that 'Pob Peth' in the same volume is a variant of 'Caingc Llywelyn', an example of a new name to a familiar air.

It is important to remember that there was more than one early Welsh music manuscript extant at this time. As noted earlier, two of the most important – those of John Thomas and Morris Edwards – were both for the fiddle, although very little is known of either collector.

John Thomas, a working fiddler active in the period between c.1730–60, notated over 400 tunes, including a number of non-Welsh examples, in a leather-bound book together with essays on music and, bizarrely, fishing.[17] The wide variety of music in this manuscript, and the lack of information regarding the writer, invites speculation about his background. Judging from his dialect, he came from Powys in north-east Wales, and judging from his writings he was literate in Welsh and in English. The music suggests that he was a working musician from perhaps the 1720s through until the 1750s, and one whose audience came from all walks of Welsh life. John Thomas's remarkable collection contains the music of theatre pieces, parlour songs, minuets for the gentry, ballad airs, country dance tunes and much else including the bawdy dances of the *anterliwt*. Among the salon songs are 'The Ravish'd Lover' by William Boyce (called 'Fanny Blooming Fair' in the manuscript) and 'The Cuckoo' by Thomas Arne, from a 1738 production of *As You Like It*, in addition to classical solos featuring some of Handel's music.

Many of the tunes arranged for harp in *Antient British Music* can be found in John Thomas's fiddle manuscript, but only one, 'Ffarwel Philip Ystwyth', is identical. The other airs vary considerably and it is obvious that they were not copied from the printed book. By the same token, numerous airs were copied from country dance books, among them 'Jenny Dang the Weaver', 'Bonny Laddy', 'Jack Latin' and 'Tit for Tat', noted exactly as they appear in Walsh's *Caledonian Country Dances* of 1735.

The fiddler Morris Edwards lived at the western end of north Wales on Anglesey. His manuscript collection, bearing the date 1778 on the cover, is more carefully written but considerably smaller in scope and more Welsh in content than John Thomas's.[18] A mere handful of tunes appear to have come from country dance books, and only a few with names like 'Queen Fancy' or 'Pretty Peggy' are from obviously non-Welsh sources. About forty per cent of the tunes are related to airs in the collections of John Parry and Edward Jones, although only a few are close variants, suggesting that most were airs in common use in north Wales. Morris Edwards, like John Thomas, includes no words to his music, but he does note some ballad tunes like 'Ffarwel Gwŷr Aberffraw' or 'Ffarwel Ned Pugh'. More interestingly, he has set down some of the tunes from oral tradition. Underneath his notation of 'Green Sleeves', he writes 'cant y nhaid' (as my grandfather sang it); and about 'Cynsêt Gwŷr Penn Morfa' he notes 'Am a glowis i Maurice Edward 1776' (As I heard it Maurice Edward 1776).

Nothing more is known of Morris Edwards apart from a few possible references. In the papers of Bodorgan, an Anglesey estate, there is a note dated 11 October 1773: 'Pd. Maurice Edward Fiddler for his music for a fortnight. 2.02.0.' Two guineas for a fortnight's music was a very substantial amount in the eighteenth century. There is a certain Mr Morris Edwards, Bangor, on the list of subscribers to *British Harmony* as well as a Mr Edwards who subscribed to *Relicks* (1784). But the name is not uncommon in Wales, and we can do no more than speculate about the identity of the subscribers. Without the fiddle manuscripts of John Thomas and Morris Edwards, knowledge of traditional music in eighteenth-century Wales would be meagre indeed.

The Welsh harp manuscripts extant from the middle of the eighteenth century are considerably shorter than the fiddle manuscripts and, in the main, contain composed music by Handel, Corelli, or Vivaldi, airs with variations by John Parry of Ruabon (including many published in 1761), minuets, gavottes, marches, concertos and so on.[19] It is known that Edward Jones visited gentry homes from time to time to give harp lessons or to play the harp for dancing, and it is possible that he may have seen such manuscripts and copied music from them during his visits. Regardless of where he found his old tunes, it is generally true that his settings do not reflect the period suggested by the titles.

Edward Jones's method of preparing the airs for publication is described in the introduction to *Bardic Museum*:

> I have given these native Melodies as genuine as possible; and have added new Basses, and Composed Variations to several of them: those Tunes to which I have not given Variations, are arranged two or three together, in the same key, so that they may be played to follow each other, as little Lessons.
>
> These old Airs differ much in structure from the modern music, and I found it very difficult to adapt regular Basses to them, according to the strict rule of counterpoint, as their fundamental harmonies are often

ambiguous, and even the keys are sometimes but obscurely indicated by the wild modulation. However, as melody is the soul of music, and harmony a secondary consideration, or an assistant; I have generally preferred steering by the original melody, and to aid it with a characteristic harmony, in its own native manner, and the conveniency of the Harp, in preference to that of a complicated modern bass, too regularly managed.[20]

Bardic Museum is more instrumental than Jones's earlier volumes. There are a good many dance tunes, including seven well known from country dance books, two older dances in three self-repeating sections, minuets, jigs and hornpipes. Twelve tunes were published with variations, a higher percentage than in Jones's previous publications, with a degree of difficulty ranging from a simple variation in 'Codiad yr Haul', suitable for a pupil or amateur, to five variations on 'Meillionen', an obvious show-piece to display the special qualities of the harp including harmonics, rapid running passages and arpeggios.

A good deal of Edward Jones's income must have come from teaching, and it seems short pieces on the same page and bearing the same key-signature could be combined into little lessons with variety in mode, style and tempo suitable for pupils. On page 89 of *Bardic Museum*, for example, 'Blodeu Gwynedd', a graceful major-mode minuet, is followed by 'Lady Puleston's Delight', a melancholy minor-mode piece in common time, and then by 'Troiad y Droell', a lively 3/8 dance in the major. There are several more examples of such lessons in the volume.

Edward Jones's final volume, *Hen Ganiadau Cymru*, was the product of his old age when he was in poverty and ailing. Part I, containing thirty-seven airs, appeared in 1820; Part II, containing seventeen airs, was prepared by him but not published until 1825, after his death. Taking the work as a whole, there are some similarities with earlier volumes, but the differences are great. There is no antiquarian introduction and no mention of druids.

Like *Bardic Museum* the emphasis is on instrumental music, with the inclusion for the first time of the pianoforte along with harp, violin and flute. Eleven airs are printed with variations, and there are numerous dances including five country dance tunes. Five airs are printed with English words and the author includes only ten airs called for by Welsh poets, a much smaller proportion than in previous volumes. *Hen Ganiadau Cymru* is the smallest of Jones's volumes, and only forty-four of its fifty-four airs were new since ten had already appeared in his earlier works in various guises. 'Mwynen Meirionydd' was first printed in *Bardic Museum* and the second version in *Hen Ganiadau Cymru* does not differ materially. The same is true of 'Malltraeth', an air closely related to an earlier version in *Relicks* (1794). 'Syr Harri Ddu' (*Relicks* (1784)) became 'Syr Harri Ddû' (*Hen Ganiadau Cymru*), with different ornamentation and added variations, and 'Lady Puleston's Delight' (*Bardic Museum*) became 'Diddanwch Arglwyddes Puleston' (*Hen Ganiadau Cymru*) with different ornamentation and a change of key. Some airs had appeared in earlier volumes under totally different names: 'Blodau Ffestiniog' (*Hen Ganiadau Cymru*) is a version of 'Ragad or, Reged' (*Relicks* (1784)); 'Hûd Tynghedven' appeared earlier as 'Y Stwffwl' (*Relicks* (1794)); 'Talaith Aberffraw' is a version of 'Blodau Gwynwydd' (*Relicks* (1794)). Jones also published three different versions of one air variously titled 'Ffarwel Ednyfed Fychan' (*Relicks* (1784)), 'Castell Towyn' (*Relicks* (1794)) and 'Hafren' (*Hen Ganiadau Cymru*). Three instrumental tunes acquired English words: 'Dewisol Gân Dafydd o'r Garreg-Wen', 'Serch Hudol', and 'Torriad y Dydd', all to be found in *Relicks* (1784, 1794). Some repetition of tunes can probably be attributed to different versions played by Welsh country harpers, but in the case of 'Mwynen Meirionydd' and 'Malltraeth' it seems more likely that the duplication was a result of forgetfulness in Edward Jones's old age.

The collection of airs in *Hen Ganiadau Cymru* did not reflect the Welsh oral tradition to the same extent as the earlier volumes. Almost a third of the tunes had no antecedents in Wales, and many unfamiliar airs had titles such as 'Difyrrwch Madam Eyton', 'Castell Moreton; or Moreton Castle in Shropshire', 'Miss Corbett of Shawbury Park's Minuet' or 'Diddanwch Madam Edwards', all of which connect the airs with members of the gentry in Wales and the Borders. A few airs were popular ones, such as 'Pêr Oslev: neu Sweet Richard', 'Dafydd y Garreg-Wen', 'Torriad y Dydd' and 'Serch Hudol'. The latter can be found almost unchanged in *Pills to Purge Melancholy*,[21] and both words and music of 'Torriad y Dydd' have affinities with a version printed in the first volume of Thomson's *Select Collection of Original Welsh Airs*. 'Dewisol Gân Dafydd' is almost unsingable as it stands, being set to words by Sir Walter Scott in a metre which does not fit the music.

Five tunes in these collections are noted by Edward Jones as having been recorded from manuscripts. 'Caingc Dafydd Brophwyd', mentioned earlier; 'Cil y Fwyalch', a strongly motival tune, was well known in seventeenth-century Wales; 'Dewis Howel', said to be 'from a manuscript of Queen Elizabeth's time', is the name of a musical measure found in sixteenth-century Welsh musical treatises (the setting in *Hen Ganiadau Cymru* is quite different from Edward Jones's usual arrangements and he may have copied both air and setting from the manuscript); 'Hûd Tynghedven', said to be 'From a M.S. of 1685', is a version of 'Y Stwffwl', a name that appears in the Robert ap Huw manuscript; 'Yr Eos-Lais' is a very florid version of a mid-seventeenth-century tune popular in England called 'The Nightingale'.

As already mentioned, very few eighteenth-century Welsh music manuscripts are extant for comparison with Edward Jones's collection. About fifty of the tunes in the manuscript of John Thomas are versions of airs which also appear in Edward Jones's collection, but most are not closely related and it does not seem likely that he noted tunes from this manuscript.

However, the manuscript of fiddler Morris Edwards was almost certainly one of Edward Jones's sources.[22] Just over a third of the tunes in this manuscript also appear in Jones's collections, and twenty-three of these are very closely related – some are almost identical. Although Morris Edwards appears to have copied some material from printed sources such as *The Dancing Master*, *Antient British Music* and *British Harmony*, he has much that does not appear elsewhere and it is quite possible that

Edward Jones had access to the manuscript. The tunes, which he included in his printed collection, were adapted by changing the key or the spelling of the titles of the airs, so that 'Agoriad y Cwrw' (The Opening of the Ale) became 'Agoriad y Cywair' (The Opening of the Key), 'Ela Salmon' became 'Alaw Salmon' and 'Hûd y Biball' (an Anglesey dialect pronunciation) became 'Hûd y Bibell'. In some airs there are small alterations in the figuration, but in others the changes are more significant. In 'Croeso Gwraig y Ty' the air is identical with that in the Morris Edwards manuscript except for two bars in the B section that have been changed, perhaps to make them more felicitous musically.

Similarly, 'Hoffedd Abram ab Ifan' is identical with 'Conset Abram Evan' in Morris Edwards, except that the mode has been changed from minor to major. Edward Jones may have planned to publish more of Morris Edwards's tunes. A pocket notebook exists in which he kept 'A List of the Names of Welsh Tunes & Songs, & some with Variations, which are already arranged for the Third Volume of the Bards',[23] containing the titles of 177 airs, of which he published fifty-seven, most of them in *Hen Ganiadau Cymru*. Among those in the notebook that he never published are titles of thirteen tunes from the Morris Edwards manuscript.

Edward Jones also had airs from musical friends, from fellow harpers, from members of his family – two of his brothers were also harpers – and from members of the Welsh community in London and Wales who were interested in preserving Welsh culture. About seventy-seven of the airs listed by Richard Morris in 1779 appear in Edward Jones's collections. Among his correspondents in Wales were poets such as David Thomas ('Dafydd Ddu Eryri'; 1759–1822), literary parsons such as John Jenkins ('Ifor Ceri') and farmers such as William Jones of Llangadfan whom Edward Jones employed as a copyist and benefited from the farmer's supply of songs, verses, tales and folk dances. There were also contributions from William Owen Pughe and others in London. Edward Jones seems never to have been short of material for his projected books, but it is notable that he did not include in his collections the tunes to popular Welsh ballads and carols such as 'Y Fedle Fawr', 'Susannah', and 'Gwêl yr Adeilad', or tunes connected with folk customs such as 'Mwynen Mai' or 'Calennig'. Unlike the *penillion* tunes, these airs had no special connection with the harp and perhaps Edward Jones considered them unsuitable for a volume that professed to promote the musical relics of a proud bardic past. Whatever the reason, though John Parry, Ruabon, may have included such tunes, Jones did not.

The importance of Edward Jones's contribution to Welsh music cannot be overstated. Throughout the nineteenth century, tunes first printed in his collections reappeared in various guises, frequently with English words and invariably with different arrangements. Between 1809 and 1822, John Parry ('Bardd Alaw') printed several volumes of 'Welsh Melodies', with simpler arrangements of airs that came, for the most part, from Edward Jones's collections. These were followed in 1839 by the first volume of *The Welsh Harper*,[24] which reprinted most of the tunes in *Relicks* (1794) and *Bardic Museum*. As late as 1873, over a third of the airs in *Songs of Wales*, an immensely popular volume, had first appeared in Edward Jones's eighteenth-century books, though by now the piano had displaced the harp, melodies and arrangements were simplified, and harp tunes were supplied with English and Welsh words by contemporary poets.[25]

Of almost equal importance with the music are the introductions to Edward Jones's works. Most of the antiquarian footnotes that attempt to link tunes to noble families or ancient events are worthless, but there is much of interest in the 'Historical Account of the Welsh Bards', the description of Welsh musical instruments, lengthy quotations from Welsh heroic and saga poetry, Giraldus Cambrensis and much more – especially, perhaps, the collection of *hen benillion*, the most substantial of the early collections of *penillion*.

5

Seasonal Festivities

BY NOW it is clear that the professional musicians of eighteenth-century Wales confined their attention almost exclusively to the publicising and publishing of what they considered to be traditional Welsh airs. They did this primarily in London, ignoring almost completely a body of popular music that flourished among their compatriots back home.

Early in the eighteenth century, Wales was almost entirely rural. It was a country on the fringe of Europe without cities or a capital and with a small population – more people lived in London than in the whole of Wales – which was largely dependent on agriculture and ruled by the seasons.

It was in the isolated farmhouses and cottages of the countryside that most Welsh social life of this period took place. Throughout the year, even in the desperately hard-working agricultural community, there were occasions for informal convivial meetings. Sheep-shearing brought together farmers who met on that day to work, but they enlivened the chore by telling stories, singing ballads and a good deal of leg-pulling. The women too who met to prepare the meals would have had a break from the usual routine in much the same way, making the day a special occasion. The sheep's wool provided another opportunity for social gathering on knitting evenings, which took place after the autumn equinox when the knitters would meet at various houses in the neighbourhood to work, usually on moonlit nights to save the expense of candles or with a blazing fire to give light. The time would pass in asking riddles, singing *penillion* and impromptu verses, or story-telling. And, of course, a celebration would be held at the end of harvest with feasting, drinking, singing and dancing. These isolated rural communities also combined helping those in need with an evening's entertainment, as with the custom of the cwrw bach or 'bid ale'. This was a social occasion in which home-brewed small beer or mead was offered and small cakes sold for a charitable purpose, perhaps assisting a newly-married couple to set up a home, or raising a sum of money to pay a neighbour's rent. Raffles might be held for prizes such as a pig or a sheep, and there would be singing and dancing, usually to the harp.

During the winter half of the year when the days grew short, especially in the period around the solstice, a number of festivities took place. Christmas Day in Pembrokeshire, and probably elsewhere, denoted the beginning of *Y Gwyliau* (The

Holidays), a period of three weeks in which comparatively little work was done on the farm. The farmworkers brought in the plough and placed it under the table in the *rŵm ford* (table room) where meals were served. After Christmas,

> parties of men went about from house to house and were invited into the *rŵm ford*, where they sat around the table, regaling themselves with beer, which was always kept warm in small neat brass pans in every farm house ready for callers. But the peculiar custom which existed amongst these holiday-makers was that they always wetted the plough which lay dormant under the table with their beer before partaking of it themselves, thus indicating that though they had dispensed with its service for the time, they had not forgotten it, and that it would again, in due course, be brought out on the green sward and turn it.[1]

It was during this period that two ritual customs took place: the *Mari Lwyd* horse ceremony and *Hela'r Dryw* (Hunting the Wren) – both forms of luck visiting, in which the wassailers wish good fortune to the family inside.

MARI LWYD

The *Mari Lwyd* was a horse's skull draped in yards of white canvas and looking like a ghostly spirit except for the adornments of coloured ribbons, black bottle-glass eyes and black cloth or leather ears. Hidden underneath the canvas, a man with a five-foot pole operated the *Mari*'s jaw, which was on a spring, enabling it to snap.

This horse figure was accompanied from door to door by a retinue, usually about six in all, depending on the number available. The Ostler or Leader carried a stick and led the *Mari* by a rein with bells attached, followed by the other members of the company who traditionally bore such names as 'Corporal', 'Sergeant', 'Punch', 'Judy' and 'Merryman'. In some accounts, Merryman played the fiddle while Punch and Judy, dressed in rags and, with blackened faces, danced. But members of the company would be chosen primarily for their skill at making up verses impromptu or remembering some scores of traditional ones, since the ritual involved a Contest for the House in which the *Mari Lwyd* party had to defeat the members of the household in verse before they could enter and demand wassail.

In a ritual as old as this one, it is not surprising that different accounts of the tradition have survived. The fullest description lists five occasions for music: (a) the arrival of the *Mari Lwyd* with introductory verses greeting the householders and challenging them to a contest; (b) the *pwnco* or debate in verse; (c) the song to close the *pwnco*; (d) the singing and dancing after the *Mari Lwyd* party enters the house; (e) the *Mari*'s farewell. In some examples of the tradition, the opening verses announced that the *Mari Lwyd* party had come asking permission to sing, describing the difficulties of the journey and suggesting that the householders prepare food for them and 'tap the barrel':[2]

Example 5.1: 'Wel Dyma Ni'n Dwad' – from the singing of two traditional Mari Lwyd men from Llangynwyd in the mid-1960s

The *pwnco* did not begin until the family inside responded, usually by asking how many were in the *Mari Lwyd* party and requesting their names. The debate proper then began with alternating verses, not in question and answer style but rather a series of humorous lampoons, each side against the other, in good-natured mockery and leg-pulling. When both parties contained able versifiers, the contest could go on for some time. In the end, however, if the party inside gave up, the *Mari Lwyd* was allowed to enter. At this point special verses were sung by the company to close the debate before the dancing, singing and inevitable horse-play began:[3]

Example 5.2: 'Cân Gloi'r Pwnco'

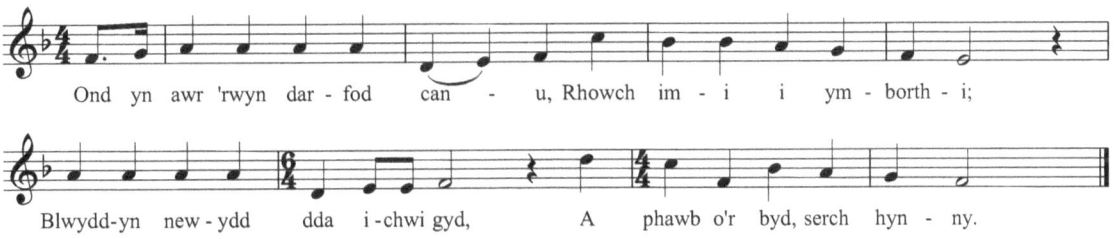

According to Margaretta Thomas, who remembered the *Mari Lwyd* party in Nantgarw between 1880 and 1920:

> There was great merriment, the singing of ballads and love songs, such as *The Maid of Cefn Ydfa* and *The Maid of Sker*, dancing to the fiddle and harp and after some hours the Feri would sing her farewell at the door.[4]

Example 5.3: 'Mari Lwyd Farewell' – sung at the door on leaving

It is important not to assume that this framework was always followed exactly by each company.[5] In the long course of tradition it is unlikely that every detail was adhered to in every performance. Within the formal structure of the ritual, there was room for enough creativity and spontaneity to allow it to survive in oral tradition almost to the present day.

The *Mari Lwyd* ritual has been described as 'a pre-Christian horse ceremony which may be associated with similar customs spread over many parts of the world',[6] and there are aspects of some of the airs connected with it that may indicate considerable age.

Several tunes noted at various times in the period between 1850 and 1960 appear to be variants of a single air. The basic characteristics which mark these tunes as members of the same group are: (a) the opening processional words, '*Wel dyma ni'n dwad ...*'; (b) the octave leaps in the melody at particular points; (c) the syncopated rhythm that derives from the tendency often found in Welsh folk-songs to extend the unaccented syllable; and (d) the general melodic shape that tends to oscillate between major and minor. There is a distinct pentatonic aspect to some of these tunes, as in Example 5.4, though none remains strictly in that scale pattern throughout:[7]

Example 5.4: 'Wel dyma ni'n dwad'

'Canu Cwnsela', noted in a manuscript submitted by a Glamorganshire musician to the Llangollen Eisteddfod of 1858,[8] is an extended version of the air. It has a slightly wider range than the average, with a chordal structure that oscillates between minor and major, and is longer due to increased repetition. Such repetition would not be unusual in a custom demanding a high degree of improvisation:[9]

Example 5.5: 'Canu Cwnsela'

There are several differences in both words and music between examples noted from traditional singers and the song as published in *Ancient National Airs of Gwent and Morganwg* (1844):[10]

Example 5.6: 'Hyd Yma Bu'n Cerdded'

'Hyd Yma Bu'n Cerdded' is firmly in the major, stepwise motion is prominent, there is no syncopation, and the traditional opening of *'Wel dyma ni'n dwad ...'* is missing. It is possible that the tune was edited to conform to the musical taste of the day. Nevertheless, from the formal structure, melodic style and nature of the words, it belongs with the others of this group.

An interesting innovation in 'O Wela Ni'n Dyfod' is the inclusion of a variant tune to be sung in answer to the Mari Lwyd party:[11]

Example 5.7: 'O Wela Ni'n Dyfod'

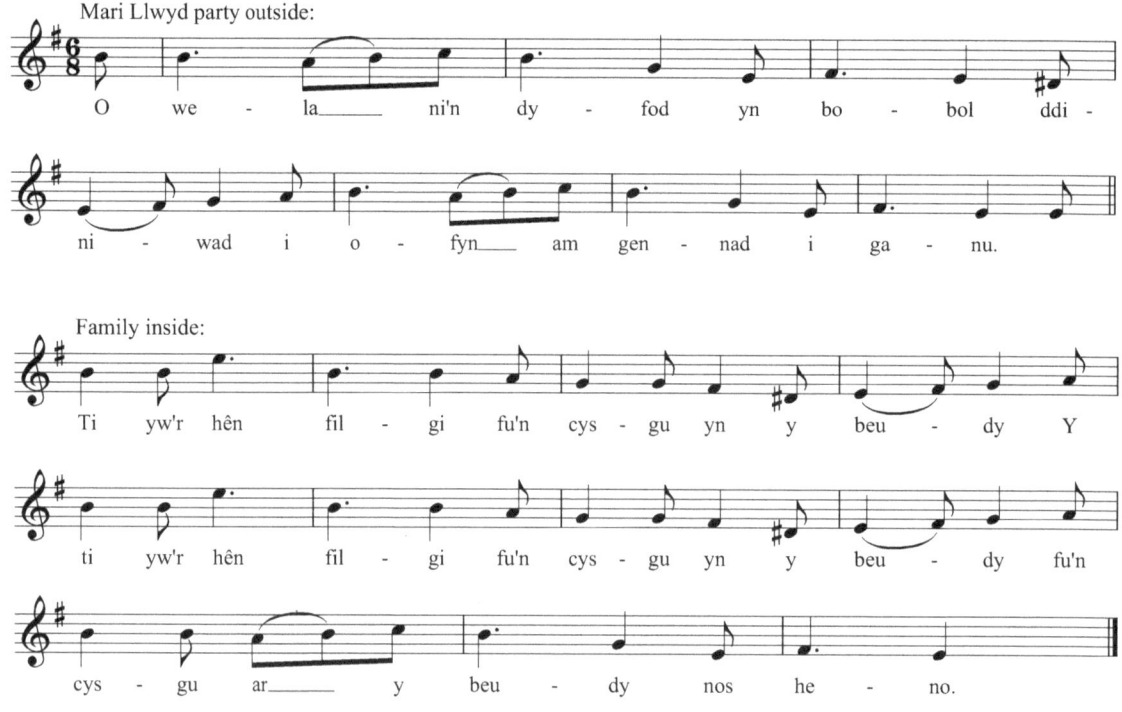

The oldest of these wassailing airs (in terms of the date of its notation) was set down by Iolo Morganwg. This is a repetitive chant with a jogging rhythm in stepwise movement, and although Iolo set it down without key/time signatures, barlines or words, the title given as 'Hen Gainc Washaela Morganwg' (An Old Glamorgan Wassailing Tune) indicates that the style and the *Mari Lwyd* words will fit:[12]

Example 5.8: 'Hen Gainc Washaela Morganwg'

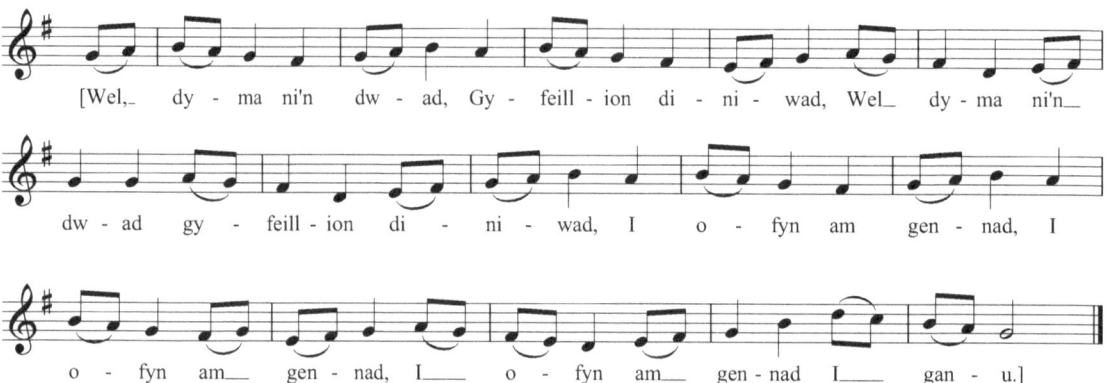

Iolo's tune is in sharp contrast to a sprightly major key air, 'Daeth Mari Lwyd Lawen', from Lampeter in Cardiganshire, the farthest north of any of the *Mari Lwyd* tunes:[13]

Example 5.9: 'Daeth Mari Lwyd Lawen'

The two Llangynwyd men who sang the *Mari Lwyd* song noted as Example 5.1 were thought to be the last of the traditional singers, but the custom has been revived in more than one area of south Wales predominantly through the persistence of folk dance groups and local poets, not all of whom are first-language Welsh speakers. During the final years of the twentieth century participation grew and, although the cultural ambience is changing, enthusiasm has not waned, even to the point where the *Mari Lwyd* custom was celebrated for the first time in north Wales in 2002 at Dinas Mawddwy.[14]

HELA'R DRYW (HUNTING THE WREN)

Another popular custom connected with *Y Gwyliau* and said to have been widespread in Europe at one time was Hunting the Wren,[15] and this, unlike the *Mari Lwyd*, was also found in north Wales. It was part of the celebrations around the winter solstice and appears to have had a long tradition in Wales. The earliest extant reference may be in a verse by a fourteenth-century Welsh bard in *Llyfr Coch Hergest* (The Red Book of Hergest), which describes striking a wren with a stone and wounding it grievously.[16] Apart from that, the earliest description of wren hunting is by the late seventeenth-century antiquarian and scholar, Edward Lhuyd:

> They are accustomed in Pembrokeshire etc. to carry a wren in a bier on Twelfth Night; from a young man to his sweetheart, that is two or three bear it in a bier (covered) with ribbons, and sing carols. They also go to other houses where there are no sweethearts and there will be beer etc. And a bier from the country they call Cutty Wran.[17]

The main features of his description are the locality, Pembrokeshire; the time, Twelfth Night (January 6); the participants, young men bearing a wren in a bier decorated with ribbons; the singing; and the ale. The description also suggests a fertility custom. In mid nineteenth-century Pembrokeshire, the Tenby procession involved an ornamented wren-house mounted on poles carried by four men, singing as they went and pretending to groan under the heavy weight of their tiny burden. In Marloes, the wren-house was carried in procession on Twelfth Day.

Although wren-hunt songs are found in other parts of Wales, there are no detailed descriptions of the custom outside of Pembrokeshire or its environs. In the early nineteenth century John Jenkins ('Ifor Ceri') noted two tunes connected with Hunting the Wren:[18]

Example 5.10: 'Halsing y Dryw' tune no. 1, as noted by Ifor Ceri

Example 5.11: 'Halsing y Dryw' tune no. 2, as noted by Ifor Ceri

He described the ritual as follows:

> In the Vicinity of Cardigan the following Singular Custom prevails and which is probably of Druidical origin: On the Night of the Fifth of January a certain Number of young men, generally four, take a Wren which is considered a Sacred Bird, and confine him in a cage (which they call his (elor) Bier) decked with all the Ribbons they can procure from the Girls of the neighbourhood. With the Wren thus gaudily housed they visit the Families of the District, singing alternate Stanzas in his praise as King of the Birds and as procuring for them many Blessings during the ensuing year, on account of his being made a Captive and a Victim.[19]

Ifor Ceri was born and raised in the Teifi Valley in southwest Wales and one of the two tunes that he called 'Halsing y Dryw' was well known in Pembrokeshire. Although he noted only the airs, words that fit both tunes can be found among wren-song verses popular in Pembrokeshire. Two examples have been noted in brackets underneath the music.

At least half a century after Ifor Ceri jotted down his airs, variants of 'Halsing y Dryw' no. 2, such as 'Dryw Bach Ydi'r Gŵr', were collected in Pembrokeshire; it is worth noting that Ifor Ceri's tune 'Halsing y Dryw' no. 1 is circular in form, whereas this example, comes to a full cadence at the end of each verse:[20]

Example 5.12: 'Dryw Bach Ydi'r Gŵr', a variant of 'Halsing y Dryw' no. 2

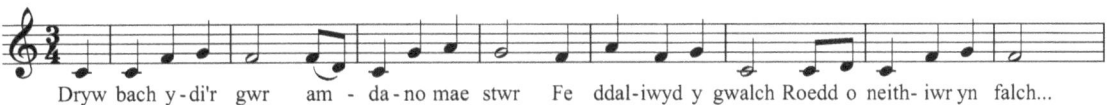

Perhaps the most interesting version is 'Joy, Health, Love and Peace', recorded by the National History Museum at St Fagans.[21] In this English-language version the melody is much more ornamented, but the metrical and rhyme structure of the Welsh words has been retained. The metre is *cywydd deuair fyrion*:

> Joy, health, love and peace / be all here in this place
> By your leave we will sing / concerning our King
> Our King is well dressed / in the silks of the best
> In ribbons so rare / no king can compare
> We have travelled many miles / over hedges and stiles
> In search of our King / unto you we bring
> We have powder and shot / to conquer the lot
> We have cannon and ball / to conquer them all
> Old Christmas is past / Twelfth-tide is the last
> And we bid you adieu / great joy to the new.

Example 5.13: 'Joy, Health, Love and Peace'

The above variant was noted in Pembrokeshire from two retired schoolteachers, Dorothy and Elizabeth Phillips, who sang it and also gave first-hand reminiscences of the custom, which they remembered from the 1920s. The wren party would go to 'any manor houses in the neighbourhood where they would have food and drink and sometimes money' during the period between the sixth and the twelfth of January, the period they called 'Twelfth-tide'. The wren house was 'a little wooden cottage and dressed with ribbons – really crêpe paper – and the wren was inside and when they entered the house of course they all looked in and wanted to see the king'. After the wren party entered there was another reference to wassailing:

> We are not dry, we can drink no small
> But tap you the barrel that's next to the wall
> And sing Ffol-de-rol, ffol-de-rol, ffol-de-rol dee dee

In Kidwelly, Carmarthenshire, a different form of the wren ritual was practised. A version of the Kidwelly wren song beginning 'Gyda ni mae perllan, A dryw bach ynddi'n hedfan ... [We have a *perllan* with a little wren flying in it] exists in manuscript under the title 'Cân y Berllan'. Both the words and music of 'Cân y Berllan' appear to be somewhat corrupt and have here been edited:[22]

Example 5.14: 'Cân y Berllan', Kidwelly wren song variant (edited)

The *perllan* was 'a small rectangular board with a circle marked in the centre and ribs of wood running from the centre to each of the four angles. At each corner of the board an apple was fixed, and within the circle a tree with a miniature bird thereon.'[23] The *phiol* was a bowl or cup, and the reference to wassailing is unmistakable.

Several wren songs were collected in north Wales, but there is no account of the custom there except for the tantalising mention of an illiterate farm labourer near Llanrhaeadr-ym-Mochnant who sang a version of the wren-hunt song.[24] 'He used to render it in a kind of chant exceedingly interesting to listen to, and often have I seen his fellow servants crowding to the stable-loft to hear him sing and to see him act it.'[25] Most of the north Wales wren songs are lively medium compass tunes in the major, but a rare minor key example collected in 1976 is in a narrow 5-tone compass with a chant-like rhythm:[26]

Example 5.15: North Wales wren song, collected in 1976

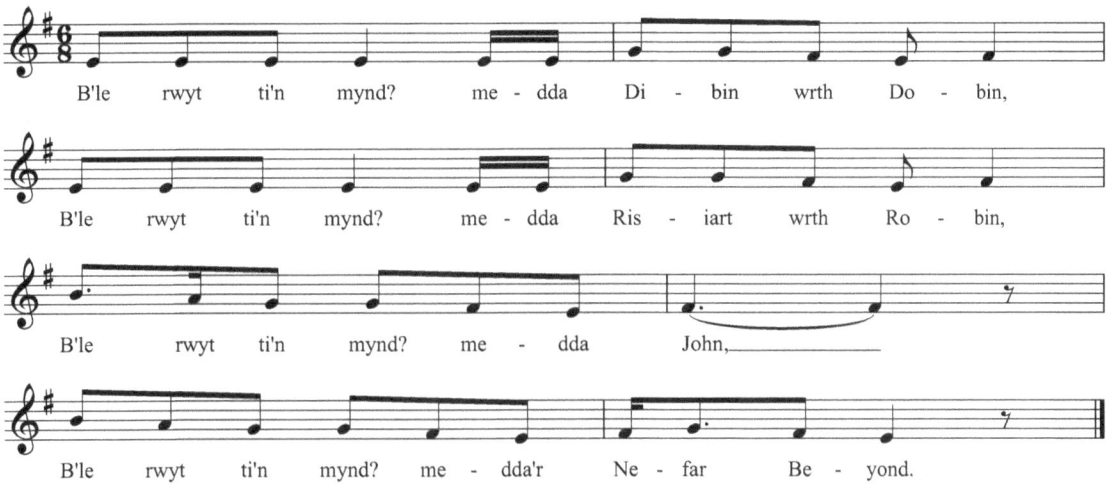

The north Wales songs in question and answer form are quite unlike the Pembrokeshire examples in both melody and poetic metre. Some of the airs from areas close to the English border are similar in type to surviving English examples, and may have been derived from the same general source.[27] The question and answer patterns are very similar with the final English word, 'everyone', being echoed in Welsh in various ways: *'cwbwl i gyd'*, *'bod ac yn un'*, and particularly *'Nefar Beyond'*, evidently a mis-hearing of 'everyone'.

Two Pembrokeshire 'Cutty Wren' songs, though melodically related, are quite different from each other in style. 'Milder to Melder' is a wren song in English[28] of a type found also in Scotland.[29]

Example 5.16: 'Milder to Melder' ('Cutty Wren' song 1)

continued

woods says John the red nose. We're going to the woods says John the red nose.

'Milder to Melder', in a strongly rhythmical triple metre with a compass of 9 tones and much repetition of phrases, is in considerable contrast to another 'Cutty Wren' song that is chant-like in style with a repeated rise to the 5th, a characteristic often found in Welsh folk-songs:[30]

Example 5.17: 'Cutty Wren' song 2

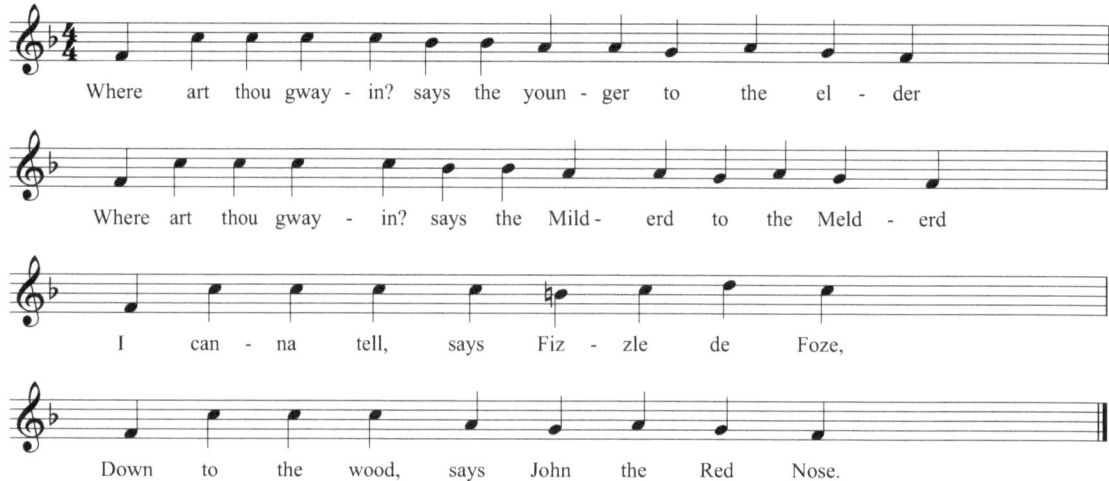

The wren songs of Wales exhibit considerable variety, from the lively question and answer songs of the north-east to the more distinctive songs in *cywydd deuair fyrion* metre found in the south-west, the *perllan* song from Kidwelly, and the Pembrokeshire 'Cutty Wren' songs.

If the custom of Hunting the Wren was once widespread in Europe, its origins must lie far back in time. There are faint hints: an account of wren hunting in *Bye-Gones* 1885 states that companies of young men would visit couples who had been married within the year; this, along with Edward Lhuyd's mention of taking the wren from a young man to his sweetheart, and an Irish wren song that says 'Although he is little his family's great', suggest a connection with fertility. Certainly there was a strong superstition in many European countries that killing a wren brought bad luck, but by today the reversal involved in the annual hunt and death of a wren, the smallest native European bird, in order to display and honour him as king has become meaningless. James Frazer, in *The Golden Bough*, wrote at length about the annual hunt and sacrifice of animals that were sacred for all but one day of the year. However, according to Ronald Hutton:

His [Frazer's] theory may well be correct, but is not susceptible of proof or disproof because of the total lack of any record of the hunt in any ancient or medieval literature. It may have been instead a striking demonstration of a festive suspension of norms, developed at a time when the old superstition about killing the bird had decayed to the point where it could be mocked.[31]

CALENNIG

Another popular and ancient wassailing custom during the period around the winter solstice was connected with the giving and receiving of *calennig* (a New Year's gift), a New Year ritual common to rich and poor alike. It was known to the Romans, who may have brought it to Wales. Valuable gifts of jewels or sums of money were an important part of New Year celebrations in wealthy households but in poor rural societies a small gift of money or food to the singer at the door was a reward for the luck that such a visit brought to the house. At an earlier period it was the men who went round the houses singing *calennig* songs and wishing good luck to the family, but in time the custom was also carried on by children, usually under the age of twelve or so. They would take a purse for any money or food they might receive, in the form of a bag tied around the neck with a long string. This left the singer's hands free to hold the *calennig*, a sprig of holly stuck into the top of an apple or orange which was set on three or four sticks with one serving as a handle. The illustration shows young luck visitors in Llangynwyd, Glamorgan, about 1908, displaying their *calennig* for the family to see.

The custom still goes on in attenuated form, though the *calennig* is no longer carried by the children nor do they by now wear a bag around their necks as they go round the

PLATE 7: *Illustration of the Llangynwyd* calennig *from the archive of St Fagans: National History Museum.* By permission of Amgueddfa Cymru/National Museum Wales.

neighbourhood houses singing on New Year's morning. A good many *calennig* songs have been preserved in the sound archives of St Fagans and in various manuscripts. The oldest in the St Fagans collection may be two songs from Pembrokeshire with a chant-like tune in a restricted melodic compass. One of these, 'Deffrwch Ben Teulu', is in the *cywydd deuair fyrion* metre and the 'luck visit' motif is strong:[32]

Example 5.18: 'Deffrwch Ben Teulu'

In some luck visits, the singer would go to the houses with staff in hand to knock on the door and rouse the family. In Example 5.19, the request for *calennig* is extended to include the singer's hard-working father and mother who patched his shoes and mended his stockings:[33]

Example 5.19: Calennig Song

Sometimes a short song is extended by an interpolated chant between the verses, as in 'Codais Heddiw'n Fore':[34]

Example 5.20: 'Codais Heddiw'n Fore'

In the popular variant, 'Blwyddyn Newydd Dda i Chi', the emphasis is on wishing a good New Year to the family:

Example 5.21: 'Blwyddyn Newydd Dda i Chi'

The tune of the New Year jingle is the chorus of a popular nineteenth-century gospel hymn, 'The Bright For-Evermore'.[35] The tune was obviously popular in Wales, for the chorus turns up more than once in *calennig* songs. Many gospel hymns became popular in Wales largely due to the great hymn writer and reformer, Reverend John Roberts ('Ieuan Gwyllt'), who published volumes of them with Welsh translations in the last quarter of the nineteenth century, including 'Cawn Fynd Adref Fory'. According to one notator, who remembered her mother singing it, 'Hon oedd cân boblogaidd plant yr ardal wrth grynhoi calennig gyda throad y ganrif' ('This was the popular song of the neighbourhood children when they collected *calennig* at the turn of the century').[36]

Example 5.22: 'Cawn Fynd Adref Fory', a *calennig* song sung in the Llandysul area of southern Ceredigion

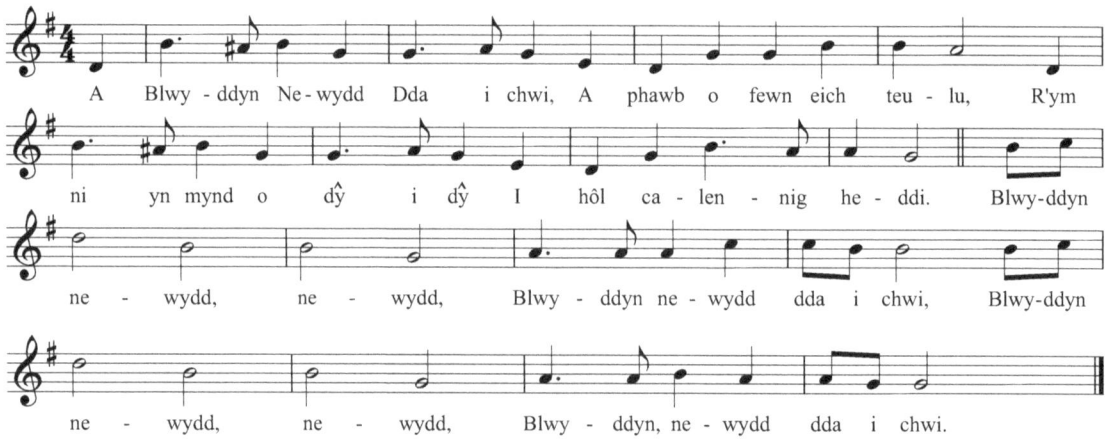

In contrast to the extant *Mari Lwyd* and wren tunes that, for the most part, tend to be variants of traditional models, the *calennig* luck visitors often used any familiar tunes that would fit their words. This may have come about when the *calennig* ritual was no longer carried out by adults who were concerned with maintaining tradition, but by children who sang the tunes they knew.

The minstrel song, 'So Early in the Morning', occurs more than once along with 'Home Sweet Home' and 'The Belle-Isle March', a popular eighteenth and nineteenth-century ballad tune.

Calennig words were also fitted to familiar Welsh harp tunes, including two found in Edward Jones's eighteenth-century collections, 'Gwŷr Harlech' and 'Llwyn Onn'. 'Mi Godais yn Fora' is how some children sang *calennig* in Llanegryn, Merionethshire, in the early twentieth century:[37]

Example 5.23: 'Mi Godais yn Fora', as sung by Meredydd Evans

GŴYL FAIR (CANDLEMAS)

The pagan Festival of Light celebrated at the beginning of February became Candlemas in the Christian calendar, commemorating the Purification of the Virgin Mary. The last of the winter wassailing customs took place at this time, and was celebrated in north Wales as a Christian ceremony with religious carols by Welsh bards and as a secular occasion for carousing and feasting. The secular *Gŵyl Fair* celebrations began with the 'contest for the house', known in north Wales as *canu yn drws* (singing by the door). Like the *Mari Lwyd* ceremony in south Wales, the wassailing party outside the house had to defeat those inside in poetic contention before they could enter and take part in the feasting, but the form of the custom was different. Since the *Gŵyl Fair* ritual did not survive into the twentieth century, present-day knowledge of its form and content comes from documents and descriptions. Fortunately, a good many wassailing verses were noted down by young Richard Morris in the early years of the eighteenth century when *Gŵyl Fair* festivities were still an important part of Anglesey life. His manuscript gives the words to about three dozen wassail carols to be sung outside the house along with several sets of words to be sung in response by those inside. These indicate that in north Wales the feat also involved setting puzzles and answering them, guessing riddles, performing tongue-twisting words faster than anyone else or singing long cumulative songs without memory lapses or slips of the tongue. The words to the wassail carols in his manuscript, usually called simply *carol gwirod yn drws* (wassail carol at the door), are in a variety of poetic metres, suggesting a high degree of preparation on the part of the participants. The wassailers, who needed more than a good memory and a talent for improvisation, would probably have learned many different types of song in contrasting poetic metres beforehand so as to be well prepared. Although there is no music in the manuscript, Richard Morris occasionally names the tunes to be used, including traditional Welsh airs such as 'Triban Morg[anwg]' and 'Ffarwel Trefaldwyn', as well as English tunes like 'Peg a Ramsey' or 'Colliers Daughter'. Usually a name, such as 'Tôn Deuair' or 'Tri Chwarter Tôn', indicates a metre rather than a specific tune.

'Carol Gwirod yn Drws ar Fesur Triban Morg' (A wassailing carol at the doorway on the measure Triban Morgannwg), which bears the date 1717 in Richard Morris's collection, begins in typical wassail style stating the number who set out through wind and rain. The following form involves some adaptation of the air:[38]

Example 5.24: 'Carol Gwirod yn Drws ar Fesur Triban Morg' (adapted from *Melus-seiniau*)

The wassailer goes on to describe the difficulties on the way: one of the company has fallen into a ditch; one has stumbled into the river and needs to dry out by the fire; another hurt himself going over a stile; another suffers from chilblains; and the wassailer himself hurt his back by falling in the gorse and is bleeding from head to foot. He concludes by challenging those inside to join in the singing.

That was the signal for the contention to begin. Richard Morris's manuscript gives several examples of the kind of feat-singing that formed such an important part of the competition. The most common metres used were the folk metres of *triban*, *awdl-gywydd* and *tri thrawiad*, and most of the airs would have been familiar folk melodies easy to remember and to sing in a contest where it was the words rather than the tune that mattered. In this study of the *Gŵyl Fair* ritual, if no specific tune is called for, the verses have been set to traditional tunes that fit the poetic metre and, if possible, the period and place.

The first carol in the manuscript is a typical example of the word-play involved. Its twenty-two lines break down into four sections, the first three in different metres and the fourth a repeat of the first metre. The words, as paraphrased in English, announce the challenge:

> We have come before daybreak to drink your beer and make merry.
> My party and I are here at your door to sing and we are sure there is
> no one inside who can outsing us. I ask for a response to our singing
> because it is freezing out here and we are suffering greatly waiting
> for you to answer. We are good singers with a substantial repertoire,
> those inside will never beat us. It's a long time till daylight and we say
> to the people inside by the fire, let us in quickly to enjoy the courtesy
> of your house.

The wassailers could of course sing all the different metres to the same tune so that the only alteration is in the rhythm. But it is possible that part of the feat would be to change the tune with the change of metre. If the responders were expected to follow the changes of tune as well as of metre, the airs would need to be familiar ones such as the folk tunes (Wassail song variants 1–4), which might have been known to Anglesey singers in the early eighteenth century. They have had to be adapted here to fit the different metres:[39]

Example 5.25: Wassail song variant 1, air 'Llanerch-y-medd'

Example 5.26: Wassail song variant 2, air 'Y Gog Lwydlas'

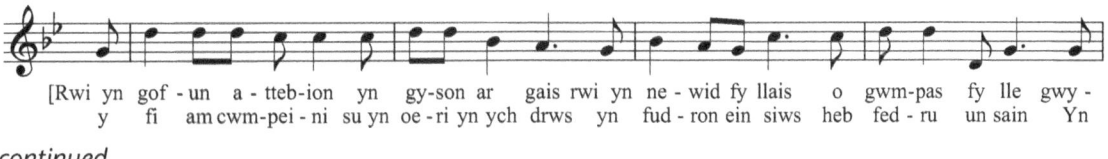

continued

Seasonal Festivities

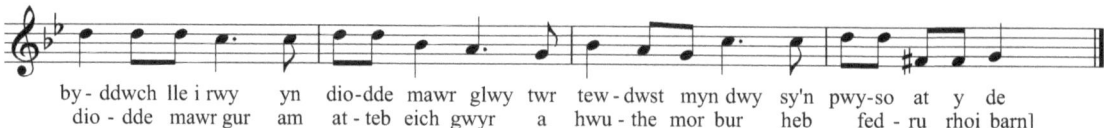

by-ddwch lle i rwy yn dio-dde mawr glwy twr tew-dwst myn dwy sy'n pwy-so at y de
dio-dde mawr gur am at-teb eich gwyr a hwu-the mor bur heb fed-ru rhoi barn]

Example 5.27: Wassail song variant 3, air 'Y Dôn Fechan'

[Barn a heu-ddan am na fed-ran y-nill ych ty drwy hir ga-nu

ag yn gos-od gwyr mor ba-rod ai a-wen be-redd be-rai cerdd la-wer]

Example 5.28: Wassail song variant 4, air 'Llanerch-y-medd'

[Lla-wer sudd dan y dydd gwnawn heb gudd hap-pus gân y
un or ddau heb nac-au gwnewch yn frau y sawl sy ai bryd go-

fi am llu doe-da i'n hu ar gwyr sy'n tu wrth y tan
llyng-wch Rus i fewn ar frus i na-du ich llus fod mewn llud]

Further trials occurred in the setting and solving of riddles. The subjects were simple elements of country life, such as a meat pasty, a roasting spit or a flagon and cup. In 'Beth Su Mor Feinion', one verse asks 'what are slender with yellow petticoats and red heads …?'.[40] The responders were expected not only to guess the answers to the riddles (in this case, the answer is 'candles in brass candlesticks'), but also to reply in the same metre.

Example 5.29: 'Beth Su Mor Feinion', Tri Tharawiad – Hen Dôn Llyfr Ficer

[Beth su mor fein-ion ai peisiau yn fel-

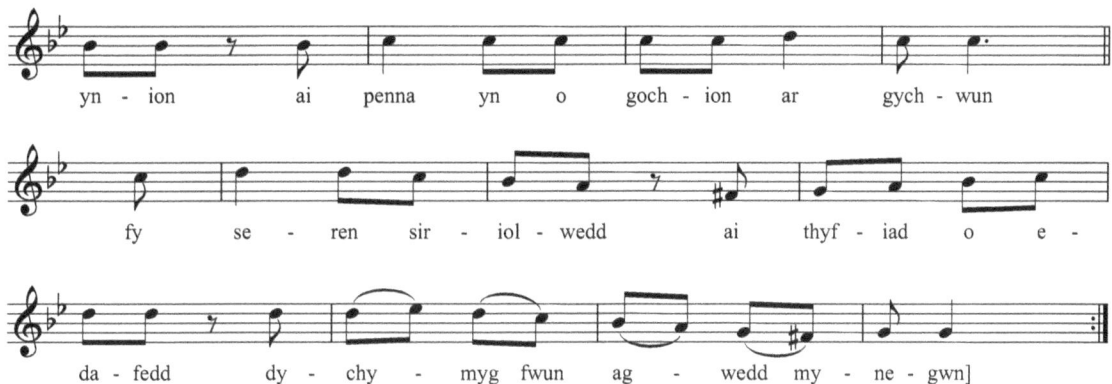

The same rule applied to the family members inside the house, who might themselves challenge the wassailers to match their metrical skill. An eighteenth-century manuscript[41] gives the words to such a challenge and names five different tunes to which the words were sung: 'Caniad Gwyl Fair iw Ganu ar Bum Mesur' (A Gŵyl Fair song to be sung on five metres); 'Fedle fawr yn gynta' (Fedle fawr first); 'Bredi Ban'; 'Marts'; 'Gonsead Gwyr y Berffro'; 'Hobi horse'; 'Fedle Fawr yn ddiwaetha' (Fedle fawr to finish).

Some of the tune-names given are perplexing and in most cases it would be necessary to edit the tunes to fit the words in the manuscript. 'Y Fedle Fawr' was a well-known tune popular in the sixteenth century, but 'Bredi Ban' is a puzzle – perhaps a corruption of the eighteenth-century ballad tune-name 'Betty Brown', popular in eighteenth-century Wales, which can be adapted to fit the words. 'Marts' calls for a march tune and 'Gonsead Gwyr y Berffro' (Consêt Gwŷr Aberffraw) will fit with some juggling. 'Hobby Horse' was more difficult and much adaptation was needed.

A challenge of this sort was a more onerous task than improvising verses in the *Mari Lwyd* metre, which provides opportunities for repetition, giving the singer time to construct the next line. In the *Gŵyl Fair* contention both parties would have needed a very large stock of wassail songs of all kinds on the tip of the tongue in order to fulfil their role in the contest. At the beginning of the eighteenth century, when young Richard Morris jotted down his wassail carols, the majority of Welsh people were still illiterate and needed to have excellent memories. When both questions and answers were common stock, it was easier for the wassailers and the families they visited to learn the verses beforehand and, significantly, Richard Morris included the answers to more than one wassail carol in his manuscript. But a response such as the six-verse carol above to five different tunes would of necessity have been devised and learned well beforehand.

Feat songs such as cumulative songs, which involved remembering long lines of words in reverse order, played an important part in *Gŵyl Fair* contests for the house. Several versions of 'Y Cyntaf Dydd o'r Gwyliau' ('The Twelve Days of Christmas') have been recovered in Wales, probably sung at Christmas wassailing festivities, but perhaps also at *Gŵyl Fair*.[42]

Seasonal Festivities

Example 5.30: 'Y Cyntaf Dydd o'r Gwyliau' (adapted)

Verse 1

Y cyn-taf dydd o'r gwyl-iau fy nghar-iad an-fo-nodd i mi bet-ri-sen ar y pren ger-llyg.

Verse 2

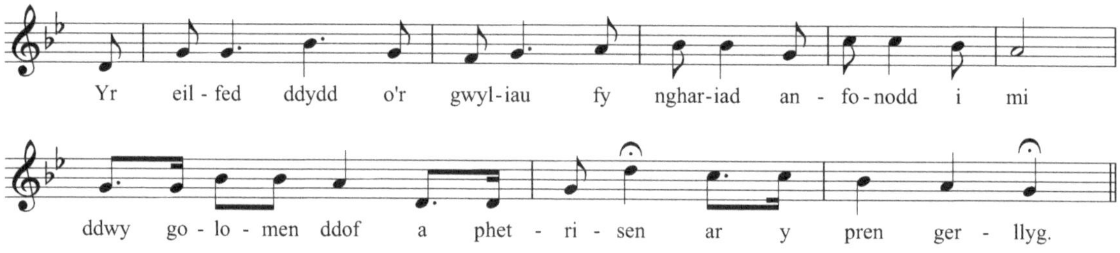

Yr eil-fed ddydd o'r gwyl-iau fy nghar-iad an-fo-nodd i mi ddwy go-lo-men ddof a phet-ri-sen ar y pren ger-llyg.

Verse 3

Y try-dydd dydd o'r gwyl-iau fy nghar-iad an-fon-odd i mi tair iar Ffrainc a dwy go-lo-men ddof a phet-ri-sen ar y pren ger-llyg.

Verse 12

Y deu-ddeg-fed dydd o'r gwyl-iau fy nghar-iad an-fon-odd i mi deu ddeg my lord yn camp-io, un drym-ar-ddeg yn drym-io, deg my la-di yn dawn-sio, naw tarw yn rhu-o, wyth mul yn ras-io, saith a-larch yn no-fio, chwe gwydd yn fyw, pum mod-rwy aur, ped-war a-der-yn ffeind, tair iar Ffrainc a dwy go-lo-men ddof, a phet-ri-sen ar y pren ger-llyg.

Although the Welsh words are very similar to the best-known English version, especially verses 1 to 7, the tune is distinctively Welsh in style.

Among the cumulative songs known to have been used at Candlemas wassailing is 'Un o Fy Mrodyr I', which was still popular enough on Anglesey to be noted down and published 200 years later:[43]

Example 5.31: 'Un o Fy Mrodyr I'

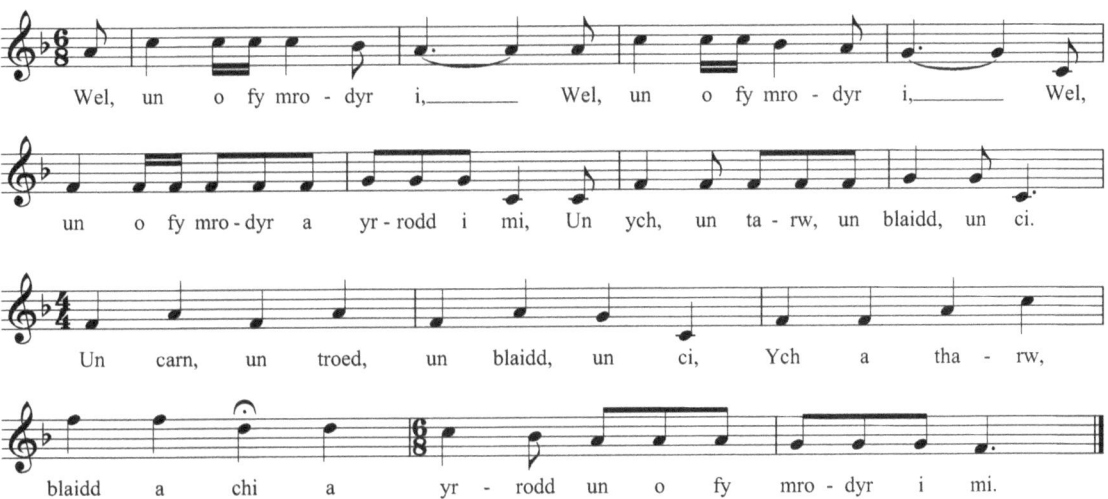

There is a reference to an old chap in Chwilog, half singing and half dancing, while going through the verses of 'Un o Fy Mrodyr I'. The trick was to sing each verse on one breath, and the singer went through the nine verses, each successively longer, on one breath for each verse while 'half dancing'.[44] An element of dancing is suggested by some of the words in the jingle: *'un cam, un tro'* (one step, one turn), although there are other versions with *'un carn, un troed'* (one hoof, one foot). There are also hints of animal guising in the words of this song: *'un ych, un tarw, un blaidd, un ci'* (an ox, a bull, a wolf, a dog), and other songs in the manuscript mention a stag, a bear and a lion, although animal guising may no longer have been part of the wassail procession by Richard Morris's time.

The most popular cumulative song in Welsh is one which is still sung with gusto in convivial gatherings. Usually called 'Cyfri'r Geifr' (Counting the Goats) or 'Oes gafr eto?' (Is There Another Goat?), it was one of the songs used at *Gŵyl Fair* celebrations in north Wales according to David Thomas ('Dafydd Ddu Eryri') in a letter to Edward Jones ('Bardd y Brenin'), dated 1799:

> I humbly apprehend that it is now too late to send anything towards completing your Book, otherwise I might send you some kind of a

Copy of Naw Gafr gorniog [Nine horned goats], which after a long and diligent enquiry I found at Caernarvon, but I do not believe it to be very perfect, neither can I find any great beauty in the same. It appears that it was sung on *Noswyl Fair* [Candlemas Eve] that is to say during the contest for the house.[45]

The earliest extant example of these cumulative goat songs is in *Ancient National Airs of Gwent and Morganwg* – there called 'Canu'r Bugail – The Shepherd's Song'. The background note says that the tune was taken down from an old harper in the area but that the words came 'from Edward Williams's ('Iolo Morganwg') MS collection of ancient Welsh songs'. The two opening bars are slightly edited:[46]

Example 5.32: 'Canu'r Bugail'

The pattern established here is of a song in two sections. The opening section mentions the goat, sometimes in the form of a question, and the second section describes the goat's colour which changes in each verse: white, black, red, grey, blue, pink, and sometimes more unusual colours. The tempo also quickens, making it more difficult to sing the nonsense words clearly. In some ways, however, the song is not typical of the goat songs generally. The compass is over an octave, wider than most of the others, and the melody is ornamented with slurs and passing tones.

According to J. Lloyd Williams, who published several goat songs in the *Journal of the Welsh Folk-Song Society*:

> These songs are peculiarly Welsh, and, in some form or other may be heard in every part of the Principality … In all the variants the words

were repeated with a change in the colour specified – the last part being generally sung much quicker than the first.⁴⁷

He noted an example from north Wales, 'Oes Gafr Eto?', version 1, which is still sung throughout Wales:⁴⁸

Example 5.33: 'Oes Gafr Eto?', version 1

Sometimes the question and answers are in different rhythms. For instance another version of 'Oes Gafr Eto?' begins in duple time with a chorus in triple time:⁴⁹

Example 5.34: 'Oes Gafr Eto?', version 2

Perhaps the most interesting goat song is 'Cyfri'r Geifr', an Anglesey tune noted by Grace Gwyneddon Davies at the beginning of the twentieth century. It differs from the others both in musical structure and in words, which pose the question and answer rather differently: 'Why are there rough short hairs on the point of a goat's beard? Because it browses among the hazel and the holly on the banks, that is why there are rough short hairs on the point of a goat's beard. Red goat, quite red, with a red tail, flank and beard.' The Welsh words are real tongue-twisters, much more difficult to sing at a fast speed than any of the other goat songs – exactly the kind of competitive piece which might have been used on Anglesey at *Gŵyl Fair* contentions:[50]

Example 5.35: 'Cyfri'r Geifr'

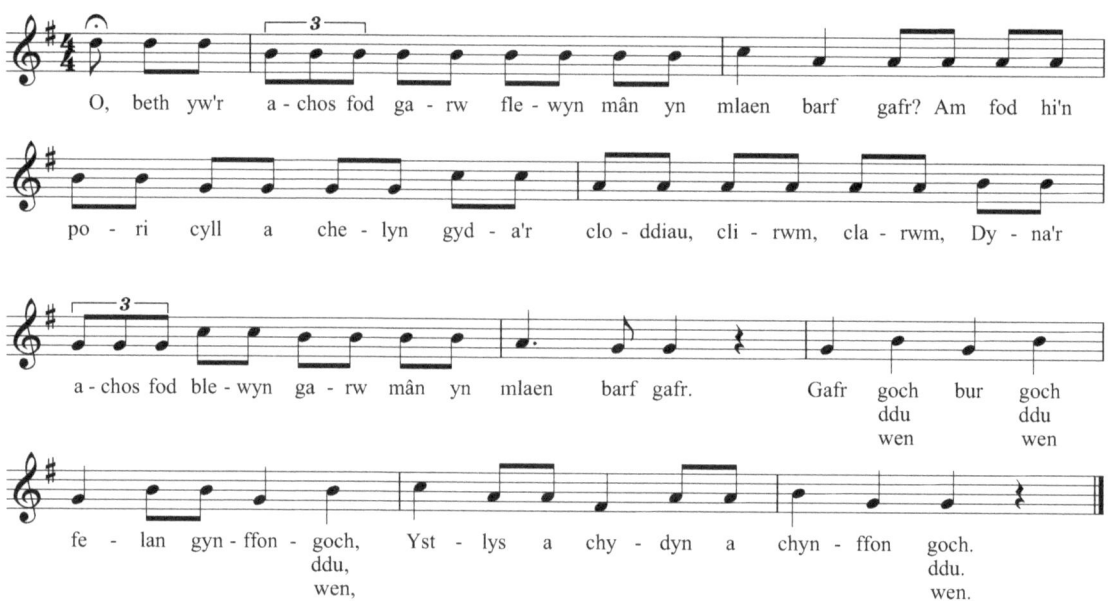

Information about the ceremonial after the *Gŵyl Fair* wassailers had entered the house comes from descriptions of the ritual as practised a half century or more later in northern Caernarvonshire, neighbouring on Anglesey.[51] After the wassailers won the right to enter, they came in two by two, greeting the family in song, complaining that their voices are hoarse and that their feet and hands are cold, but that they are hoping for a welcome. According to William Williams of Llandygái, writing in 1806:

> On their entering, they demanded in rhyming words, a chair to be placed on the middle of the floor, and a Virgin, as pure as Mary to be placed in it: but the women, I suppose sensible of their own frailties,

always placed in the chair an Infant girl: afterwards the Wassail cup was brought, which usually held 2 or 3 quarts of sugared ale and toasted slices of bread, with pieces of wax candles stuck round the edge and lighted. The foreman of the gang, with this between his hands went round the chair, and the others followed him in procession singing, then he would, after first pledging the Virgin, drink to her health; in doing this he must be careful to keep his eyebrows and hair from being singed. After this ceremony was over, the company were entertained with supper and plenty of Wassail, and in parting they all joined in a song of thanks to the good man of the house for his bounteous treat ...[52]

The very elaborate ritual connected with *Gŵyl Fair* celebrations, both outside and inside the house, implies a more formal structure than that of the *Mari Lwyd* or of the wren party, and less scope for improvisation. The variety of poetic metres used and the necessity in some cases for the responders to answer in the same metres argues a high degree of preparation on both sides. After entering the house, the *Gŵyl Fair* wassailers took part in a ceremony that, although sadly in decline by the end of the eighteenth century, had its roots in Catholic tradition. Undoubtedly, the repugnance felt toward Roman Catholicism by Nonconformists, who were by then prospering in Wales, was to a large extent responsible for the fact that *Gŵyl Fair* celebrations appear to have died out in the early nineteenth century.

There was one custom not connected with the calendar festivals, which involved the same kind of *pwnco* as the *Mari Lwyd* or *Gŵyl Fair*, and that was the contest for the bride at the door of her home before the wedding. The groom's party would arrive at the house to be greeted by a barred door and asked why they had come. The banter would go back and forth between the two sides – in one recorded case it lasted for thirty-four verses – until the party was allowed to enter. The metre of the verses was usually the *triban*. The verse quoted here is from a bridal-contest song:[53]

Example 5.36: Bridal-contest song

SPRING CELEBRATIONS

The coming of spring and summer brought their own holidays. Shrove Tuesday, just before the forty-day Lenten fast, was known in Wales as *Dydd Mawrth Ynyd* or *Dydd Mawrth Crempog* (Pancake Tuesday). Like New Year's Day, it was an opportunity for children to go through the neighbourhood begging – not for money in this case, but for food such as butter and sugar, which would be forbidden during Lent. The practice survived in some areas into the early twentieth century, as shown in 'Os Gwelwch yn Dda Ga'i Grempog':[54]

Example 5.37: 'Os Gwelwch yn Dda Ga'i Grempog'

Easter was the most important feast in the Christian calendar, and Welsh poets celebrated it with Easter carols written in the same metrical patterns as the Christmas carols and sung to many of the same tunes. However, the May carols sung outside the house on May mornings, especially May Day, were rather different. These luck visit songs were written to a simpler metre that became associated with May carols, and their chief purpose was to proclaim the coming of summer and wish good luck to the family. Although May Day celebrations began as a pagan festival, by the seventeenth century a strong religious element had become prominent. There is an occasional suggestion in some of the carols that May singers were accompanied by instruments, specifically *tannau* (strings). One set of verses in the May carol metre was directed to be sung by two men and two boys with harp and fiddle, and there is more direct evidence of instrumental accompaniment. John Thomas noted a tune called 'Mwynen Mai' (Gentle May) in his fiddle manuscript,[55] and another version was published by the harper John Parry.[56]

Almost all the airs to May carols collected by Ifor Ceri are without ornamentation, apart from the occasional passing tone. One notable exception is 'Fy Mrodyr a Chwiorydd', a carol air that is very highly ornamented and includes a short melisma. The barring has been slightly changed and only the first half of the verse has been included here:[57]

Example 5.38: 'Fy Mrodyr a Chwiorydd'

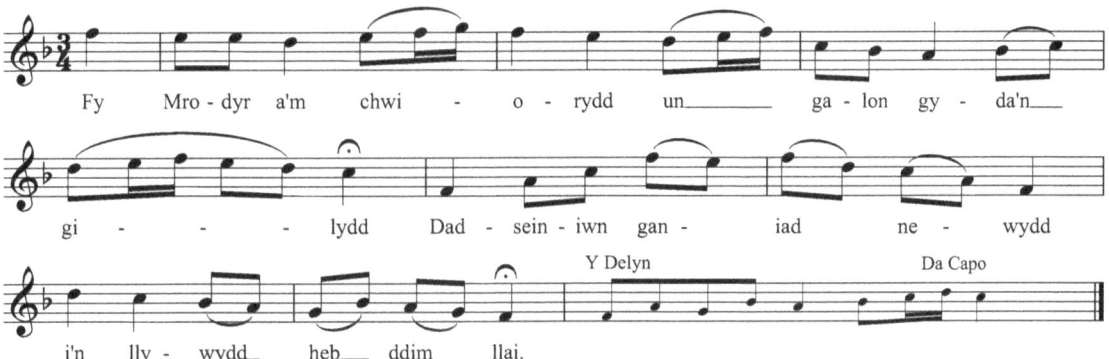

In contrast to the religious tone of the carols, the May dancing or *dawnsio haf* was unashamedly secular. Accounts vary, but the main components were male dancers with instrumental accompaniment and a decorated ritual object. In south Wales this object was the Maypole, but in north Wales it was the *cangen haf* (summer branch). An account from 1825 describes the *cangen haf* as a long pole with a frame covered in white linen to which ornaments were fixed. An early twentieth-century report says it was a large piece of gorse. and a later description speaks of it as 'a leafy bough'. Most agree that it was beautifully decorated with glittering objects such as watches, silver spoons and cups. The *cangen haf* was borne through the village and along rural roads by the revellers who danced the 'Cadi Ha!'.[58]

Example 5.39: 'Cadi Ha!'

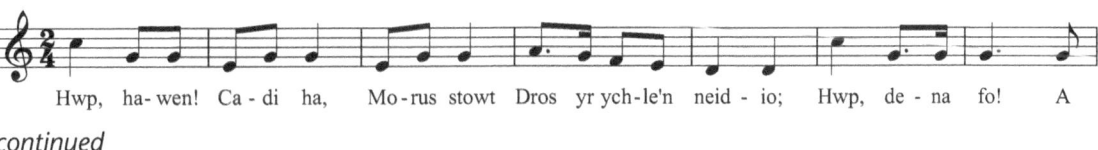

continued

chyn-ffon buwch a chyn-ffon llo, A chyn-ffon Ri-chard Par-ri fo; Hwp, de-na fo!

The number of participants involved in this north Wales custom varied from twelve to twenty young men. The revellers consisted of dancers dressed in white with knots of brightly coloured ribbon adorning their clothes, one or possibly two instrumentalists playing the harp, fiddle or, in one case, a concertina, and most importantly the *Cadi* and the *Fool*. According to the earliest recorded description, the *Cadi* was a man 'always arrayed in comic attire … a coat and waistcoat being used for the upper part of the body, and for the lower petticoats …'.[59] His face would be blackened or he would wear a mask. The *Cadi* in early twentieth-century Holywell was dressed entirely as a woman, but with a blackened face and brandishing a broomstick (see Plate 8).

The *Cadi* was usually accompanied by the *Fool* and their activities were similar to the antics of the Punch and Judy that sometimes accompanied the *Mari Lwyd* in south Wales. According to one writer, 'Nid oedd dim neillduol ond y canu a'r dawnsio, ynghyd a'r Morus-dawns, yn yr holl ddefod, heblaw digrifwch y *Ffwl* a'r *Gadi*' ('There was nothing remarkable but the singing and the dancing, along with the morris dance, in the entire ceremony apart from the entertainment of the *Fool* and the *Cadi*').[60] Although with the passage of time some of the words have been corrupted, references to the tails of the cow, the calf or the dog in the 'Cadi Ha!' song 'La-da Li, a La-da Lo' suggest animal guising, and it is clear that shouting and leaping high was an important part of the dance:[61]

PLATE 8: *The Holywell Cadi, from the archive of St Fagans: National History Museum.*
By permission of Amgueddfa Cymru/National Museum Wales.

Example 5.40: 'La-da Li, a La-da Lo'

In south Wales, the chief ritual connected with the arrival of summer was the raising of the Maypole, sometimes called the *bedwen haf* (summer birch), and sometimes *bedwen Ifan* (St John's birch) since it was also connected with festivities at the summer solstice (the feast of St John the Baptist was on 24 June). There would be morris dancing around the Maypole accompanied by harp or fiddle, ballad singing and story-telling. A poem from the first half of the eighteenth century invites the young people of the neighbourhood to dance around the *bedwen haf* on *Gŵyl Ifan* (St John's Day), and goes on to describe decking the Maypole with coloured ribbons as well as warning the young men of neighbouring villages against trying to steal it. This is followed by a poem in the same metre naming the eight morris dancers and their musician, said to be the best fiddler in Glamorganshire. These verses, with lines suitable for a join-in chorus persuading the onlookers to come to Gwenfô (Wenvoe) and join in the fun, were certainly meant to be sung. Although there is no tune direction with the poem, the words will fit an adaptation of Iolo Morganwg's Glamorganshire morris dance tune (Example 2.5):[62]

Example 5.41: Iolo Morganwg's morris dance tune adaptation

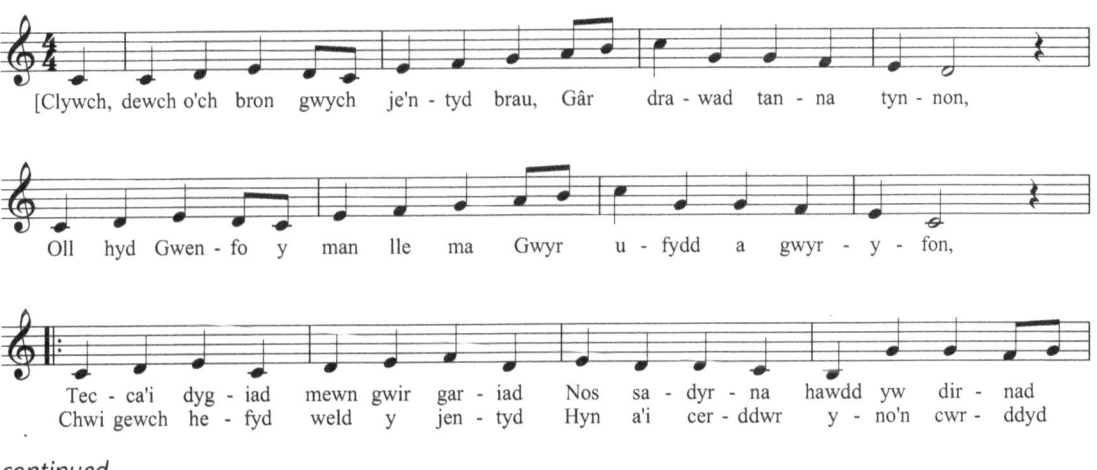

continued

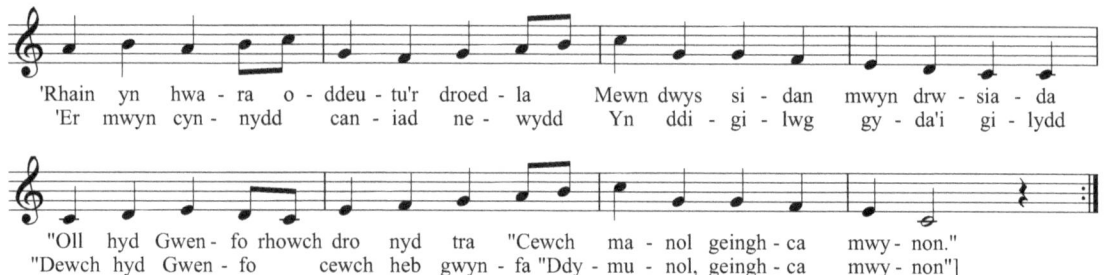

The Anglican Church was still frequented by the vast majority of Welsh people at this time and the parish church was the centre of village life. Both religious observance and recreation took place on Sundays, holy days, and patronal festivals; Sunday was as much an occasion for merriment as for worship, as can be seen in this account by John Evans of Bala in 1813:

> Ar y dyddiau gwyliau a'r gwylmabsantau tyrrai miloedd at ei gilydd, gan ddechrau ar y Saboth. Byddai'r siopau i gyd yn agored, a gwerth llawer o bunnau'n cael eu gwerthu o eiddo. Yr amaethwyr a fyddent yn cyflogi eu gweinidogion. Y nos aent i'r tafarndai i yfed i ganu ac i ddawnsio, ac yn y diwedd yn curo ac yn labio'i gilydd yn y modd creulonaf.
> [On the holidays and *gŵyl mabsantau* thousands flocked together beginning on the Sabbath. All the shops would be open and many pounds' worth of goods would be sold. The farmers would hire workers. At night they would go to the taverns to drink and sing and dance, and at the end hitting and beating each other most cruelly.][63]

The festival known as *gŵyl mabsant* was originally the feastday of the patron saint, a solemn occasion when the relics of the saint were brought out and carried about the parish. The following account appears in Simon Thomas, *Hanes y Byd a'r Amseroedd*, published in London in 1721:

> Ar y nos o flaen y Diwrnod hwnnw … arfer y plwyfolion oedd ymgynnull i'r Eglwys neu'r Llan i wylio, i ymprydio, a gweddio, ac i losci canhwyllau gerbron yr escyrn … fe fyddai iddynt ar y diwrnod trannoeth yr hwn a elwid Dydd Gwyl y Mabsanct, ymroddi yn llwyr i lawenydd: Canys hwy a dreulient yr holl ddydd mewn gwleddau, chwareyddiaethu, cerddoriaeth, a phob math o ddifyrrwch. Y gwyliau hyn a gynhaliwyd ym mhob plwyf, yn strict, ac yn ddefosiynol iawn trwy yr holl amser ac y bu y grefydd Babaidd yn y wlad. Nid ydys yn awr yn gwneuthur cymaint gyfrif Nos-wyl y Mabsanct ac oeddid yn yr amseroedd hynny: eithr am y diwrnod fe'i cedwir byth yn dra cyffelyb i'r modd y cedwid gynt, canys yr ydys nid yn unig yn ymgynull i wledda,

campio a difyrru, eithr hefyd mewn mannau o Gymru yn rhoddi rhyw fath o offrymau "Er mwyn Duw, a Mair a'r Mabsant gan ei goffa wrth ei enw".

[The night before the festival … it was the parishioners' practice to gather in the church to keep vigil, fast, pray and light candles before the relics … on the following day which they called Patron Saint's Day, they gave themselves completely to merriment. They spent the whole day in feasting, games, music and all kinds of entertainment. These festivals, which were held conscientiously in every parish, were very devotional during the time that the country followed the Papist religion. Less attention is paid now to the night before the festival than was done in those times, but the day itself is kept very much as it used to be because they not only gather to feast, play and amuse themselves but in some parts of Wales they also give a kind of offering "For the sake of God and Mary and the Patron Saint celebrating him by name".][64]

This account is reminiscent of the description of the Poulton vigil mentioned in chapter 2. In the beginning, the festival went on for a whole week, but by the eighteenth century it lasted only three or four days. It provided a respite for the people of the parish when no work was done and relatives returned to their native area to join in the celebrations. As its religious significance faded, all sorts of sports and games were held along with singing, dancing, feasting and interlude performances.

In rural Wales, with few towns and very poor roads, the fair and the market played an important role. Fairs that had some of the characteristics of the *gŵyl mabsant* and were originally often associated with the feastday of a saint occurred at least twice a year in many towns, and provided a long-anticipated break in the daily grind of labouring, as in the old Welsh saying:

Dim ond heddiw tan yfory
Dim ond 'fory tan y ffair.
[Only today until tomorrow
Only tomorrow till the fair.]

Carols, Ballads and the *Anterliwt*

PLYGAIN CAROLS

Most of the great Christian celebrations had a sacred and a secular side and Christmas wassailers might also have been among the church worshippers for the *plygain* service early on Christmas morning. The Welsh word *plygain* comes from the Latin *pulli cantus* or 'cock crow' and, originally, the start of the service might vary between three and six o'clock in the morning. By the eighteenth century, many prospective church-goers did not go to bed at all on Christmas eve, but stayed up drinking and playing cards, or singing and dancing to the harp, or making treacle toffee and generally enjoying themselves. An Englishwoman, Elizabeth Baker, living in Dolgellau, north Wales, described her visit to the *plygain* with members of the gentry in 1785:

> Equipping in my Great Coat and woollen gloves I set forth to celebrate what is here named *A Plugen*. Coffee and Tea commenced it ... The Beverage ended cards succeeded; ... The cards continued till supper which was a hot and plentiful one and resumed again after: about three in the morning coffee and Tea, etc. was again served as at our first coming and after that was mulled Ebillon and warm Punch for the males. The cards ceased. Sir John was the principal winner ... Humph[rey] Owen was too much fatigued with his guests revelry to stay till the bell summoned us to church; neither he nor his uncle of Dolserai or Sir John ... accompanied us there. We set forth with abundance of candles. Prayers were begun and the Church quite filled where we stayed till eight and broad daylight, hearing the different carols sung. The congregation behaved quietly ... I perceived no drunkenness in the assembly.[1]

Another description from Dolgellau, written about a century later, paints a different picture:

> Now the church is in a blaze, now crammed, body, aisles, gallery, now Shon Robert, the club-footed shoemaker, and his wife ... strike

up alternately, and without artificial aid of pitch pipe, the long, long carol and old favourite describing the Worship of Kings and of the Wise Men, and the Flight into Egypt, and the terrible wickedness of Herod. The crowds are wholly silent and rapt in admiration. Then the good Rector and his curate ... stand up, and read the Morning Service abbreviated ... – restless and somewhat surging is the congregation during prayers – the Rector obliged sometimes to stop short in his office and look direct at some part or persons, but no verbal admonishment. Prayers over, the singers begin again more carols, new singers, old carols in solos, duets, trios, choruses, then silence in the audience, broken at appropriate pauses by the suppressed hum, of delight and approval, till between eight and nine, hunger telling on the singers, the Plygain is over and the Bells strike out a round peal.[2]

'Ar Fore Dydd Nadolig', the oldest Welsh Christmas carol still extant with music, may have originated in pre-Reformation times. It was noted from oral tradition in Cardiganshire in the mid-twentieth century, but both words and musical style point to a much earlier origin. The pentachordal melody is plainsong-like in movement, and there are references to Roman Catholic practice in the words:[3]

Example 6.1: 'Ar Fore Dydd Nadolig'

The *plygain* appears to be a survival of the Catholic midnight Christmas mass, which evolved into a form of carol service when the country became Protestant. Undoubtedly the *plygain*'s long-lasting appeal came from the carols that were sung as solos, duets, trios or in small groups by members of the congregation. Although music played a prominent part, there can be no doubt that the poetry was of supreme importance; both illustrious and humble poets in Wales wrote words for carols to be sung in *plygain* services on familiar tunes. These carols, often running to a great many verses, were a means of relating Bible stories and of teaching religious doctrine to all at a time when few could read. The earliest printed Welsh Christmas carols were those of Vicar Prichard in the seventeenth century, with words in popular Welsh metres. These homely carols fitted easily on traditional tunes and were long remembered not only in Wales but further afield. This version of 'Awn i Fethlem', one of the Vicar's carols, came from a member of the Welsh colony in Argentina:[4]

Example 6.2: 'Awn i Fethlem' (from the singing of Sara MacDonald, Gaiman, Patagonia)

The carols printed in Thomas Jones's *Carolau a Dyriau Duwiol* in 1696, although more ambitious poetically than the Vicar's verses, were also for the most part in familiar metres, often *tri thrawiad*. Three carols in the volume were noted with the words '*iw ganu gyda thannau*' (to be sung with strings), indicating an instrumental accompaniment. Although most of the metres used for the carols are traditional Welsh ones, more complex tunes such as 'Ffarwel Ned Puw' and 'Crimson Velvet' also make their appearance. Over half a century later, *Blodeu-gerdd Cymry*[5] printed over fifty poems in *tri thrawiad* metre, many of them *plygain* carols, but already their popularity was waning. Still later in the century, William Jones, Llangadfan, the passionately Welsh eighteenth-century auto-didact with wide interests, sent a letter to Edward Jones in London in which he says:

> Your endeavors to preserve the remains of our music & poetry, induce me to send you the tunes of the May & Christmas carrols, as they were sung in this Country, but now begin to be neglected & likely to be intirely lost to the next generation.[6]

He appends tunes to a May carol and to a Christmas carol in *tri thrawiad* metre which he calls 'Hên Fesur' (Old Measure):[7]

Carols, Ballads and the *Anterliwt*

Example 6.3: 'Awn Heddyw er Mwyn Haeddiant i Ganu Gogoniant' – 'Hên Fesur'

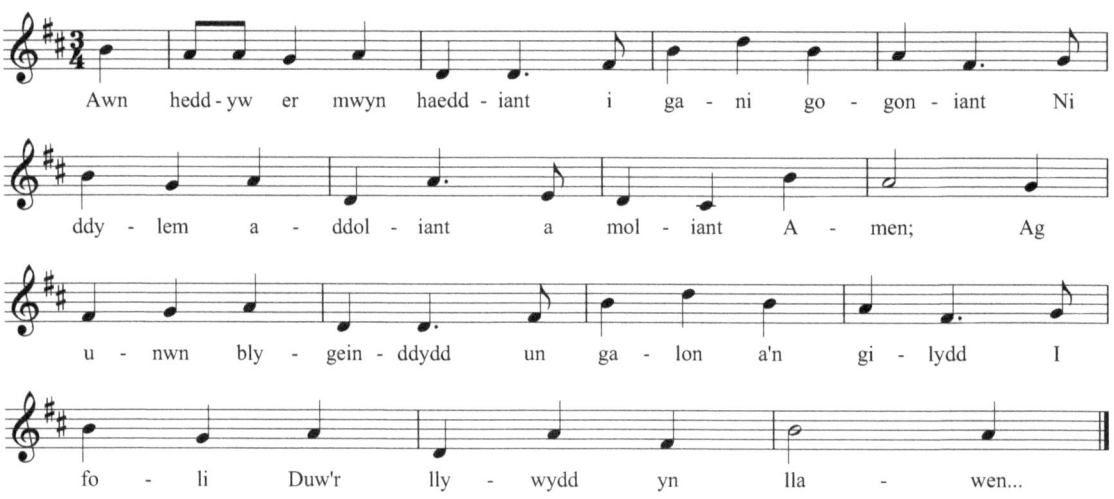

The most popular of the Welsh *plygain* tunes in terms of length of tradition and number of variants was 'Ffarwel Ned Puw/Pugh'. Numerous sets of words were printed to be sung on it from the seventeenth century well into the nineteenth, and it is still heard in *plygain* services at the present day. The 'Ffarwel Ned Puw' metre has given birth to at least eight different tunes, but the most popular version begins with a smooth flowing melody similar to the opening bars of the English carols, 'Tomorrow Shall Be My Dancing Day' and 'Rejoice and Be Merry'. However, the remainder of the Welsh carol tune is quite different and it seems likely that the opening was simply a familiar formula. *Plygain* singing was not entirely a masculine prerogative, as is shown by the antiphonal singing of the shoemaker and his wife in an earlier quotation. Nonetheless, the singing of carols by a male trio with the melody line in the middle and the harmony taken by tenor and bass was, and still is, a favourite with *plygain* congregations. A popular version was noted from the singing of three Montgomeryshire brothers in 1967:[8]

Example 6.4: 'Ffarwel Ned Puw', from the singing of three Montgomeryshire brothers, 1967

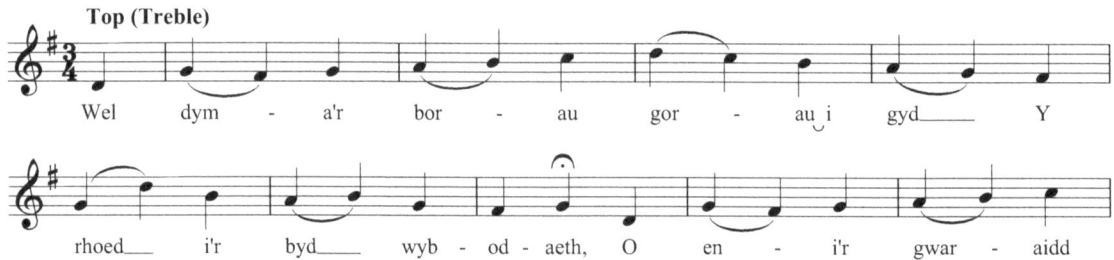

The majority of the 'Ffarwel Ned Puw' tunes are in the major, but there are a few in the minor, such as this narrow compass version from Anglesey which is extremely plain, rhythmically and melodically:[9]

Example 6.5: 'Ffarwel Ned Puw', Anglesey variant in the minor

'Ffarwel Ned Puw' was also called for in secular ballads and dances. John Parry, Ruabon, and Edward Jones ('Bardd y Brenin'), printed tunes called 'Ffarwel Ned Puw/Pugh' and there are variants in the fiddle manuscripts of John Thomas and Morris Edwards. At first glance, these instrumental airs bear little resemblance to the carol tunes. However, the formal dance pattern of three self-repeating sections is found in most of them, and carol words can be fitted to the dances if allowance is made for the feminine endings of the carol phrases so that the voice finishes a beat or so before the instrumental cadence.

One of the seventeenth-century English ballad tunes that attracted the attention of Welsh poets was 'See the Building'. By the end of the century, it had fallen out of fashion in England just when it was becoming immensely popular in Wales as a ballad and carol tune. Richard Morris, in early eighteenth-century Anglesey, noted Welsh and English verses in his manuscript to be sung to 'See the Building' and versions of the tune under its Welsh name, 'Gwêl yr Adeilad', continued to be sung as late as the twentieth century, especially as a carol tune:[10]

Example 6.6: 'Gwêl yr Adeilad' variant

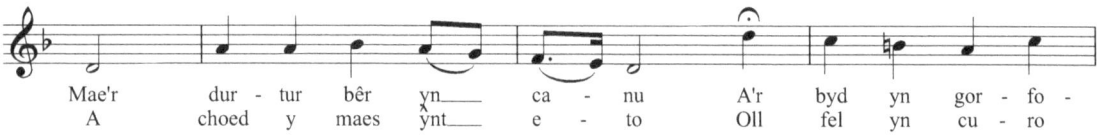

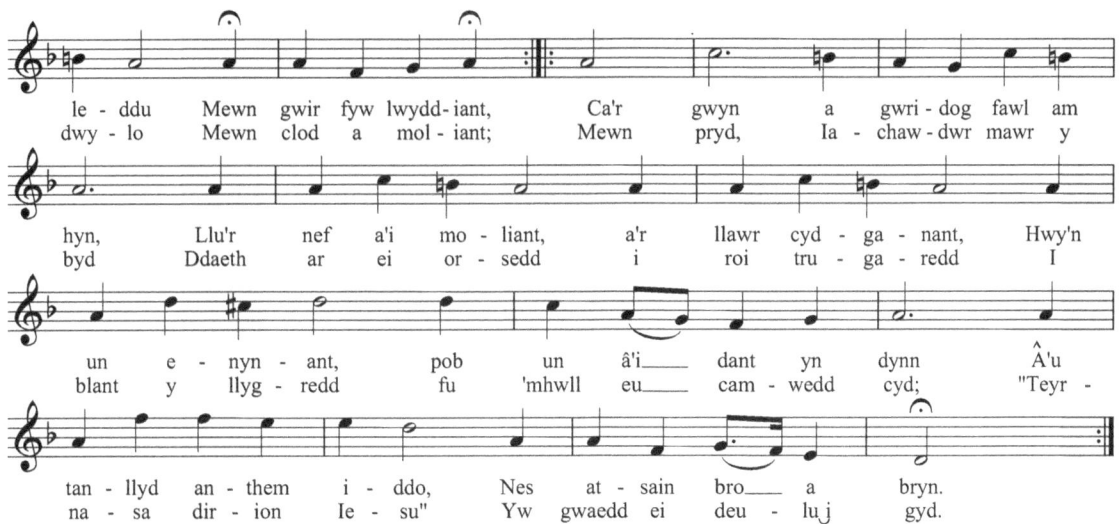

In contrast to the wide compass and strong melody of 'Gwêl yr Adeilad', the old carol 'Ffarwel Gwŷr Aberffraw', has a chant-like melody in an indeterminate mode with a narrow compass of five tones. The irregular rhythm grows out of the words and emphasises the intricate rhyme scheme:[11]

Example 6.7: 'Ffarwel Gwŷr Aberffraw'

continued

Carols, Ballads and the *Anterliwt*

o - dol wledd, Dydd yd - yw hedd - yw o hedd.

Clyw ddae - ar oer - ddu, Mae'r nef yn ca - nu,

Os bu yn gw - gu'i gwedd. A

gwyl yw hi O la - wen Jiw - bi -

li. Ple mae'r ty - lod - ion, Cloff - ion

deill - ion? Cânt rodd - ion yn ddi - ri.

'Mentra Gwen', like 'Gwêl yr Adeilad', appears to have origins outside Wales. The distinctive stanza pattern can be found in Scotland as far back as the sixteenth century, and it continued to be used in popular songs and ballads such as 'Captain Kid's Farewel to the Seas'. The earliest known appearance of the Welsh name was in Richard Morris's manuscript, where it is called 'Mentria Gwen', a name perhaps taken from a Welsh ballad now lost. 'Mentra Gwen' became increasingly popular with carol and ballad writers, with considerable diversity in the tune modes and the metre of the words. The earliest Welsh version of the tune was set down without words by the fiddler John Thomas in the mid-eighteenth century, and over a century later a variant of it was sung in an Anglesey Christmas carol service:[12]

Example 6.8: 'Mentra Gwen' variant as sung on Anglesey

Ar gy - fer he - ddiw'r bo - re'n Fab - an bach, 'Fa - ban bach, Y

Carols, Ballads and the *Anterliwt*

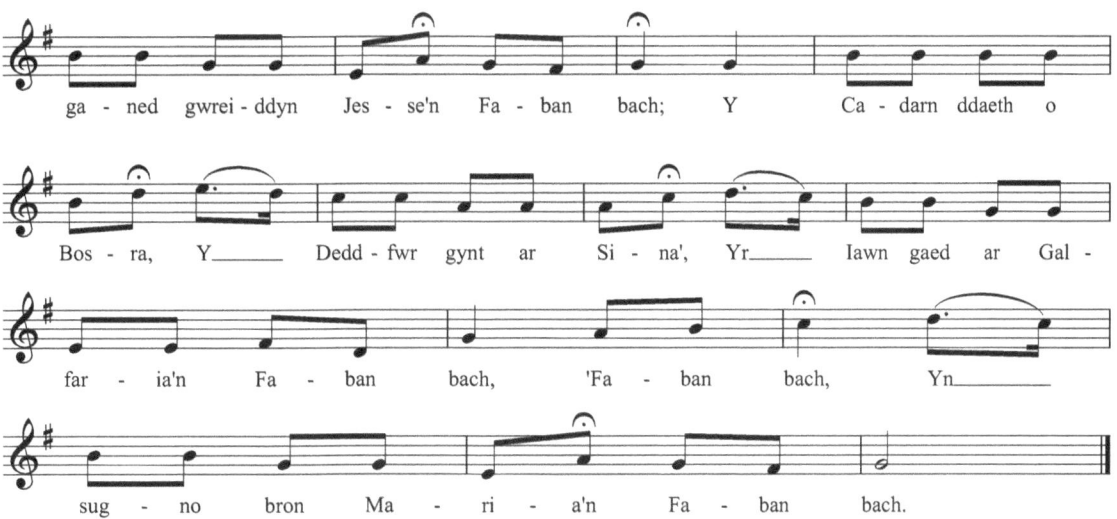

An unusual example of a 'Mentra Gwen' tune in the dorian/re mode with melismas on two of the cadences was collected in Cardiganshire:[13]

Example 6.9: 'Mentra Gwen' variant in the dorian/re mode

Marches as well as ballad tunes and dances caught the attention of the carol writers, and eighteenth-century carols were sung to 'The Belle-Isle March' and 'Gwŷr Harlech' among others. Perhaps the most interesting of these is a carol called 'Galar Gwŷr Ffrainc' (The Lamentation of the Men of France) a version of 'La Carmagnole', a popular dance and song at the time of the French Revolution:[14]

Example 6.10: 'Galar Gwŷr Ffrainc'

[Musical score with lyrics:]

Dowch, dowch, yn awr o fawr i fân I seinio clod i'r Ies-u glân;
Mae Messiah wed-i dod, I'w enw glân datseiniwn glod. Mawr
sain gorfoledd sydd! Daeth Crëwr mawr y dydd! Dofn, dofn ry-fe-ddod
yw Gweld Duw yn ddyn a dyn yn Dduw! Dofn, dofn ry-fe-ddod
yw Gweld Duw yn ddyn a dyn___ yn Dduw!

BALLADS

The fair fulfilled, among other things, the functions of an enormous bazaar and open-air amusement arcade. A wide variety of items would be sold there, including cattle, books, stockings, tawdry gewgaws and anything else that might fetch a penny or two. There was plenty of entertainment in the taverns, which were open all day and most of the night, with opportunities for dancing and singing to the harp. But there would also be ballad-mongers who came to the fair to peddle their wares, which they offered for sale in flimsy paper pamphlets containing two or three songs. The best of these wrote the ballads they sang but the lesser balladeers, pedlars or beggars sang whatever songs they could find that would bring in some money. The ballad singer acted as moral counselor, reporter of exciting events, amusing entertainer and voice of the oppressed. His themes were varied and included carols, full of worthy advice and religious in content, comic adventures, and dialogues between young lovers, but in a country without newspapers the great attraction for the public would be the sensational ballads of murders, shipwrecks or strange happenings. The ballads were also popular as one of the few ways the poor could protest openly about the tyranny of landlords or the bullying of rapacious stewards. They were sung on popular airs familiar to a public who would want to sing for themselves the ballads they purchased.

The declaiming of poetry in fairs was not new in the eighteenth century. Long before this, *datgeiniaid pen pastwn*, that is inferior bards who could not declaim their poetry to an instrument, plied their craft in fairs by declaiming to the thump of a staff, as mentioned earlier in chapter 2. Other more proficient poets, like Robin Clidro, no doubt sang in fairs and taverns as well as at the houses of the gentry. It is worth noting here that, at this period, the language of these ballads was still mainly Welsh rather than English. Some of these songs were light-hearted and amusing but at least one murder ballad survives in manuscript from about 1600.[15]

Although eighteenth-century ballad pamphlets were flimsy and not meant to last, enough have survived to allow a study of the ballad airs which took the public's fancy, giving a vivid picture of the life of the period and popular musical taste. Seventeenth and eighteenth-century Welsh ballad poetry, especially in north Wales, was heavily under the influence of poets like Huw Morys who combined bardic technique with the metres of the new tunes from England and the Continent. However, it should be noted that Welsh poets did not embrace foreign balladry indiscriminately. The 'most popular single tune associated with ballads [in England] before 1700 [is "Packington's Pound"]',[16] but neither that name nor those of 'Fortune My Foe' or 'Greensleeves', the next most popular, can be found among eighteenth-century Welsh ballad tunes (although 'Greensleeves' was well known in Wales). The five most popular ballad tunes in eighteenth-century Wales were 'See the Building' (Gwêl yr Adeilad), 'Crimson Velvet' (Y Ffion Felfed), 'The Banks of Ireland' (Bryniau Werddon), 'Loath to Depart' (Anhawdd Ymadael), and 'Gerard's Mistress' (Gwledd Angharad).[17] However, despite the profusion of foreign tunes, there were also strong indigenous Welsh contenders, often known by both Welsh and English titles such as 'Heavy Heart/Calon Drom', 'Leave Land/Gadael Tir', 'Ffarwel Dai Llwyd' and 'Neithiwr ac Echnos', all favourites with Huw Morys and other poets of the period. Less ambitious folk poets continued to be attracted by the *triban* metre and the trochaic tetrameter quatrain so numerous in collections of *penillion*.

Murder ballads are always popular, and none more so than the story of the son who returns home after a long period away and is killed by his parents who do not recognise him. Versions of the theme are found in many European cultures, including Wales, where the ballad is called 'Y Blotyn Du' (The Black Spot) after the black spot on the man's arm that proves to the murderers that the man they have killed is their own son. According to Lady Herbert Lewis, writing in 1911, 'I have heard it sung to four different tunes in Flintshire. The words of the ballad are still sold by pedlars.'[18]

Example 6.11: 'Y Blotyn Du'

Gwran - dewch ar stor - i greul - on Fu gynt yn ngwlad y Saes - on,
Ger - llaw Caer - au pen - tre Caer, O fewn i Gorn - wal dir - ion.

In a long ballad such as 'Y Blotyn Du', a simple air might be varied by changing the mode in different verses, altering the melody or rhythm, or extending it by repetition. One country singer sang all but the last verse of the ballad in the major, altering the tune in many a verse to bring out the story and finishing with the final sad verse in the minor.

One of the most popular folk metres for Welsh ballad singers was the ubiquitous trochaic tetrameter quatrain: four lines, rhyming AABB, in which all four lines end on an unaccented syllable. The metre suits the Welsh language perfectly and hundreds of these unassuming verses were passed along orally. When a printed collection of Welsh *penillion* appeared in 1940,[19] considerably over half the verses in the book were in trochaic tetrameter quatrains, twice as many as verses in *triban*, *awdl-gywydd* and *tri thrawiad* metres combined. These little quatrains are sung to a variety of tunes, from the artless to the more polished. One of the most popular, and certainly one of the oldest, is the tune known as 'Y Dôn Fechan'. First published in *Relicks* (1794), at least thirteen versions of this simple melody are still extant. The *Relicks* version sung to the old ballad of 'Hên Ŵr o'r Coed' shows it at its simplest:[20]

Example 6.12: 'Y Dôn Fechan' variant (Hên Ŵr o'r Coed')

This 8-bar pentachordal tune in ABBA form with the third degree major is replicated, changed and expanded in various ways. Most of the extant versions are in triple time, but the blind ballad singer Dic Dywyll was heard singing a duple time variant in Caernarfon in the 1830s. He sang it with the third degree minor, well suited to the tragic love ballad of 'Morgan Jones o'r Dolau Gwyrddion':[21]

Example 6.13: 'Y Dôn Fechan' variant ('Morgan Jones o'r Dolau Gwyrddion')

Ballads on folk metres which were easy to compose and easy to sing provided no real challenge to Welsh poets. When English tunes began to appear in broadsides and printed collections in the seventeenth century, the music became generally available to those who could read music, although many of the versions found in Welsh manuscripts have obviously been passed on orally. 'Let Mary Live Long' is a case in point. The tune and its name came from a 1692 broadside wishing long life to King William and Queen Mary, and remained popular in England until the 1730s. But its popularity in Wales, which continued long after it had died out in England, came from the elaborate eleven-line stanza pattern that gave full rein to Welsh verbal ingenuity, expressed here in formal patterns of consonantal assonance and internal rhyme:[22]

Example 6.14: 'Hir Oes i Fair' ('Let Mary Live Long')

Among the most unusual adaptations of an English tune to Welsh poetic purposes are the versions of 'God Save the King', known in Welsh as 'Duw Gadwo'r Brenin'. The earliest Welsh ballads to be published in this metre come from the last quarter of the eighteenth century, a period when the country was at war with the American colonies, as well as the French, and patriotism was well to the fore. In general, the Welsh examples follow the basic melodic pattern of the first half of 'God Save the King', and part of the second, but the tune is considerably extended in both halves. Tune-names such as 'God Save the King, Yr hen ffordd' (the old way), or 'Duw Gadwo'r Brenin, Yr hen ffordd Gymreig' (God Save the King, the old Welsh way), indicate that the Welsh versions are metrically quite distinct from the familiar English pattern. Jonathan Hughes was just one of the eighteenth-century poets who used the metre, in his case in a ballad poking fun at tea-drinking, which was just coming into fashion:[23]

Example 6.15: 'Duw Gadwo'r Brenin, Yr hen ffordd Gymreig'

The metre was equally popular for Christmas carols, and in 'Roedd yn y Wlad Honno' it is easy to see how country singers would stretch the rhythm by lingering on certain syllables; in the case of this Flintshire version, it acted as a means of bringing out the intricate rhyme scheme:[24]

Example 6.16: 'Roedd yn y Wlad Honno'

In addition to the circulation of ballads in fairs and on other public occasions, much eighteenth-century poetry printed in almanacs was accompanied by words such as '*i'w canu ar ...*' (to be sung on ...) or '*ar y mesur a elwir ...*' (on the measure called ...). An analysis of the metres of these poems and the tunes called for gives some interesting results. In the almanacs printed between 1681 and 1800, about 250 poems are in 'song' metres. These include traditional Welsh metres such as *tri thrawiad*, *awdl-gywydd*, *triban*, *carolau haf* (May carols) and metres connected with Welsh tunes such as 'Heavy Heart', 'Ffarwel Ned Puw' and 'Ffarwel Dai Llwyd'.

One of the most popular ballads in Wales was 'Y Bachgen Main', in which a mother tries to persuade her daughter to marry a rich man. If she marries him, she will have servants and wealth and social position, but the girl answers that even if she were offered the silks of Persia and the gold of Peru she would rather have the lad she loves, and to him she will remain true:[25]

Example 6.17: 'Y Bachgen Main'

continued

wnes yn nes-nes at-ynt Nes o'wn i yn y lle a'r man, A phwy oedd

y-no yn ym-go-mio ond f'ann-wyl gar-iad gy-da'i mam.

The words to the song 'Merch Ifanc o'n Ben Boreu' are sad: 'I was a young girl in the morning, a young wife at mid-day, and before the night I was a widow with my heart broken'. The music matches the sadness of the words. Only one verse was collected, until some years later an Anglesey man sang a long ballad with a verse that contained the words, 'Merch ifanc oedd hi'r bore … A chyn y nos yn widw, A'i dwylo bach yn rhydd' ('In the morning she was a young girl … Before night a widow, with her hands free'). The ballad tells the story of a young man who became a sailor because the girl he loved was prevented, misleadingly, by her family from marrying him and given to another. On the sailor's return from his long voyage, he finds she is free to marry again and consents readily to marry him:[26]

Example 6.18: 'Merch Ifanc o'n Ben Boreu'

Merch i-fanc o'n ben bo-reu Gwraig i-fanc ga-nol dydd A chyn y nos yn we-ddw A chyn y nos yn we-ddw A chyn y nos yn we-ddw A'm ca-lon fach yn brudd.

'Gwn Dafydd Ifan' is a satirical ballad about Dafydd Ifan, said to be a veteran of the Battle of Waterloo. He always carried his gun because he was fond of sport, but in his old age he lost his reason and the lock of his gun was removed so it could not be fired. The air, however, appears to be older than the words and may have been adapted from an earlier song:[27]

Example 6.19: 'Gwn Dafydd Ifan'

Before the middle of the eighteenth century, about eighty-five per cent of the poetry printed in the almanacs was in the traditional short Welsh metres. From the middle of the eighteenth century onward, almanacs show the steady decline of poems in traditional Welsh metres as the preference grew for English tunes with new and challenging metres such as 'Belle-Isle March', 'Monday Morning' (Dydd Llun y Bore), 'Black-Eyed Susan' (Susan Lygad-ddu) and 'Princess Royal'. A similar change was to be seen in the metres of sacred poetry. In contrast to the seventeenth-century vicar, Rhys Prichard, whose book *Canwyll y Cymry* was full of verses in traditional Welsh metres familiar to his readers, the great Welsh hymn-writer William Williams, Pantycelyn wrote in 1763 that he wished to write another book, 'ond aros yr wyf i gael amryw fesurau newyddion oddiwrth y Saeson, fel na bo'r Cymry yn fyrr o'u braint hwy mewn dim i foli Duw' ('but I am waiting to get some new metres from the English so that the Welsh will not lack anything to praise God').[28]

ANTERLIWT (INTERLUDE)

Many of the tunes used for carols and ballads can also be found in the music of the *anterliwt*, dramas in verse that were particularly popular in north Wales country areas in the seventeenth and eighteenth centuries. The Welsh word *anterliwt*, which appears as early as the sixteenth century, is derived from the English 'interlude', but the mode in which the plays were presented is Welsh. The purpose of the *anterliwt* was partly to provide bawdy entertainment, but also to deliver moral maxims.

> The performance would be by the roadside, in the market square or in an inn yard. The stage would be a cart, a trestle-table or a door laid

on two barrels. There would be no curtain to go up, no stage-lights to come on, and very little by way of a set. I would have to stand, unless I could climb to the top of a wall or the branch of a tree. When the players were satisfied that they had enough of a crowd, they would begin.[29]

The same Englishwoman, Elizabeth Baker, who went to the *plygain* service in Dolgellau, also attended an 'Interlude' that year and found it:

amazing that from a single penny for admittance of each person these Buffoons get from 25s. to 30s. a night for two or three nights successively ... some lamented that I had not mentioned my intention [of going] that the Dialogue might have been more delicate; for it is, without an injunction to the contrary, grossly obscene ... there was a Welsh song in tune and a Hornpipe danced better than I expected.[30]

The two essential characters in the *anterliwt* are the Fool and the Miser. The Fool, with his ribald songs and suggestive dancing, represents the phallic element of the horseplay. The Miser is treated as a laughing-stock – an unpleasant, rapacious man who has become wealthy by oppressing his tenants, stealing, and bearing false witness – and one of the basic themes of many an *anterliwt* is the Fool's humiliation of the Miser. Other characters appear as called for by the main story, which the *anterliwt* writer often adapted from a popular source such as a well-known ballad, historical situation or folk-tale.

There was no established theatre in Wales at this period, and typically it was men such as carters, coopers or sextons who wrote and sometimes performed in these dramas, since they made their living in occupations that could be left for a time. All the characters were played by male actors, and in small companies they would of necessity double roles. Music was essential with songs for the various characters, and in most cases dancing was usually accompanied by the fiddle. A glance at the tunes used in the *anterliwts* shows that a great many of them were airs familiar to ballad-mongers and writers of *plygain* carols. Indeed, many *anterliwt* authors, such as Huw Morys (1622–1709), Jonathan Hughes (1721–1805), Thomas Edwards ('Twm o'r Nant'; 1739–1810), Elis Roberts (d. 1789) and Hugh Jones (1700?–82) were proficient in all of these *genres*, and suited their verse to the company.

Since dancing was usually part of the entertainment, there is more variety in the music of the *anterliwt* than the ballad or carol. Jigs and hornpipes were popular; 'Buttered Pease' was called for in *Llur*, and 'Jack Latin' in *Cwymp Dyn*, but more often than not no particular tune was named. The phallic dances by the Fool were an important element in the entertainment. 'Sbonc bogel' (belly jerk; the least obscene of the phallic dance names) is called for in at least three *anterliwts*, and the tune must have been popular in Wales over an extended period for the melody is a variant of the Elizabethan dance tune, 'Pepper is Black':[31]

Example 6.20: 'Sbonc bogel'

There were dances of various types for other characters as well. Sometimes the Fool and the Miser dance together, as in *Jeils*,[32] where they dance and sing a song with the chorus 'ffylanti tw tam tylo'. In 1717, Richard Morris wrote that he could play 'ffyrling ting teen' on the viol but the earliest extant form of the air in Wales was a melody called 'Fflanti Too' set down in an abbreviated violin notation by John Thomas in his 1752 manuscript. This notation may have been devised by him as a kind of musical shorthand, which places dots in a pattern, but gives almost no rhythmic indications and is not easy to read without other versions for comparison. However, when transcribed in conventional musical notation, it becomes clear that the tune is related to 'Dadl Dau – Flaunting Two':[33]

Example 6.21: 'Dadl Dau – Flaunting Two'

Y Dywysoges Genefetha (Princess Genefetha), written in 1744, calls for the Fool and the Miser to sing a song with each verse ending 'Ffylan tin tw tawn teulo' and, although dancing isn't mentioned, it is hard to believe that they would not have danced together in the chorus. A verse from the song mentioned is attached here to John Thomas's 'Fflanti Too':[34]

Example 6.22: 'Ffylan Tin Tw' from *Y Dywysoges Genefetha*

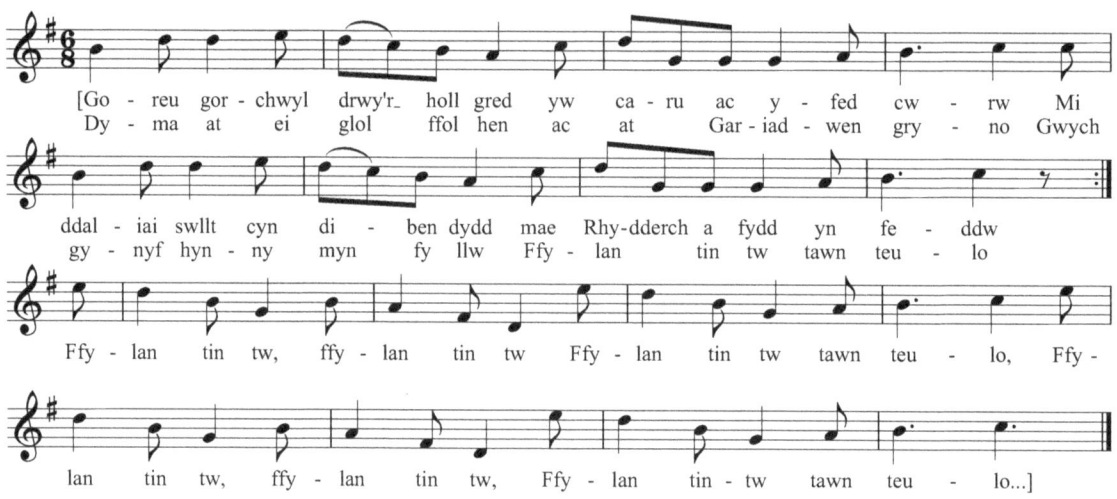

John Thomas is also responsible for the earliest notation of an air that became familiar through its appearance in *Relicks* (1784). 'Ar Hyd y Nos' was called for in *Ffrewyll y Methodistiaid* (Whipping the Methodists), an anti-Methodist *anterliwt* written in the early 1740s. Here too the air is written in abbreviated violin notation, but there is little difference between the tune printed in *Relicks* some forty years later and John Thomas's version:[35]

Example 6.23: 'Ar Hyd y Nos' from the John Thomas manuscript

Most *anterliwt* songs were set to familiar tunes of the period. 'Queen's Dream' had long been known in Wales, but the original name of the sixteenth-century air was 'Nutmegs and Ginger'. The same melody was used in a setting for lute called 'The Parlement', a name that may have been taken from Thomas Deloney's ballad of 1602 in the same metre called 'The Queenes Goeing to the Parliament'.[36] Perhaps that is where the Welsh tune acquired its association with the word 'Queen', though it does not explain the 'Dream'. At any rate, it was called 'Queen's Dream' in Wales until later in the eighteenth century, when it was cymricised as 'Breuddwyd y Frenhines':[37]

Example 6.24: 'Queen's Dream/Breuddwyd y Frenhines'

The oral tradition in Wales at this period was still very strong and John Thomas's fiddle manuscript, together with that of Morris Edwards, is a significant and rare written example of Welsh traditional music before the nineteenth century. John Thomas's manuscript is by far the most important. Understandably dance tunes formed a large part of the collection of working fiddlers, but it is obvious that John Thomas also played popular ballad tunes of the day for he includes variants of such well-known airs as 'Gwêl yr Adeilad', 'Brynie'r Werddon', 'Heavy Heart',

'Diniweidrwydd', 'Charity Mistress', 'Ffarwel Ned Puw', 'Black-eyed Susan' and 'Y Cowper Mwyn', among many others.

Above all it is obvious that John Thomas followed the *anterliwt* as a fiddler and at least half of the tunes known to have been used in the numerous *anterliwt*s that entertained north Wales in the eighteenth century can be found in his manuscript in one form or another. However, it is the phallic dances, such as 'Sbonc bogel' and 'Contar dreinsiwr', that connect John Thomas particularly closely to the *anterliwt*.

The Early Collectors: Iolo Morganwg and Ifor Ceri

THE EIGHTEENTH CENTURY in Wales produced some notable polymaths. Educational opportunities were increasing in spite of the lack of national institutions or financial resources, and by the end of the century the reading public in Wales had expanded considerably. Many of these versatile scholars were craftsmen, clergymen or well-to-do farmers who had time to pursue interests other than scraping a living. Lewis Morris, Richard Morris's brilliant elder brother, was a surveyor who interested himself in science, engineering, cartography, history, philology, literature, agriculture, music and a host of other topics. William Jones, the Llangadfan farmer, became an expert in classical studies, literature, astronomy, medicine and much else. Undoubtedly, the most extraordinary of these was Edward Williams ('Iolo Morganwg'; 1747–1826), a Glamorgan mason by trade who never went to school or college and had an astonishing range of scholarly and antiquarian interests, including the history of Wales and Welsh literature, architecture, sculpture, botany, geology, agriculture, horticulture, theology, music and much more. He was far ahead of his time in the scholarly interest he took in all aspects of traditional life, including old customs, seasonal games and diversions, legends and folk-songs. Long before today's National History Museum in St Fagans had been thought of, Iolo had advocated the establishment of an institution for the study of ancient traditional songs, tales and music.[1]

Iolo was fiercely proud of Glamorgan's cultural heritage and determined to prove it superior to that of any other part of Wales, especially the north. In the process of trying to establish this he became, among other things, Wales's most famous literary faker, forging manuscripts and antiquarian documents of history, poetry, archaeology – anything that would serve to glorify Glamorgan. His intellectual brilliance was so formidable that it was many years after he died before his forgeries began to be widely questioned and a century before they were finally unravelled.

However, there is no reason to think that Iolo's notations of traditional music are anything but the genuine product of his time and place. For the most part, they are records of the music-making of ordinary people in Glamorgan, often jotted down hastily in notebooks or on the backs of envelopes. His collection reflects a very different kind of music from the airs in the books published by John Parry and Edward Jones, and it is clear from Iolo's manuscripts that, unlike the harper/collectors of north Wales, it was tunes connected with words that most interested him. He includes words to well over a quarter of the airs in the collection; where no words are given, the title of the air indicates that words were sung to it, such as 'Cobler Coch o Hengoed', the subject of a set of humorous verses, or 'Hwp y Diri Dando', a popular tune in song-and-chorus style. When no title is given, a tune is often called by its poetic metre, such as 'Cainc ar y Cyhydedd Hir', 'Cywydd Deuair Morganwg', 'Triban Deublyg' or simply 'Morganwg cyhydedd 8 a 7'. These were tunes that were suitable for the singing of *penillion* and any verses in a suitable metre could be used.

Iolo Morganwg's activities in gathering traditional songs and dances make him the earliest collector in Wales – as well as one of the first in Europe – and his remarks on the differences between singing styles in north and south Wales are of considerable interest (always allowing for Iolo's prejudice against the north):

> The ancient Northwalian singing is a kind of chaunt which is to this day retained, and it is adapted to every kind of verse and stanza ... In singing to the harp whatever tune is played whether solemn or gay, slow or brisk the songster sings his very various kinds of stanzas, and those on a strange variety of subjects, heroic or pastoral, Elegiac or comic, to the same dull chant, which to say the best that can [be] said of it, is nothing better than a tollerable drone to the harp. – The South Walian Music has much of the Scotish Manner, and is more lively than the No. Wal^n. which has in it something grand. In Southwales the manner of singing is for the instrument to play the song's appropriate tune which, and not a chaunt, the singer also uses. The North Walian chaunt is something similar to, but less pleasing than, the Glamorgan oxen or plow chant, which like the former can be adapted to all metres.[2]

This appears to be a description of what was called *canu gyda'r tannau* or *canu penillion* in north Wales, and is especially interesting for the light it throws on the contrasting styles of singing in south and north Wales.

Judging by the existing manuscripts, Iolo collected almost seventy songs and airs of various kinds. Unfortunately, his enthusiasm for collecting was not matched by an equal facility for notating tunes. He almost never gives time or key signatures, and in the rare cases where these appear it is probably an indication that the piece has been copied from another source. Barlines are used to indicate phrase endings of the verse rather than marking rhythmic groupings, and it is sometimes difficult to work out the rhythm. Fortunately, almost half of the airs in the collection are in the traditional Welsh metres of *cywydd deuair fyrion*, *awdl-gywydd* and *triban* so that if an air fits one of those metres it is comparatively easy to know where the barlines should go. Sometimes Iolo names the metre, at other times he merely notes the number of syllables in each line, as in 'Morganwg cyhydedd 8 a 7' (where he notes 8 syllables in the first line and 7 in the second).

The question of tonality is equally complicated. Although it is usually possible to work out the keynote, even without a key signature or accidentals, it is difficult to be sure without other references whether the air is in the major or the minor, or perhaps the dorian/re mode so popular in Wales.[3] About two-thirds of the airs are written with G as the keynote. Major mode versions of about a dozen of these are to be found in other collections, and it would appear that Iolo set down major mode airs in the key of G. Similarly, it is possible that examples written with the keynote A are meant to be in the minor mode. Those are the most popular keynotes, although there are a few in C and D, and one in F. Perhaps the airs written in D were sung in the dorian/re mode but there is no evidence one way or the other.

Iolo Morganwg's wide interests are reflected in the songs he noted, several of which are connected with occupations. The oldest may be the ox-ploughing songs, a type mentioned by Giraldus Cambrensis in the twelfth century (see chapter 1). Many examples of oxen songs have been collected over the years, but Iolo's song 'Cainc y Cathreiwr' was the earliest. It is unusual in its rhythmic freedom (even allowing for his unconventional notation) and again this may reflect the style in which the lads sang to the oxen as they were ploughing. There was no need to keep a steady rhythm as if they were soldiers marching; their job was to sing 'to keep the oxen in good heart'.[4]

Example 7.1: 'Cainc y Cathreiwr'

The same rhythmic freedom is found in the milkmaid's song, 'Cainc yr Odryddes', calling the cows to be milked. The extended phrases on vowels were suitable for projecting the voice over long distances to bring the cows in from the pastures. Iolo was aware of the *Ranz des Vaches*, Swiss mountain songs sung to summon the cows, songs that were improvisatory in character, reiterating short phrases with changes of tempo and accent, a description that also applies to Iolo's song:[5]

Example 7.2: 'Cainc yr Odryddes'

[Musical notation with lyrics:]

hai haw haw Bri-thi i'r bu-arth h. h. h. B i'r B.

h. h. h. B h. h. h. B--- fach

h. h. h. B--- h. h. h. B--- fach h. h. B--- f

h. h. h. h. h. h. h. h. h. B--- i B---

h. B--- f h. h. h. h. h. h. h. h. h. B--- i B---

Songs noted by Iolo connected with various rituals include religious songs, wassail carols and spring carols, as well as a Christmas carol. Among these were two songs that he said used to be sung in Glamorgan's parish churches as well as in some Nonconformist congregations: one was correctly written with a time signature and barlines in the proper places (obviously copied from a manuscript or printed source); the second tune, 'Hen Erddigan Morganwg' 'mesur byrr', with traditional secular words, is much freer (for ease of reading the rhythm has been edited in this example and a number of those that follow): [6]

Example 7.3: 'Hen Erddigan Morganwg' 'mesur byrr' (edited)

Gwyn fyd y ber fwy-al-chen Sy'n ddig-rif ar y gang-en

Heb awr o-fa-lus y-no bydd Drwy gorph y dydd yn lla-wen.

Iolo also noted examples of May carol tunes. Here again he included no words, but traditional May carol words will fit:[7]

Example 7.4: May carol tune, 'Mesur Carol Haf' (edited)

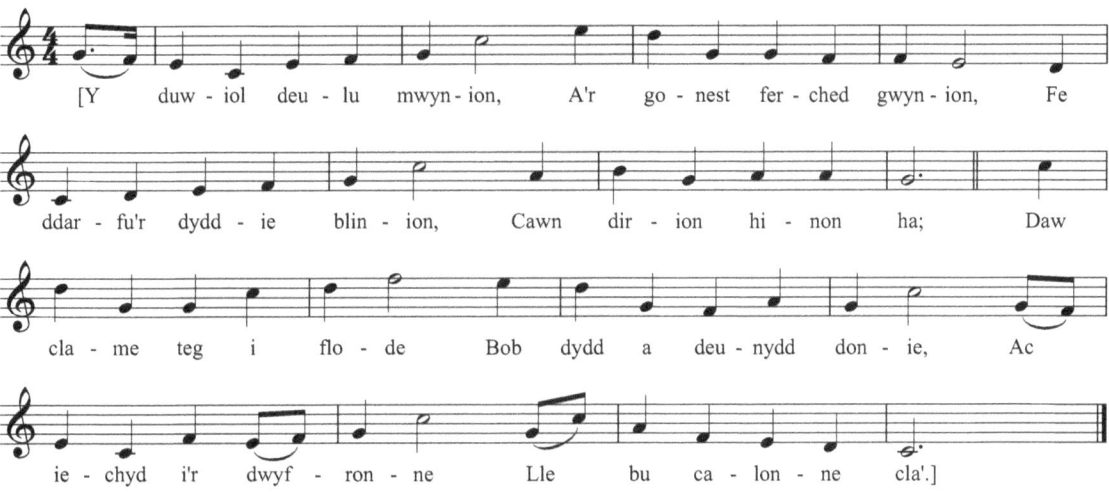

Morris dancing played an important part in spring celebrations and Iolo set down a morris dance air that appears to be an early version of the Helston Furry Dance tune (see Example 2.5). It is difficult to know how many of the airs in Iolo's manuscripts were used for dancing. An untitled variant of the first half of the early eighteenth-century dance tune 'Meillionen' appears in this collection, but Iolo himself used the word 'dance' in connection with only three: the morris dance tune, and the two *triban* airs 'Llanbedr ar Fynydd. Cainc ar fesur Triban (a dance)' and 'Dawns Triban Deublyg':[8]

Example 7.5: 'Dawns Triban Deublyg' (edited)

continued

Many of Iolo's lively *triban* tunes would have been suitable for dancing, and this was also true of some of the great number of tunes in *awdl-gywydd* metre (for example, 8.7.FM). Iolo called one of these, which he noted without words, 'Sigl Din ar y Drain (mesur "Y Gelynen" – "Y Gelynen" metre)'. The words of 'Y Gelynen' sung with a nonsense chorus were well known in north Wales, and they fit equally well on Iolo's tune:[9]

Example 7.6: 'Sigl Din ar y Drain (mesur "Y Gelynen" – "Y Gelynen" metre)'

Among the best known traditional love lyrics to come out of south Wales are those usually titled 'Bugeilio'r Gwenith Gwyn'. They were printed in *Ancient National Airs of Gwent and Morganwg*, set to a tune that became associated with the words. Iolo's much earlier collection includes the same ballad words set to a different but equally attractive melody that he calls 'Pebyll Penon'.[10]

Example 7.7: 'Pebyll Penon' (rhythm revised)

His unmetred rhythmic notation, oscillating between duple and triple time, gives a certain leisurely quality to the air, but the general flow of the melody indicates common time. It is worth noting that the compass of the air is unusually wide for traditional Welsh airs, and this is true of several other songs in Iolo's collection. The same characteristic of wide vocal compass is found in many songs in *Ancient National Airs of Gwent and Morganwg* and contrasts with the north Wales song tradition in which a medium compass of about an octave is quite common, due perhaps to the influence of *canu gyda'r tannau*; in this form of singing, the words are of primary importance and the vocal compass is, therefore, comparatively narrow in order to allow the words to take precedence.

Communal songs that could be sung at informal gatherings, such as game songs or songs with a join-in chorus, must have played an important part in the entertainment of the area. Words from *Tribannau Morganwg*, fitted to an edited version of a communal song tune noted by Iolo, 'Pwyo Pen y Gofid', give the flavour of the singing style:[11]

Example 7.8: 'Pwyo Pen y Gofid' (edited)

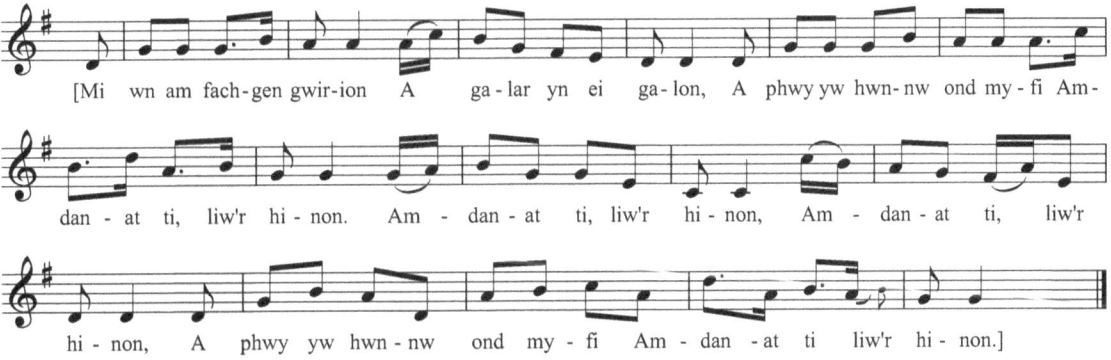

Iolo noted some songs intended for harp and voice, including a version of the popular Glamorganshire ballad 'Y Ferch o'r Scer'. Easily the most interesting of these is Iolo's notation of 'Triban Morganwg' with alternate sections for harp and voice. The earliest printed version of the tune appeared as 'Treban Morganough' in a 1730 collection by Walsh, and was reprinted a year later in *Thirty New and Choice Country Dances*. The earliest Welsh printed version did not appear until almost half a century later, after William Jones of Llangadfan sent a copy of 'Triban Morganwg' to Edward Jones in London (see Plate 6). He printed the air in *Relicks* (1784) without words or any indication that words were sung to it, and when the air next appeared it was with English words and the harp part as accompaniment rather than as an equal partner with the singer. Iolo, however, keeps to the alternate voice-and-harp principle and, although he did not set down words under the voice part, he noted instrumental and vocal sections with the words 'sym' (symphony) and 'air'.[12] As a Glamorgan man, he would have known scores of *triban* verses, any of which would fit:

Example 7.9: 'Triban Morganwg' (Iolo Morganwg's notation)

Almost half of Iolo's airs are in rhythmic patterns that fit traditional Welsh poetic metres such as the *triban* and *awdl-gywydd*. As already mentioned, one of the oldest of the Welsh bardic metres is *cywydd deuair fyrion*, and the words 'deff-rowch ben teulu mae'r flwyddyn newy', set to 'Ton Deuair', come from a New Year *calennig* song:[13]

Example 7.10: 'Ton Deuair' 'deffrowch ben teulu mae'r flwyddyn newy' (edited)

Perhaps the most tantalising of all Iolo's airs is his copy of 'Hun Gwenllian', a name connected with one of the pieces in tablature in the Robert ap Huw manuscript. Eighteenth-century antiquarian interest in old Welsh music led to the discovery of important manuscripts in the libraries of collectors. In the ferment of this curiosity about the culture of the past, William Owen Pughe wrote to Iolo urging him to bring out his history of the Bards of Ynys Prydain:

> This work is so looked for by the literary world, that I am sure its completion would be the making of you (as they say here) especially so by combining the ancient Music with the poetry ... which you will be able to do most completely as it seems, from your discoveries at Havod. Even if you had not found there the key you mention, perhaps it might have been done by Hun Gwenllian, which is in the old Book and also pretty common in N Wales.[14]

In a later note, William Owen Pughe asks him if he remembered to lay hold of 'Hun Gwenllian' when he was in north Wales.

It appears that Iolo did indeed get hold of 'Hun Gwenllian' through Twm o'r Nant, the poet and *anterliwt* author, who seems to have given him a copy of the air 'as sung by some poets'. It is in considerable contrast to other versions noted by north-Walian collectors. What they do seem to have in common is a degree of sequential treatment at certain points, and this may have some relevance to the example in the Robert ap Huw manuscript. The earliest printed version is Aria XXI in *Antient British Music*, written in the style of a march (see Example 3.4), whereas the version Iolo had from Twm o'r Nant later in the century may be closer to the ap Huw manuscript.[15]

Example 7.11: 'Hun Gwenllian' (from Twm o'r Nant)

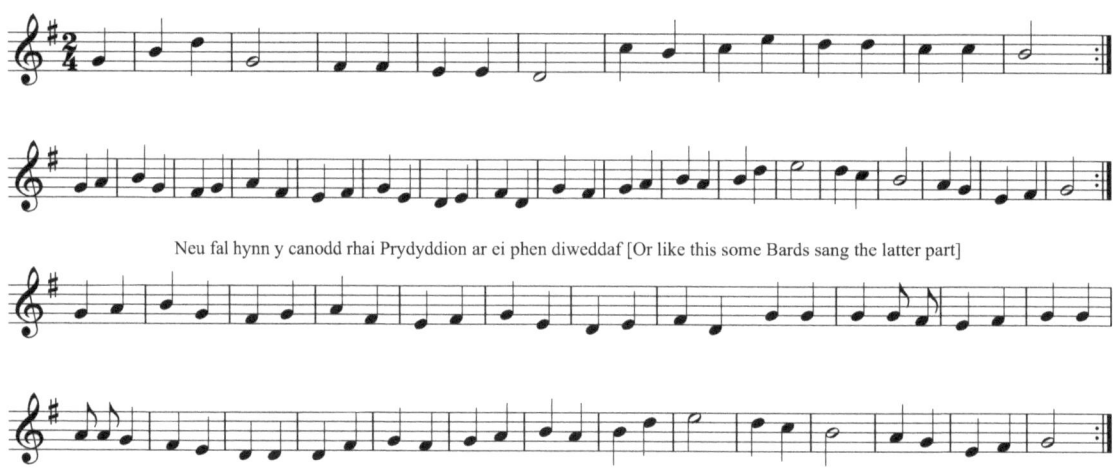

Neu fal hynn y canodd rhai Prydyddion ar ei phen diweddaf [Or like this some Bards sang the latter part]

There is considerable variety in the examples noted subsequently,[16] with less and less relationship to any bardic exemplar, and the most recent example published in *Songs of Wales* (1873) was set out in typical nineteenth-century style as a salon song:[17]

Example 7.12: 'Hun Gwenllian', 'Philomusus's' Collection for the 1824 Welshpool Eisteddfod

Example 7.13: 'Hun Gwenllian' from Bangor MS 2255 (E. Ylltyr Williams)

Example 7.14: 'A gentle maid in secret sigh'd' (Erddigan Hun Gwenllian) from *The Songs of Wales*

The harp air from *Antient British Music* and the example sent by Twm o'r Nant (which is the only one to refer to its use by poets) date back to the eighteenth century, in contrast to the other airs that are later. What the three manuscript examples (Examples 7.11, 7.12 and 7.13) appear to have in common is a 4-bar downward chordal sequence not found in the published airs, and this may have some significance with music of an earlier period. The only example to include words is in *Songs of Wales* (Example 7.14), with Welsh verses by the nineteenth-century poet Ceiriog in a metre that does not fit the earlier airs.

Iolo Morganwg's collection as a whole presents some interesting points and shows significant differences between the music noted by the north Wales harpers of the period and the singers of Glamorgan. There are no examples here of the intricate interweaving of words so beloved of the seventeenth and eighteenth-century north Wales ballad and carol singers. In contrast, the Glamorgan songs are notable for a more highly decorated vocal line with numerous slurs and frequently a wide vocal compass. Their favourite metres are the simpler *triban* and *awdl-gywydd*, and this has its effect on the airs that are in general more lyrical than the north Wales tunes connected with complex poetry. For all its faults of notation, Iolo Morganwg's collection is a vitally important contribution to Welsh traditional music.

When Iolo was in his sixties, a country vicar in another part of Wales was noting down Welsh ballads and traditional airs in a compilation that vastly eclipsed Iolo's collection in size, importance and variety. The collector was John Jenkins (1770–1829), a native of Ceredigion in south Wales who graduated from Oxford, served as chaplain aboard various British warships, and eventually became vicar of Kerry (*Ceri* in Welsh), a village in mid-Wales. The early nineteenth century was a period of ferment in Welsh culture, which saw the establishment of literary societies and the development of the eisteddfod, especially from 1819 onwards. The vicar of Kerry, a cultured churchman deeply interested in Welsh music and poetry, was an important figure in these activities with considerable influence on his bishop and his fellow-clergymen in Wales. It was at this time that he acquired the name by which he is known in Welsh literary and musical circles: 'Ifor Ceri'. It was fashionable in this period for Welsh poets, musicians and antiquarians to use a pseudonym for their writings, and John Jenkins decided to call himself 'Ioan Ceri' (John Kerry). But his kindness and generosity in welcoming men of letters and fellow enthusiasts to his home led them to call him 'Ifor Ceri' after Ifor Hael (Ifor the Generous) the fourteenth-century patron of Dafydd ap Gwilym, and the name stuck.[18]

Unlike the great eighteenth-century harper/collectors, Ifor Ceri's chief interest was music connected with words. Poetry was commonly published with the instruction 'To be sung to the tune of ...', and the assumption was that the reader would be familiar with the air. For instance, the poetry in *Blodeu-gerdd Cymry*, first published in 1759, called for some sixty different airs, but by Ifor Ceri's time many of the tunes had been forgotten:

> I began my collection about eight or nine years ago [1817–18] after reading the Blodeugerdd and two or three books of the same sort. As a rapid change was taking place in the habits and manners of our country people, I thought that unless a collection was made at present of the Hen Donau [Old Airs], Marwnadau [Elegies], Carolau [Carols], &c. Cymru, it would be in vain to look for them in thirty years time; they would be superseded by strains of a very different description (and in my opinion of very inferior quality) under the name of hymns. And perhaps the attempt to recover them was now too late. I however commenced my noting what tunes I was myself acquainted with; and communicating my wish of preserving the old tunes to my musical friends in different parts of Wales, I find now, contrary to my expectation, that my collection contains within a small number (and those I shall probably recover) all the tunes to which our lyric poetry has been composed from the time of Queen Elizabeth downwards.[19]

The volumes of songs noted by Ifor Ceri that survive present a remarkable picture of Welsh music in his time. The first of these, called *Melus-geingciau Deheubarth Cymru* (The Melodies of South Wales), was probably compiled about 1815, a few years after he came to live in mid-Wales, though he must have been gathering songs from his native region long before that.[20] The manuscript contains forty-two songs of various kinds (thirteen with words), three instrumental jigs and several unfinished airs. The first piece sets out the air on the treble staff with empty bars in the bass, presumably for an accompaniment, and a single verse of words at the bottom of the page in praise of a young woman. This was the general pattern at the beginning of the manuscript, but by song number thirteen, 'Siani Aeth am Serch', Ifor Ceri began to use the bass staves to jot down other tunes, sometimes scribbling the notes as if he were taking them down from a singer:[21]

Example 7.15: 'Siani Aeth am Serch'

After this point, it would appear that he decided to favour songs of a more serious nature, especially those in the complex metres so popular in the north. Just over half the songs in *Melus-geingciau* were retained for the two volumes that followed: *Melus-seiniau Cymru*[22] and *Per-seiniau Cymru*.[23] Among the songs that Ifor Ceri did not recopy were ballads and love songs such as 'Cwyn y Prentis':[24]

Example 7.16: 'Cwyn y Prentis'

Also, 'Annerch i'r Derin Du', a song sending a bird as love messenger (*llatai* = love messenger). The air is a rather four-square version of 'Ffanni Blodau'r Ffair', itself a version of William Boyce's song, 'The Ravished Lover', which was exceptionally popular in south Wales.[25] In *Melus-seiniau* there is another version of the same air, but the *llatai* words have been discarded in favour of words to 'Ffanni Blodau'r Ffair':

Example 7.17: 'Annerch i'r Derin Du'

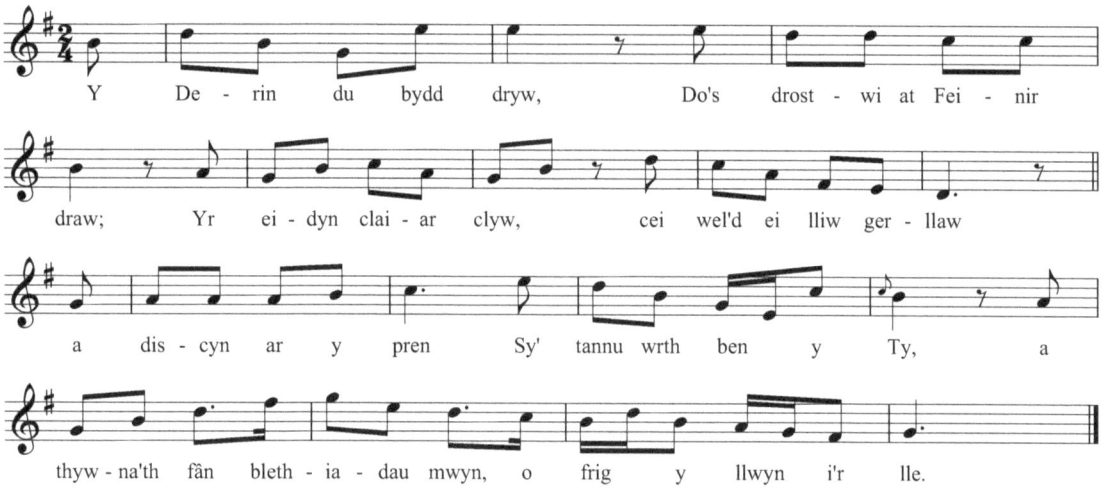

'Dewch Ymlaen' is a regimental marching song:[26]

Example 7.18: 'Dewch Ymlaen' ('Haf etti'r Glocsen')

Two songs connected with the wren-hunt custom were also left out, perhaps because it was felt they were not suited to the more serious purpose of the new collection.

Ifor Ceri sometimes altered the airs that he transferred from *Melus-geingciau* to the later volumes; for example, 'Clod Gwen' was renamed 'Lliw'r Gwinwydd' in *Melus-seiniau* and noted in a different key, with alterations in music and words. Publishers such as Edward Jones and George Thomson felt free to change the traditional airs in their books, and collectors of this period were clearly less concerned with authenticity than with artistic quality. Ifor Ceri also undoubtedly edited airs sent to him by others. It is noticeable that there are no modal tunes in his collection although dorian/re mode and aeolian/la[27] mode airs were popular in Wales, and perhaps his musical training led him to change tunes that he regarded as 'incorrect'. The principle of notating a song exactly as it was sung was still far in the future.

Melus-seiniau is Ifor Ceri's second and much larger manuscript, and he usually added the names of those who collected the airs in it. Thirty-six airs are marked with his own initials 'JJ', and presumably these came from tunes he himself knew or had collected. Numerous airs were sent to him by other collectors, not all equally proficient in noting down tunes from singers. Some thirty tunes were sent to him by friends in south Wales – poets, musicians and schoolmasters for the most part – as well as twenty-nine from collectors in mid-Wales. He wrote that among the latter was a man who was 'third in lineal descent from a person who used to sing them to Huw Morus with his unrivalled songs'.[28] Ifor Ceri seems to have had no collectors in north Wales. Seventeen airs in the north Wales style came from Darowen in Powys, where his friends the cultured clerical Richards family lived, and at least some of these appear to have been noted by Ifor Ceri himself from singers in the area. Apart from the Darowen airs, he also took ten airs from the printed books of the great north Wales harpers Edward Jones and John Parry, Ruabon.

In all there are 125 separate pieces of music in *Melus-seiniau*, although some are different versions of the same air or different airs that bear the same title. Ballads and plygain carols from eighteenth and early nineteenth-century books of poetry, such as *Blodeu-gerdd Cymry, Dewisol Ganiadau yr Oes Hon* and works by Twm o'r Nant and Jonathan Hughes, were set to about half of the airs in *Melus-seiniau*.

> I have, whenever I had an opportunity of taking down a tune, preferred the vocalist to the harper, as more likely to furnish me with the original simple air, and the manner in which it was sung by our lyric bards and their contemporaries.[29]

However, it is unlikely that Ifor Ceri actually heard all or even most of the airs in his collection sung to words from these books. His achievement was to marry the airs he had gathered to the poetry that called for them, but there are many songs in Ifor Ceri's manuscript where the words are an awkward fit and in more than one case he appears to have adapted an old ballad to an unsuitable air of the right title, which had been sent to him or which he had heard sung to different words.

Melus-seiniau is divided into different categories. Part 1 is devoted to hymn tunes with a few based on traditional airs.[30] Part 2, titled 'Marwnadau, Carolau, a

Chaniadau Moesol' (Elegies, Carols, and Moral Songs), opens with five examples in *tri thrawiad* metre such as 'Y Tri Tharawiad Deheubarth neu Gadael Tir y Ffordd Hwyaf'. A comparison with songs in the same metre from north Wales shows that those from south Wales are freer in fitting the words to the music, including the use of slurs to tie two or more notes together, a custom that would have been frowned on in the north:[31]

Example 7.19: 'Y Tri Tharawiad Deheubarth neu Gadael Tir y Ffordd Hwyaf'

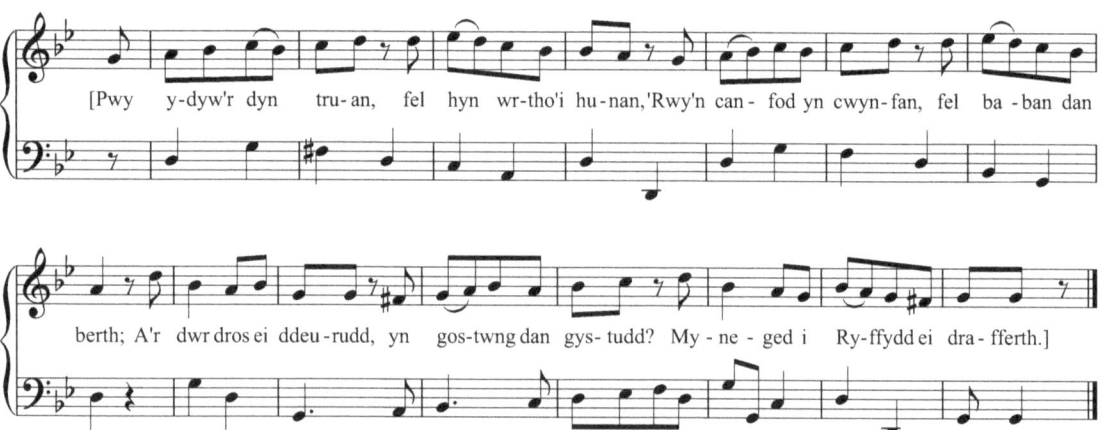

Ifor Ceri also includes 'Tri Tharawiad Gwynedd' from north Wales, which fits the air without slurs.[32] Among the examples of *tri thrawiad* in *Melus-seiniau* is a very different setting noted down as 'Gwaith Mr Parry o Lundain' (the work of Mr Parry of London) – undoubtedly John Parry ('Bardd Alaw'), professional harpist, composer and musical entrepreneur, born in Wales but living and working in London. Parry's setting of an elegy to Sir Thomas Picton of Pembrokeshire, who was killed at the battle of Waterloo in 1815, is in sharp contrast to the simple settings of the other examples that are for the most part unaccompanied. It is written for voice and instrumental accompaniment suitable for harp or piano, with a vocal line that would be more acceptable in a concert song – flowing, in a wide compass, soaring and dipping, modulating twice and with a bass line that adds a throbbing rhythm from time to time.[33] Nothing could be more unsuitable for its purpose or more calculated to take attention away from the intricate verbal *cynghanedd* of Welsh poetry.

Very few songs in *Melus-seiniau* are in the traditional Welsh metres that are so prominent in Iolo Morganwg's collection. Apart from the examples of *tri thrawiad*, there are four May carols and only one song in *awdl-gywydd* metre where it appears that neither words nor air came to Ifor Ceri by traditional means: the melody was adapted from 'Gadael Tir' in Edward Jones's *Relicks*, and the verse taken from *Corph y Gaingc* by David Thomas ('Dafydd Ddu Eryri'). The most interesting traditional metre in this collection is the *triban*, with examples in a variety of styles including 'Triban Morganwg' and phrases for the singer interwoven with instrumental symphonies.[34] Ifor Ceri notes that this is the way the *triban* is generally sung in Glamorganshire:

Example 7.20: 'Triban Morganwg' (with symphonies), 'J. Howells Fel y cenir Mesur Triban yn gyffredin yn awr yn Morganwg'

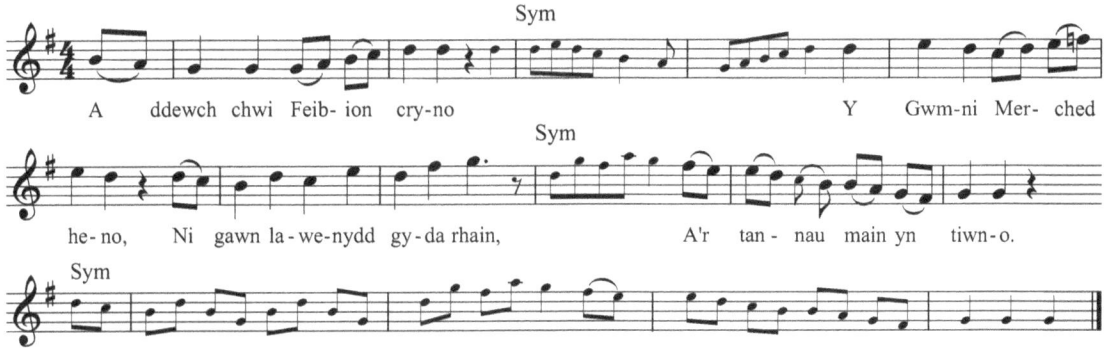

The largest part of *Melus-seiniau* is devoted to the ballad tunes called for in Welsh books of poetry. Almost half of these ballads came from *Blodeu-gerdd Cymry*, a substantial collection of poetry written to be sung to named tunes, many of which were not Welsh. These tended to be much more complex than airs in traditional Welsh metres, and were sometimes divided into two or three sections with changes of rhythm as in 'Hoffedd y Prins Rupert neu Tyb y Tywysog' (Prince Rupert's Delight or the Prince's Fancy). The title of the air places it in the seventeenth century when Prince Rupert fought in the English Civil War:[35]

Example 7.21: 'Hoffedd y Prins Rupert ney Tyb y Tywysog'

continued

Edward Jones in *Relicks* also prints an air called 'Tyb y Tywysog', but it is in a different form and rhythm that does not fit the *Blodeu-gerdd* words. By contrast, Ifor Ceri's air that does fit was noted in Darowen, and appears to have come down to the singer through long oral tradition.

The old ballad airs were also popular farther south. 'Mel Wefus Deheubarth' is a south Wales air that Ifor Ceri noted to words from the *Blodeu-gerdd* condemning miserliness. Whether he actually heard them sung to this air is uncertain:[36]

Example 7.22: 'Mel Wefus Deheubarth'

Ifor Ceri's collection contains almost all of the best-known ballad tunes in Wales, judging by the number of times they were called for on ballad sheets and the books of the period. They include such enduringly popular tunes as 'Gwêl yr Adeilad', 'Y Ffion Felfed', 'Bryniau Iwerddon', 'Anhawdd Ymadael', 'Y Fedle Fawr', 'Gwledd Angharad', 'Ffarwel Dai Llwyd', 'Calon Drom', 'Mentra Gwen' and a host of others. About a third of these are Welsh, and the others had settled in Wales long before Ifor Ceri's time.

Although the airs to 'Elegies, Carols, and Moral Songs' form the largest element of this section of *Melus-seiniau*, the final fifteen songs that were set down without full details, six with no details at all apart from their names, are of a different order. 'Caingc y Fflemynes'[37] and 'Y Saith Rhyfeddod'[38] have all the characteristics of folksongs in style, rhyme scheme, lyrics and form:

Example 7.23: 'Caingc y Fflemynes' ('Caingc o Syr Penfro. J. Parry')

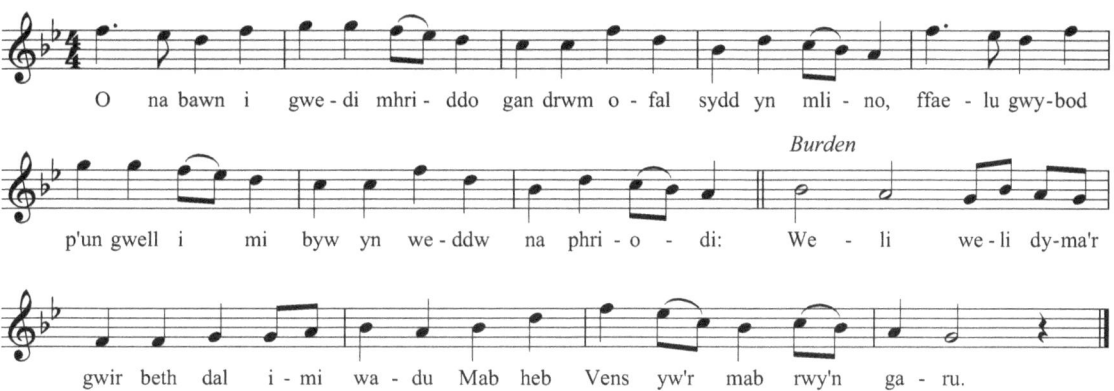

'Y Saith Rhyfeddod' in the same group is a lively tune with a join-in chorus after each line. It is written with a little instrumental flourish at the end of the third line, and may have been noted at a gathering where there was a harp or fiddle:

Example 7.24: 'Y Saith Rhyfeddod'

The same collector, one J. Parry from south Wales, probably Carmarthenshire, contributed to Ifor Ceri's collection a number of airs that included only the first few words of each song. Nevertheless, like the two examples above, these are undoubtedly traditional airs and not tunes to published ballads. Only 'Caingc y Fflemynes' and 'Y Saith Rhyfeddod' have both titles and words; the other six airs bear titles that merely refer to the places they came from, such as 'Mwynen Llangyndeyrn' or

'Tri Tharawiad Trichwmwd', and have no more than half a line of words. One of the most interesting of these is 'Caingc Llandyfaelog'.[39] The half-line of words to this air comes from a well-known ballad in *triban* metre, which, when set down in full, could give an unusual setting with numerous repetitions:

Example 7.25: 'Caingc Llandyfaelog' (the words in brackets have been added from the *llatai* song 'Adar Mân y Mynydd')

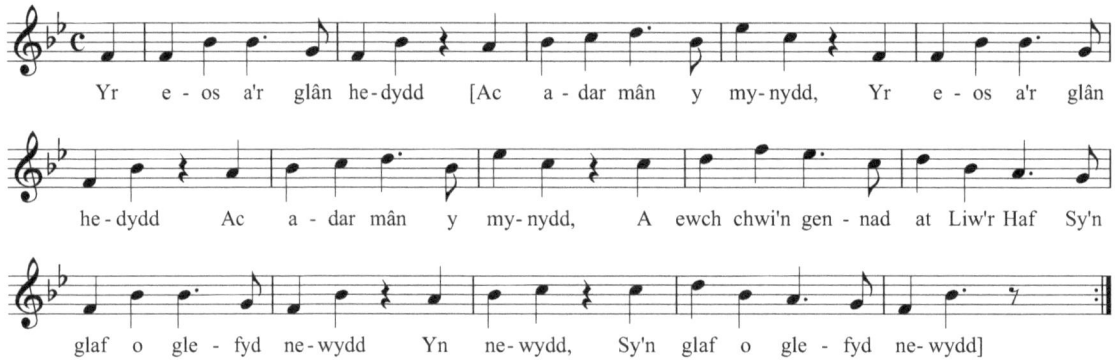

Alternatively, it could be an example of interaction between voice and instrumental accompaniment with bars 5–8 and the final three bars as symphonies.

Part 3 of *Melus-seiniau* contains 'Caniadau ar Filwriaeth, Carwriaeth, ac amryw destynau difyr a digrif' (Songs on Warfare, Love, and various interesting and amusing Subjects). The mood of this section is generally lighter in tone in both music and poetry. It opens with five songs on military subjects, including praise of valiant soldiers such as Duke William, the Merthyr Tydfil Volunteers and General Sir Thomas Picton. The airs themselves are not particularly military, and two of them were also used as hymn tunes. Perhaps the most 'soldierly' of them is 'Hoffedd Duwc William', a four-square tune suitable for marching, with words wishing success and long life to Duke William, 'truehearted and a brave fighter':[40]

Example 7.26: 'Hoffedd Duwc William' ('D. S. Morgan Ceredigion' (Dafydd Siencyn Morgan))

The remainder of Part 3 is loosely divided between ballad airs and traditional airs. As in Part 2, over half of the ballad airs are set to words from published works such as the *Blodeu-gerdd* and *Blwch o Bleser*,[41] although the words do not always fit Ifor Ceri's tunes. An interesting example of this is 'Morfa Rhuddlan', an air that probably goes back at least to the seventeenth century in Welsh oral tradition. It was well known to Richard Morris, who set down words to be sung to it and noted that he could play it on the viol some nine years before its first appearance in print in *Aria di Camera*. The air has continued in popularity to the present day, printed in a wide variety of instrumental versions used for dancing, for singing ballads and as a piece for the harp. Ifor Ceri's version is closest to 'Rhydlan Marsh' in *Airs* 1761, though there are numerous differences:[42]

Example 7.27: 'Morfa Rhuddlan'

Almost certainly, Ifor Ceri copied the example in *Melus-seiniau* from a book or the manuscript of a competent musician, for the bass line is considerably better than Ifor Ceri's usual harmonisations. Unfortunately, the words from the *Blodeu-gerdd* to be sung to the tune were set down at the bottom of the page, as was his usual practice. If he had set them instead under the notes, he might have seen how badly they suit their purpose. The verse contains a number of internal rhymes that occur on a series of strong beats:

> Gwrando gwyn, Fenws fwyn, Dyn Sy'n dwyn dolur
> Wedi ymroi, oni ddoi, ar gais i roi cysur ...

A competent singer/declaimer would be expected to bring out these rhymes, but in this example the poetry is in a duple metre with rhymes on strong beats, whereas the music is in triple time so that the rhymes fall on weak beats and the emphasis is lost. Obviously, something is wrong with the setting. Were these words sung to a different tune with the same name? Were they sung without accompaniment, or sung in a different manner, perhaps declaimed against instrumental accompaniment? In the early twentieth century, a folk tune was published called 'Morfa Rhuddlan (Yn ôl yr hen ffurf)' (Morfa Rhuddlan (according to the old form)), which suits the metre of the words perfectly. It is in a basic 5-tone scale with the 3rd degree flat and a chordal and melodic pattern, which has certain similarities with the eighteenth-century harp air when the florid nature of the arrangement is discounted:[43]

Example 7.28: 'Morfa Rhuddlan (Yn ôl yr hen ffurf)' noted by Tom Powell of Pwllheli

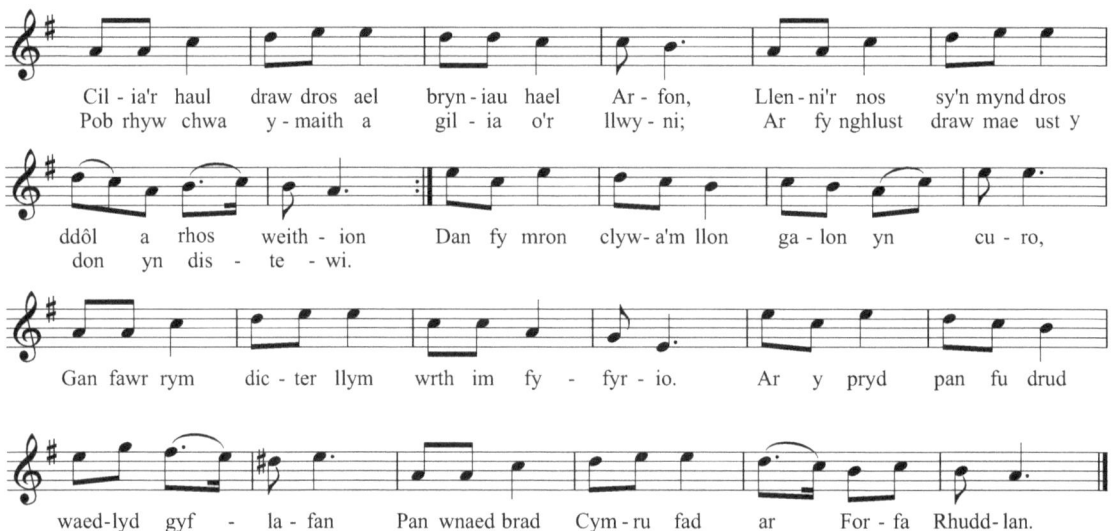

The same melody was used in the nineteenth century to sing 'Cân y Gaethes Ddu', a ballad about a black slave woman and her baby:[44]

Example 7.29: 'Morfa Rhuddlan' ('Cân y Gaethes Ddu')

Is there any relationship between these ballad airs? All the instrumental versions, whether in print or manuscript, have certain characteristics in common: all are in triple time and in three main sections, with the opening section in the minor, the middle section major and the final section modulating back to finish in the minor. On the other hand, the two songs that are in the minor throughout are in duple time and in two sections only. But if the middle section in the major is omitted, it can be seen that there is a strong similarity between the instrumental air and the two songs. It appears that the same air gave birth to two different traditions – the older vocal/declamatory style and the instrumental/melodic style that may have developed out of it – and that Ifor Ceri was unaware of the older tradition.

The last half of Part 3 of *Melus-seiniau* contains a number of traditional airs and folk ballads. In most cases, Ifor Ceri has noted the traditional words along with the air, but occasionally he sets down words from the *Blodeu-gerdd* or *Blwch o Bleser*. Fortunately, there are enough examples of folk airs with folk words to give a picture of traditional singing in south and mid-Wales during Ifor Ceri's time. There are several jig tunes, some with humorous words such as 'Can ar Owain Cordolen – Y Siacced Fral', a song from Ceredigion with a short join-in chorus at the end of each line, suitable for singing at a *noson lawen* (a 'merry evening' with singing and story-telling) or an evening at the tavern:[45]

Example 7.30: 'Can ar Owain Cordolen' ('Y Siacced Fral' 'JJ Ceredigion')

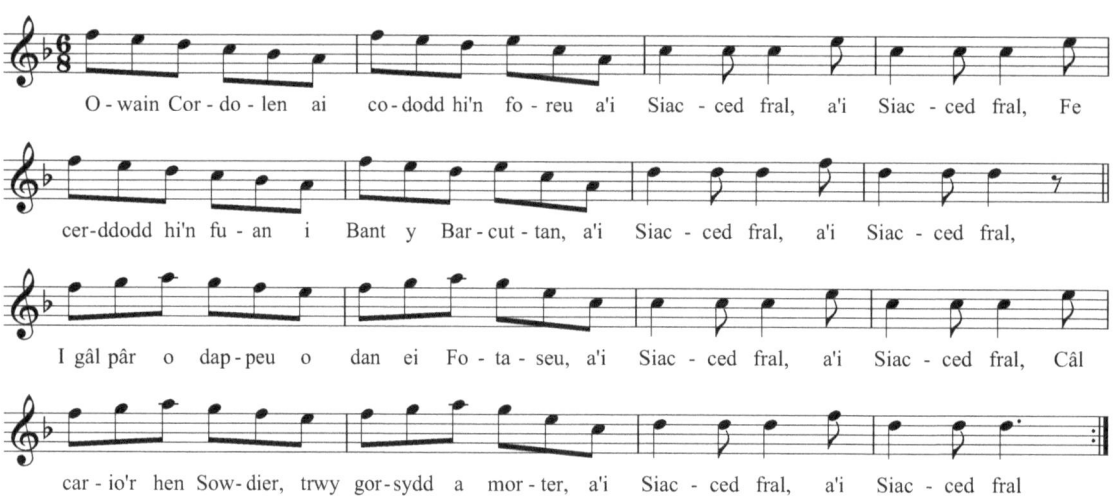

Ifor Ceri noted another jig which he learned from his uncle Dr Lewes, perhaps when he was his curate at the tail-end of the eighteenth century or possibly even earlier when he was a lad:[46]

Example 7.31: 'Mi Welais Rhyfeddod' (learned from 'Dr Lewes, Syr Penfro')

The manuscript ends with a section of seventeen items, which Ifor Ceri calls 'Chwanegiad' (Supplement), a catch-all of ballads, harp airs, songs in traditional metres, oxen songs and settings for harp and voice. There are seven ballads in various styles, all but one with words selected by Ifor Ceri from printed works. Among these is 'Nutmeg and Ginger', an air that can be traced back to sixteenth-century England. Ifor Ceri's melody is a relative of 'Breuddwyd y Frenhines' or 'Queen's Dream', but lacking two sections of four bars each – a metre known as 'Queen's Dream ffordd fyrraf' (Queen's Dream the shortest way). He noted another version of the air in *Melus-geingciau* no. 24, 'Yr Hen Cwmpeiniwr Mwyn' and, although no words were included, the title suggests folk verses. For the air in *Melus-seiniau*, Ifor Ceri chose a plaintive verse from *Blwch o Bleser*, but he might equally well have chosen the humorous words from *Gwaith y Bardd Bach*, a manuscript in his library that he knew well:[47]

Example 7.32: 'Can i ddosbarthwr y Llythurau [Post Master] ar Nutmeg and Ginger'.

Some of the most unusual pieces in *Melus-seiniau* can be found in the 'Chwanegiad'. 'The Duke of Gloucester's March', sent to Ifor Ceri by John Howell ('Eos Glandyfroedd'; 1774–1830), a Carmarthenshire poet, is an unusual setting of words, rich in *cynghanedd*, to an English military march:[48]

Example 7.33: 'Hoffedd Glandyfroedd' ('The Duke of Gloucester's March')

The song as noted has a compass of twelve tones leading up to a top B flat, which would make clear diction almost impossible in a song where the words were the most important feature. The air was probably taken from an instrumental source, and the singer would adjust the melody to bring it into a singable range. In the archives at St Fagans, there is a song in similar style to be sung to 'The Duke of York's March'[49] with a range of eleven tones, but noted in a more singable tessitura.

John Howell also sent Ifor Ceri an even more interesting example of this type of singing. The words come from the *Blodeu-gerdd*, which calls for them to be set to the tune 'Cudun-wynn Ffrainc', a Welsh adaptation of 'Whitelock's Coranto', written by Bulstrode Whitelocke in 1633 for a Christmas masque. Verses to that air became popular in Welsh oral tradition, resulting in such misnomers as 'Locs gyranto' and 'Chwet cloci'r anto'. The fiddler John Thomas called it 'whit locs arandum', but some years later the fiddler Morris Edwards noted it under the name 'Cudun Gwyn Ffrainc', and the air finally appeared in print in *British Harmony* and *Relicks* as 'Cudun Gwyn'. However, John Howell's example as it appears in *Melus-seiniau* is very different from any other, whether in manuscript or print.[50]

Melus-seiniau is an astonishingly varied collection with regard to the period in which Ifor Ceri lived. Although it was begun with the purpose of finding airs called for in the literature of seventeenth and eighteenth-century Welsh poets, his lively interest in music resulted in a great deal of other music as well, including hymn tunes, songs in *tri thrawiad* metre, dance tunes, *llatai* songs, oxen songs (probably under the influence of Iolo Morganwg), love songs, songs sung with the harp, *penillion* songs, marching songs and join-in songs for social gatherings. It is a formidable compilation, only spoiled by his frequent disregard of folk words in favour of those from books and his determination to set all these songs in major or minor keys to the neglect of the folk modes.

Ifor Ceri's final book of airs was handsomely laid out to hold 101 airs, a favourite number for anthologies. He started to call it *Melus-Seiniau Cymru*, but crossed out the word *Melus* and substituted the word *Per-* (Sweet-), possibly to distinguish this volume from the one that preceded it. The contents of *Per-Seiniau Cymru* indicate that Ifor Ceri organised his collection with considerable care, which suggests that by this stage he may have had a printed work in view. Many of the tune names were connected with ballads by acknowledged Welsh poets. Variants of the same tune-name, for example 'Mentra Gwen' or 'Bryniau Werddon', were collected into family groups rather than scattered throughout the volume, which simplified comparison of the airs. The purpose of this compilation is serious for there are no examples of folk ballads, oxen songs, *llatai* songs or songs for social diversion.

Forty-eight of the songs in *Per-seiniau* do not appear in his previous collections. One of the most interesting of these is 'Y Mynach Dû or Black Friar fel y cenir yn Nglyn Ceiriog'. It was sent to him by one of his regular correspondents, John Cain Jones, and is in four main sections musically – ABCD – but in five different poetic metres. Until the final eight bars, the air stays within the compass of an octave, a suitable range for a singer whose primary objective is to bring out the words. Unusually, Ifor Ceri has set it for voice and accompaniment, probably harp. There is no other example in this collection that illustrates so well the effect of mixing different poetical metres in a song with accompaniment:[51]

Example 7.34: 'Y Mynach Dû or Black Friar fel y cenir yn Nglyn Ceiriog'

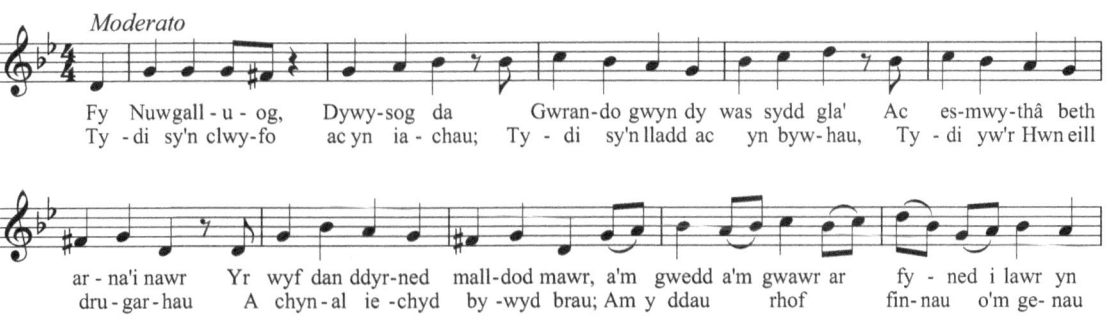

continued

The Early Collectors: Iolo Morganwg and Ifor Ceri

Only two other pieces in *Per-seiniau* are laid out in two staves for voice and accompaniment; the well-known Welsh ballad tune 'Ffarwel Prydain' with fourteen verses, and the hymn-like arrangement of 'Trymder' (a dialogue between poet and Church):[52]

Example 7.35: 'Trymder'

One distinctive aspect of *Per-seiniau Cymru* is the inclusion of four carol tunes, all unfortunately without words. Three were collected in east Wales, and one (Example 7.36) in the area of Offa's Dyke on the border with England:[53]

Example 7.36: 'Ton Carol ar Gyffiniau Clawdd Offa' ('Carol tune from the area of Offa's Dyke')

A similar version called 'Hosanna Mwy' was noted many years later 'from the singing of an old gravedigger at Garn Dolbenmaen, Caernarvonshire':[54]

Example 7.37: 'Hosanna Mwy'

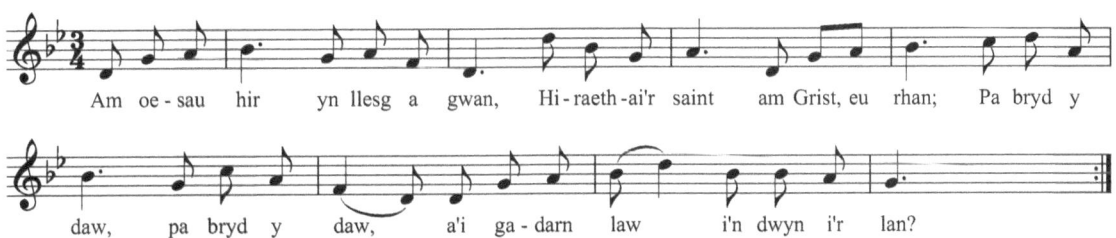

As in Ifor Ceri's earlier compilations, some pieces were taken from printed works: 'Dini-weidrwydd y Golomen' and 'Calenig' came directly from *British Harmony* and 'Breud-dwyd Dafydd Rhys' is very close to Aria XIV in *Antient British Music*. Occasionally, Ifor Ceri made changes in the pieces he borrowed: 'Mentra Gwen' (*Per-seiniau*, no. 90) is almost identical with *British Harmony*, but in a lower key, and 'Cwympiad y Dail' is noted in 4/4 time, though similar versions in *British Harmony* and *Relicks* are in 3/4.[55]

Ifor Ceri's surviving collection, *Melus-geingciau*, *Melus-seiniau* and *Per-seiniau*, as well as numerous separate music manuscripts and papers, is a priceless contribution to the study of Welsh traditional music. He was an indefatigable collector and a capable musician with a wide circle of friends and acquaintances who sent him material. His main faults as a collector were rhythmic strictness and an insistence on setting all his airs in either major or minor keys, to the neglect of the popular folk modes. But this is splitting hairs. Ifor Ceri's service to Welsh traditional music is inestimable, and without his great collection Welsh traditional music would be immeasurably poorer.

8

The Great Change

THE NINETEENTH CENTURY saw an immense change in Welsh life and culture. It began in a country where agriculture and minor industries such as weaving were the chief means of earning a livelihood, but by the beginning of the twentieth century more Welsh people were working in industries such as coal or iron and steel than in farming. The change was equally remarkable in other aspects of Welsh life. Religion underwent an upheaval of mountainous proportions, in which Methodism, an eighteenth-century movement to reform the established Church, grew mightily and transformed the nature of religious practice in Wales. Cultural changes became prominent as the small eighteenth-century eisteddfods, which consisted of a few poets around a table in a tavern, swelled into a movement that by the end of the century had become a symbol of Welshness in the face of increasing anglicisation.

This was the period that saw an outpouring of editions and arrangements of Welsh music, almost entirely based on the harp airs of the great eighteenth-century collections of John Parry, Ruabon, and Edward Jones ('Bardd y Brenin'). However, by the nineteenth century, few of those who published arrangements of Welsh folk airs had collected the tunes themselves, and some of those who did were not Welsh. In most cases their purpose was to fit English words to previously published airs, which they arranged with pianoforte accompaniment within the capacity of the amateur.

This became apparent early in the century. When, in 1803, the Reverend William Bingley published his volume of *Sixty of the most admired Welsh airs*,[1] they were set to English words and arranged for the pianoforte, not the harp. From then on, although the harp continued to be mentioned, it was frequently 'for the pianoforte or harp' and more rarely 'for the harp or the pianoforte', until, in 1873, Brinley Richards published *The Songs of Wales*, a volume containing some sixty-four airs arranged as salon songs with pianoforte accompaniment and no mention of the harp.

Many of the airs in Bingley's collection came from printed sources, usually *British Harmony*, *Relicks* and *Bardic Museum*. Frequently, the melody lines were identical to the source, although the bass lines were new and sometimes the changes were slight, but occasionally there were considerable differences and this seemed to be the pattern for most of the songbooks that followed. This was not, however, the pattern for the collection *Specimens of Various Styles of Music*,[2] made by William

Crotch with the help of his friend, the violinist Jean-Baptiste Malchair, and printed in 1806–7. It was originally intended to illustrate lectures given in Oxford and London, and the Welsh examples were only part of a course that included 'Welch, English, Irish and Scotch' music. In the preface to the published work, Dr Crotch makes the point that 'the regular measure and diatonic scale of the Welch music is more congenial to English taste in general, and appears at first more natural to experienced musicians than those of the Irish or Scotch ... Welch music not only solicits an accompaniment, but being chiefly composed for the harp is usually found with one.'

There were forty-two musical items from Wales, all without words. Most are either harp airs (such as 'Erddigan Tro'r Tant', 'Caingc Dafydd Brophwyd', 'Mwynder Meirionydd') or ballad tunes (such as 'Ffarwel Ned Puw', 'Toriad y Dydd', 'Y Fedle Fawr'). Only a few items, such as 'Ar Hyd y Nos', 'Glan Meddwdod Mwyn' and 'Distyll y Don', could be called songs. Unlike Bingley, Crotch is interested in musical evaluation and sometimes gives more than one version of the same air for comparison. He has three versions of 'Sweet Richard':[3]

Version (a), 'as Danced in England 1796':

Example 8.1: 'Sweet Richard' (version 'a' from *Specimens*)

Version (b), 'Another and Older Edition ...' from *Antient British Music* (1742):

Example 8.2: 'Sweet Richard' (version 'b' from *Specimens*)

Version (c), 'Another Edition of the Same Tune from an old MS' (a very ornate version from an unknown source):

Example 8.3: 'Sweet Richard' (version 'c' from *Specimens*)

There are also three versions of 'Whitelock's Coranto' and two versions of 'Ffarwel Ned Puw' and of 'Merch Megan'. Dr Crotch's *Specimens* is in considerable contrast to the other printed collections of traditional Welsh tunes in the nineteenth century. It is a scholarly collection, not merely a compilaton of airs.

From the point of view of traditional music, the most interesting item is one which Malchair 'heard sung' in Harlech Castle. He noted the tune and Crotch included it in the collection. With its narrow 5-note compass in AABA form, it is quite different in style from all the other airs, but the melody is clearly related to a popular Welsh folk-song air that has several variants:[4]

Example 8.4: 'Malchair Example' from *Specimens*

continued

Unfortunately, Malchair did not note any words (which were, in any case, probably sung in Welsh), and it was about a century later that his manuscript book containing the music was discovered by chance in a second-hand book stall in north Wales.

Most of the collections that followed Crotch are of less interest to the historian because many of the airs had already been published and were merely set to different accompaniments. George Thomson, an Edinburgh publisher, deserves mention because he persuaded two of the greatest musicians of his time, Haydn and Beethoven, to make arrangements for voice and piano of airs which, for the most part, he got from printed collections. In addition to the collections of songs from his native Scotland, many to poetry by Burns, Thomson published three volumes of airs from Wales in 1809, 1811 and 1817, as well as airs from Ireland.[5] He was a competent amateur musician himself, with decided ideas as to the kind of arrangements he wanted for his books, and he was not above editing Beethoven's piano accompaniments to any of the airs if he felt they were too difficult. He was even more drastic with the songs, adding notes or deleting them as the mood took him. He explains his approach to the music thus:

> Of the air *Farewel Frances*, he [the editor, that is Thomson himself] has adopted little more than half the number of bars to be found in the ordinary copies, because the rest appeared to him not only deficient in melody, but more like patch-work than a part of one connected air. In the ordinary notation of the air, called *Venture Gwen*, there are but seven bars in the first strain, while in the second there are nine. It probably received that awkward shape from the blunder of some early copyist; but as it would have puzzled the Poet to write for the Air in such a shape, the Editor equalized the length of each strain, and perhaps he has thus restored the air to its original state.[6]

'Venture Gwen' is a member of the 'Mentra Gwen' family, and one of its outstanding characteristics is precisely the odd number of bars that Thomson was so concerned to 'correct'. Compare the version from *Relicks*[7] with the one from Thomson:[8]

Example 8.5: 'Mentra Gwen' (from *Relicks* (1784))

Example 8.6: 'Mentra Gwen' (Thomson's version)

In his introduction to 'Tros y Garreg', Thomson writes:

> A very few of the Airs in which monotonous and dry repetitions occurred, have been shortened of these, – while some others have been lengthened by a single repetition of the first strain, when that strain happened to be but half the length of the second.[9]

In Thomson's version of 'Tros y Garreg',[10] he shortened the B section by four bars so that it matches the A section and thereby loses the splendid climax of the air:

Example 8.7: 'Tros y Garreg' (from *Relicks* (1794))

Example 8.8: 'Tros y Garreg' (Thomson's version)

During this period, the blind harper Richard Roberts was making his living through performing, teaching, and adjudicating at eisteddfods in Wales and at meetings of Cymdeithas y Gwyneddigion in London. In 1829, some of his arrangements were published in *Cambrian Harmony*.[11] This book differs from the usual Welsh music books of the period, which took most of their airs from the earlier published collections. Almost half of the thirty-three airs in this compilation can be found in the manuscript collection of the fiddler Morris Edwards and only a few of them were taken from the great harp collections. Since Richard Roberts was blind, it would have been his amanuensis who prepared the book for print, presumably from Roberts's playing, indicating that the oral/manuscript tradition was still important in the nineteenth century.

The most prolific of the collectors and arrangers of Welsh music in the nineteenth century was undoubtedly the John Parry who is usually known by his bardic name of 'Bardd Alaw' to differentiate him from the earlier John Parry, Ruabon, compiler of *Antient British Music* and *British Harmony*. Bardd Alaw was born in 1776, when John Parry, Ruabon, and Edward Jones were still alive, but he represented a new generation and a new attitude to traditional Welsh music. He had some musical training on the harp in his native Denbigh, but his specialty was wind instruments, and at the age of seventeen he joined the Denbigh band. His ability was such that within a short time he had become the bandmaster. In 1807, he settled in London where he quickly made his name as writer and conductor of his own music for Vauxhall Gardens. But Bardd Alaw, unlike his predecessor Edward Jones, was not a collector. He was a composer, performer and musical entrepreneur who did much to popularise Welsh traditional airs among his fellow Welshmen as well as the English middle class. In 1809, Bardd Alaw brought out *A Selection of Welsh melodies*, the first of his series of publications of Welsh airs.[12] All of the airs had been published previously in Edward Jones's collections, but Bardd Alaw printed them here in new arrangements with English lyrics and 'editorial' comments on each one. This was quickly followed by a succession of publications including *A Collection of Welch Airs*[13] and *National Melodies of England, Ireland, Scotland and Wales*.[14]

In 1839 Bardd Alaw brought out the first volume of *The Welsh Harper* and nine years later followed it with volume two.[15] There is very little in them that is new, apart from his arrangements of the airs. Most of the pieces in volume one were taken from Edward Jones's collections, and much of volume two came from Ifor Ceri's manuscripts. Bardd Alaw was a good businessman who edited these publications with a marketing eye on the English and the anglicised Welsh, in the process mangling the tunes and changing the titles arbitrarily, but he also published them out of pride in his country and a desire to show its unique culture.

It is not surprising that Bardd Alaw, along with Edward Jones, should have found himself involved in the revival of the eisteddfod in the first half of the nineteenth century. The eisteddfod is an institution that has had a long history in Wales, although the word has entailed different things at different times.

Bardic contention in Welsh goes back a long way. There is a sixth-century tale about a competitive meeting between bards and musicians under the patronage of Maelgwn Gwynedd. Because he favoured the bards, he cunningly insisted that first of all the competitors had to swim the river, which did no harm to the poets but ruined the harps so that the musicians could no longer compete. As previously noted, the Laws of Hywel Dda acknowledge the privileged status of poets and musicians. *Brut y Tywysogion* (Chronicle of the Princes) describes the twelfth-century feast held by the Lord Rhys in Cardigan Castle, and mentions that it included a contest for two chairs, one for the best bard and one for the best musician. In the fifteenth century, an eisteddfod convened in Carmarthen and, in addition to adjudicating performances by bards and musicians, it tightened the rules and created new bardic metres. Most important were the two Caerwys eisteddfods in the sixteenth century, held for the purpose of safeguarding and regulating the bardic tradition.

In spite of these efforts, Welsh culture declined in the seventeenth century and by the beginning of the eighteenth century the classical bardic tradition was in a sorry state. There are occasional mentions of poetic competitions such as a meeting c.1600 in the home of the chancellor of Llandaf Cathedral, where bards competed on the *englyn* (an intricate poetic form), and in 1663 there was a bardic meeting in Bala that one of the poets called an 'eisteddfod'. But the eisteddfod really began to be prominent once again in the eighteenth century when bardic meetings were promoted through the popular Welsh almanacs of the period, and they became known as the 'Almanac Eisteddfods'. They were advertised ahead of time in the almanacs, and the meetings were usually held in taverns with a small audience to enjoy the competition. The bards sat around a long table with bread and beer in front of them. After the subject of the competition was announced, each poet in turn went to the Chair to declaim his poem. At the end of the meeting the name of the winning bard was announced, and he then sat in the Chair while each of the losing poets in turn would drink his health and pay for his beer. The meetings were haphazard, the winning poems printed in the almanacs were uninspired, and the standard had fallen so low that by the end of the eighteenth century a London Welsh society, *Cymdeithas y Gwyneddigion* (The Society of the Men of Gwynedd), felt that something must be done to safeguard Welsh literary standards. Between

1789 and 1795, the *Gwyneddigion* promoted an eisteddfod annually. The subject was chosen a year in advance, and the poems were sent in anonymously to the adjudicators who would choose the best. On the first day of the eisteddfod, the name of the winning bard was announced and he would be seated in the bardic Chair for the duration of the eisteddfod. These competitive meetings proved popular; in Caerwys, in 1798, the gathering included twenty bards, eighteen musicians and twelve harpers.

Nevertheless, after a few years enthusiasm began to wane. The disappointed *Gwyneddigion* had hoped that the eisteddfod would enrich Welsh culture and perhaps promote plans for establishing an academy as a centre of Welsh literary life to make up for the lack of other educational facilities. Instead, it was Ifor Ceri and his cultured circle of patriotic churchmen who were prominent in reviving the eisteddfod. Their plan attracted the attention of the bishop of St David's, Thomas Burgess, an Englishman who encouraged the promotion of Welsh culture. Carmarthen town was chosen to hold the first of what developed into a series of 'Provincial Eisteddfods', in 1819, and Iolo Morganwg used this opportunity to link his version of Druidism to the eisteddfod movement for the first time.

The Society that initiated this series of Provincial Eisteddfods was *Cymdeithas Gymroaidd Dyfed* (The Cambrian Society of Dyfed). Within a few months, *Cymdeithas Gymroaidd Gwynedd* (The Gwynedd Cambrian Society) was established in north Wales with Sir Robert Vaughan as President, closely followed by the Powys Cymmrodorion Society of mid Wales under the Presidency of Sir Watkin Williams Wynne, and later by the Cambrian Society of Gwent under the leadership of Sir Charles Morgan. It was felt important to have the backing of the gentry for such a new venture, but it changed the nature of the eisteddfod from the start for the Welsh gentry, with very few exceptions, were by now anglicised and could not appreciate or participate in the poetic competitions that were the basis of the eisteddfod. So it was decided to hold concerts in the evenings as entertainments that all could enjoy.

Because poetry held the most prominent place in eisteddfod competitions, the musical side had been represented by harp contests and *penillion* singing. However, by the nineteenth century, music was gaining in importance as a separate art freed from the restraints of the rules of Welsh poetry. It was a Swansea-born Welsh cleric from Bath, the Reverend John Bowen, who offered to bring his group of Bath singers to the Carmarthen Eisteddfod in 1819, so that they might perform in concerts during the eisteddfod with the profits going to good causes. The opening concert of the eisteddfod was completely English with glees and works by composers like Henry Bishop, but on the following night an effort was made to give a Welsh flavour to the proceedings with songs from the published collections of J. F. M. Dovaston, a Shropshire Englishman, and John Parry ('Bardd Alaw').

However, in the Welshpool Eisteddfod of 1824, a prize was offered for 'The best Collection of Old Welsh Tunes' never before published, the first time such a competition had been held in a Welsh eisteddfod. Ifor Ceri was the patron and adjudicator of the competition, and two substantial collections of over one hundred airs each were submitted, one by 'Aneurin' (Aneurin Owen of Nantglyn), a scholar of distinction deeply interested in Welsh culture, and the other by 'Philomusus' (John Gwynne of Darowen). Between them, the two collections presented over 200 different musical items, since they used almost none of the same material – only four items were common to both entries: 'Dydd Llun y Bore', 'Dydd Trwy'r Ffenestr', 'Merch Megan' and 'Y Cowper Mwyn'.

'Aneurin's winning collection of 105 airs, none with words, is neatly laid out. In general, it consists of a few seventeenth and eighteenth-century ballad tunes, airs from Edward Jones's collection, numerous airs for the harp and one (presumably for the *crwth*) called 'Caingc y Crythor Garw'. It is an interesting collection and well presented.

'Philomusus', the other entrant, was criticised by the adjudicator for his 'inaccuracy of notation and many of the tunes being already published'. Notes are omitted in some airs, there are too many notes in others, and barlines are often misplaced. There are many instances of incorrect rhythm, much of it due to treating the opening anacrusis as the first note of the bar, thus putting the stress on the wrong notes. In spite of these drawbacks, Philomusus's entry is of interest because he noted, however badly, variants of airs found in printed collections as well as airs not previously published. It is unfortunate that he included no words with the airs, since it is obvious that words were sung to a good many of them.[16]

Bardd Alaw, the musical entrepreneur, was appointed 'Registrar of Music' to the Cymmrodorion for the purpose of arranging the Provincial Eisteddfod concerts and he did his work effectively, demanding high standards in the performances. Ifor Ceri foresaw the problems that these 'Anglo-Italian farces', as he sarcastically called them, would bring : 'Our great people [that is, the gentry] as they have in a measure lost their nationality can only be brought together by Musical Entertainments of a superior style'.[17] Between 1819 and 1834, ten 'Provincial' eisteddfods were held in various parts of the country, generally with poetry competitions as well as harp and *penillion* singing during the day, and concerts in the evening. But Bardd Alaw's expensive evening concerts with performers from London left debts that had to be cleared by the gentry, and after 1834 the provincial eisteddfod ceased to exist.

However, the eisteddfod as an institution was by no means dead. Many Welsh societies staged their own eisteddfods, but the most prestigious by far was *Cymreigyddion y Fenni* (the Abergavenny Cymreigyddion Society). Their patroness, Lady Augusta Hall (later Lady Llanover), was an Englishwoman who had learned Welsh and, with the wise encouragement of Thomas Price ('Carnhuanawc'; 1787–1848), vicar, historian and eloquent patriot, she became the guiding spirit of the *Cymreigyddion*. Between 1834 and 1853, ten eisteddfods were held in the area. Her position in society and forceful character meant that the eisteddfod had considerable backing, and she and her family were extremely generous in their patronage. In order to promote the triple harp she gave harps to the winning harpists in each eisteddfod – thirty-seven over the years – and she encouraged others to support the aims of the eisteddfod. In 1837, Lady Coffin Greenly offered a prize 'For the best collection of original unpublished Welsh airs, with the words as sung by the peasantry of Wales'. The prize was won by another member of the gentry, Maria Jane Williams (1795–1873) from the Aberpergwm estate in the Vale of Neath, and forty-three songs from her collection, with accompaniments for harp or piano, were later published in *Ancient National Airs of Gwent and Morganwg*.[18] Many of the songs in this elegant book, including 'Y Bore Glas', 'Y Deryn Pur', 'Merch y Melinydd' and 'Bugeila'r Gwenith Gwyn', among others, became generally popular in Wales through inclusion in *The Songs of Wales* years later.

Maria Jane Williams's book was an important milestone in Welsh traditional music because it was the first book of traditional Welsh airs to be published with Welsh words to all the melodies. This was very different from the volumes of the eighteenth-century north Wales harper-collectors. Although ballads could be sung to many of their airs, it was rare for words to be included with the tune. John Parry, Ruabon, added no words to the tunes in his printed books and, although Edward Jones does note a few airs with Welsh words, the proportion is tiny. In contrast, the south Wales collection made by Maria Jane Williams represents a more expansive musical style in which words and music are meant to fit together. The vast majority of the airs in this volume are in the major mode, the next most popular scale pattern is the dorian, and least popular is the harmonic minor. Her airs are, with one exception, ornamented – some considerably so, such as 'Pan O'wn y Gwanwyn' set in the dorian mode:[19]

Example 8.9: 'Pan O'wn y Gwanwyn'

This air has a wide compass of ten tones, and it is noticeable that the airs in this collection are generally in a wider compass than those of north Wales. 'Cerais Ferch', another love song, which Maria Jane Williams said she took down from the singing of Iolo Morganwg, has a range of thirteen notes with wide leaps in the melody and is very unlikely to have been sung in that form by an old man of Iolo's age, or indeed most untrained singers:[20]

Example 8.10: 'Cerais Ferch'

Many, such as 'Y Ferch o'r Scer', are conspicuous for their beauty of melody.[21] The setting of the air is more elaborate than the version noted by Thomas David Llewelyn ('Llewelyn Alaw'; 1828–79), which he called 'Hyd y Frwynen Las':

Example 8.11: 'Y Ferch o'r Scer'

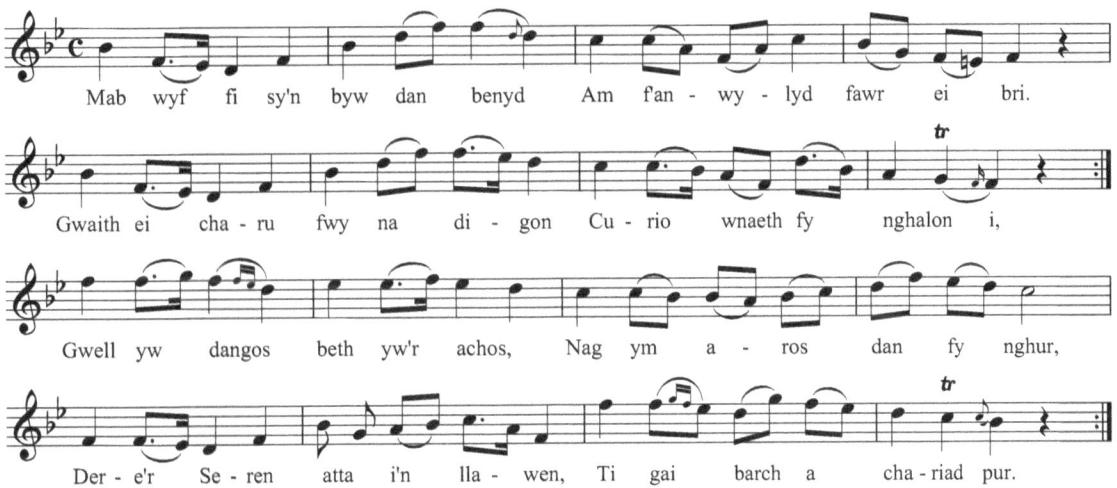

There is considerable variety in the song-types in Maria Jane Williams's collection. In addition to the love songs, there are wassail songs connected with the *Mari Lwyd* custom so popular in Glamorgan, one for the *pwnco* (debate) outside the door, and another that was sung after the wassailers gained entry. In addition, there are songs, such as 'Triban Morgannwg', calling for the singing of *penillion* to the harp:[22]

Example 8.12: 'Triban Morganwg'

'Y Ddafad Gyrnig' was a favourite children's song:[23]

Example 8.13: 'Y Ddafad Gyrnig'

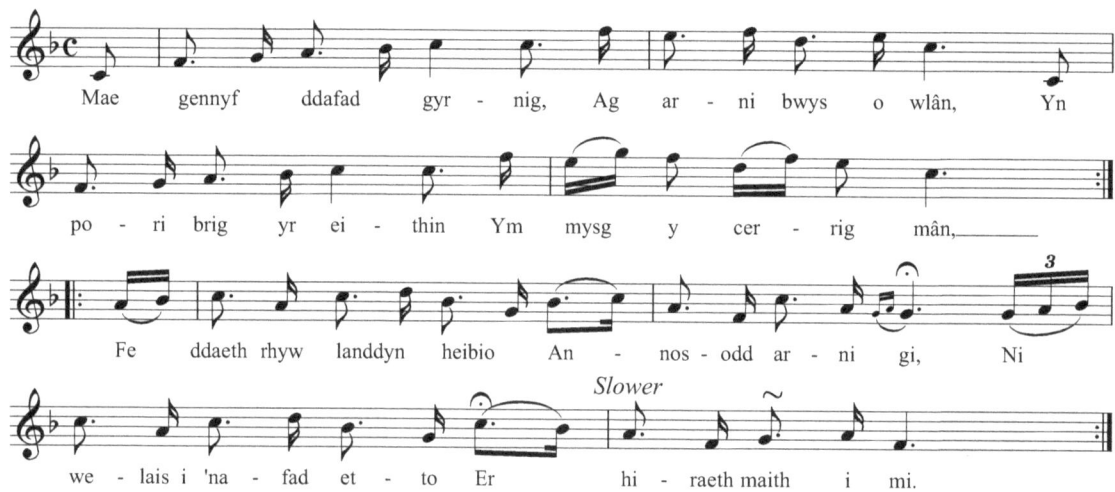

In 'Y Deryn Du Pigfelyn', the blackbird is again treated as a love messenger:[24]

Example 8.14: 'Y Deryn Du Pigfelyn'

The Great Change

Included is 'Cân Aberhonddu', a soldier's farewell ballad. The air is a variant of 'Cwynfan Prydain'.[25]

Example 8.15: 'Cân Aberhonddu'

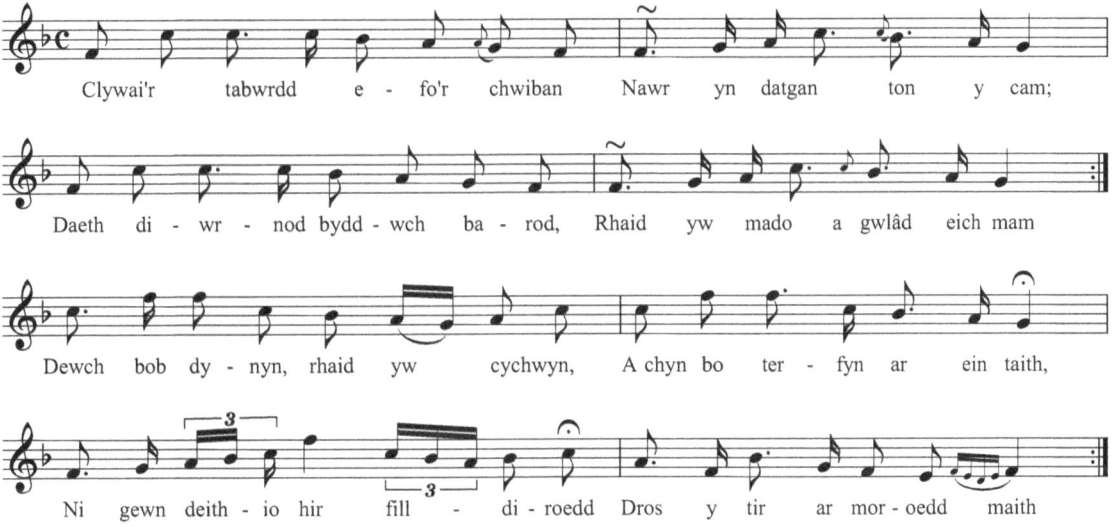

'Breuddwyd', a dream-vision song, describes a beautiful goddess-like apparition:[26]

Example 8.16: 'Breuddwyd'

continued

Some of the attributes of Maria Jane Williams's songs are undoubtedly due to the discriminating musical taste of the author, but other songs of the period collected in south Wales by Iolo Morganwg, John Thomas ('Ieuan Ddu') and D. Thomas Llewelyn ('Llewelyn Alaw') show many of the same characteristics, including wide melodic compass and lyrical phrasing. It is possible that the north Wales emphasis on *canu penillion* (singing short verses to the harp) is in part responsible for the narrow melodic compass of many songs from that area. Whatever the cause, it seems that in the early nineteenth century the expressive songs of south Wales gave a different tinge to Welsh traditional music.

The second-placed competitor for Lady Coffin Greenly's prize in the 1837 eisteddfod was John Thomas ('Ieuan Ddu'; 1795–1871), also from south Wales and born in the same year as Maria Jane Williams, but from a very different background. His boyhood home was a comfortable farmhouse, Pibwr Lwyd in Carmarthenshire, where he had a good education including some formal musical training, and he was said to have led the local band when he was sixteen. For some time he kept a school in the area but in about 1830 he moved to Merthyr Tydfil, which was in those days a lively industrial town with a population that increased daily as people left the land to find work in the town's new industries. The place was a ferment of eisteddfods, literary societies, chapel activities, concerts large and small and, of course, taverns where harpers played and penillion and ballads were sung. More formalised music was to be heard in the singing of choirs, including the temperance choirs that became popular in the 1830s. Ieuan Ddu played an important part on the musical side as a musician and voice trainer, but he was also an eisteddfod adjudicator and competitor. A year after the appearance of *Ancient National Airs of Gwent and Morganwg* in 1844, he brought out *The Cambrian Minstrel/Y Caniedydd Cymreig*.[27]

There are 106 airs on the treble stave only, without accompaniment, in his book, and verses by Ieuan Ddu himself in Welsh and/or English. He wanted to have Welsh airs, suitable for singing, in permanent form as cheaply as possible, with the intention:

> to furnish that class which was least likely to purchase more expensive works of the same nature, with a tolerably complete volume of our National Melodies, and to add to such as were already published, as many as possible of the unpublished ones, which, in another half a century, if not now snatched from oblivion, would, in all probability be irretrievably lost.[28]

The general contents include airs taken from the harp volumes of John Parry, Ruabon, and Edward Jones, as well as a number of songs that Ieuan Ddu composed to his own words. He also noted some forty-three songs from traditional singers – four men from the Merthyr area – which would have been a fitting addition to the songs in Maria Jane Williams's book if he had not discarded the traditional words and replaced them with his own, considerably diminishing the value of the collection.

In places where the notation is poorly done, it is sometimes difficult to know what mode or key is intended. 'Dros yr Afon', for example (a variant of the popular Welsh ballad air, 'Diniweidrwydd'), alternates between major, minor and dorian:[29]

Example 8.17: 'Dros yr Afon'

One of the most attractive songs in the book is the air called 'Pa Bryd y Deui Etto?'. Undoubtedly, this was the first line of the song he heard originally, which he then replaced with some mundane words of his own. It is a rare example in this collection of an unaltered dorian mode:[30]

Example 8.18: 'Pa Bryd y Deui Etto?'

continued

The Great Change

The compass of the traditional songs that Ieuan Ddu collected is frequently wide and the melodies are ornamented – characteristics also found in airs noted by Iolo Morganwg and Maria Jane Williams. 'Hen Wr o'r Coed Yn ol Dull Dyfed' is Ieuan Ddu's version of 'Y Dôn Fechan':[31]

Example 8.19: 'Hen Wr o'r Coed Yn ol Dull Dyfed'

In a footnote to the song, Ieuan Ddu points out that it is heard sung in very different styles in different parts of Wales, all equally pleasant, and sometimes in different keys.

Some of the items included are arranged as part-songs for use by groups of singers in concerts or eisteddfods. Occasionally, he prints a simple unadorned air in a medium compass, such as 'Pe Cawn i Hon', which he learned from his mother:[32]

Example 8.20: 'Pe Cawn i Hon'

It is a great pity that Ieuan Ddu was not a more careful notator – although undoubtedly some of the blame for the numerous mistakes should fall on the printer. *Cambrian Minstrel* contains many attractive and interesting pieces, but it is irretrievably damaged by the omission throughout of the traditional words and the many errors in notation.

The burgeoning eisteddfod had the backing of many members of the established Church, such as Ifor Ceri and his fellow-churchmen, who were supported in their efforts to preserve and extend Welsh culture by their bishop. But the nineteenth century saw the culmination of religious turbulence which had begun in the period when Henry VIII broke with the Church in Rome, and the established Church of England became Protestant. The Puritan element broke away from the Church and formed small dissenting groups, which in the seventeenth century grew into Baptists, Presbyterians, Independents and Quakers. After the restoration of the monarchy in 1660, these sects were persecuted in various ways and many Nonconformists, especially the Quakers, fled to America.

A more serious break came in the eighteenth century with the increase in groups of churchmen like Howel Harris, Daniel Rowland and William Williams of Pantycelyn, who wanted to reform the Church from within. The end result for their followers was a break from the established Church in 1811, along with the spread of Nonconformist worship in which the hymn played an important part.

Music in the eighteenth-century Church was provided by the choir and not the congregation, but when the revival meetings started it became the custom to sing a hymn at the end of the service. This became an essential part of worship, through the genius of Williams, Pantycelyn and others, whose hymns generated great excitement. According to John Wesley, the same verse might be sung over and over 'with all their might, perhaps above thirty, yea forty times'.[33]

Until the end of the eighteenth century, there were no standard books in Welsh for teaching the principles of music and, except for a few professional musicians, songs and airs were passed on orally. But the new interest in music, prompted by the necessity of teaching revival hymn tunes, led to the publication in 1797 of *Cyfaill mewn Llogell* (A Friend in the Pocket),[34] the first book in the Welsh language to teach the principles of music. The author was John Williams, a peripatetic music teacher in north Wales, known as Siôn Singer, and in a letter to the reader at the beginning of the book he makes it clear that his purpose is to improve congregational singing. The book, which was so small it would fit into a pocket, consisted of a short opening section on the 'Scale of Music', or Gamut. This was followed by music lessons set out in the form of a discussion between teacher and pupil dealing with the various octaves, treble, counter and bass; time values of the notes; the symbols that indicate accidentals; the meaning of the various time signatures; tables of consonances and dissonances – in short, all that the budding musician needs to know. The book concludes with words to a number of hymns in a variety of metres. It was a momentous step forward in Welsh music, and the beginning of the end for the oral tradition in Wales.

The nineteenth century saw an eruption of hymn books, some with sections similar to *Cyfaill mewn Llogell* explaining the principles of music, but also containing the music of the hymns. In 1816, John Ellis published *Mawl yr Arglwydd* (a collection of psalms and hymns).[35] This gave musical training in addition to a number of sacred pieces set out for two or three voices; but the author's guiding purpose was to ensure that the music should be the servant of the holy word and not the other way around – even if the music was discordant as a result. Singing schools were established in various parts of the country for the purpose of teaching the music of the hymns. One of the most effective of these was *Cymdeithas y Cantorion Crefyddol, Bethesda* (The Society of Religious Singers, Bethesda). The leader was Robert Williams, a young man who came to Bethesda in 1819 and started music classes in the chapel. On Saturday night, at six o'clock after work, the singers would meet to learn the hymn-tunes for the Sunday service. They were divided into classes according to knowledge and ability, and each week they learned the hymns to be sung in the chapel that coming Sunday. But there were also meetings during the week that taught them to read music and understand its principles. Before long, the congregational singing in Bethesda became famous throughout Wales, and in order to maintain their high standards the society set out a list of rules that governed the behaviour of its members. Among its prohibitions was that anybody found guilty of drunkenness, fornication, thievery, murder, falsehood, desecrating the Sabbath, swearing, etc., would be denied membership. The society was successful for many years, and through hard work and dedication Bethesda became one of the most important musical centres of mid-nineteenth-century Wales.

This society was only one of many in a patchwork across Wales. In Aberystwyth, a musical union was formed from various religious denominations and its choral and congregational singing became famous. With little formal music education, the union members taught themselves the basic principles of music and then passed on their knowledge to others. By the 1820s, more and more books of sacred songs were beginning to be published, but most of the airs were from English collections. Until *Caniadau y Cyssegr* (Songs of the Sanctuary) appeared in 1839, no one had published a collection of the old hymn tunes that were composed and sung in the heat of the religious revivals in eighteenth and early nineteenth-century Wales. The author, John Roberts of Henllan, called it '... gasgliad o donau hen a diweddar, gan mwyaf o gyfansoddiad Cymreig' ('... a collection of old and recent hymn-tunes, the majority of Welsh composition').[36] In his introduction, he says that the melodies have been sung in Wales for more than half a century, and that his contribution was to collect the tunes and harmonise them in four parts: the trebles to sing the melody and the men to sing the rest. Of the fifty-five hymn-tunes in his book, the majority are in the major, with nine in the minor and two in the dorian mode. The melody to the hymn 'Y Seren Ddydd' is one of the many versions of the old ballad air 'Diniweidrwydd':[37]

Example 8.21: 'Y Seren Ddydd'

One of the most important of these musical societies was pioneered by the Mills family in Llanidloes, mid-Wales, described as 'a humble Welsh equivalent of the Bach dynasty'.[38] The family made an important contribution to sacred music in Wales, beginning with Henry Mills, born in 1757. He joined the Methodists and was appointed an accredited teacher in the area. Initial opposition arose to his appointment partly because he was very young and partly because he could play two or three instruments. There was enormous prejudice against musical instruments among some chapel-goers who felt that instruments came between the worshipper and the purity of the Word. This was especially true of the harp, which was associated with the tavern. However, through hard work and considerable ability, Henry Mills and his sons turned Llanidloes into one of the most musical places in mid-nineteenth-century Wales. The Mills sons made an immense contribution: James was Precentor of the Llanidloes Choral Society, excelling as a conductor and composer of hymns and anthems; and his brother, Richard, also began to compose while young and his gifts earned the praise of Bardd Alaw. Richard's great contribution was *Caniadau Seion*, a book dedicated to Bardd Alaw 'am ei lafur diflin, a'i ymdrechion canmoladwy er gwasanaeth a diwylliant Cerddoriaeth Gymreig' ('for his untiring labour and praiseworthy efforts in the service and culture of Welsh Music').[39]

There are over 200 hymns in this substantial book, and the airs were taken from a variety of sources, including Mozart, Handel, Haydn's *Creation*, and two anthems by the American composer William Billings.

'Joanna' is a variant of an air that was popular in the chapel and the tavern:[40]

Example 8.22: 'Joanna' (adapted from Richard Mills's original four-part setting)

Sometimes old songs are tidied up: 'Llantrisant' is a rhythmically strict version of an air used to sing a seventeenth-century Christmas carol 'Awn i Fethlem':[41]

Example 8.23: 'Llantrisant'

This was also the period of the rise of the temperance movement in Wales. There had been a tremendous growth in the number of taverns, especially in industrial areas, where drunkenness became a serious problem. It was answered by a rise in temperance societies that held meetings at which temperance songs were sung with gusto. The first temperance festival in Wales was held in 1836, and temperance marches were also popular.

There were also temperance eisteddfods. Previously local eisteddfods had been held in taverns, but by the middle of the century the eisteddfod had left the tavern for the chapel. It was a period of change and growth in which the chapel and eisteddfod culture, with its hymns, singing festivals and music classes, was widespread. This was true throughout Wales, but in the south Wales valleys the rapidly expanding population resulting from industrial growth had other outlets as well. Sizeable south Wales towns, such as Swansea, Carmarthen and later Cardiff, were large enough to support theatres featuring plays, operas, and orchestras.

However, it was becoming more and more apparent that education – or rather the lack of education – was proving a problem in Wales as in the rest of Britain. Astonishingly, for a wealthy country the British state provided no systematic education for its citizens who were instructed, if at all, by a jumble of methods. The established Church played a part in educating the citizenry, but in mid-nineteenth-century Wales the majority of the Welsh had left the Church for the chapel and thus the lack of a state education was a more serious issue. The government in London sent a commission of three Englishmen, all lawyers and members of the Anglican Church, who did not speak or understand Welsh, to investigate the condition of education in Wales. Because of their inability to communicate with monoglot Welsh people, they relied chiefly on the clergy of the Church of England to interpret – and some of these clergy members were all too ready to blacken the reputations of the Nonconformists in their midst. Many Welsh people were aware of the inadequacy of their schools, and were ready to cooperate with the commission in the expectation that the government would take measures to improve educational provision in Wales: 'They were prepared to hear that they were poorly educated; they had not expected to be told that they were drunken, dirty, superstitious and sexually promiscuous liars and cheats. The response was immediate and bitter.'[42]

The effect of this infamous report on Welsh life and especially on the Welsh language was galvanic. The period that followed saw campaigns to present Wales as a virtuous nation. Singing with the harp had already fallen out of favour with the advent of the Methodist Revival. The great preacher Thomas Charles wrote, in 1791, 'No harps, but the *golden* harps of which St John speaks, have been played in this neighbourhood for several months past',[43] and one writer at the end of the nineteenth century noted:

> The introduction of Methodism made a great change in the habits of the people. Dancing was altogether discouraged as profane. My father told me that he remembered an old man, I think about Llangammarch or Abergwessin, who played the harp, but who joined the Methodists or Dissenters, and then gave up the harp, and threw it under the bed, where it lay till it got unglewed and wormeaten, and fell to pieces.[44]

Indeed had it not been for the Welsh gypsies, traditional music in Wales might have lost even more of its support during this period. Fortunately, Welsh gypsies continued to play the harp for singing and dancing. They were known as *teulu Abram Wood* (Abram Wood's family) and seem to have appeared in Wales about the middle of the eighteenth century. Abram Wood's great-grand-daughter described him as being a tall man with a dark complexion, who always rode on a thoroughbred horse. He wore a cocked hat trimmed with gold lace, and a silk swallow-tailed coat with white breeches. The Gypsies that settled in Wales not only became fluent Welsh speakers, but they adopted the Welsh triple harp as their own, playing it in a unique style. They were already good fiddlers and, together with the harp, were welcome at neighbourhood farms to play for dancing. Their ability was such that they competed at various eisteddfods and frequently won. Although most were itinerant, travelling from farm to village to town, making music when and where they might find an audience, one or two were so proficient that they became domestic harpers to gentry families. Jeremiah Wood was known as 'Jerry Bach Gogerddan' because he was the domestic harper to the Price family of Gogerddan in Cardiganshire. He was with the same family for fifty years, and when he died the family had his tombstone carved with a harp.

The gypsy harpists also played for royalty on more than one occasion. The most famous of them, John Roberts of Newtown, known as 'Telynor Cymru' (The Harpist of Wales), was the eldest son of a Welshman who married a gypsy. After doing service in the army, where he learned to read music and to play a variety of instruments, he became so skilled that he was invited on more than one occasion to play the harp for the young Princess Victoria. When he had enough money to buy himself out of the army, he left to embark on a career as a harpist playing at private parties in the houses of the gentry, competing at various eisteddfods where he won a number of prizes, and performing at concerts held in hotels and assembly rooms. He had nine sons, all of whom played the harp, and when they were old enough to perform in public they called themselves 'The Cambrian Minstrels' and travelled about Wales giving performances, culminating in an invitation to perform for Queen Victoria in 1889 when she was visiting Palé Hall in Merionethshire. John Roberts and his nine sons performed for the Queen, playing during dinner and then performing a special program that included John Roberts himself singing *penillion*.

Although the oral tradition was still important at this period, it was not unusual for harpists and other musicians to note down music in a book. Fortunately, a few of these have survived to illustrate the music-making of the period. In Llanbrynmair, Montgomeryshire, William Peate, a cobbler who was very fond of music, had a close friend called 'John Roberts y Cynjer', who was known as a *dyn hysbys* (one who it was believed could reveal the future and who could heal and safeguard people and animals). 'John Roberts y Cynjer' was also a musician who could note down music as well as compose, and after he died his book of Welsh music was passed on to his friend. In the process, it became known as 'William Peate's Book'.[45]

The contents comprise some 115 airs of various kinds. Most are written for treble and bass with a few for treble only, and many of these arrangements of well-known airs can be found in the collections of John Parry, Ruabon, Edward Jones and Richard Roberts. The most interesting part of the manuscript is at the back, where a number of *plygain* carol tunes have been noted. Some of these are set in typical *plygain* style for three voices, invariably male, with tenor on top, bass on the bottom and the air in the middle. That is the case with 'Difyrwch Gwyr Caernarfon', which seems to have been accurately notated except that the notator has put the time signature as 3/4 whereas the air is obviously in 6/8 time:[46]

Example 8.24: 'Difyrwch Gwyr Caernarfon'

The folk tradition and the eisteddfod tradition continued to be important in nineteenth-century Wales. Although the Fenni eisteddfods came to an end in 1853, the tradition survived and indeed flourished, as will be seen in the next chapter.

9
The Momentum Continues

IN 1858, an eisteddfod was organised in Llangollen. It lasted four days and for the first time cheap railway excursions were arranged for the crowds who wanted to attend. Among the prizes offered at the eisteddfod was one for an unpublished collection of Welsh airs. Two of the entrants to this competition were from south Wales and both were harpists. The winner was David Thomas Llewelyn ('Llewelyn Alaw'); his reputed prize-winning collection is now preserved in the National Library of Wales as NLW MS 331D.

Unusually, the losing entry was also preserved, submitted under the pseudonym 'Orpheus'. The manuscript eventually passed through various hands until, some thirty years later, Lewis Hartley of Bangor found it in a second-hand bookshop and gave it to a friend as a wedding present. The friend was the bride, Mary Davies, a well known singer who later became one of the pillars of the infant Welsh Folk-Song Society, and thus the manuscript was saved for study.[1]

Containing eighty songs, this manuscript is divided into two parts: Part I: Traditional and Part II: Modern and Original. Unfortunately, 'Orpheus' discarded most of the traditional words and added others, sometimes of his own invention. In two introductory pages of 'Notes and Observations', he gives the original names of some of the airs, and occasionally a traditional verse that he had heard sung. But the absence of the original words throughout seriously impairs the value of the collection. The compilation shows a degree of variety for it contains ballads on old and new airs, *llatai* songs and a song connected with the *Mari Lwyd* custom. For the first fourteen airs in the collection, 'Orpheus' provides information about the singer and frequently adds details about where the air was collected. The first song in the manuscript is 'Llangollen Market', sung in English by an old ballad singer from Radnorshire on the English border and set here to Welsh words. But the oldest song in the collection may well be 'Yr Eira', one of a large family of Welsh traditional tunes that derive ultimately from the sixteenth-century song 'King Solomon'. Over the years the air has been sung in Wales to a wide variety of words. According to the collector, this version was 'known in Carmarthen and Cardiganshire':[2]

Example 9.1: 'Yr Eira'

'A'i Di Perot Purion Per' is another example of sending a bird as love messenger to a sweetheart; in this case the messenger is a parrot, quite suitably since parrots could be taught to speak![3]

Example 9.2: 'A'i Di Perot Purion Per'

The love song, 'Yn Mhontypridd Mae Mwriad', has a fine dorian air. The form of this example is unusual in Welsh folk-song because the fifth phrase does not come to a cadence, but leads back to the beginning:[4]

Example 9.3: 'Yn Mhontypridd Mae Mwriad'

'Y Fwyalchen Ddu Bigfelen' is a member of the large family of Welsh tunes derived from 'St Patrick's Day in the Morning'.[5] As usual, 'Orpheus' has written other words to the air, but in 'Notes and Observations' he set down a traditional verse which is macaronic with lines alternately in Welsh and English:[6]

Example 9.4: 'Y Fwyalchen Ddu Bigfelen'

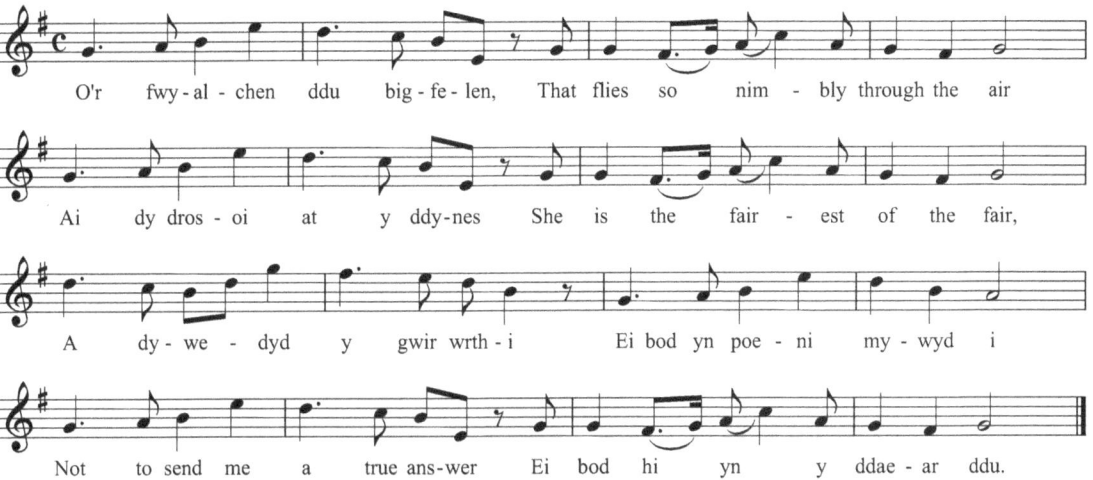

The collection as a whole is interesting for showing the wide variety of airs that were sung in Wales in the middle of the nineteenth century. About a quarter of these appear to come from the Welsh folk tradition. The remainder of the collection consists of taproom songs, parlour songs, English ballads and harp airs, most of which were most likely composed – many by 'Orpheus' himself – for the competition. Perhaps the most interesting is the song called 'Glan Rhondda'. It is now known that 'Orpheus' was James James, that he wrote the air 'Glan Rhondda' and that his father, Evan James, wrote the words. By now, the song has been adopted as the Welsh national anthem.

The winning competitor, Thomas David Llewelyn ('Llewelyn Alaw'), born a year before the death of Ifor Ceri, represented a different type of collector. He learned to play the harp at the age of eight, but when he was eleven he went to work in the coal mines. In his twenties, however, Llewelyn Alaw decided to make his career as a harpist and for the rest of his life he was in demand as a performer and teacher. He played the harp in public concerts and private recitals, in tavern eisteddfods and temperance singing festivals, country dances and grand balls, club dinners, public meetings and chapel gatherings. The nine volumes of his manuscripts in the National Library of Wales testify to the variety of his musical interests; more than 250 of the airs are of Welsh origin or were adopted by the Welsh over the years, including airs from the works of John Parry, Ruabon, Edward Jones and John Parry ('Bardd Alaw').

As might be expected, Llewelyn Alaw's manuscripts are full of the dances of the period: waltzes, hornpipes, polkas, quadrilles, galops, quicksteps and reels to popular dance tunes like 'The Dashing White Sergeant', 'Queen of Prussia's Waltz', 'Napoleon's Retreat March' and 'Hungarian Gallopade'. Many were so popular in Wales that they lost their English titles, and a dance tune like 'Haste to the Wedding' became 'Hast i'r Briodas'. But Llewelyn Alaw's large Welsh repertoire was equally wide-ranging and included a number of Welsh dance tunes, such as the 'Aberdare Railway Polka', 'Carmarthenshire Hornpipe' and 'Dinevor Waltz', and many of these tunes were his own compositions. Llewelyn Alaw noted seventeenth and eighteenth-century ballad airs, some copied from books, such as 'Ffarwel Ned Pugh' (*British Harmony*), 'Sweet Richard' (*Cambrian Harmony*) and 'Merch Megan' (*Relicks*), as well as numerous other favourites like 'Ymadawiad y Brenin', 'Llef Caerwent', 'Bryniau Werddon' and 'Diniweidrwydd'. His collection also includes a large number of Welsh traditional song airs, such as 'Tôn y Melinydd', 'Y Blotyn Du' and 'Y Bachgen Main'. However, he is comparatively sparing in noting words to the airs – there are no words or accompaniments to songs in the numbered section of the manuscript that was said to have won the eisteddfod prize, and some of the music is carelessly written.[7] Clearly, this could not have been the manuscript that was submitted to the contest judges, but it was probably a working copy in which Llewelyn Alaw noted the pieces he intended to include in the finished work. Occasional titles suggest that words were sung to some of the airs, such as 'Trigolion Plwyf Merthyr', which appears to be the first line of a ballad addressing the people of Merthyr Tydfil:[8]

Example 9.5: 'Trigolion Plwyf Merthyr'

One of the oldest songs in Llewelyn Alaw's collection is 'Gwrandewch ar Ferch sy'n Serchog', with words by the seventeenth-century poet Huw Morys. It is set here to the English air 'Gerard's Mistress', known in Wales as 'Charity Mistress'. The song appears to have been taken down from a singer rather than copied from a manuscript, since there are difficulties here and there in the notation. Nevertheless, it is a significant clue to the way the poem was sung and an important remnant from an earlier period:[9]

Example 9.6: 'Gwrandewch ar Ferch sy'n Serchog'

Many of Llewelyn Alaw's examples were songs, but he rarely included the words since his manuscripts were for his work as a harper and clearly not intended for publication. Where he noted only the music, a clue to the words can sometimes be found in the title. A song entitled 'Betty o Lan Sant Ffraid' suggests a well-known erotic ballad by John Jones ('Jac Glan-y-Gors'; 1766–1821) and the ballad words fit the tune with ease:[10]

Example 9.7: 'Betty o Lan Sant Ffraid'

In some cases, however, Llewelyn Alaw gives the first verse of a song, enough to show how the words fit the music. 'Y Carwr Gwirion' may have been noted from oral tradition as Llewelyn Alaw made two attempts to write it. He included words at the bottom of the page, and lines such as 'Mi roes fy serch ar ferch fach fain goch liwgar giwrain lygad' ('I loved a slender, red-haired, fine-eyed girl') appear to be the product of a gifted folk poet. However, he seems to have set down the music as a harp air rather than as a song. The wide intervals, grace notes and succession of running notes are instrumental rather than vocal:[11]

Example 9.8: 'Y Carwr Gwirion'

'Carwriaeth' is a night-visit song. Here too the lyrics are the work of an accomplished versifier, telling of a poet who goes on a moonlit night to see his sweetheart. Llewelyn Alaw sets the song in a high key – perhaps intended as a tenor solo – but in a lower key it would make a suitable song for any voice:[12]

Example 9.9: 'Carwriaeth'

Llewelyn Alaw and Maria Jane Williams, both from south Wales, were contemporaries, though he was much younger than she, and it is not surprising that they shared some of the same repertoire. A comparison of 'Y Ferch o'r Scer' (see Example 8.11) and 'Hyd y Frwynen Las' in Llewelyn Alaw's manuscript shows how Maria Jane Williams refined a simple air into a salon song:[13]

Example 9.10: 'Hyd y Frwynen Las'

continued

It may have been Llewelyn Alaw's training as an instrumentalist that kept his musical notation in the major or minor keys, ignoring the modal element of traditional singing. Ballad airs are often shared, and it is not surprising that some of them came to Wales from across the border. The melody of 'Yn Nhloty'r Sir yr Wyf yn Byw' is a distant variant of the ballad air 'Gilderoy', which became popular in Ireland as 'The Star of the County Down' and in England as 'Dives and Lazarus':[14]

Example 9.11: 'Yn Nhloty'r Sir yr Wyf yn Byw'

The ballad of 'Y Blotyn Du' was popular throughout Wales and sung to many different airs (see Example 6.11), including, as here, the old drinking tune 'Landlord Fill the Flowing Bowl':[15]

Example 9.12: 'Y Blotyn Du'

'Snapping' the unaccented syllable is often found in Welsh folk-song, perhaps even more in the days before traditional music began to be published in books. Llewelyn Alaw notes one air, 'Mae Gwyr Ifanc', which is full of 'snap'. Although he gives no time signature, it appears to be in 6/8 time and 'snapping' the unaccented syllable gives a dancing/skipping rhythm to the words that refer to young men planting trees:[16]

Example 9.13: 'Mae Gwyr Ifanc'

Another very interesting example in Llewelyn Alaw's collection of snapping the note is 'Old Darby', a popular air for ballads and carols in the eighteenth and nineteenth centuries. As a hymn tune, it was sung in phrases of straight 9.8., with end accents alternately feminine and masculine. But in Llewelyn Alaw's notation for three voices (perhaps for singing a *plygain* carol), the snapping of the first note of the bar gives a special pulse to the air:[17]

Example 9.14: 'Old Darby' (3-part harmony)

continued

One of the most popular song-forms in Wales was the four-line verse with interlaced refrain, which could be sung with nonsense syllables or played as an instrumental burden. Llewelyn Alaw noted a number of airs in this style, often calling them simply 'Welsh Air':[18]

Example 9.15: 'Welsh Air' (Mesur Nos Galan)

'Hob y Deri Dando', a very popular song-type, appeared in print for the first time in Edward Jones's *Relicks*, and examples of the air copied or adapted from the *Relicks* versions appeared in the publications of Bingley, Bardd Alaw and Thomson, as well as in the manuscript collections of Iolo Morganwg, Aneurin Owen and William

Peate. Llewelyn Alaw's version, 'As sung in south Wales', is similar to a song in Iolo Morganwg's collection called 'Hwp i Diri Dando Arwest Salmau':[19]

Example 9.16: 'Hob y Deri Dan Do'

Llewelyn Alaw has several versions of the air 'Fy Ngwen Mae'r Eira ar y Bannau', instrumental and vocal. In one version, the rather flowery words suggest that Llewelyn Alaw may have intended it as a parlour song, and in another manuscript he noted the same song in two parts, perhaps for local concerts or small musical gatherings:[20]

Example 9.17: 'Fy Ngwen Mae'r Eira ar y Bannau'

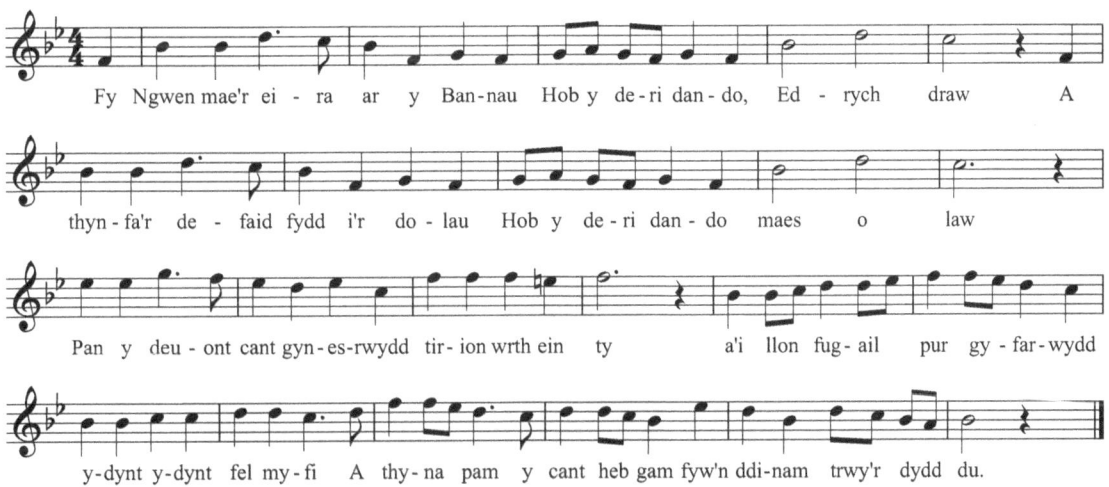

Llewelyn Alaw's manuscripts differ from the collections of cultured amateurs like Ifor Ceri because Llewelyn Alaw was, first and foremost, a professional musician. It is clear from the wide variety of music in his collection that he was a man of extraordinary ability, and his death at the comparatively early age of fifty-one was a serious loss to Welsh traditional music.

In the Llangollen 1858 eisteddfod, it was decided to ensure that a national eisteddfod should be a permanent institution, and by 1860 a council and a general committee were set up to rule the new establishment. A 'reform bill' resolved that an eisteddfod was to be held yearly, in south and north Wales alternately, and the first of the national eisteddfods under the new regime was held in Aberdare in 1861. They continued to be held annually until 1868, but by then the eisteddfod was in serious financial trouble and the council was disbanded. However, at the Caernarfon Eisteddfod of 1880, it was decided to establish *Cymdeithas yr Eisteddfod Genedlaethol* (The National Eisteddfod Society), and the first eisteddfod under its authority was held at Merthyr Tydfil in 1881. Since then, with the exception of the war years of 1914 and 1940, the National Eisteddfod has been held annually.

The nineteenth century in Wales was a time of change and upheaval, when much of the old singing tradition disappeared or was altered to fit new forms of worship and a different lifestyle. For many, there was less interest in noting the old songs than in composing new ones. By the second half of the century, there was a noticeable increase in musical publications and, in addition to making available previously unpublished airs, there were numerous arrangements of old ones, often for choirs or schools. The *cymanfa ganu* (a hymn-singing festival) to a great extent replaced the singing in the tavern, and was associated with the popularity of a new form of musical notation known as 'Tonic Sol-Fa'. The system was developed in England in the mid-nineteenth century as a popular method of teaching a congregation of all ages to sing using letters of the alphabet representing the notes of the scale. Not only was Tonic Sol-Fa easy to read, it was cheap to print and when the system was presented in Welsh it swept through Wales like a whirlwind. Children learned Tonic Sol-Fa at school and adults attended sol-fa classes in the evenings. Tonic Sol-Fa enabled amateur singers to learn great works such as *Judas Maccabeus* or *Elijah*, and resulted in an eruption of choral singing. The Welsh hymn profited even more from this new system. Welsh congregational singing improved immensely and became more polished, with congregations singing four-part hymns with ease, where previously the singing had been in unison. Without the development of Tonic Sol-Fa, Welsh choral singing might never have reached the musical heights it attained in the nineteenth century.

Instrumental music also flourished in Wales during this period, with the piano gradually replacing the harp as the instrument of choice for most Welsh people. Books of Welsh music were now printed with accompaniments for the piano, and undoubtedly the most popular of these was *The Songs of Wales*.[21] Its author, Henry Brinley Richards (1817–85) was brought up in a musical family in Carmarthen, and showed so much early promise that he went to the Royal Academy of Music in London, and from there to Paris where he studied with Chopin. Brinley Richards composed a good deal of music, including symphonic music for orchestra, but by now his reputation rests upon *The Songs of Wales*, a book that was so popular it was said to be on the piano in every music-loving miner's cottage. Brinley Richards was not a collector of unknown Welsh songs, but rather an arranger of familiar airs. Of the seventy songs in this volume, the majority came from the publications of John Parry, Bardd Alaw (who had taken most of them from the collections of Edward Jones), together with several songs from *Ancient National Airs of Gwent and Morganwg* and one from Ieuan Ddu's volume. In general, Brinley Richards's contribution was the attractive piano accompaniments that are within the compass of the competent amateur.

In at least one case, the nature of the original air was completely changed. 'Yn Iach i Ti Gymru' is a poignant farewell song with words by a contemporary poet, set to an air that Bardd Alaw called 'Llandovery'. The original air, which came from Ifor Ceri's collection, *Melus-Seiniau*, is a rollicking jig with a join-in chorus,[22] and it was Bardd Alaw who apparently changed it:[23]

Example 9.18: 'Yn Iach i Ti Gymru'

continued

The most important collector/editor in the second half of the nineteenth century was John Owen ('Owain Alaw'; 1821–83). He was born into a Welsh-speaking family in Chester, where he had a good education including music lessons from a professional teacher. His ability was so outstanding that at a young age he was appointed organist in Lady Huntingdon's Chapel and conductor of an orchestral society, and when he was twenty-three he gave up a business career in favour of music. He became well known as a composer, arranger, organist, choir-master, accompanist and baritone soloist. Owain Alaw was one of the stalwarts of the eisteddfod, both as competitor and adjudicator of competitions such as the one in Llangollen where he awarded the prize to Llewelyn Alaw. Between 1860 and 1864, he published in serial form *Gems of Welsh Melody*, and in 1873 the various issues were collected, with a few modifications, into one book.[24]

This important collection is in considerable contrast to *The Songs of Wales*. There is plenty of variety in the music: although about half the airs come from the works of Edward Jones plus a few from the publications of John Parry, Ruabon, and Maria Jane Williams, the contents also include songs not previously printed; composed songs in traditional style; 'national' songs; instrumental pieces; songs arranged for two or more voices; and the first printed collection of 'specimens of pennillion singing after the manner of North Wales'. The accompaniments are sometimes for

'Pianoforte or Harp', but more often for the piano, even in the specimens of *penillion* singing that traditionally were connected with the harp.

The introductory notes to the first issue of *Gems* in 1860 emphasise the 'antiquity' of Welsh music, even going so far as to suggest that 'there is no reason to doubt ... that the tune called "Glan Meddwdod Mwyn" came to us from the time of the Druids; and it is probably a correct specimen of Welsh music of that early period'. That kind of statement was not uncommon in the period before serious studies in Welsh musicology had begun. However, Owain Alaw also gives a pertinent description of *penillion* singing with the harp at the eisteddfod as well as discussing award-winning compositions and performances, adding that the eisteddfod meetings 'have been the means of bringing into public notice almost all the Poets, Literary men, and Musicians of Wales, and have been of great service in furthering native talent, and fostering the latent genius of the Welsh people'.

The contents of *Gems* show that Owain Alaw was aiming at a very different public from that of *The Songs of Wales*. His connection with Welsh eisteddfodic culture, whether the national eisteddfod of several days or the rural eisteddfod of an afternoon and evening, meant that traditional Welsh airs were arranged as vocal solos, duets, quartets or choruses with harp or piano accompaniment, as well as instrumental solos. He composed some pieces himself and made numerous arrangements of others, for by now there were calls for music of all kinds to fill the expanding social needs of an increasingly educated society. *Gems*, published in 1873, gathered in one large volume the contents of previous issues, some of which were edited by changing the accompaniment, setting different words or adding 'antiquarian' notes. He divided the contents into 'Songs with English and Welsh words'; 'Specimens of Pennillion Singing'; and 'Welsh National Airs'. Owain Alaw included patriotic airs like 'Saint David's Day' and his own composition, 'Cymru Lân, Gwlad y Gân', but none achieved the popularity of 'Hen Wlad Fy Nhadau'. Owain Alaw's arrangement of this, made with the permission of the composer James James, is effectively the same as that sung today.

There is considerable difference in the style of the lyrics written for Owain Alaw's collection of airs and the lyrics in earlier collections. By the second half of the nineteenth century, Victorian mores had infiltrated the style and subjects of poetry, including traditional Welsh songs. 'Galar Gwraig y Milwr', an attractive major-mode air in triple time, is burdened with dolorous words full of mournful predictions, quite unsuited to the tune:[25]

Example 9.19: 'Galar Gwraig y Milwr'

continued

'Tôn y Melinydd' is a rollicking tune with a join-in chorus, the kind of song to be heard in a *noson lawen* or sung in the stable-loft by farm workers at the end of the day:[26]

Example 9.20: 'Tôn y Melinydd'

In contrast, 'Plygeingan' is an elegant air with a wide compass, which Owain Alaw says was 'taken from a collection of unpublished Welsh airs':[27]

Example 9.21: 'Plygeingan'

'Alawon Fy Ngwlad' is the name that Owain Alaw gave to an air, probably a dance tune, originally called 'Hobed o Hilion'. He slowed it down and turned it into a ballad with rather saccharine words about the songs of Wales:[28]

Example 9.22: 'Alawon Fy Ngwlad'

The beautiful love song, 'Lloer Dirion Lliw'r Dydd', is the most interesting one in the collection. Owain Alaw himself took down this song from the singing of David Morgan of Llanidloes, who had learned the air and the first verse from his mother. Owain Alaw's note to the song says 'This plaintive Melody is a good specimen of the Welsh Style'. It appears to have been set down as it was sung, and the style is declamatory rather than lyrical. The tendency to hold the unaccented syllable longer than the accented one in words like 'dirion', 'penyd', 'gwla' or 'ddolur' is a Welsh characteristic that gives impetus to the vocal line:[29]

Example 9.23: 'Lloer Dirion Lliw'r Dydd'

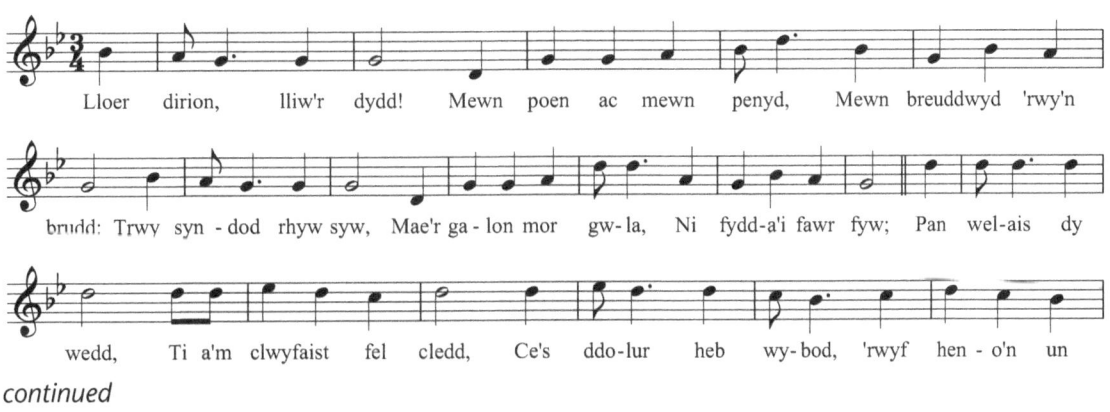

continued

During the second half of the nineteenth century as more people became literate many Welsh periodicals were launched including some devoted to music. A few started and failed through lack of support, but in 1861 Reverend John Roberts ('Ieuan Gwyllt') brought out the first issue of *Y Cerddor Cymreig* aimed at educating the Welsh in music. The editor's plan was to include the history of music; training in the principles of music; publication of original music in each issue; musical criticism of Welsh music in print; and correspondence on musical matters. This ambitious programme of musical education included a column entitled *Ystafell yr Hen Alawon* ('The Old Tune Room'). During this period, a number of Welsh traditional tunes and 'national airs' appeared in this column, sometimes including comments on the airs and their background.

Among the regular contributors to 'The Old Tune Room' were Ylltyr Williams, who had been a quarryman and schoolmaster in north Wales before becoming a bookseller, and David Lewis from mid-Wales, a music teacher and adjudicator who was aware of the importance of the old airs. Unfortunately, very few of the airs printed in these periodicals included the words sung to them, which is a serious drawback to any study of the music of the period. After *Y Cerddor Cymreig* ceased publication, others took its place with occasional contributions of traditional music. In 1883, *Cerddor y Cymry* included a column titled *Ystafell yr Hen Alawon – Moesol a Chysegredig* ('The Old Tune Room – Moral and Sacred'), which appeared occasionally, and in 1889 *Y Cerddor*, the most important of the periodicals, was launched under the leadership of two acknowledged musicians, D. Emlyn Evans and David Jenkins. Here again, very few traditional airs were printed with words. Many came from collections that noted music only, but the attitudes of the period also contributed to the lack of words to many tunes. The heading 'Moral and Sacred' excluded many of the traditional songs sung in the fair or by the farmhands, which were considered coarse or even indecent. Frequently, when a tune was printed without words, a poet would be invited to write 'respectable' words to it. In spite of these drawbacks, the musical periodicals prepared the way for the more serious discussion of traditional music that was to come in the following century.

Many of the tunes printed in 'The Old Tune Room' were popular with ballad singers who, for centuries, had plied their trade in fairs, markets and public places. Sometimes, ballad singers performed and sold ballads that they themselves had written to traditional tunes, while at other times they used the words of established poets. In addition, there were hawkers who merely sold ballads, written by others, from door to door. In this way a great body of popular song was spread throughout the country. There was scarcely a town that did not possess a printing press. Altogether, they produced a huge number of ballad sheets.

More prestigious presses published volumes by poets who realised that there was a ready market for songs in local concerts, eisteddfods, temperance meetings and so on. In most cases they set their poems to popular tunes, traditional or contemporary, doing for Wales what Robert Burns did for Scotland and Thomas Moore did for Ireland. The most prominent of these poets were John Ceiriog Hughes ('Ceiriog'; 1832–87), John Jones ('Talhaiarn'; 1810–70) and Richard Davies ('Mynyddog'; 1833–77). Their books had wide circulation and their songs became so popular that they were imitated by many lesser poets responding to the needs of local performers.

Tunes flooded in from outside Wales. The music hall was a source of many new airs, including 'Polly Perkins of Paddington Green' and 'Not for Joe'. Parlour songs, such as 'The Last Rose of Summer' and English folk-songs like 'The Three Ravens', were provided with Welsh words. Of particular interest was the influx of American tunes, both sacred and secular, in the second half of the century. Stephen Collins Foster's songs became very popular, along with many minstrel show tunes. In contrast were the evangelising songs of Sankey and Moody. Over the years, a great many of these tunes became deeply embedded in the Welsh oral tradition.

In 1896, a collection of 'Old Welsh Airs' was published in two sumptuous volumes under the title of *Alawon Fy Ngwlad – The Lays of My Land*.[30] Nicholas Bennett, the squire of Glanyrafon in Montgomeryshire, who put together the collection from various sources, was a direct descendant of the Nicholas Bennett who bought Glanyrafon in 1628. The squire appears to have been a genial man who enjoyed hunting and fishing and kept a pack of beagles, but he was also a cultured man who was fond of Welsh music and poetry. He would send his friends birds, fish or hares that he had caught, and thanks came back in the form of *englynion* written especially for him. The poet Ceiriog and the declaimer John Jones ('Idris Fychan'; 1825–87) were among those who were on the lookout for airs on his behalf, and over a period of time Nicholas Bennett seems to have bought or borrowed various manuscripts of Welsh music. At some point he decided to publish the Welsh airs in his manuscript collection. More than a third of the airs in *Alawon Fy Ngwlad* were taken from Llewelyn Alaw's collection, others were taken from *Melus-Seiniau* and William Peate's manuscript. Some airs were noted from *British Harmony* or such periodicals as *Y Cerddor*, *Y Cerddor Cymreig* and the *Red Dragon*. But the provenance of at least half of the airs in *Alawon Fy Ngwlad* is unknown – a serious loss to Welsh music scholarship.

This huge collection of just over 500 airs contains many different types and styles of Welsh traditional music, as well as portraits of well-known Welsh harpists and *penillion* singers and an essay on *penillion* singing. Among the airs are ballad and carol tunes, love songs, *plygain* airs, numerous dance tunes and marches, humorous songs and songs connected with folk customs, such as May songs, a wren song and a *calennig* song. There is tremendous variety in the music of these airs, but without the words many of them sound odd when merely played as arrangements for the piano. The old connection between words and music was broken when airs were published in books and periodicals without any words to accompany them, and many airs in 'irregular' forms due to the missing poetry were incorrectly barred. There is a strong tendency in D. Emlyn Evans's arrangements of the airs in *Alawon Fy Ngwlad* to coerce traditional music into regular evenly-barred phrases. 'Trymder' is a typical example. The words of the Christmas carol from *Diliau Barddas*, by Robert Davies ('Bardd Nantglyn'; 1769–1835), are in an unusual Welsh metre, and when set to music (as in 'Trymder' (version no. 1)) they result in an irregular form consisting of three and four-bar phrases (A: 3.3. B: 4.3):[31]

Example 9.24: 'Trymder' (version no. 1)

In 'Trymder' (version no. 2), D. Emlyn Evans regularised the form into four four-bar phrases (A:8 B:8), making it impossible to sing any of the poems in the 'Trymder' metre to this air:[32]

Example 9.25: 'Trymder' (version no. 2)

The piano accompaniments also detract from those folk airs that were traditionally unaccompanied, or accompanied by the harp. Modal airs, such as dorian or aeolian, are generally 'corrected' here to major or minor. 'Bryniau'r Iwerddon', which is in the dorian mode in Llewelyn Alaw's manuscript, has been changed to the minor in *Alawon fy Ngwlad*. Sometimes the changes are more drastic as extra bars are added, leading tones are sharpened, and there is a tendency to ensure that there is an even number of bars in each section of an air. Too many of the accompaniments are overly fussy and difficult to play for the average amateur. 'Balaclafa' is basically a simple four-phrase air, but D. Emlyn Evans has given it a running accompaniment in the bass and a highly chordal and syncopated melody line with unnecessary chromaticisms in the harmony:[33]

Example 9.26: 'Balaclafa'

continued

Throughout the two volumes, simple melodies are often spoiled by unnecessary chromaticism. Many of these problems arose because the arranger was more concerned with following the rules of nineteenth-century musical composition than in setting down Welsh music as it was played and sung. The most grievous omission was the lack of words to the songs, and it appears that Nicholas Bennett wanted to reissue the volumes with the missing words. T. Soley Thomas, a farmer and folk-song collector from the same area, wrote in 1910:

> A few years ago I caught the patriotic fever of collecting old melodies from Mr Nicholas Bennett Llawryglyn Montg[omeryshire] who sent a letter 'Please copy old W[elsh] airs in the rural districts of Montg[omeryshire], so that I may republish my collectn of airs in four vols with the airs and words and add a few to them'.[34]

Bennett died before this could be put into effect and *Alawon fy Ngwlad*, two expensive volumes with no words to the songs and with unsuitable accompaniments, never appealed to the audience it was meant for: the lovers of Welsh traditional music.

At the beginning of the nineteenth century Wales was a country with a strong oral tradition in music and in literature; by the end of the century, the Welsh had become literate in both, a change that had a powerful effect on traditional culture. The cultural differences between the agricultural and industrial areas of Wales became more pronounced, as industrialisation led to a different kind of music-making by the great choirs of the mining areas that sang the works of Handel and Mendelssohn. The growing importance of the eisteddfod also led to performances of composed music and widened Welsh musical horizons. The 1870 Education Act, which at last provided schooling for all, was in fact a serious blow to Welsh traditional culture for the education provided was in English only and the songs children sang in school were English songs. In twentieth-century Wales, the approach to traditional music would concentrate on preserving the Welsh tradition in the face of increasing anglicisation.

10
J. Lloyd Williams and the Welsh Folk-Song Society

THE TWENTIETH CENTURY opened with the last of the religious revivals, which had the overall effect of replacing the folk-song with the hymn. At the same time, the new century saw the formation of a society with the purpose of preserving the folk-song. The religious revival flamed briefly and then subsided – the Welsh Folk-Song Society, on the other hand, went on to celebrate its centenary in 2006.

The society's success was due above all to John Lloyd Williams (1854–1945), a towering figure who, in his long life, bridged the nineteenth and twentieth centuries. In many ways the story of his early life is a pattern of the development of Wales in that period. He was born in Llanrwst in 1854, the eldest of several children. His background was fairly typical of rural Wales at that time. There was no government school system, and education was a makeshift. The Church of England provided education through 'national' schools, but by the mid-nineteenth century the majority of Welsh people were Nonconformist and preferred to send their children to the 'British' schools. Lloyd Williams's mother had received no formal schooling, but, like many Welsh people in those days, she was educated through the Nonconformist chapel and had learned to read, passing on her interest in botany to her son. His father worked as a lead miner, and later as a quarryman in Blaenau Ffestiniog, a considerable distance from home. He walked eighteen miles overnight to work, arriving early on Monday morning, worked hard and slept in the quarry barracks during the week, before walking the eighteen miles back to Llanrwst after work finished on Saturday, arriving in time for the morning chapel service on Sunday. In spite of the paucity of educational facilities, this was a cultured family with a desire for learning.

Lloyd Williams's ability was such that when he completed elementary school, instead of going to work in the quarry with his father as most of the boys did, he continued in school and in time became a school monitor and then a student-teacher. The next step was the Normal College in Bangor where, as the holder of a Queen's Scholarship, he spent two years training to be a teacher. College life expanded his experience greatly in many fields, and it was there he learned to love the symphonies of Mozart and Beethoven, and the Handel oratorios that he sang in the college choir. After he finished his training in 1875, he became the first headmaster of a new school in Garndolbenmaen, a village not far from Porthmadog

PLATE 9: *Photograph of J. Lloyd Williams as an elderly man.*
By permission of Cymdeithas Alawon Gwerin Cymru/The Welsh Folk-Song Society.

in north-west Wales. He was there for eighteen years, educating himself as well as the children, for in addition to his school activities he taught himself to play the piano and the fiddle, composed and staged operettas for children, and established a children's choir. Outside school hours he added greatly to the music of the area by conducting hymn-singing festivals, training local soloists, conducting a mixed choir, giving public lectures on music and adjudicating in eisteddfods.

Nonetheless, his first love was botany and in 1893, at the age of thirty-nine, he left Wales to begin an extended course of study at the Royal College of Science in London. During the four years he spent in the city, Lloyd Williams took the opportunity to hear as much good music as possible and expanded his knowledge of musical form, harmony and orchestration. In 1897 he returned to Wales as assistant lecturer in Botany at the newly established University College of North Wales, Bangor, where he was later appointed to the additional post of Director of Music. Here again his contribution to Welsh culture was important. Before he came to Bangor the standard of music at the college had come under considerable criticism, and he was asked by the Principal to improve the situation. He did so in a short time and his enthusiasm and interest brought new vigour to the musical life of the college.

The period around 1900 was formative for Welsh education and culture and saw the establishment of the University of Wales, the National Library of Wales and the National Museum of Wales – and it was during this time that the Welsh Folk-Song Society was founded (1906). Although the English and Irish folk-song societies had been established slightly earlier, the Welsh society was not a direct imitation of them and its 1914–15 report states that 'The Society owes its origin to the Eisteddfod and to the Honourable Society of Cymmrodorion'.[1]

The budding Welsh Folk-Song Society was strongly supported by two Irishmen; Harry Reichel, Principal of the University College of North Wales, Bangor, and A. P. Graves, who had a home in Harlech. Their influence and guidance was crucial to the development of the society in its early days, as was the organising ability of the society's first secretary, L. D. Jones ('Llew Tegid'; 1851–1928). But it was Lloyd Williams who encouraged the early collectors of Welsh folk-songs. As Director of Music for the college in 1907, he established a singing group of young men called the *Canorion*. According to his own account:

> The first Society that was ever formed with the prime object of collecting and singing Welsh Folk-songs was a small Society of Students at the Bangor University College ... The little group of Students called themselves 'Y CANORION', and their warmest supporter was Sir Harry Reichel. He paid, out of his own pocket, the rent of the small room in the town of Bangor in which they met for song and discussion; and he and Lady Reichel invited them to take part in College Concerts and other functions. At that time our professional Welsh musicians pooh-poohed the whole thing. It was said and written that all important Welsh airs were already known, and that in any case the chief interest of Folk Music was antiquarian. If I may make a personal confession – it was in one of these College functions held in the grounds of the old College that I first fully realised the significance of the work in which we were engaged. A Brass Band was playing in the grounds, but as is usual in such places, conversation filled the air. Our small group of 'CANORION' assembled quietly under a tree and started singing. There was a sudden hush. The guests drew nearer. Tune after tune were sung; and it was with difficulty that we were allowed to leave off. Then it was that the real power of the Folk-song first revealed itself to me.[2]

With Lloyd Williams's encouragement, the members of the *Canorion* began to look for folk-songs in their native areas and the results were astonishing. They gathered together over one hundred songs, with one member, John Morris, collecting as many as forty songs, including 'Adar Mân y Mynydd', in which the lover sends his ailing sweetheart a nightingale, a lark and the little mountain birds. They return with the sad news that she is dying. He will mourn her death to the sound of viol, harp and tolling bell.[3]

Example 10.1: 'Adar Mân y Mynydd'

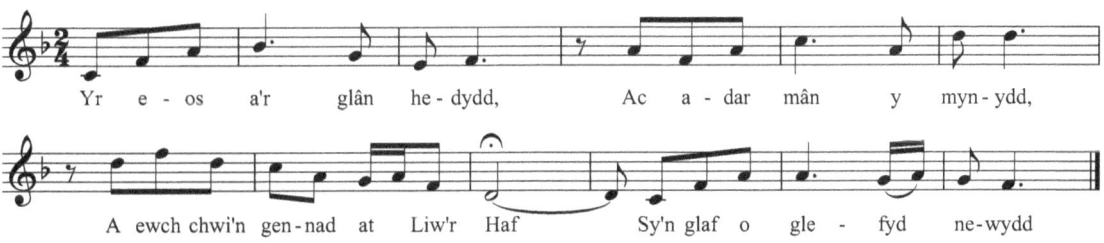

Another John Morris find, 'Yr Hen Ŵr Mwyn', a version of a widespread dialogue song in question-and-answer form, opens slowly in declamatory fashion with 'Betti' asking the 'kind old man' where he has been this night. He answers in rollicking fashion that he has been hunting the hare and that he will sell it for beer – and if he gets drunk, so be it![4]

Example 10.2: 'Yr Hen Ŵr Mwyn'

Although the folk-song tradition had largely been extinguished in the late nineteenth century by the religious revivals, much survived within families or on the less respectable fringes of society, and the launching of the Welsh Folk-Song Society gave the tradition new life. As Lloyd Williams wrote in the first issue of the *Cylchgrawn Cymdeithas Alawon Gwerin Cymru/Journal of the Welsh Folk-Song Society* (1909):

> The Society has been established for the purpose of collecting and preserving Welsh folk-songs, ballads and tunes, and of publishing such of these as may be deemed advisable; in short, to carry out for Wales, the work that is already being done by the Folk-Song Society for England and by the Irish Folk-Song Society for Ireland.[5]

The committee members of the infant society were an interesting mixture of Welsh and non-Welsh, musicians and non-musicians, upper-middle class and ordinary members of society. But they had in common a wish to preserve the best of the old folk culture at a time of rapid change. The greatest of these collectors was J. Lloyd Williams himself, who seems to have noted down songs everywhere he went. As a highly-educated Welsh-speaker from a humble background, he was able to communicate easily at every social level, and his involvement in the preservation and analysis of Welsh folk-song is unsurpassed. His most important early contribution was his lecture before the Honourable Society of Cymmrodorion in London, in 1908, titled

'Welsh National Melodies and Folk-Song',[6] and this was followed in 1909 by the first issue of the *Journal of the Welsh Folk-Song Society*, which he edited.

The editor's introduction to this issue gives a brief discussion of the past history of Welsh harp airs, the nineteenth-century collections of Maria Jane Williams and John Thomas ('Ieuan Ddu'), and the effect of religious prejudice on the folk-song. He warns against the inclusion of foreign and composed tunes, but also makes the point that even if mistakes are made, it is better to include too many tunes than too few:

> The Society does not confine its efforts to the discovery of beautiful melodies for the use of the singer. The student has also to be considered, and it is highly desirable to store up such melodies as will supply some information on the history of Welsh minstrelsy, and on the characteristic forms, rhythmic figures, and melodic curves that serve to distinguish Welsh music from that of other nationalities. For this purpose the transformations undergone by airs of foreign origin during their naturalization in Wales, are frequently quite as illuminating as undoubtedly native melodies.[7]

In the same introductory notes to the first edition of the *JWFSS*, he lists three types of airs in Welsh traditional music: harp airs, ballad and carol tunes, and folk tunes. The harp airs could serve as instrumental solos, either as songs, sometimes with English words, or as airs to which *penillion* might be sung. The ballad and carol tunes are meant to be sung with words; they are frequently lengthy and many are borrowed from English sources. The typical folktune, unlike the harp air, almost always has words, in simple direct verses that become changed over the course of time. The numerous varieties of Welsh folk-songs include 'solo-and-chorus', songs associated with customs, question-and-answer songs, and cumulative songs. They were sung in the farm kitchen or the dairy, in the stable-loft, in the quarry barracks or in the village alehouse, and Lloyd Williams noted with regret the disappearance of so many songs in recent years, noting how:

> old people who came under the influence of the religious revival of the earlier part of the [nineteenth] century, are so accustomed to regard these songs as frivolous if not immoral, that they can only with the greatest difficulty be persuaded to sing any that they happen to know.[8]

There is a brief reference to *penillion*, which north Wales singers chant to a 'simple counterpoint ... when accompanied by the melody on the harp'. Although changed social conditions and improved means of transport had a strong effect on musical taste in both town and country, the Welsh folk-song could still be heard in the workshop, on the train, in the farm house or the tavern, not only in Wales and England, but farther afield in the United States, Australia, New Zealand and the Welsh colony in Patagonia.

The aim of the *JWFSS* editor was to print 'examples of different types of tunes ... [and] of the various lines of investigation'.[9] From the beginning, it is clear that Lloyd Williams was preparing to examine Welsh folk-songs as both scientist and musician. His analytical mind was of crucial importance to this aspect of his work, but he was also determined to make the songs available for use in schools, in concert programmes and by Welsh people generally 'to make the national melody a means of fostering the musical development of the country on truly national lines'.[10] This was in the spirit of the time, when composers such as Vaughan Williams gave voice to the increasing nationalism of the period by the use of 'folk' airs.

J. Lloyd Williams was aided in these aims by the committee of the Welsh Folk-Song Society. Mary Davies, Ruth Lewis and Grace Gwyneddon Davies were members who enjoyed the leisure to go about the country with the sole purpose of collecting songs, and they published some of these songs in collections. Mary Davies, a well-known professional singer in the world of oratorio and classical concerts, had strong Welsh family connections and was a member of the Nassau Street Welsh chapel in London. She married William Cadwaladr Davies, who became the first Registrar of the new university college in Bangor, and went with him to north Wales where she became interested in Welsh traditional music. When her husband died in 1904, Mary Davies asked J. Lloyd Williams to arrange the music for the funeral. As a thank you, she sent him the 'Orpheus' manuscript that had been given to her as a wedding present and, when the first issue of the *JWFSS* appeared in 1909, it opened with ten songs taken from this manuscript. It was the beginning of a long association, in which her experience as a practical musician played its part in the budding Welsh folk-song movement.

Mary Davies's social position within influential circles of the early twentieth century was of considerable help to the young Society. She knew David Lloyd George, the leading Welsh politician of his day, and persuaded him to back the folk-song movement in Wales. In addition, she knew Cecil Sharp and Frank Kidson of the English folk-song movement, and Lucy Broadwood was a close friend. Mary Davies was able to bring all these people in touch with the new Welsh Folk-Song Society. She was also a close friend of the Lewis family.

Ruth Caine, an Englishwoman, had married Herbert Lewis, Member of Parliament for Flintshire, and he had been largely instrumental in establishing the National Library of Wales. The family had a home in Wales, and Ruth Lewis learned Welsh. Although she was not a fluent speaker, she made sure that her children, Kitty and Mostyn, were proud of their Welsh heritage.

In 1909, at the National Eisteddfod of Wales held in London, J. Lloyd Williams gave a lecture on collecting Welsh folk-songs, which resulted in tremendous enthusiasm for this aspect of Welsh traditional life. Despite this, some highly regarded Welsh musicians still maintained that everything of value had already been published, and any other folk tunes that might be discovered would prove to be worthless. They even asserted that the modal tunes had been wrongly remembered and sung, and should not be published until they had been 'corrected' by a competent musician. Nevertheless, the collectors persevered and one day Mary Davies arrived at the Lewis home carrying a new invention, a portable phonograph, with which Ruth Lewis later recorded a local Flintshire man singing an old Welsh carol, 'O Deued Pob Cristion':[11]

Example 10.3: 'O Deued Pob Cristion'

From that beginning, Ruth Lewis went on to collect songs in south and mid-Wales, as well as in the north-east where she lived. It was not always easy. Many of the people she went to see were unwilling, in the wake of the religious revival of 1904–5, to sing anything but hymns:

> Much tact and patience is required and worthless productions of modern date must be suffered before the real old song appears. This, however, has never been the case with Mrs. Jane Williams. Her songs, whether Welsh or English, are all old and worth recording, because she is nearly ninety years of age, and being unable to read or write, she remembers the things of long ago better than those of today.[12]

Jane Williams, who was recorded by Ruth Lewis at the Holywell workhouse, proved to be an important source of Welsh folk-songs, and among the most popular of these was 'Lliw Gwyn Rhosyn yr Haf', a humorous dialogue in which the girl scornfully rebuffs the young man's protestations of love, but accepts him in the end:[13]

Example 10.4: 'Lliw Gwyn Rhosyn yr Haf'

With good humour and perseverance, Ruth Lewis managed to record not only singers but also an occasional instrumentalist, such as Wil Ffidler who played for the 'Cadi Ha' dancing in Mostyn:[14]

Example 10.5: 'Cadi Ha' (as played by Wil Ffidler)

J. Lloyd Williams and the Welsh Folk-Song Society

Wherever possible, Ruth Lewis tried to find someone who knew the area and could locate suitable people willing to sing into the phonograph. Sometimes, to get them started, her daughter Kitty would sing a few Welsh airs and with patience they got songs from farmers and blacksmiths, weavers and housewives, including some country-dwellers who could speak only Welsh. In this way they collected a number of songs, some of which were published, but many more can be found in her unpublished collections in the National Library of Wales, Aberystwyth, and at the Welsh National History Museum in St Fagans.

The phonograph was an invaluable tool for collectors like Ruth Lewis who were not able to note songs directly from the singer. Mary Davies, however, could note songs directly as well as use the phonograph. One example of such documentation is 'Dacw 'Nghariad', noted in Cardiff from the singing of a woman who had heard it sung by a travelling tailor:[15]

Example 10.6: 'Dacw 'Nghariad'

'Y Cariad Cyntaf', with words and music from an earlier period, was transcribed from her phonograph recording of the singing of an Aberystwyth van driver:[16]

Example 10.7: 'Y Cariad Cyntaf'

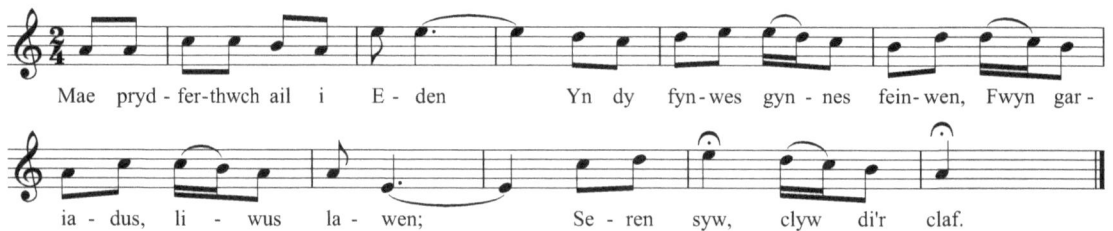

'Y Ddau Farch', with the older of two steeds complaining bitterly to the other about the misfortunes of old age, was sung into the phonograph at Cwrtmawr, Cardiganshire in 1910:[17]

Example 10.8: 'Y Ddau Farch'

Occasionally, songs were sent to her, as in this letter from D. Jones of Llanidloes, dated 1913:

> Here is a bit of a song which my father sang to us when we were children ... There was an old character who lived between Pontarfynach and Pontrhydygroes who was sometimes called 'Twm y Sane' [Tom the

Stockings] or 'Twm y Weaver' [Tom the Weaver] or 'Twm y Dafedd' [Tom the Yarn]. He got these different names because he made his living from selling the items above. He had a mule and a small cart and travelled around from fair to fair and from market to market. On his travels he was always humming /singing a tune. The mule's name was 'Jerry' ... And Twm considered that Jerry was important enough to be part of the conversation so he told Jerry all his problems and troubles. In between verses – and sometimes in the middle of the song – Twm would talk to him like this ...[18]

Example 10.9: 'Cân Twm y Sane'

In Wales, where Welsh and English are both spoken, there are some macaronic songs which combine the two languages. 'Cân Merthyr' is just such a song, about a brow-beaten husband and his masterful wife, heard from an old ballad singer on the streets of the town.[19]

Example 10.10: 'Cân Merthyr'

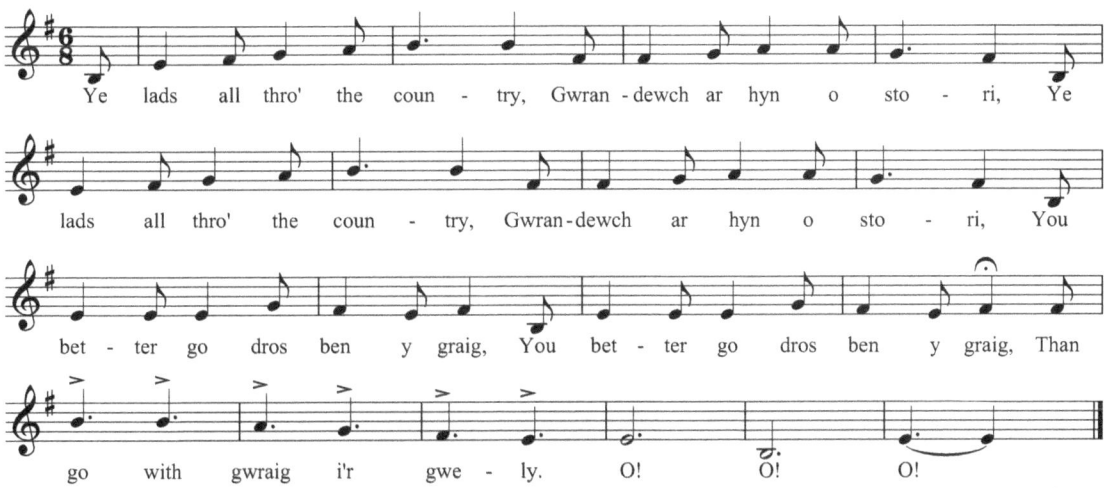

The cuckoo was important as the harbinger of spring. In the song 'O Gwcw, O Gwcw', he is late in arriving and the singer asks where he has been so long. The cuckoo answers that it was the cold north wind that kept him back.[20]

Example 10.11: 'O Gwcw, O Gwcw'

Mary Davies's niece, Grace Roberts of Liverpool, was a professional singer who had sung in France and Italy. She began collecting folk-songs on Anglesey, where her father's family lived, and eventually published three collections of them. In Dwyran, she found a farmer, Owen Parry, who sang the songs he had learned in his youth or had heard sung in the stable-loft at the end of the working day. Among them was 'Y Gelynen', in praise of the holly tree:[21]

Example 10.12: 'Y Gelynen'

'Titrwm Tatrwm' is a tender love song, in which the lover taps on his sweetheart's window complaining about the bitter weather outside:[22]

Example 10.13: 'Titrwm Tatrwm'

In 'Cwyn Mam yng Nghyfraith', a mother-in-law complains because her daughter-in-law's washing is too white and she is afraid that her son has been buying soap (an expensive commodity in those days) for his wife:[23]

Example 10.14: 'Cwyn Mam yng Nghyfraith'

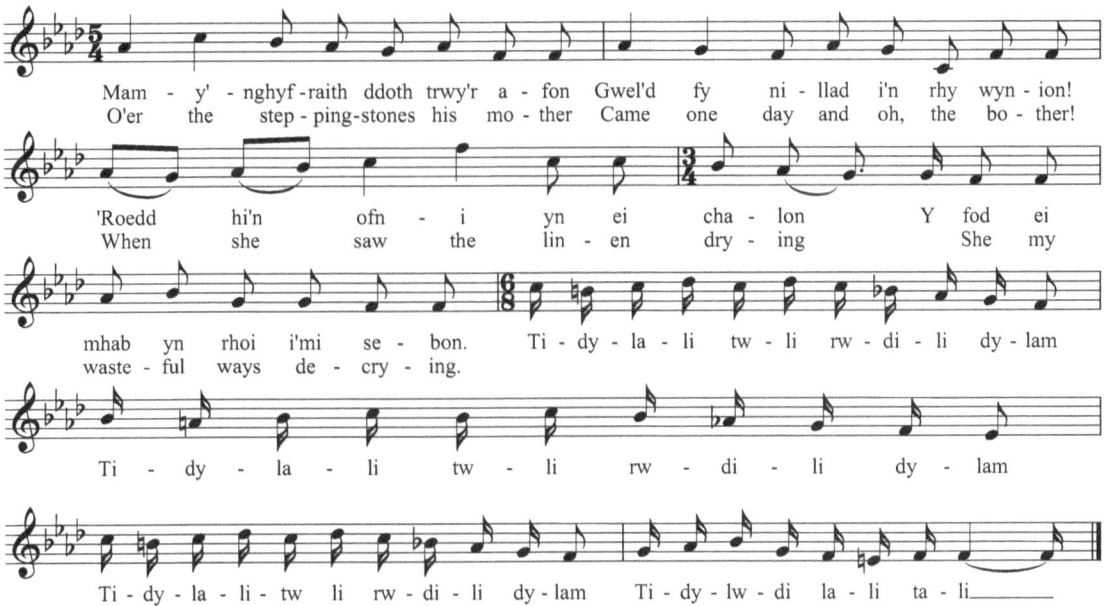

The most prolific collector by far was J. Lloyd Williams himself. His substantial collection is housed in the National Library of Wales and shows the wide variety of music he collected. He was in the habit of carrying a small notebook in his pocket, and when he heard an interesting song he jotted it down using an abbreviated form of

Tonic Sol-Fa notation giving the basic melody, form and rhythm which could be fleshed out later. This enabled him to note down songs anywhere from a variety of people – on trains and buses or walking down the street, on the eisteddfod field or adjudicating in folk-song competitions, from farm labourers and college students, housewives and preachers. One such song was 'Hiraeth', which he sent to Grace Gwyneddon Davies. This song, which undoubtedly has roots in earlier times, has a declamatory opening phrase, limited compass and emphasis on the 5th of the scale until the final phrase, when it soars up to the octave:[24]

Example 10.15: 'Hiraeth'

The love song, 'Tra Bo Dau', was noted by J. Lloyd Williams from the singing of his wife and sister-in-law, who had learned it from their father some time in the nineteenth century. The form is unusual, opening with a quatrain in triple time, followed by a short declamatory section in 6/8 time, and ending with a couplet in triple time that echoes the last four bars of the opening. There is no other song in a similar style in the *JWFSS*.[25]

Example 10.16: 'Tra Bo Dau'

'Yr Hen Fyharen' is a nonsense song that was popular with farm workers. Like many other Welsh songs, it has a declamatory opening but then the melody moves steadily downwards and the verse finishes with a short tail. This, in most cases, is where the 'joke' occurs in the words.[26]

Example 10.17: 'Yr Hen Fyharen'

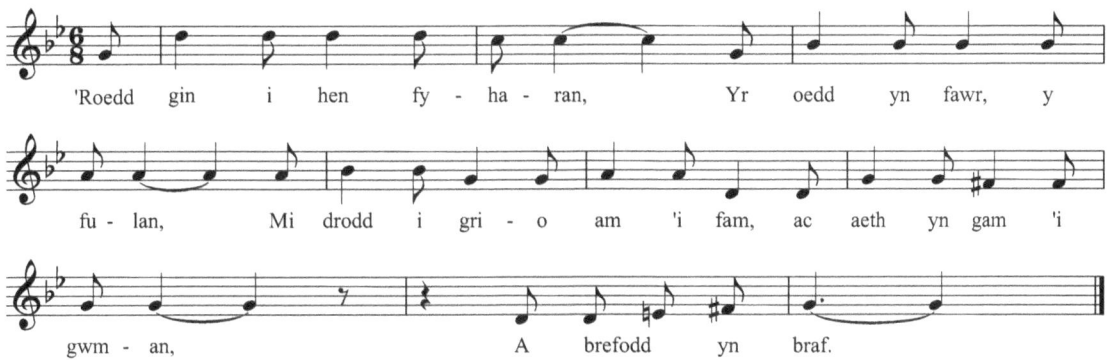

In 'Y Fwyalchen', the blackbird is a love-messenger sent by a young man to his sweetheart.[27] The song is pentatonic, that is it has no semi-tones. Pentatonic songs are rare in Welsh folk-song, and this air may have been brought into Wales from outside, perhaps from Scotland. The well known folk-song scholar, A. G. Gilchrist, claimed that a variant of the air was noted in Aberdeenshire in 1906 and printed in *Last Leaves of traditional Ballads and Ballad Airs*.[28]

Example 10.18: 'Y Fwyalchen'

'Ar Lan y Môr' is one of a number of love songs that have a declamatory opening. In this case, the first three musical phrases open in the same fashion, with a change in the final phrase. The words are significant as belonging to the language of flowers in which the rose stands for love, the lily for purity, rosemary for faithfulness and thyme for virginity. According to J. Lloyd Williams:

The words are a typical example of the 'Triads' so well-known in old Welsh literature. Of the three objects or ideas mentioned, the third often forms a climax to the other two ... But what is of equal interest is that the first three lines of the tune generally begin with the same formula, the fourth being different.[29]

Example 10.19: 'Ar Lan y Môr'

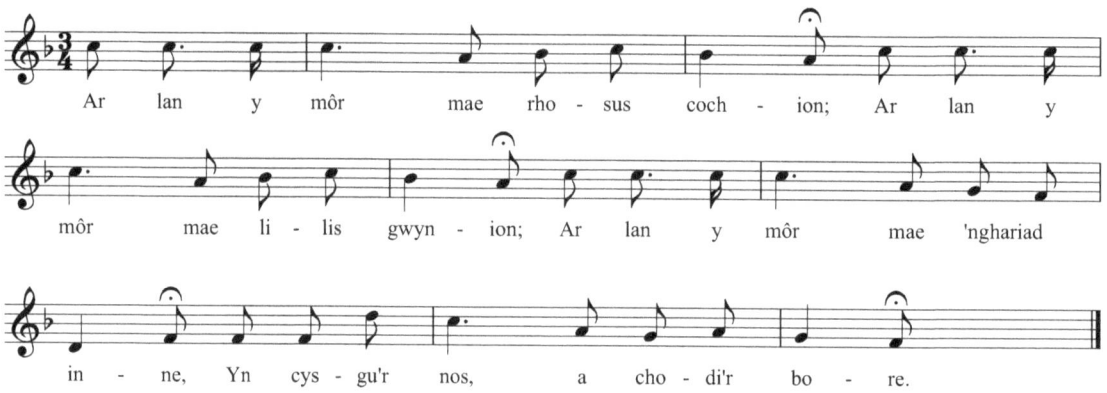

Farewell songs play a significant role in traditional Welsh music, perhaps because Wales is bounded by the sea on three sides, and many of the songs are connected with leaving the land. In the song 'Ffarwel i Blwy Llangywer', the singer is sad because he is leaving Wales to go to England, 'with a heart like lead, to dance before the harp and play before the drum'. Was he perhaps a member of a troupe of performers – actors, singers, musicians – on the way to England to try their luck?[30]

Example 10.20: 'Ffarwel i Blwy Llangywer'

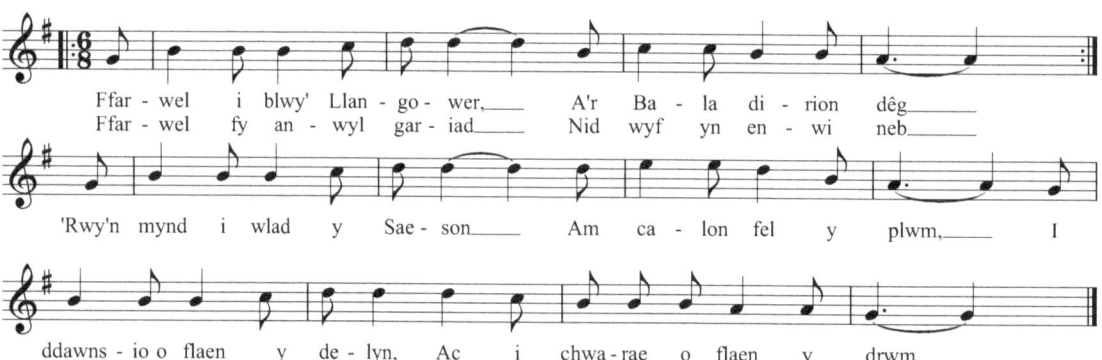

The song 'Ffarwel i Aberystwyth' notes well known features of Aberystwyth – Pen Maesglas, the Castle Tower, the Morfa – and nearby places such as Pen y Parciau, Figure Four and Llanrhystud. The air of this farewell song, sung by a young man who goes to sea because he was disappointed in love, goes back to the eighteenth century in Wales, and still earlier in England where it was known as 'Grim King of the Ghosts'.[31]

Example 10.21: 'Ffarwel i Aberystwyth'

Lloyd Williams noted the song 'Y Deryn Du Sy'n Rhodio'r Gwledydd' from the singing of John Morris, the Canorion Society member, who had heard it sung in the Ffestiniog and Trawsfynydd areas. In it, a young man asks a blackbird for matrimonial advice:[32]

Example 10.22: 'Y Deryn Du Sy'n Rhodio'r Gwledydd'

Lloyd Williams was a tenacious collector. This was certainly the case with a version of the song 'Ffarwel Gwŷr Aberffraw' (see Example 6.7), which one of the *Canorion* had tried to take down but without success. The singer himself said that he could take down ordinary notation, but was puzzled by this one. Lloyd Williams made a special journey to record it, and noted that the singer's performance was 'easy and natural':

Friends and colleagues sent him songs, sometimes with background notes. One contributor sent 'Y Glomen', a love song, after 'hearing it sung by Richard Jones, the grave digger of Garn Dolbenmaen':[33]

Example 10.23: 'Y Glomen'

Volume II, Part 1, of the *JWFSS* appeared in 1914 and, according to the editor's notes, the number of collectors continued to increase although 'some of our professionals still insist that the folk-song is cultivated at the expense of the art song', a reflection of the antagonism to traditional music still found in a number of highly regarded Welsh musicians. Later, the editor asks if the neglect by Welsh musicians of their own folkmusic is 'an evidence of the inferiority of native songs, or of their own lack of vision?'.[34] Lloyd Williams's interest in musical analysis is very apparent in this volume. In Part 2, which appeared in 1919, he noted twelve airs that he believed stemmed originally from the same melody, found in manuscripts and books or noted from singers. The examples show how the air developed in mode, melody and rhythm at different periods and in different places. 'Mwynen Merch', which he heard sung in Bangor, displays characteristics of earlier times: it is a love song in the dorian mode and the rhythmic irregularity emphasises the *cynghanedd* in the words:[35]

Example 10.24: 'Mwynen Merch'

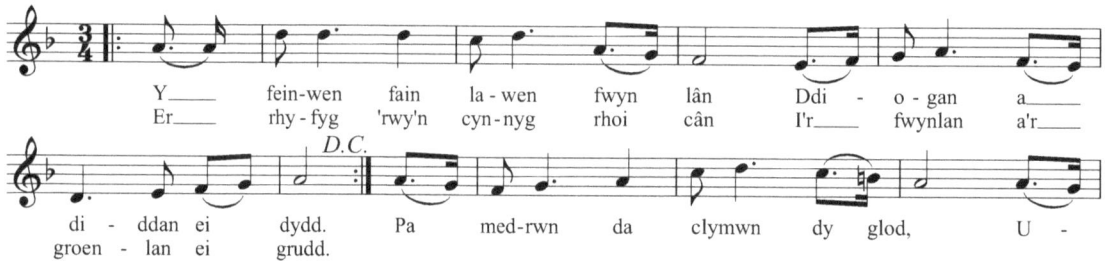

Ifor Ceri, Llewelyn Alaw, 'Philomusus', Maria Jane Williams and Ieuan Ddu all noted variants of the air, in which the lengthy, declamatory style of the earlier song gave way to a shorter and smoother ballad style. 'Y Mab Addfwyn' is a typical example:[36]

Example 10.25: 'Y Mab Addfwyn'

When John Thomas printed a variant of the air in *Cambrian Minstrel*, it was in the major, in 6/8 time, the syncopation gone and the ending shortened. It appears in the *JWFSS* as 'Mae Gennyf Fi Fwthyn a Gardd':[37]

Example 10.26: 'Mae Gennyf Fi Fwthyn a Gardd'

continued

The collecting and noting of Welsh folk-songs went on throughout the years of the First World War and the difficult years that followed. Mary Davies, who had been so much help to Lloyd Williams in collecting songs, died in 1930 and was succeeded as president of the society by Ruth Lewis, now Lady Lewis. The musician and publisher W. S. Gwynn Williams became secretary, but in spite of Lloyd Williams's advanced age (he was 80 in 1934) he remained as editor of the *JWFSS* and the issues continued to be full of interest, with collections of nursery songs, carol and ballad tunes, May carols and dances, and miscellaneous folk-songs and airs.

With the death of J. Lloyd Williams in 1945, the Folk-Song Society lost its spark. In 1951, the *JWFSS* was revived under the editorship of W. S. Gwynn Williams who, though an able musician, was a publisher and not a collector, and had other interests in addition to the society. During his years as editor, he printed songs sent in by members of the society but they were relatively few in number. W. S. Gwynn Williams's main contributions to Welsh traditional music were as the author of the useful book *Welsh National Music and Dance* (1932) and as the publisher of volumes containing folk-song collections. The most popular of the latter was *Caneuon Traddodiadol y Cymry*, comprising 124 songs taken from various issues of the *JWFSS* and reprinted by his press in two volumes.

In 1948, the Welsh Folk Museum (now the National History Museum) opened at St Fagans Castle. The outdoor museum is a collection of traditional Welsh buildings, but there is also an indoor museum housing a library with archives for the scholar interested in Welsh life and language, including the songs people sang. In its early years, the museum promoted an active campaign of field recording, especially by D. Roy Saer. The resulting collection of tape recordings of traditional singers, such as Bob Roberts, Tai'r Felin, John Thomas, Maes-y-Fedw, Ben Phillips and Bertie Stephens is an indispensable asset to scholars interested in singing styles. The museum also acquired a number of important manuscripts related to Welsh folk life, among them traditional songs collected by Ruth Lewis, J. Ffos Davies and Tal Griffith.

By 1957, the museum was tape-recording Welsh songs from traditional singers, which included humorous songs, love songs, seasonal songs, cumulative songs, Christmas carols, nursery songs, and work songs, learned from oral tradition and sung unaccompanied. Sixty of these songs have appeared in the two volumes of *Caneuon Llafar Gwlad (Songs from Oral Tradition)* (1974 and 1994), edited by D. Roy Saer and published by the museum. The first volume included notes in Welsh and English, often extensive, about the songs, and indicated a significant development in Welsh folk-song collecting. In addition, the museum in association with the Welsh Folk-Song Society published *Hen Alawon (Carolau a Cherddi)*, a book of forty-six *plygain* carols noted on Anglesey in the late nineteenth century. Two LP recordings of songs from the archives were also produced – one of 'Plygain Carols' and the other of 'Stable-Loft Songs' – both of which are currently available on one CD.[38]

The availability of Welsh songs in print and on record undoubtedly contributed to the awareness of Welsh traditional music during the 1960s and 70s. Some of the best song and ballad singers, such as Bertie Stephens, Ben Phillips and John Thomas, could be heard on Welsh radio programmes and a Welsh film of 1949, *Noson Lawen*, featured the traditional singer Bob Roberts, Tai'r Felin. It was a time when folk-songs and folk-singers were to be heard on all the media in Europe and America and, especially among young people, it sparked an interest in Welsh folk-songs. They were sung by folk groups and rock groups, trios and choirs, young and old solo singers. In this way the songs, which had to date been primarily preserved between the covers of books, were given back to the singers.

In 1963, an annual weekend course in Welsh folk-song was established with lectures, often on important topics such as 'Candlemas Singing in Arfon' by Trefor M. Owen, or 'The Tonal Limits of Welsh Folk-song' by Peter Crossley-Holland, which were later printed in the *JWFSS*. In 1977, the *Journal of the Welsh Folk-Song Society* published its last issue and was, from 1978, replaced by the annual publication *Canu Gwerin* (Folk-Song) under the editorship of D. Roy Saer. In the period since then, more than one hundred folk-songs have appeared on its pages, in addition to articles on topics related to Welsh folk-song.

'Y Gwydr Glas', printed in *Canu Gwerin*, is one of a number of songs where the lover comes to knock on his sweetheart's window. In this case, it is the girl who sings, asking that if her sweetheart comes courting this evening, he is to have a sympathetic answer, not an unkind one – tell him that she is not at home and that a young man from another parish has taken her away.[39]

Example 10.27: 'Y Gwydr Glas'

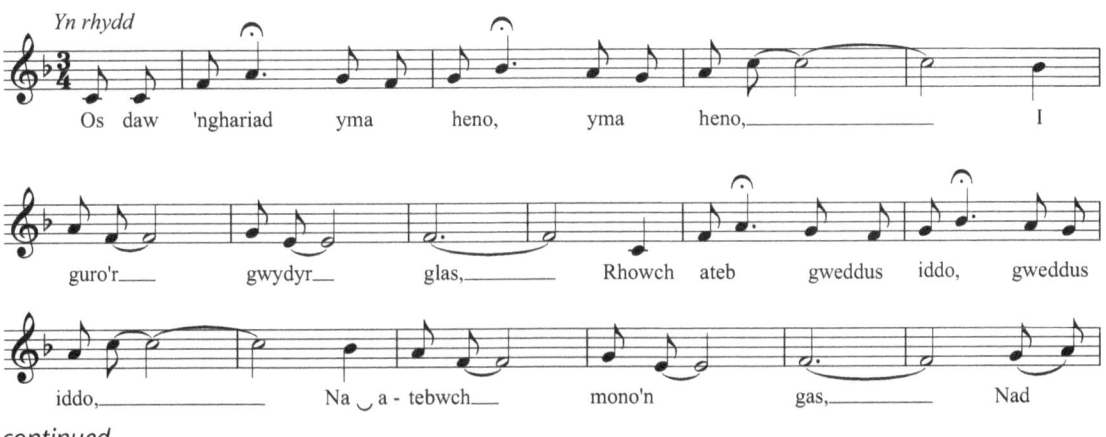

continued

'Cân y Cardi', a drinking song from south Wales, is a rare example of a jolly song reflecting an industrial background. The singer has just come down from rural Cardiganshire boasting about his abilities as a workman, and after each verse comes a chorus: 'Cered y byd i'r sawl a fynno, A finna'n llawan iach: Llym(a)id nawr ac yn y man O gwrw melyn bach!' ('Let the world go as it will, I will be merry with a little drink now and then'). The song works at another level too, the workman's mining tools serving as erotic symbols.[40]

Example 10.28: 'Cân y Cardi'

About half a century ago in mid-Wales, a labourer on the water scheme at Nant y Moch, Cardiganshire, sang 'Ar y Bryn Mae Caseg Felen' – a song of longing to be free like the chestnut mare on the hill. The supervisor heard it, and liked it so much that he began to sing it himself. A friend noted it down and later it was published in *Canu Gwerin*.[41]

Example 10.29: 'Ar y Bryn Mae Caseg Felen'

The singer of 'Mi Fuais yn Medi'r Cynhaea' was greatly dissatisfied with his work. He used to be a reaper and followed the plough until late in the day. He also did the threshing some mornings – and he didn't like any part of the job! The song was collected by Ruth Lewis in south-west Wales in 1913. Unfortunately, only one verse was noted.[42]

Example 10.30: 'Mi Fuais yn Medi'r Cynhaea'

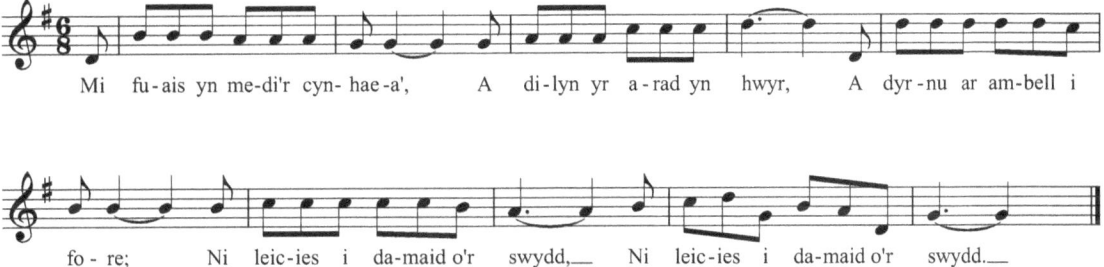

The museum at St Fagans collected traditional songs, music and tales from all over Wales. 'I Ysgafnhau ein Gwaith', an industrial worker's song from north-east Wales, came from one of their collections and was noted by a man who had heard his grandmother sing it – according to the chorus words, they sang this song from time to time to lighten their work.[43]

Example 10.31: 'I Ysgafnhau ein Gwaith'

continued

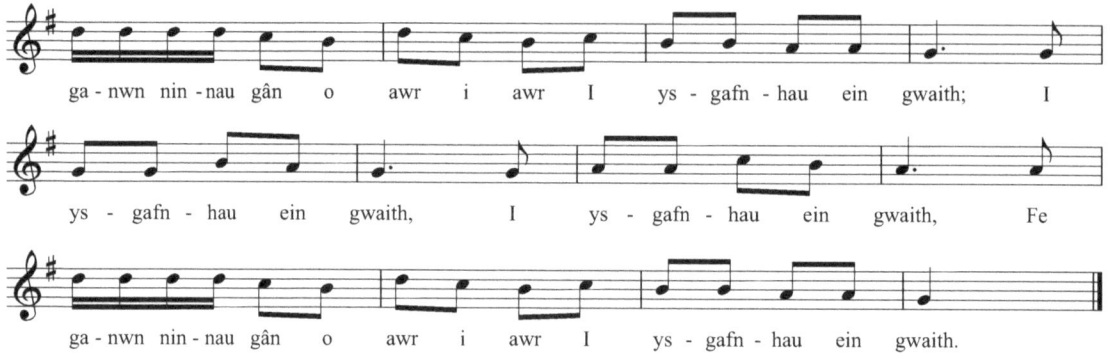

The Welsh shanty 'Fe Hwyliwyd Llestr Egwan' is a rare, perhaps unique, example of the type in the Welsh language. The recorder of the song, Meredydd Evans, knew from his father, who had been a seaman under sail for eighteen years, that there was a good deal of singing on board ship. However, the songs they sang were not work songs but songs in the forecastle after work, to lighten a journey that was long and at times monotonous. 'Fe Hwyliwyd Llestr Egwan' was used as a capstan shanty on Bangor to Boston slate ships.[44]

Example 10.32: 'Fe Hwyliwyd Llestr Egwan'

'Mae Gen i Swllt', collected by Tal Griffith in 1921, is one of many versions of 'I've Got Sixpence'. The relationship is in the words only, for the air itself is very Welsh in style, with its declamatory opening and narrow compass.[45]

Example 10.33: 'Mae Gen i Swllt'

One of the more remarkable survivals of traditional music into the twenty-first century is the *plygain* carol service during the Christmas season – and since the mid-twentieth century its popularity has expanded considerably. The late Canon Geraint Vaughan Jones, Rector of Mallwyd, in an area where the *plygain* continues to thrive, published two sizeable volumes of *plygain* carols, almost all in the three-voice arrangements popular with traditional *plygain* singers.[46]

In part, as a result of the revival of interest in Welsh traditional music, University College of North Wales, Bangor (now Bangor University), appointed a Research Assistant in Welsh Folk Music, Wyn Thomas, in 1979. This was the first such appoinment in Wales. By 1982, he had compiled the first bibliography of Welsh Traditional Music; the third edition of which, considerably augmented, was published in 2006.[47] In recent years, the School of Music at Bangor University has made a substantial and important contribution to the study of Welsh traditional music, through courses, weekend schools, performances, research and publications including the bilingual periodical *Welsh Music History/Hanes Cerddoriaeth Cymru*.

One of the most significant features of Welsh traditional music has always been the interaction between the scholarly and the popular approach in all its aspects, including instrumental music. *Cymdeithas Offerynnau Traddodiadol Cymru* (The Society for the Traditional Instruments of Wales) was established in 1996, but from 2004 on it became known as *Clera*. Its development has been the most exciting event in Welsh traditional music since the establishment of the Welsh Folk-Song Society. *Clera* concentrates on furthering instrumental music and organises working sessions and public performances throughout the country, appealing to both young and old performers. To celebrate *Clera*'s tenth anniversary, they presented a stunning evening performance at *Y Galeri* in

Caernarfon that included all aspects of traditional music from a dozen harps, a folk orchestra of forty members, singers, instrumentalists and Welsh dances by performers of all ages.

Cymdeithas Alawon Gwerin Cymru/The Welsh Folk-Song Society, born just over a century ago, continues the work of collecting and publishing Welsh traditional music for a contemporary audience. Wales has seen numerous developments – political, educational and social – that have influenced Welsh life over the last century. Traditional music too has undergone significant changes through the years and has shown its ability to adapt to changing popular tastes. The increase in musical literacy had resulted in more musicians who could note the songs they heard and more singers who learned songs from books rather than from other singers. Nowadays radio, television, recordings and the internet provide a wide variety of music that undoubtedly affects singing styles in folk-song as in other fields. That is the way it should be. Traditional music can only live if each generation sees in it something essential to itself. Otherwise it will only exist between the covers of books.

EPILOGUE

At the beginning of the twentieth century, according to J. Lloyd Williams, it was being said that 'all important Welsh airs were already known, and that in any case the chief interest of Folk Music was antiquarian'. Could the same thing be said today, at the beginning of the twenty-first century?

As for 'Folk Music' being of merely 'antiquatrian' interest, nothing could be further from the truth. Human nature has not noticeably changed over the last century – we continue to dance and sing, alone and in groups, and we continue to socialise against a background of music. While the *canu llofft stabal* and *noson lawen* may no longer be the informal coming-together at the end of the day that they once were, people still feel the need to relax and enjoy themselves by making music together. The repertoire of Welsh traditional music continues to evolve and grow in response to this need. Musicians, some with formal musical training and many without, continue to vary and adapt traditional Welsh tunes – often for instruments comparatively new to the genre/repertoire, such as guitar and button accordion.[48]

New songs and tunes are still being learned 'by ear', although the methods of transmission may be very different from those of the past. New generations are constantly coming into contact with traditional music by going to gigs, surfing the 'net or listening to CDs and PMP devices. However they come across it, audiences are continuing to sing and play music that is part of a tradition going back over centuries. As it always has been, and will be well into the future, Welsh traditional music is one of the most vibrant of the many threads running through the life and culture of Wales.

Notes

Chapter 1

1. C. Page, 'Instruments and instrumental music before 1300', in R. Crocker and D. Hiley (eds), *The New Oxford History of Music: The Early Middle Ages to 1300,* vol. 2 (Oxford, 1990), p. 459.
2. *Memoirs of the Right Honourable the Marquis of Clanricarde* (London, 1722), p. clxx.
3. Thomas Jones (ed.), *Brut y Tywysogion or The Chronicle of the Princes* (Cardiff, 1955), p. 167. In the original Welsh text, refer to p. 166.
4. See 'Cainc y Cathreiwr' in chapter 7, an example of an oxen song collected by Iolo Morganwg.
5. Gerald of Wales, *Journey through Wales/The Description of Wales: translated with an introduction by Lewis Thorpe* (London, 1978), pp. 242–3.
6. L. Hibberd, 'Giraldus Cambrensis on Welsh popular singing', in *Essays on Music in Honor of Archibald Thompson Davison / by his associates* (Cambridge, Mass., 1957), p. 21.
7. Ieuan Gwyllt, *Llyfr Tonau Cynulleidfaol*, second edition (Llundain, 1859), p. xiii.
8. *Y Cerddor Cymreig*, 2, 29 (Merthyr Tydfil, 1863), 37.
9. E. H. Sanders, 'Rondellus', in S. Sadie (ed.), *The New Grove Dictionary of Music and Musicians*, vol. 16 (London, 1980), pp. 170–1.
10. Ibid., p. 170.
11. Owain T. Edwards, *Matins, Lauds and Vespers for St David's Day* (Cambridge, 1990), p. 148. For a general discussion of medieval ecclesiastical music in Wales, see Sally Harper, *Music in Welsh Culture before 1650: a Study of the Principal Sources* (Aldershot, 2007).
12. John Gwynfor Jones, 'Cerdd a bonedd yng Nghymru', *Welsh Music/Cerddoriaeth Cymru*, 6, 9 (1981–2), 26–7.
13. See the facsimile edition, Henry Lewis (ed.), *Musica: B.M. Additional MS. 14905* (Cardiff, 1936). Another facsimile edition was published in 1987, edited by Wyn Thomas.
14. Hugh Owen (ed.), *Additional Letters of the Morrises of Anglesey*, I, (London, 1947–9), p. 370. See also the reference by Lewis Morris on p. 22 of the Robert ap Huw manuscript.
15. NLW MS 171E, p. 36.
16. Sally Harper, 'The Robert ap Huw manuscript and the canon of sixteenth-century Welsh harp music', in *Welsh Music History/Hanes Cerddoriaeth Cymru*, 3 (1999), 130.
17. For a recent symposium on the Robert ap Huw manuscript, see *Welsh Music History/Hanes Cerdd-oriaeth Cymru*, 3 (1999), which is devoted to various aspects of the manuscript and its author.
18. Peter Crossley-Holland, 'Secular homophonic music in Wales in the middle ages', *Music & Letters*, 23 (1942), 136.
19. Robert Wedderburn, *The Complaynt of Scotland, vyth ane Exortatione to the three Estaits, to be vigilante in the Deffens of their Public Veil,* first edn, reprinted with an introduction by A. M. Stewart (Edinburgh, 1979), pp. 49–52.
20. Charles Burney, *A General History of Music from the Earliest Ages to the Present Period, to which is prefixed a Dissertation on the Music of the Ancients*, vol. II (London, 1782), p. 487.

21 Edward Jones, *The Bardic Museum* (London, 1802).
22 Owen Jones, William Owen Pughe and Edward Williams (eds), *The Myvyrian Archaiology of Wales: collected out of ancient manuscripts* (Denbigh, 1870), pp. 1211–12
23 *Welsh Music History/Hanes Cerddoriaeth Cymru*, 3 (1999).
24 Osian Ellis, *The Story of the Harp in Wales* (Cardiff, 1991), p. 27.
25 Dafydd Jones, *Blodeu-gerdd Cymry*, third edition (Treffynnon, 1823), p. xv. First published in 1759, but running to later editions.
26 John Parry, *British Harmony* (London and Ruabon, 1781).
27 Edward Jones, *Musical and Poetical Relicks of the Welsh Bards* (London, 1784). A later, enlarged, edition was published in 1794.
28 Parry, *British Harmony*, pp. 14–15.
29 Edward Jones, *Hen Ganiadau Cymru* (London, 1820).
30 Bangor MS 2294, ff. 90–1.

Chapter 2

1 Ifor Williams, 'Cerddorion a cherddau yn Lleweni, Nadolig 1595', *BBCS* VIII (1935), 8. See also Harper, *Music in Welsh Culture*, pp. 319–26.
2 Clement Robinson, *A handefull of pleasant delites, containing sundrie new sonets and delectable histories, in divers kindes of meeter . . . by Clement Robinson, and divers others* (London, 1584).
3 Thomas Nashe, *Have with you to Saffron-walden. Or, Gabriell Harvey's hunt is up* (London, 1596).
4 Cardiff Public Libraries, Central Library, MS 3.42, p. 157.
5 Thomas Robinson, *New citharen lessons, with perfect tunings of the same . . . By Thomas Robinson, student in all the seven liberall sciences* (London, 1609).
6 'Cywydd Rhys Goch Eryri i Robert ap Meredudd', in H. Lewis, T. Roberts, I. Williams (eds), *Cywyddau Iolo Goch ac Eraill*, Argraffiad Newydd (Caerdydd, 1937), p. 302, ll. 11–29.
7 'Ymddiddan rhwng yr Wtreswr a'r Dylluan', in T. H. Parry-Williams (ed.) *Canu Rhydd Cynnar* (Caerdydd, 1932), p. 439, ll. 103–16. 'School' (line 11) refers to the teaching of the strict bardic system; 'is gywair' (line 14) is an accredited harp tuning; 'englyn' (line 14) is a type of verse (author's translation).
8 G. J. Williams and E. J. Jones, *Gramadegau'r Penceirddiaid* (Cardiff, 1934), p. 223 (author's translation).
9 NLW MS 171E, letter to Edward Jones, p. 40.
10 For an example, see Ifor Williams, *Canu Taliesin* (Caerdydd, 1960), p. 4, poem IV.
11 'Cywydd deuair: Morganwg', Iolo Morganwg's notation is taken from NLW, Iolo A. Williams MSS, uncatalogued. 'Cywydd deuair fyrion' comes from NLW 13089E, p. 253, and is reproduced by permission of Dr Meredydd Evans from his article 'Deuair Fyrion ac Alawon', *CG*, 8 (1985), 16–31.
12 D. Roy Saer (ed.), *Caneuon Llafar Gwlad (Songs from Oral Tradition)* vol. I (Cardiff, 1974), p. 19.
13 David Klausner (ed.), *Records of Early Drama: Wales* (Toronto, 2005), p. 29.
14 Prys Morgan, *The Eighteenth Century Renaissance* (Llandybïe, 1982), p. 26. The excerpt was translated from Edward Lhuyd's *Parochialia*, ii, p. 59.
15 For an excellent English-language introduction to the art and craft of cynghanedd, see Mererid Hopwood, *Singing in Chains: Listening to Welsh Verse* (Llandysul, 2004).
16 T. H. Parry-Williams (ed.) *Canu Rhydd Cynnar* (Caerdydd, 1932), pp. 396–9.
17 *Bardic Museum* (London, 1802).
18 John Playford, *The English Dancing Master; or, plaine and easie Rules for the dancing of Country Dances, with the tune to each Dance. Published by J. Playford* (London, 1651).
19 See *JWFSS*, I/2 (1910), 107. Note that the tune has been misbarred in this example. For a more detailed discussion of wren-hunting, see chapter 5.
20 See T. H. Parry-Williams (ed.), *Llawysgrif Richard Morris o Gerddi, &c [BL Add. MS 14992]* (Cardiff, 1931).

21 NLW, J. Lloyd Williams MS AH1/36. Edited in Cass Meurig, *Alawon John Thomas: a fiddler's tune book from eighteenth-century Wales* (Aberystwyth, 2004).
22 NLW MS 171E, pp. 37 and 40. Copies by William Jones, Llangadfan of the tunes and words of the May and Christmas carols as they were sung in Montgomeryshire.
23 'Hopcyn' and 'Cadrawd', *Hen Gwndidau, Carolau, a Chywyddau* (Bangor, 1910), p. 181, ll. 21–4.
24 I. Williams, 'Penityas', *BBCS* VIII (1936), 138.
25 John M. Ward, 'The Morris Tune', *Journal of the American Musicological Society* XXXIX (1986), 300.
26 Alex Urquahart; Dermot O'Connar; Hugh Edwards, *Aria di Camera* (London, c.1726).
27 NLW MS 13089E, p. 419.
28 There was probably the singing of bardic religious poetry in church, but this was naturally not choral.
29 *Canwyll y Cymry/The Welshman's Candle: sef gwaith y Parchedig Mr. Rees Prichard* (Llundain, 1646). A great many further editions were published.
30 'Awn i Fethlem': *JWFSS*, III/1 (1930), 55; 'Clychau Rhiwabon' in Phyllis Kinney and Meredydd Evans (eds) *Hen Alawon (Carolau a Cherddi), Casgliad John Owen, Dwyran* (Aberystwyth, 1993), no. 30.
31 Geraint H. Jenkins, *The Foundations of Modern Wales 1642–1780* (Oxford, 1987), p. 3.
32 Erasmus Saunders, *A View of the State of Religion in the Diocese of St David's* (London, 1721); facsimile (Cardiff, 1949), p. 33.
33 *CG*, 18 (1995), 47.
34 Hugh Owen (ed.), *Additional Letters of the Morrises of Anglesey (1735–1786)*, II, (London, 1947–9), pp. 552–3.
35 John Ward, 'Music for *A Handefull of pleasant delites*', *Journal of the American Musicological Society*, X (1957), p. 180.
36 NLW MS 1940Ai. '*Melus-seiniau Cymru*', f. 53.
37 Words: Huw Morus: *Eos Ceiriog*, Llyfr 2 (Wrecsam, 1823), p. 195; tune: Kinney and Evans, *Hen Alawon*, no. 5 (the tune has been adapted to fit the poem).

Chapter 3

1 T. H. Parry-Williams (ed.), *Llawysgrif Richard Morris o Gerddi, &c [BL Add. MS 14992]* (Cardiff, 1931).
2 Ibid., pp. 108–9.
3 '"Englynion" y Misoedd', in T. H. Parry-Williams (ed.), *Canu Rhydd Cynnar* (Caerdydd, 1932), p. 246, ll. 15–16.
4 John Playford, *The English Dancing Master* (London, 1651). See also Jeremy Barlow (ed.), *The Complete Country Dance Tunes from Playford's Dancing Master (1651–ca. 1728)* (London, 1985).
5 Thomas D'Urfey, *Wit and Mirth: or Pills to Purge Melancholy; Being a Collection of the best Merry Ballads and Songs, Old and New* (London, 1719). This is a collection of songs, some with printed music, published in 6 volumes between 1719 and 1720. See also the facsimile reproduction of the 1876 reprint published by Folklore Library Publishers, New York, in 1959.
6 *JWFSS* I/2 (1910), 115–18.
7 Margaret Dean-Smith, *Playford's English Dancing Master 1651: A Facsimile Reprint with an Introduction, Bibliography and Notes* (London, 1957), p. ix.
8 William Crotch, *Specimens of Various Styles of Music* (London, 1806–7). See examples 8.1, 8.2 and 8.3.
9 Robert ap Huw was said to have played at the court of James I; a harper named Evans played for Charles II; the Powels, father and son, were famous harpers in London and the son played at the court of George II.
10 P. Toynbee and L. Whibley (eds), *Correspondence of Thomas Gray*, vol. II (Oxford, 1935), pp. 501–2. *Odikle* [ode] refers to Gray's poem, 'The Bard'.

11 John Parry; Evan Williams, *Antient British Music* (London, 1742).
12 See J. Lloyd Williams, 'Antient British Music', *JWFSS* II/1 (1914), 15–28.
13 Words: *Blodeu-gerdd Cymry*, pp. 247–9.
14 Simon McVeigh, *Concert Life in London from Mozart to Haydn* (Cambridge, 1993), p. 84.
15 J. Lloyd Williams, *Y Tri Thelynor* (Llundain, 1945), p. 64.
16 *Relicks* (1794), p. 61.
17 John Parry, *A Collection of Welsh, English and Scotch Airs* (London, 1761).
18 John Parry, *The Welsh Harper*, vol. II (London, 1848), p. 88.
19 Air, *BH*, no. 3, p. 7; words, *JWFSS* III/1 (1930), 31–2. For a fuller discussion of the calennig festivities, see chapter 5.
20 *BH*, no. 39, p. 37.
21 Air, *BH*, no. 7, p. 12; words, T. H. Parry-Williams, *Hen Benillion* (Llandysul, 1965), rhif 215.
22 Air, *BH*, no. 8, p. 13; words, NLW MS 9168A, f. 46r.
23 For a more detailed discussion of the Plygain, see chapter 6.

Chapter 4

1 See Tecwyn Ellis, *Edward Jones 'Bardd y Brenin' 1752–1824* (Caerdydd, 1957) and Joan Rimmer, 'Edward Jones's musical and poetical relicks of the Welsh bards, 1784' *CG*, 10 (1987), 26–42.
2 *Bardic Museum*, p. xi.
3 'Hob y Deri Danno', 'Hob y Deri Dando', 'Distyll y Donn', 'Dadl Dau'.
4 *Relicks* (1825), p. 55.
5 NLW MS 171E, p. 36. Copies by William Jones, Llangadfan, of the tunes and words of the May and Christmas carols, as they were sung in Montgomeryshire.
6 Thomas Pennant, *The Journey to Snowdon*, vol. I (London, 1781), pp. 91–2.
7 For a fuller discussion of *penillion* singing, see Appendix 1: Cerdd Dant.
8 See Maldwyn: The Index to Welsh Poetry in Manuscript. This is available on-line from the National Library of Wales website at *www.llgc.org.uk*.
9 In order of popularity, these were 'Gadael Tir'; 'Y Galon Drom'; 'Anhawdd Ymadael'; 'Ymadawiad y Brenin'; 'Ffarwel Ned Puw'; 'Crimson Velvet (Cwynfan Brydain)'; 'Breuddwyd y Frenhines'; 'Bwrw Gofal Ymaith'; 'Cil y Fwyalch'; 'Malldod Dolgellau'; 'Hela'r Ysgyfarnog'; 'Glan Feddwdod Mwyn'; 'Sweet Richard'; 'Tôn y Ceiliog Du'; 'Mentra Gwen'; '(Orddigan) Hun Gwenllian'; and 'Morfa Rhuddlan'.
10 *Blodeu-gerdd Cymry*, pp. 496–500.
11 Air: *Relicks* (1794), p. 126; words: MS John Jones Llanddeiniolen 1778, NLW MS 13947B, ff. 9v–10r.
12 John Parry, 'Welsh Music – No. VII', *The Cambro-Briton*, vol. I, 1820, 415–16.
13 'Tôn y Fammaeth' is related to 'Woodycock', 'Consêt Gruffydd ap Cynan' to 'Vienna', 'Tros y Garreg' to 'The Gun' and 'Ymdaith Mwngc' to 'Monk's March'.
14 NLW MS 171E, p. 40.
15 *Relicks* (1784), p. 105.
16 Some copies of *Antient British Music*; Maurice Edwards MS, Bangor MS 2294.
17 John Thomas MS.
18 Bangor MS 2294.
19 Daniel Huws, 'Tair o Lawysgrifau Telynorion' (Three Harpers' Manuscripts) *Welsh Music/Cerddoriaeth Cymru*, 4, 9 (1975), 19.
20 *Bardic Museum*, pp. xi–xii.
21 D'Urfey, *Pills to Purge Melancholy*, vol. V, p. 306.
22 Bangor MS 2294.
23 Cardiff Public Libraries, Central Library, MS 1.40, ff. 51–7.

24 John Parry, *The Welsh Harper*, vol. I (London, 1839).
25 Brinley Richards: *The Songs of Wales: with English words by Sir Walter Scott, [et. al.]. . .; and a complete Welsh adaptation by Ceiriog Hughes; the music edited with new symphonies and arrangements by Brinley Richards* (London, 1873).

Chapter 5

1 Quoted in Trefor M. Owen, *Welsh Folk Customs* (Cardiff, 1959), pp. 27–8.
2 From the singing of two traditional *Mari Lwyd* men from Llangynwyd in the mid-1960s.
3 *CG*, 1 (1978), 28.
4 Peter Kennedy (ed.), *Folksongs of Britain and Ireland* (London, 1975), p. 172.
5 *Y Cerddor*, 1 Mehefin 1906, 62. Transcribed from the original sol-fa.
6 Owen, *Welsh Folk Customs*, p. 49.
7 *Cymanfa Urdd Gobaith Cymru 1935*, t. 5. Transcribed from the original sol-fa.
8 Orpheus MS – NLW Minor Deposit 150. For a more detailed discussion of the manuscript and its author, see chapter 9.
9 Orpheus MS, no. 40.
10 Maria Jane Williams, *Ancient National Airs of Gwent and Morganwg* (Llandovery, 1844), p. 31.
11 NLW, J. Lloyd Williams Music MS AH3/3.
12 Air: NLW Iolo A Williams MS 145, f. 10.
13 NLW, J. Lloyd Williams MS AH3/14.
14 The only other recorded appearance of the *Mari Lwyd* in north Wales was at Christmas, as part of the celebrations for the Festival of Britain 1951.
15 Much of the content of this section first appeared in Phyllis Kinney, 'Hunting the Wren', *WMH*, 6 (2004), 104–18.
16 J. Gwenogfryn Evans (ed.), *The Poetry in the Red Book of Hergest* (Llanbedrog, 1911), col. 1358, lines 39–41. This interpretation was suggested by Sir Ifor Williams in a letter to Dr Iorwerth C. Peate (then Curator of the Welsh Folk Museum), dated 9 February 1938.
17 Edward Lhuyd, *Parochialia*: 'Arverant yn swydh Benfro &c. dhwyn driw mewn elor nos ystwylh; odhiwrth gwr Ivank at i Gariad, sef day nae dri ai dygant mewn elor a ribane; ag a ganant gorolion. Ant hevyd i day ereilh lhe ni bo kariadon a bydh kwrw v. &c. A elor o'r wlad ai galwant Kwlli (sic. Kwtti) wran.' Quoted in *Welsh Folk Customs*, p. 63.
18 'Halsing y Dryw tune no. 1'; air, *Melus-geingciau*, no. 26; words, *Welsh Folk Customs*, p. 67. 'Halsing y Dryw tune no. 2'; air, *Melus-geingciau*, no. 27; words, Rhiannon Ifans, *Sêrs a rybana: astudiaeth o'r canu gwasael* (Llandysul, 1983), p. 138.
19 *Melus-geingciau*, no. 28.
20 NLW, J. Lloyd Williams MS AH3/13.
21 St Fagans: National History Museum Tape Archive no. 6508.
22 NLW, J. Lloyd Williams MS AH3/2 (edited).
23 Quoted in Owen, *Welsh Folk Customs*, p. 59.
24 *JWFSS* I/2 (1910), 107.
25 Ibid., 106. Quoted in a footnote. The article 'Hunting the Wren', by L. D. Jones ('Llew Tegid'; 1851–1928), contains interesting material.
26 Meredydd Evans and Phyllis Kinney, *Canu'r Cymru* I (Penygroes, 1984), p. 11.
27 Compare English wren-hunt songs in the *Journal of the Folk-Song Society*, V, no. 18, 75–7.
28 *JWFSS* I/2 (1910), 105.
29 See *Ancient and Modern Scottish Songs, Heroic Ballads, Etc. . . edited with a glossary by David Herd* Vol. II (Edinburgh, 1776), pp. 210–11.
30 Cardiff Public Libraries, Central Library, MS 4.308 (Cadrawd XIIF, The Folklore of South Pembrokeshire).

31 Ronald Hutton, *The Stations of the Sun* (Oxford, 1996), p. 97.
32 D. Roy Saer (ed.), *Caneuon Llafar Gwlad (Songs from Oral Tradition)*, vol. I (Cardiff, 1974), p. 29.
33 *JWFSS* III/1 (1930), 31–2.
34 David de Lloyd, *Forty Welsh Traditional Tunes* (London, 1929), p. 56.
35 Ira D. Sankey, *Sacred Songs and Solos* (London, 188?), no. 91.
36 Nansi Martin, *Caneuon Gwynionydd* (Llandysul, 1973), Nodiadau ar y Caneuon, Rhif 6 (author's translation).
37 As sung by Meredydd Evans.
38 Words: *Llawysgrif Richard Morris*, p. 6; tune adapted from *Melus-seiniau*, 'Triban Morganwg', omitting the symphonies.
39 Airs: Wassail song variant 1, 'Llanerch-y-medd', *Caneuon Llafar Gwlad* I, 19; Wassail song variant 2, 'Y Gog Lwydlas', *JWFSS* II/4 (1925), 273; Wassail song variant 3, 'Y Dôn Fechan', *JWFSS* I/4 (1912), 160; Wassail song variant 4, 'Llanerch-y-medd', *Caneuon Llafar Gwlad* I, 19; words to all variants, *Llawysgrif Richard Morris*, pp. 4–5.
40 Words, *Llawysgrif Richard Morris*, p. 8; air, *Per-seiniau*, no. 18.
41 NLW MS 9168A (a collection of Welsh-language poems and carols from the eighteenth century).
42 Adapted from *JWFSS* I/4 (1912), 175.
43 Grace Gwyneddon Davies, *Alawon Gwerin Môn/Folk-Songs from Anglesey*, (Wrexham, 1914), p. 16.
44 *Llawysgrif Richard Morris*, pp. lxxxviii–lxxxix.
45 Quoted in Meredydd Evans, 'Canu Gorchest/Contest Singing', *WMH*, 1, (1996), p. 89.
46 *ANAGM*, p. 62.
47 *JWFSS* I/2 (1910), 91.
48 Ibid., p. 90.
49 *Cymanfa Ganu Alawon Gwerin* 1937, p. 7. Transcribed from the original sol-fa.
50 Davies, *Alawon Gwerin Môn*, p. 18.
51 Trefor M. Owen, 'The Celebration of Candlemas in Wales', *Folklore*, 84, (1973), 238–51.
52 NLW MS 821, A Survey of the County of Caernarvonshire by William Williams, (1806), ff. 447v–8v.
53 Air, *JWFSS* III/4 (1941), 191; words, *Sêrs a Rybana*, p. 212.
54 *JWFSS* III/1 (1930), 26–7.
55 John Thomas MS, f. 91v.
56 *BH* 1781, p. 37.
57 *Per-seiniau*, no. 22.
58 *JWFSS* III/1 (1930), 69.
59 W. S. Gwynn Williams, *Welsh National Music and Dance* (London, 1932), p. 115.
60 W. Roberts, *Crefydd yr Oesau Tywyll* (Caerfyrddin, 1852), p. 95 (author's translation).
61 *JWFSS* III/1 (1930), 72.
62 Air, NLW 13089; words, *Llên Cymru* III (1954), 48–50.
63 Goronwy P. Owen (ed.), *Atgofion John Evans y Bala* (Caernarfon, 1997), p. 125 (author's translation).
64 Quoted in R. W. Jones, *Bywyd cymdeithasol Cymru yn y ddeunawfed ganrif* (Llundain, 1931), p. 115 (author's translation).

Chapter 6

1 Ben Bowen Thomas, *The Old Order: based on the Diary of Elizabeth Baker (Dolgelley, 1778–1786)* (Cardiff, 1945), pp. 34–5.
2 Quoted in 'Carolau Plygain/Plygain Carols', a booklet by D. Roy Saer to accompany the LP record of carols from the sound archives of St Fagans: National History Museum.

3   NLW Facsimile 7, Myra Evans songbook, no. 2.
4   Phyllis Kinney and Meredydd Evans, *Canu'r Cymry* II (Penygroes, 1987), p. 10.
5   Dafydd Jones, *Blodeu-gerdd Cymry* (1759).
6   NLW MS 171E, p. 35.
7   Ibid.
8   *Folk Life*, 7 (1969), 41–2.
9   Phyllis Kinney and Meredydd Evans (eds), *Hen Alawon (Carolau a Cherddi), Casgliad John Owen, Dwyran* (Aberystwyth, 1993), no. 11. Transcribed from the original sol-fa.
10 Kinney and Evans, *Hen Alawon*, no. 16. Transcribed from the original sol-fa.
11 *JWFSS* I/2 (1910), 75–6.
12 Kinney & Evans, *Hen Alawon*, no 34. Transcribed from the original sol-fa.
13 Kinney & Evans, *Canu'r Cymry* II, p. 17.
14 *CG*, 6 (1983), 56. Edited and transcribed from the original sol-fa.
15 Meredydd Evans, 'Canu Cymru yn yr unfed ganrif ar Bymtheg', *Cof Cenedl* XIII, p. 65.
16 Claude M. Simpson, *The British Broadside Ballad and its Music* (New Brunswick, 1966), p. 564.
17 This information is taken from an analysis of ballad tunes carried out by the author.
18 Mrs Herbert Lewis, 'Y Blotyn Du', *Folk-Songs Collected in Flintshire and the Vale of Clwyd* (Cardiff and Wrexham, 1914), p. xii.
19 T. H. Parry-Williams, *Hen Benillion* (Llandysul, 1940).
20 Air, *Relicks* (1794), p. 135 (titled 'Cerdd yr hên-ŵr o'r Coed').
21 *JWFSS* I/1 (1909), 58.
22 Air, Bangor MS 2254, f. 242; words, *Bardd a Byrddau*, p. 251.
23 *Melus-seiniau*, no. 55.
24 Air, 'Duw Gadwo'r Brenin', Lady Herbert Lewis, *Second Collection of Welsh Folk-Songs* (Wrexham and Cardiff, 1934), pp. 8–9.
25 Evans and Kinney, *Canu'r Cymry* I, p. 46.
26 *JWFSS* I/1 (1909), 35.
27 Lewis, *Folk-Songs collected in Flintshire and the Vale of Clwyd*, pp. 34–5.
28 Quoted in R. D. Griffith, 'Hanes dechrau canu cynulleidfaol yng Nghymru', *Y Cerddor* II, Mawrth (March) 1932, 72 (author's translation).
29 Dafydd Glyn Jones, 'The Interludes', in Branwen Jarvis (ed.), *A Guide to Welsh Literature* vol. IV, c.1700–1800, (Cardiff, 2000), p. 212.
30 Thomas, *The Old Order*, p. 51.
31 John Thomas MS, f. 58v.
32 *Jeils: anterliwt* by Ellis Roberts [18th cent.] Bangor MSS 1733.
33 *Relicks* (1794), p. 176.
34 Air, John Thomas MS, f. 72r.; words, Jonathan Hughes, *Y Dywysoges Genefetha*, 1744 (NLW Cwrtmawr 120A MS 120 and NLW Cwrtmawr 161B MS 161).
35 Air, John Thomas MS, f. 76v.; words from the Anterliwt *Ffrewyll y Methodistiaid*.
36 For a fuller explanation of the derivation of the name, see John M. Ward, 'Apropos the British broadside ballad and its Music', *Journal of the American Musicological Society*, XX (1967), 60–1.
37 Air, John Thomas MS, f. 74v; words, Anon, *Y Brenin Llur* (NLW Cwrtmawr 212 c.1700–1750).

Chapter 7

1   On Iolo Morganwg and his activities, see G. J. Williams, *Iolo Morganwg: Y Gyfrol Gyntaf* (Cardiff, 1956); Prys Morgan, *Iolo Morganwg* (Cardiff, 1975); Ceri W. Lewis, *Iolo Morganwg* (Caernarfon, 1995); Geraint H. Jenkins (ed.), *A Rattleskull Genius: the Many Faces of Iolo Morganwg* (Cardiff, 2005); Geraint H. Jenkins, Ffion Mair Jones and David Ceri Jones (eds), *The Correspondence of Iolo Morganwg* (3 vols, Cardiff, 2007); Mary-Ann Constantine, *The Truth Against the World:*

Notes

Iolo Morganwg and Romantic Forgery (Cardiff, 2007); Cathryn A. Charnell-White, *Bardic Circles: National, Regional and Personal Identity in the Bardic Vision of Iolo Morganwg* (Cardiff, 2007); Marion Löffler, *The Literary and Historical Legacy of Iolo Morganwg 1826-1926* (Cardiff, 2007); Ffion Mair Jones, *'The Bard is a Very Singular Character': Iolo Morganwg, Marginalia and Print Culture* (Cardiff, 2010).

2. NLW MS 13118B, p. 136. See also Williams, *Iolo Morganwg* pp. 60–1, 49.
3. The dorian/re mode is the scale on D with no accidentals.
4. NLW MS 13146A, p. 436.
5. Ibid., p. 435 ('Casgledydd Penn Ffordd').
6. NLW MS 21421E, 131/4, Barddoniaeth Gymraeg &c. A copy in the hand of Edward Williams ('Iolo Morganwg') of a melody described as 'Hen erddigan Morganwg' ('mesur byrr') and of verses attributed to Thomas Llywelyn o Regoes 'allan o Lyfr George Tudur Y Salmwr', beginning 'Gwyn fyd y ber fwyalchen'. The air has been edited.
7. Air, NLW, Iolo A. Williams MS 145, f. 15 (edited); words, *JWFSS* III/1 (1930), 62. NLW, Iolo A. Williams MS 145 consists of an envelope of loose sheets of music manuscripts, written in the hand of Iolo Morganwg.
8. NLW, Iolo A. Williams MS 145, f. 10 (edited).
9. NLW, Iolo A. Williams uncatalogued MSS, 1802.
10. NLW, Iolo A. Williams MS 145, f. 7 (rhythm revised).
11. Air, NLW, Iolo A. Williams MS 145, f. 10 (edited); words, NLW MS 13146A, p. 202. See also Tegwyn Jones, *Tribannau Morgannwg* (Llandysul, 1976), p. 110, no. 297.
12. NLW MS 13174A, f. 91. Iolo's directions as to 'air' or 'symphony' are not always clear. For a somewhat different interpretation of the same air, see Daniel Huws, 'Caneuon llafar gwlad ac Iolo a'i fath', *Darlith Goffa Amy Parry-Williams*, 1993 (Aberystwyth, Cymdeithas Alawon Gwerin Cymru).
13. Air, NLW, Iolo A. Williams MS 145, f. 12 (edited); words, *CG* 8 (1985), 27.
14. G. H. Jenkins, Ff. M. Jones and D. C. Jones (eds) *The Correspondence of Iolo Morganwg* vol. II, pp. 175–6. Letter No. 497 from William Owen Pughe to Iolo Morganwg, dated 3 June 179[9]; source NLW 21282E, no. 334.
15. NLW, Iolo A. Williams MS 145, f. 1.
16. Example 5.12: 'Philomusus's' Collection for the 1824 Welshpool Eisteddfod in NLW MS 1932D and Example 5.13: Bangor MS 2255 (E. Ylltyr Williams), f. 74.
17. Brinley Richards, *The Songs of Wales* (London, 1873), pp. 13–15.
18. On Ifor Ceri and his collections, see Daniel Huws, 'Melus-seiniau Cymru', *CG*, 8 (1985), 32–50, and 9 (1986), 47–57.
19. Daniel Huws, 'Melus-Seiniau Cymru: Atodiadau', *CG*, 9 (1986), 47.
20. NLW, J. Lloyd Williams MS AH1/34 (formerly MS 36). '*Melus-geingciau Deheubarth Cymru*', a collection made by John Jenkins ('Ifor Ceri') c.1815.
21. *Melus-geingciau*, no. 13.
22. NLW MS 1940Ai. '*Melus-seiniau Cymru*', a collection made by John Jenkins ('Ifor Ceri') in 1817–1825.
23. NLW MS 1940Aii. '*Per-seiniau Cymru*', a collection made by John Jenkins ('Ifor Ceri') in 1824–1825.
24. *Melus-geingciau*, no. 4. The repetition of words in square brackets does not appear in the manuscript.
25. *Melus-geingciau*, no. 7.
26. *Melus-geingciau*, no. 2.
27. The aeolian/la mode is the scale on A with no accidentals.
28. Huws, 'Melus-Seiniau Cymru: Atodiadau', 49.
29. Ibid., p. 48.
30. 'Dewch i'r Frwydr', 'Y Frwynen Las', 'Mentra Gwen', 'Triban'.
31. *Melus-seiniau*, f. 51. Words, John Howell, *Blodau Dyfed* (Caerfyrddin, 1824), p. 170.
32. *Melus-seiniau*, f. 53.

33 *Melus-seiniau*, f. 55.
34 *Melus-seiniau*, f. 179.
35 Air, *Melus-seiniau*, f. 79; words, *Blodeu-gerdd Cymry*, pp. 139–43.
36 Air, *Melus-seiniau*, f. 83; words, *Blodeu-gerdd Cymry*, pp. 181–2.
37 *Melus-seiniau*, f. 92.
38 *Melus-seiniau*, f. 94.
39 *Melus-seiniau*, f. 95v. The words in brackets have been added from the *Ilatai* song 'Adar Mân y Mynydd', JWFSS II/4 (1925), 219.
40 *Melus-seiniau*, f. 102.
41 *Blwch o Bleser i ieuentid Cymru* (Caerfyrddin, 1822). Many later editions of this popular work were produced.
42 *Melus-seiniau*, f. 130.
43 *New song book/Llyfr canu newydd* vol. II, (Cardiff, 1930), no. 32, pp. 12–13. Words, Evan Evans ('Ieuan Glan Geirionydd'; 1795–1855). See also Tom Parry, *Baledi'r Ddeunawfed Ganrif* (Caerdydd, 1935), pp. 150–2.
44 As sung by W. O. Jones ('Eos y Gogledd'; 1868–1928). A copy of the song is in the author's possession.
45 *Melus-seiniau*, f. 135.
46 *Melus-seiniau*, f. 141.
47 Air, 'Nutmeg a Ginger Deheubarth', *Melus-seiniau*, f. 148v; words, NLW MS 19B, f. 129. The Poetical Works of John Jenkins ('Ioan Siencyn'), of Cardigan.
48 *Melus-seiniau*, f. 182v.
49 St Fagans: National History Museum Tape archive, no. 1459/100.
50 *Melus-seiniau*, f. 142.
51 *Per-seiniau*, no. 1.
52 JWFSS II/4 (1925), 260–1. The air is from *Per-seiniau*, no. 63.
53 *Per-seiniau*, no. 95.
54 JWFSS III/3 (1937), 117.
55 It may be pertinent to say that none of the Welsh versions of 'Cwympiad y Dail' has any connection with 'The Fall of the Leafe' in the *Fitzwilliam Virginal Book*.

Chapter 8

1 William Bingley, *Sixty of the most admired Welsh airs* (London, 1803).
2 Crotch, *Specimens of Various Styles of Music. . .* (London, 1806–7).
3 All three versions appear in *Specimens*, no. 151.
4 Ibid., no. 156.
5 George Thomson, *A Selected Collection of Original Welsh Airs* (London and Edinburgh, 1809, 1811, 1817). Vol. I, 1809; vol. II, 1811; vol. III, 1817. For a recent discussion of the Haydn settings, see Marjorie E. Rycroft, 'Haydn's Welsh Songs: George Thomson's Musical and Literary Sources', in *WMH*, 7 (2007).
6 Thomson, *Original Welsh Airs*, p. 1 (footnote).
7 *Relicks* (1784), p. 71.
8 Thomson, *Original Welsh Airs*, vol. I, no. 9.
9 Ibid., p. 1.
10 Thomson, *Original Welsh Airs*, vol. I, no. 23.
11 Richard Roberts, *Cambrian Harmony* (Dublin and Caernarfon, 1829).
12 John Parry, *A selection of Welsh melodies* (London, 1809).
13 John Parry, *A collection of Welch Airs* (London, 1810).
14 John Parry, *National Melodies* (London, 1810).

15 John Parry, *The Welsh Harper*, 2 vols (London, 1839–48).
16 Both collections survive, unpublished, among the papers of Ifor Ceri in NLW MS 1932D.
17 Quoted in Hywel Teifi Edwards, *Yr Eisteddfod* (Llandysul, 1976), p. 44.
18 Maria Jane Williams, *Ancient National Airs of Gwent and Morganwg* (Llandovery, 1844).
19 Ibid., p. 20.
20 Ibid., p. 40.
21 Ibid., p. 42.
22 Ibid., p. 9.
23 Ibid., p. 53.
24 Ibid., p. 12.
25 Ibid., p. 63.
26 Ibid., p. 64.
27 John Thomas, *Y Caniedydd Cymreig; The Cambrian Minstrel* (Merthyr Tudfil, 1845). On John Thomas and his collection, see Meredydd Evans, 'Ieuan Ddu: eisteddfodwr a cherddor', *Taliesin*, 58 (1986), 61–71; Daniel Huws, 'Ieuan Ddu and Welsh traditional music', *Merthyr Historian*, 12 (2001), 63–68; and Nigel Ruddock, 'Tair cân Ieuan Ddu a'u geiriau gwreiddiol', *CG*, 28/2005, 42–51; 'Y Caniedydd Cymreig – rhagor am Ieuan Ddu a'i ganeuon', *CG*, 30/2007, 63–78; 'Y Caniedydd Cymreig – rhagor am Ieuan Ddu a'i ganeuon', *CG*, 31/2008, 95–120.
28 Ibid., p. iii.
29 Ibid., p. 14. The Welsh and English verses deal with totally different themes.
30 Ibid., p. 28.
31 Ibid., p. 140.
32 Ibid., the music is on p. 47, while the one verse is on p. 48.
33 Quoted in R. D. Griffith, *Hanes Canu Cynulleidfaol Cymru* (Caerdydd, 1948), p. 33.
34 *Cyfaill mewn Llogell* (Caerfyrddin, 1797).
35 John Ellis, *Mawl yr Arglwydd* (Trefriw, 1816).
36 John Roberts, *Caniadau y Cyssegr* (Dinbych, 1839) (author's translation).
37 Ibid., p. 44.
38 Gareth Williams, *Valleys of song: music and society in Wales, 1840–1914* (Cardiff, 1998), p. 23.
39 Richard Mills, *Caniadau Seion* (Llanidloes, 1840) (author's translation).
40 Ibid., p. 106. The example has been adapted from Richard Mills's original four-part setting.
41 Ibid., p. 14.
42 Gwyneth Tyson Roberts, *The language of the Blue Books: the perfect instrument of Empire* (Cardiff, 1998), p. 209.
43 Quoted in Ifor ap Gwilym, *Y Traddodiad Cerddorol yng Nghymru* (Abertawe, 1978), p. 27.
44 *Bye-Gones*, 16 May 1894, p. 344.
45 NLW, J. Lloyd Williams Music MS AH1/39.
46 Ibid., f. 118.

Chapter 9

1 Orpheus MS - NLW Minor Deposit 150. A collection of songs submitted to the Llangollen Eisteddfod of 1858. On this collection, and identification of its compiler as James James (Iago ap Iago), see Meredydd Evans, 'Who was "Orpheus"? of the 1858 Llangollen Eisteddfod', *WMH*, 5 (Cardiff, 2002), 65–71.
2 Orpheus MS, no. 3.
3 Ibid., no. 6. In 'Notes and Observations' at the beginning of the manuscript, this traditional verse is given (note 6).
4 Ibid., no. 10.
5 P. Kinney, 'An Irish-Welsh tune Family', *WMH*, 1 (Cardiff, 1996), pp. 114–19.

6   Orpheus MS, no. 36. In 'Notes and Observations' at the beginning of the manuscript, this traditional verse is given (note 36).
7   NLW MS 331D. A collection of Welsh airs, made by Llewelyn Alaw.
8   NLW MS 329B, no. 98. A collection, including Welsh airs, made by Llewelyn Alaw in 1855.
9   NLW MS 331D, p. 35. Air, 'Charity Mistress'; words, Huw Morys.
10   Ibid., no. 8.
11   NLW MS 337D, no. 12. A collection of Welsh airs, dances and popular tunes, from the repertoire of Llewelyn Alaw.
12   NLW MS 330A, no. 12. A collection, containing Welsh airs, made by Llewelyn Alaw.
13   NLW MS 337D, no. 36.
14   NLW MS 336D, p. 156. A collection of popular melodies arranged for the harp by Llewelyn Alaw in 1857.
15   NLW MS 329D, no. 70.
16   NLW MS 336D, p. ~~125~~/98.
17   NLW MS 337D, p. 64.
18   NLW MS 329B, no. 96.
19   NLW MS 336D, p. 191.
20   Ibid., p. 205.
21   Brinley Richards, *The Songs of Wales* (London, 1873).
22   *Melus-seiniau*, no. 53.
23   Richards, *The Songs of Wales*, p. 10.
24   John Owen, *Gems of Welsh Melody* (London and Wrexham, 1873).
25   Ibid., p. 108.
26   Ibid., p. 116.
27   Ibid., p. 114.
28   Ibid., p. 166.
29   Ibid., p. 168.
30   Nicholas Bennett, *Alawon Fy Ngwlad – The Lays of My Land* (Newtown, 1896).
31   *JWFSS* II/4 (1925), 256–7.
32   Bennett, *Alawon fy Ngwlad*, vol. I, p. 40.
33   Ibid., p. 25.
34   NLW, J. Lloyd Williams MS AH2/10.

Chapter 10

1   D. Roy Saer, *Cymdeithas Alawon Gwerin Cymru: Canrif Gron/The Welsh Folk-Song Society: A Whole Century 1908–1983* (Cardiff, 2006), p. 44.
2   J. Lloyd Williams, 'The Welsh Folk-Song Society', *Y Cerddor*, Medi (September) 1931, 314.
3   *JWFSS* II/4 (1909), 219.
4   *JWFSS* V/1 (1957), 18.
5   *JWFSS* I/1 (1909), 11.
6   J. Lloyd Williams, 'Welsh National Melodies and Folk-song', *The Transactions of the Honourable Society of Cymmrodorion* 1907–8 (1909), pp. 1–46.
7   *JWFSS* I/1 (1909), 17.
8   Ibid., 19.
9   Ibid., 20.
10   Ibid., 22.
11   *JWFSS* II/2 (1919), 127.
12   Mrs Herbert Lewis, *Folk-Songs Collected in Flintshire and the Vale of Clwyd* (Cardiff and Wrexham, 1914), p. viii.

13 Ibid., p. 19.
14 *JWFSS* III/1 (1930), 70.
15 *JWFSS* I/2 (1910), 77.
16 *JWFSS* I/4 (1912), 166.
17 *JWFSS* I/3 (1911), 146.
18 NLW, J. Lloyd Williams MS AH3/2. The air is a variant of the 'Bellisle March'. Transcribed from the original sol-fa.
19 Kinney and Evans, *Canu'r Cymry* I, p. 12.
20 *JWFSS* I/4 (1912), 206.
21 Grace Gwyneddon Davies, *Alawon Gwerin Môn/Folk-Songs from Anglesey* (Wrexham, 1914), p. 8.
22 Ibid., p. 6.
23 Ibid., pp.14–15.
24 Grace Gwyneddon Davies, *Chwech o Alawon Gwerin Cymreig/Six Welsh Folk Songs* (Cardiff, 1933), p. 10.
25 *JWFSS* I/1 (1909), 41.
26 *JWFSS* II/3 (1922), 190.
27 *JWFSS* III/1 (1930), 75.
28 Ibid., 76.
29 *JWFSS* III/3 (1937), 125–6.
30 *JWFSS* I/1 (1909), 43.
31 *JWFSS* I/4 (1912), 188.
32 *JWFSS* I/3 (1911), 123.
33 *JWFSS* I/2 (1910), 70.
34 *JWFSS* II/1 (1914), 13.
35 *JWFSS* II/2 (1919), 88.
36 *JWFSS* II/2 (1919), 96. The tune is taken from the Llewelyn Alaw MS, NLW 329.
37 *JWFSS* II/2 (1919), 99.
38 *Caneuon Plygain a Llofft Stabal/Traditional Plygain Carols and stable-loft songs from Wales*, Sain SCD 2389.
39 *CG*, 3 (1980), 29.
40 *CG*, 1 (1978), 33 (author's translation).
41 *CG*, 2 (1979), 51.
42 *CG*, 8 (1985), 56.
43 Ibid., 58.
44 *CG*, 2 (1979), 46.
45 *CG*, 3 (1980), 28.
46 Geraint Vaughan-Jones, *Hen Garolau Plygain* (Talybont, 1987) and *Mwy o Garolau Plygain* (Talybont, 1990).
47 Wyn Thomas, *Cerddoriaeth Draddodiadol yng Nghymru: Llyfryddiaeth/Traditional Music in Wales: A bibliography,* 3rd edn (Llanrwst, 2006).
48 See C. Meurig, 'Composing Traditional Music', in S. Harper and W. Thomas (eds), *Cynheiliaid y Gân/Bearers of Song: Ysgrifau i Anrhydeddu/Essays in Honour of Phyllis Kinney and Meredydd Evans*, (Caerdydd/Cardiff, 2007), pp. 240–50.

Appendix 1
Cerdd Dant

Canu penillion, canu gyda'r tannau or *cerdd dant*, the older term by which it is now generally known, is a form of singing to string accompaniment that has long existed alongside folk-song and in parallel with it. It is a distinct tradition, but one which has, in the past, had much influence on folk-song, especially in north Wales. *Canu penillion* has been popular as a form of social entertainment in Wales for centuries, and seems to be unique to the country. The terms refer to the ancient Welsh tradition of singing or declaiming verses of different poetic metres to a given air on the harp, or sometimes the crwth, a matter touched on in chapter 3 and elsewhere in passing. The harper begins with an air agreed upon beforehand with the singer, who enters later, striking into the air at a point that will allow him to finish with the instrument at certain sections of the air and at its conclusion. The singer does not follow the *cainc* (harp melody) but declaims in *cyfalaw* (in counterpoint to it). Rests of more than one beat are not allowed and the principle of *sill am dant* (one syllable for each note) forbids slurs.

In 1913, *Llyfr Cerdd Dannau* (A Book of *Cerdd Dant*) was published, in which the author Robert Griffith stated that the old Welsh way of singing to the harp had almost disappeared, and that before it completely died out he had decided to collect from the old declaimers *(datgeiniaid)* examples of the various counterpoint settings that they used. A number of these are printed in his book, and a general analysis of them shows that the melodic compass of the settings is narrow, stepwise motion is prominent, there is considerable repetition of notes, and very little rhythmic variation. 'Codiad yr Ehedydd' is a typical example:[1]

Example A.1: 'Codiad yr Ehedydd'

continued

Appendix 1

The origins of *canu penillion* have been a vexed question. Antiquaries of the eighteenth century, inspired by Lewis Morris, observing the unique qualities of this mode of singing and the fact that the remotest parts of Wales were where it most flourished, began to associate it with the druids. This became the popular view – that the tradition, if not druidical, was at least ancient. A revisionist case was made by Osian Ellis in 1973. On the strength of musical specimens of *penillion* singing prepared for publication by Evan Williams, co-editor of *Antient British Music*, in 1745 (see chapter 3), Osian Ellis proposed that *penillion* singing was partly modelled on airs from English ballad operas. Early musical evidence is scarce, but the literary evidence, it must be said, points firmly to there being a continuity, however tenuous, between the singing (or chanting) of strict-metre bardic poetry and *canu penillion* such as is published by Robert Griffith and such as is found in the few examples from the nineteenth century and in the collection of Telynor Mawddwy, *Y Tant Aur* (1911).[2] The twentieth century saw a remarkable development of the art. In contrast to Example A.1, the counterpoint became more melodic and with a much wider compass, as illustrated in 'Mantell Siani':[3]

Appendix 1

Example A.2: 'Mantell Siani'

243

Canu penillion, while still a purely oral tradition of extempore singing, in which the competitions might stretch over many hours, was a very popular feature of the eisteddfods in the early and mid-nineteenth century. By the time of the establishment of the National Eisteddfod, although a number of practitioners survived, the tradition had waned. *Cerdd dant* began to take a new direction and the National Eisteddfod had an important role in the new developments. Since 1893, *cerdd dant* has been a regular part of the National Eisteddfod competitions. After the First World War, part-singing in *cerdd dant* became popular and, in addition to solos, there were settings for duets, quartets, groups up to sixteen in number, and choirs (female, male and mixed). Over the years, the style of the settings has gradually been modernised, and airs composed more recently include many aspects of musical development such as complicated harmonies, dynamics and a degree of rhythmic sophistication, without however changing the basic elements of the craft, as in the adventurous setting by Bethan Bryn of a prose passage in Dylan Thomas's 'Under Milk Wood' (translated into Welsh by T. James Jones):[4]

Example A.3: Extract from 'Dan y Wenallt', a setting by Bethan Bryn of Dylan Thomas's 'Under Milk Wood'

Reproduced by permission of Bethan Bryn

Appendix 1

By the twentieth century, expressiveness had become an important element in the performing of *cerdd dant*. Previously, the emphasis was on a clear delivery of the words, which remains essential, but expression has been added to the art. In part, this is because many of those who currently compose *cerdd dant* settings have studied music in college and are familiar with the use of chordal patterns to add expressiveness. Devices, such as a temporary change of mode from major to minor and the use of dynamics or discords to emphasise sorrow or anger, also bring variety into the vocal parts.

Prose settings of *cerdd dant* began to appear by the 1930s. Although not part of the old *cerdd dant* tradition, they were suitable for declaiming parts of the Welsh Bible and secular prose from *The Mabinogion*, an early medieval collection of Welsh legends. More recently, Bethan Bryn's *cerdd dant* setting of 'Dan y Wenallt' has been performed – the first performance taking place at the Aberystwyth Arts Centre in 2009.

Cymdeithas Cerdd Dant Cymru (The Cerdd Dant Society of Wales), established in November 1934, was in part inspired by the work of the Welsh Folk-Song Society, but mainly by the need to bring order and direction to the ancient craft of *cerdd dant*. In 1936, the Society published the first issue of *Allwedd y Tannau*, a new journal devoted to *cerdd dant*, in which the aims of the Society are clearly stated: 'meithrin y gelfyddyd o ganu gyda'r tannau, noddi'r delyn, diogelu hanes y gelfyddyd a'r datgeiniaid, a phopeth sy'n ymwneud â'r gelfyddyd' ('to nurture the art of singing with the strings, to sponsor the harp, research the history of the art and the *datgeiniaid*, and everything to do with it').[5] This lively society has been essential to the promotion of the art. Few homes possess a harp, and the Society is able to lend harps to budding young musicians in addition to organising classes for those who wish to learn the art of setting poetry and prose to harp airs. In addition to playing an important part in the National Eisteddfod each year, the Society has held an annual *cerdd dant* festival since 1947, in north Wales and south Wales alternately. It is a competitive festival and has resulted in the composition of many new *cerdd dant* airs, some with bolder and more imaginative settings. It seems safe to say that this ancient art will continue to play an important part in the traditional music and cultural life of Wales.

Notes

1. Robert Griffith, *Llyfr Cerdd Dannau* (Caernarfon, 1913), pp. 460–1.
2. The debate about the origins of canu penillion can be followed in the following publications: Osian Ellis, 'Welsh music: history and fancy', *Transactions of the Honourable Society of Cymmrodorion*, 1972–3 (1974), 73–94; Osian Ellis, *Hanes y Delyn yng Nghymru/The Story of the Harp in Wales* (Cardiff, 1980); Meredydd Evans and Phyllis Kinney, 'Hanes a datblygiad canu gyda'r tannau', in A. Ll. Davies (gol.), *Gwŷr Wrth Gerdd* (Rhuthin, 1981), 72–91 (reprinted with an English translation in *WMH*, 6 (2004), 155–192; Meredydd Evans, review article in *Allwedd y Tannau*, 50 (1991), 48–56; reply by Osian Ellis in *Allwedd y Tannau*, 51 (1992), 48–63; Daniel Huws, 'Gwisgo merched â mesurau', in Harper, S. and Thomas, W. (eds), *Cynheiliaid y Gân/Bearers of Song: Ysgrifau i Anrhydeddu/Essays in Honour of Phyllis Kinney and Meredydd Evans* (Caerdydd/Cardiff, 2007), pp. 145–88.
3. Aled Lloyd Davies, *Cerdd Dant: Llawlyfr Gosod* (Caernarfon, 1983), pp. 58–9.
4. Extract from 'Dan y Wenallt', a *cerdd dant* setting of Dylan Thomas's 'Under Milk Wood' by Bethan Bryn. 'Nawr mae'r dreflan yn gyfnos i gyd. Pob cobl ac asyn, llwyn gwsberis a stryd yn farced agored i'r gwyll. Mae'r gwyll a'r llwch seremonïol a chwsg adar ac eira hidl cynta'r hwyrhau yn lluwcho drwy gyfnos brwd y rhandir hwn o serch. Llaregyb yw prif-ddinas y cyfnos.' ('Now the town is dusk. Each cobble, donkey, goose and gooseberry street is a thoroughfare of dusk; and dusk and ceremonial dust, and night's first darkening snow, and the sleep of birds, drift under and through the live dusk of this place of love. Llaregyb is the capital of dusk.'). From Dylan Thomas, *Under Milk Wood – A play for Voices* (London, 1954; reprint, 1959), p. 76. Translated into Welsh by T. James Jones.
5. Author's translation.

Appendix 2
Printed Music Collections referred to (including facsimiles) by date of publication

D'Urfey, Thomas, *Wit and Mirth: or Pills to Purge Melancholy* (London, 1719).
Urquahart, Alex, Dermot O'Connar and Hugh Edwards, *Aria di Camera* (London, c.1726).
Parry, John (Ruabon) and Evan Williams, *Antient British Music* (London, 1742).
Parry, John (Ruabon), *A Collection of Welsh, English and Scotch Airs* (London, 1752 or 1761).
Parry, John (Ruabon), *British Harmony* (London and Ruabon, 1781).
Jones, Edward, *Musical and Poetical Relicks of the Welsh Bards* (London, 1784). A later enlarged edition was published in 1794.
Jones, Edward, *The Bardic Museum* (London, 1802).
Bingley, William, *Sixty of the most admired Welsh airs* (London, 1803).
Crotch, William, *Specimens of Various Styles of Music* (London, 1806–7).
Parry, John ('Bardd Alaw'), *A selection of Welsh melodies* (London, 1809).
Thomson, George, *A Selected Collection of Original Welsh Airs*, vols I, II and III (London and Edinburgh, 1809, 1811 and 1817).
Parry, John ('Bardd Alaw'), *A collection of Welch Airs* (London, 1810).
Parry, John ('Bardd Alaw'), *National Melodies* (London, 1810).
Ellis, John, *Mawl yr Arglwydd* (Trefriw, 1816).
Jones, Edward, *Hen Ganiadau Cymru* (London, 1820).
Roberts, Richard, *Cambrian Harmony* (Dublin and Caernarfon, 1829).
Parry, John ('Bardd Alaw'), *The Welsh Harper*, vols I and II (London, 1839 and 1848).
Roberts, John (Henllan), *Caniadau y Cyssegr* (Dinbych, 1839).
Mills, Richard, *Caniadau Seion* (Llanidloes, 1840).
Williams, Maria Jane, *Ancient National Airs of Gwent and Morganwg* (Llandovery, 1844).
Williams, Maria Jane, *Ancient National Airs of Gwent and Morganwg: A facsimile of the 1844 edition with introduction and notes on the songs by Daniel Huws* (Cymdeithas Alawon Gwerin Cymru/The Welsh Folk-Song Society, 1988).

Thomas, John, *Y Caniedydd Cymreig – The Cambrian Minstrel* (Merthyr Tudfil, 1845).
Jones, J. D. (ed.), *Caniadau Bethlehem* (Wrexham, 1857).
Roberts, John ('Ieuan Gwyllt'), *Llyfr Tonau Cynulleidfaol* (Llundain, ail argraffiad [second edition], 1859).
Owen, John ('Owain Alaw'), *Gems of Welsh Melody* (London and Wrexham, 1873).
Richards, Brinley, *The Songs of Wales* (London, 1873).
Bennett, Nicholas, *Alawon Fy Ngwlad – The Lays of My Land* (Newtown, 1896).
Davies, Grace Gwyneddon: *Alawon Gwerin Môn/Folk-Songs from Anglesey* (Wrexham, 1914).
Lewis, Mrs Herbert, *Folk-Songs Collected in Flintshire and the Vale of Clwyd* (Cardiff and Wrexham, 1914).
Davies, Mary, *Welsh Folk-Songs/Caneuon Gwerin Cymru* (Cardiff, 1919).
Davies, Grace Gwyneddon, *Ail Gasgliad o Alawon Gwerin Môn/Second Collection of Folk-Songs from Anglesey* (Wrexham, 1924).
Williams, W. S. Gwynn, *Old Welsh Folk Songs* (London, 1927).
Lloyd, David de, *Forty Welsh Traditional Tunes* (London, 1929).
University Council of Music, *New song book/Llyfr canu newydd*, vols I–III (Cardiff, 1929–32).
Williams, W. S. Gwynn, *Welsh National Music and Dance* (London, 1932).
Davies, Grace Gwyneddon, *Chwech o Alawon Gwerin Cymreig/Six Welsh Folk Songs* (Cardiff, 1933).
Lewis, Lady Herbert, *Second Collection of Welsh Folk-Songs* (Wrexham and Cardiff, 1934).
Lewis, Henry (ed.), *Musica: B.M. Additional MS. 14905* (Cardiff, 1936). Another facsimile edition, edited by Wyn Thomas, was published in 1987.
Williams, Grace, *Six Welsh Oxen Songs* (London, 1937).
Davies, Mary, *Second Collection of Welsh Folk-Songs/Ail Gasgliad o Ganeuon Gwerin Cymru* (Wrexham, 1946).
Parry, Enid, *Wyth Gân Werin/Eight Folk Songs* (Wrexham, 1949).
Lloyd, David de, *Alawon o Gymru/Songs from Wales* (Cardiff, 1952).
Pwyllgor Cerdd Esgobaeth Bangor (The Bangor Diocesan Music Committee), Llyfr Carolau Bangor, 2 vols (Bangor, 1952–3).
Pwyllgor Undeb Noddwyr Alawon Cymru (Committee of the Patrons of Welsh Airs), *Carolau Hen a Newydd* (Tonypandy, 1954).
Dean-Smith, Margaret, *Playford's English Dancing Master 1651: A Facsimile Reprint* (London, 1957).
Williams, W. S. Gwynn, *Un ar Ddeg o Ganeuon Gwerin Cymru/Eleven Welsh Folk Songs* (Llangollen, 1958).
Williams, W. S. Gwynn, *Caneuon Traddodiadol y Cymry/Traditional Songs of the Welsh*, 2 vols (Llangollen, 1961–3).
Martin, Nansi, *Caneuon Gwynionydd* (Llandysul, 1973).
Saer, D. Roy (ed.), *Caneuon Llafar Gwlad (Songs from Oral Tradition)*, vol. 1 (Cardiff, 1974).

Kinney, Phyllis and Meredydd Evans (eds), *Caneuon Gwerin i Blant* (Llandysul, 1981).
Evans, Meredydd and Phyllis Kinney, *Canu'r Cymru*, 2 vols (Penygroes, 1984–7).
Barlow, Jeremy (ed.), *The Complete Country Dance Tunes from Playford's Dancing Master (1651–c.1728)* (London, 1985).
Vaughan-Jones, Geraint, *Hen Garolau Plygain* (Talybont, 1987).
Vaughan-Jones, Geraint, *Mwy o Garolau Plygain* (Talybont, 1990).
Kinney, Phyllis and Meredydd Evans (eds), *Hen Alawon (Carolau a Cherddi), Casgliad John Owen, Dwyran* (Aberystwyth, 1993).
Saer, D. Roy (ed.), *Caneuon Llafar Gwlad (Songs from Oral Tradition)*, vol. 2 (Cardiff, 1994).
Meurig, Cass, *Alawon John Thomas: a fiddler's tune book from eighteenth-century Wales* (Aberystwyth, 2004).

Bibliography

For a comprehensive and up-to-date bibliography of Welsh traditional music, see Wyn Thomas's *Cerddoriaeth Draddodiadol yng Nghymru: Llyfryddiaeth/Traditional Music in Wales: A Bibliography*, 3rd edn (Llanrwst, 2006).

Printed Music Collections (including facsimiles), alphabetically by collector/editor

Barlow, Jeremy (ed.), *The Complete Country Dance Tunes from Playford's Dancing Master (1651–c.1728)* (London, 1985).

Bennett, Nicholas, *Alawon Fy Ngwlad – The Lays of My Land. Collected by Nicholas Bennett, of Glanyrafon. Arranged for the harp or pianoforte by D. Emlyn Evans* (Newtown, 1896).

Bingley, William: *Sixty of the most admired Welsh airs collected principally during the excursion into Wales by the Revd. W. Bingley . . . The basses and the variations arranged for pianoforte, by William Russell, Junior, organist of the Foundling Hospital, London* (London, 1803).

Crotch, William, *Specimens of Various Styles of Music, Referred To In a Course of Lectures Read At Oxford and London and Adapted to Keyed Instruments* (London, 1806–7).

Davies, Grace Gwyneddon, *Alawon Gwerin Môn/Folk-Songs from Anglesey* (Wrexham, 1914).

Davies, Grace Gwyneddon, *Ail Gasgliad o Alawon Gwerin Môn/Second Collection of Folk-Songs from Anglesey* (Wrexham, 1924).

Davies, Grace Gwyneddon, *Chwech o Alawon Gwerin Cymreig/Six Welsh Folk Songs* (Cardiff, 1933).

Davies, Mary, *Welsh Folk-Songs/Caneuon Gwerin Cymru: Trefnwyd gan W. Hubert Davies* (Cardiff, 1919).

Davies, Mary, *Second Collection of Welsh Folk-Songs/Ail Gasgliad o Ganeuon Gwerin Cymru: wedi'u trefnu gan W. Hubert Davies* (Wrexham, 1946).

Dean-Smith, Margaret, *Playford's English Dancing Master 1651: A Facsimile Reprint with an Introduction, Bibliography and Notes* (London, 1957).

D'Urfey, Thomas: *Wit and Mirth: or Pills to Purge Melancholy; Being a Collection of the best Merry Ballads and Songs, Old and New* (London, 1719).

Ellis, John, *Mawl yr Arglwydd, sef casgliad o rannau o'r Psalmau a'r hymnau, yn attebion lleisiol, a rhai pennillion: at yr hyn y chwanegwyd cyfarwyddiadau i osod allan y synwyr wrth ddarllain ...: hefyd hyfforddiadau i ddysgu'r gelfyddyd ardderchog o gerddoriaeth* (Trefriw, 1816).

Evans, Meredydd and Phyllis Kinney, *Canu'r Cymru*, 2 vols (Penygroes, 1984–7).

Jones, Edward, *Musical and Poetical Relicks of the Welsh Bards: preserved by tradition, and authentic manuscripts, from remote antiquity; never before published. To the bardic tunes are added variations for harp, harpsichord, violin, or flute . . . likewise a history of the bards from the earliest period to the present time, and an account of their music, poetry and musical instruments with a delineation of the latter* (London, 1784). A later enlarged edition was published in 1794.

Jones, Edward, *The Bardic Museum of primitive British Literature; and other admirable rarities; forming the second volume of the musical, poetical and historical relicks of the Welsh Bards and Druids: Drawn from authentic documents of remote antiquity (with great pains now rescued from oblivion) and never before published. Containing the ancient war-tunes of the bards. To these national melodies are added new basses; with variations, for the harp or harpsichord; violin or flute* (London, 1802).

Jones, Edward, *Hen Ganiadau Cymru: Cambro-British melodies, or the national songs and airs of Wales; . . . These airs are harmonized with new basses; to which are added variations for the harp, or the piano-forte, violin or flute* (London, 1820).

Jones, J. D. (ed.), *Caniadau Bethlehem* (Wrexham, 1857).

Kinney, Phyllis and Meredydd Evans (eds), *Caneuon Gwerin i Blant* (Llandysul, 1981).

Kinney, Phyllis and Meredydd Evans (eds), *Hen Alawon (Carolau a Cherddi), Casgliad John Owen, Dwyran* (Aberystwyth, 1993).

Lewis, Henry (ed.), *Musica: B.M. Additional MS. 14905* (Cardiff, 1936). Another facsimile edition, edited by Wyn Thomas, was published in 1987.

Lewis, Mrs Herbert, *Folk-Songs Collected in Flintshire and the Vale of Clwyd* (Cardiff and Wrexham, 1914).

Lewis, Lady Herbert, *Second Collection of Welsh Folk-Songs* (Wrexham and Cardiff, 1934).

Lloyd, David de, *Forty Welsh Traditional Tunes: Issued by the Cardiganshire Antiquarian Society and arranged for two voices and piano by David de Lloyd* (London, 1929).

Lloyd, David de, *Alawon o Gymru/Songs from Wales* (Cardiff, 1952).

Martin, Nansi, *Caneuon Gwynionydd* (Llandysul, 1973).

Meurig, Cass, *Alawon John Thomas: a fiddler's tune book from eighteenth-century Wales* (Aberystwyth, 2004).

Mills, Richard, *Caniadau Seion, sef Casgliad o Donau Addas I'w Canu yn yr Addoliad Dwyfol; yn cynwys Nifer lluosog o Erddyganau gwreiddiol, yn Nghyda Phigion o'r Goreuon o Waith yr Awduron Goraf, Hen a Diweddar, wedi eu trefnu Yn Unol a*

Phriod-ddull Cerddoriaeth Eglwysig Cymreig gan Richard Mills, Llanidloes (Llanidloes, 1840).

Owen, John ('Owain Alaw'), *Gems of Welsh Melody: a selection of popular Welsh songs . . . specimens of pennillion singing . . . with symphonies and accompaniments for piano or harp arr. by John Owen (Owain Alaw)* (London and Wrexham, 1873).

Parry, Enid, *Wyth Gân Werin/Eight Folk Songs* (Wrexham, 1949).

Parry, John (Ruabon) and Evan Williams, *Antient British Music; or, a collection of tunes, never before published, which are retained by the Cambro-Britons, (more particularly in North-Wales) and supposed by the learned to be the remains of the Music of the Ancient Druids, so much famed in Roman history. Part I containing twenty-four numbered (numbered but unnamed) Airs, set for the harp, harpsichord, violin, and all within the compass of the german flute; and figured for a thorough bass. To which is prefixed, an historical account of the rise and progress of music among the ancient Britons* (London, 1742).

Parry, John (Ruabon), *A Collection of Welsh, English and Scotch Airs, With New Variations, Also Four New Lessons For The Harp Or Harpsichord. Composed by John Parry, To Which Are Added Twelve Airs For The Guittar* (London, 1752 or 1761).

Parry, John (Ruabon), *British Harmony: Being a collection of ancient Welsh airs, the traditional remains of those originally sung by the bards of Wales, carefully compiled and now first published with some additional variations* (London and Ruabon, 1781)

Parry, John ('Bardd Alaw'): *A selection of Welsh melodies; with appropriate English words/adapted for the voice, with symphonies & accompaniments for the piano forte or harp by John Parry* (London, 1809).

Parry, John ('Bardd Alaw') *A collection of Welch Airs, arranged on a plan never before attempted, forming six divertimentos, each consisting of three of the most favourite airs, expressly adapted for the pianoforte. With accompaniments for a flute and violincello. Also notes and observations on the mode of playing and singing the Welch Music. Dedicated to Sir W. W. Wynn, Bart* (London, 1810).

Parry, John ('Bardd Alaw'), *National Melodies, consisting of the most admired airs of England, Ireland, Scotland and Wales. Arranged as Rondos, or with variations for the Pianoforte . . . by the most eminent authors* (London, 1810).

Parry, John ('Bardd Alaw'), *The Welsh Harper: being an extensive collection of Welsh music, including most of the contents of the three volumes published by the late Edward Jones . . . also several airs from the publications of the late Mr. Parry of Ruabon . . . with many others never before published, by John Parry, London*, vol. I (London, 1839).

Parry, John ('Bardd Alaw'), *The Welsh Harper, containing two hundred Welsh airs: Chiefly selected from manuscript collections: Interspersed with numerous interesting historical notes and observations on the Music of Wales, arranged for the harp or pianoforte*, vol. II (London, 1848).

Pwyllgor Cerdd Esgobaeth Bangor (The Bangor Diocesan Music Committee), *Llyfr Carolau Bangor*, 2 vols (Bangor, 1952–3).

Pwyllgor Undeb Noddwyr Alawon Cymru (Committee of the Patrons of Welsh Airs), *Carolau Hen a Newydd* (Tonypandy, 1954).

Richards, Brinley, *The Songs of Wales: with English words by Sir Walter Scott, [et. al.] . . .; and a complete Welsh adaptation by Ceiriog Hughes; the music edited with new symphonies and arrangements by Brinley Richards* (London, 1873).

Roberts, John (Henllan), *Caniadau y Cyssegr, neu gasgliad o donau hen a diweddar, gan mwyaf o gyfansoddiad Cymreig. Wedi'u cynganeddu i bedwar o leisiau* (Dinbych, 1839).

Roberts, John ('Ieuan Gwyllt'): *Llyfr Tonau Cynulleidfaol* (Llundain, ail argraffiad [second edition], 1859).

Roberts, Richard, *Cambrian Harmony, being a collection of Welch airs never before published. Arranged as they were originally performed by the ancient Britons, adapted for the harp and piano forte* (Dublin and Caernarfon, 1829).

Saer, D. Roy (ed.), *Caneuon Llafar Gwlad (Songs from Oral Tradition)*, vol. 1, (Cardiff, 1974).

Saer, D. Roy (ed.), *Caneuon Llafar Gwlad (Songs from Oral Tradition)*, vol. 2 (Cardiff, 1994).

Thomas, John, *Y Caniedydd Cymreig; The Cambrian Minstrel; Being a collection of the melodies of Cambria, with original words in English and Welsh; together with several original airs by John Thomas* (Merthyr Tudfil, 1845).

Thomson, George, *A Selected Collection of Original Welsh Airs, adapted for the voice, united to characteristic English poetry never before published, with introductory and concluding symphonies and accompaniments for the piano forte or harp, violin, and violoncello*, vols I, II and III (London and Edinburgh, 1809, 1811 and 1817).

University Council of Music, *New song book/Llyfr canu newydd*, vols I–III (Cardiff, 1929–32).

Urquahart, Alex, Dermot O'Connar and Hugh Edwards, *ARIA DI CAMERA: Being a choice Collection of Scotsh, Irish, and Welsh air's for the violin and german flute, by the following masters: Mr. Alex Urquahart of Edinburgh, Mr. Dermot O'Connar of Limerick, Mr. Hugh Edwards of Carmarthen* (London, c.1726).

Vaughan-Jones, Geraint, *Hen Garolau Plygain* (Talybont, 1987).

Vaughan-Jones, Geraint, *Mwy o Garolau Plygain* (Talybont, 1990).

Williams, Grace, *Six Welsh Oxen Songs* (London, 1937).

Williams, Maria Jane, *Ancient National Airs of Gwent and Morganwg; Being a collection of original Welsh melodies, hitherto unpublished, which obtained the prize at the Eisteddfod held in celebration of the fifth anniversary of the Abergavenny Cymreigyddion, October 1838. To which are added the words usually sung thereto. Collected and arranged for the harp or piano forte* (Llandovery, 1844).

Williams, Maria Jane, *Ancient National Airs of Gwent and Morganwg: A facsimile of the 1844 edition with introduction and notes on the songs by Daniel Huws* (Cymdeithas Alawon Gwerin Cymru/The Welsh Folk-Song Society, 1988).

Williams, W. S. Gwynn, *Old Welsh Folk Songs: selected, edited and arranged with pianoforte accompaniment* (London, 1927).

Williams, W. S. Gwynn: *Welsh National Music and Dance* (London, 1932).

Williams, W. S. Gwynn: *Un ar Ddeg o Ganeuon Gwerin Cymru/Eleven Welsh Folk Songs* (Llangollen, 1958).

Williams, W. S. Gwynn: *Caneuon Traddodiadol y Cymry/Traditional Songs of the Welsh*, 2 vols (Llangollen, 1961–3).

Manuscripts

Bangor MSS

Bangor MS 2255 (E. Ylltyr Williams)
Bangor MS 2294 (Maurice/Morris Edwards MS).

Cardiff Public Libraries MSS

Central Library, MS 1.40 (Pocketbook of Edward Jones).
Central Library, MS 3.42 (The Book of Phillip Powell).
Central Library, MS 4.308 (Cadrawd XIIF, The Folklore of South Pembrokeshire).

National Library of Wales MSS

NLW MS 19B, f. 129. The Poetical Works of John Jenkins ('Ioan Siencyn'), of Cardigan.
NLW, MS 171E (Miscellanea of Edward Jones).
NLW MS 329B (A collection, including Welsh airs, made by 'Llewelyn Alaw' in 1855).
NLW MS 330A (A collection, containing Welsh airs, made by 'Llewelyn Alaw').
NLW MS 331D (A collection of Welsh airs, made by 'Llewelyn Alaw').
NLW MS 336D (A collection of popular melodies arranged for the harp by 'Llewelyn Alaw' in 1857).
NLW MS 337D (A collection of Welsh airs, dances and popular tunes, from the repertoire of 'Llewelyn Alaw').
NLW MS 821 (A Survey of the County of Caernarvonshire by William Williams, 1806).
NLW MS 1932D (Philomusus's Collection for the 1824 Welshpool Eisteddfod).
NLW, J. Lloyd Williams MS AH1/34 (formerly MS 36). 'Melus-geingciau Deheubarth Cymru' (c.1815).
NLW MS 1940Ai. 'Melus-seiniau Cymru' (1817–1825).
NLW MS 1940Aii. 'Per-seiniau Cymru' (1824–1825).
NLW MS 9168A. (A collection of Welsh-language poems and carols from the eighteenth century).
NLW MS 13089E (Miscellanea).
NLW MS 13118B (A composite volume containing transcripts of prose and verse items in the hand of Iolo Morganwg).
NLW MS 13146A (A volume containing miscellaneous prose and music items in the hand of Iolo Morganwg).

NLW MS 13174A (A journal, written in pencil by 'Iolo Morganwg' and containing an account of his journey from London to Merthyr in 1802).
NLW Facsimile 7, Myra Evans songbook.
NLW Minor Deposit 150. A collection of songs submitted to the Llangollen Eisteddfod of 1858 (Orpheus MS).
NLW, Iolo A. Williams MS 145 (This file consists of an envelope of loose sheets of music manuscripts, written in the hand of Iolo Morganwg).
NLW, Iolo A. Williams MSS, uncatalogued.
NLW, J. Lloyd Williams MS AH1/36 (John Thomas MS).
NLW, J. Lloyd Williams Music MS AH1/39.
NLW, J. Lloyd Williams MS AH2/10.
NLW, J. Lloyd Williams MS AH3/2.
NLW, J. Lloyd Williams Music MS AH3/3.
NLW, J. Lloyd Williams MS AH3/13.
NLW, J Lloyd Williams MS AH3/14.

Printed Verse Collections (in Welsh)

Blwch o Bleser i ieuenctid Cymru (Caerfyrddin, 1822). Many later editions of this popular work were produced.
Davies, Robert, *Diliau Barddas,. . . gan Robert Davies, o Nantglyn* (Dinbych, 1827).
Edwards, Thomas, *Gwaith Thomas Edwards (Twm o'r Nant)*, 2nd edn (Liverpool, 1874).
'Hopcyn' (L. J. Hopkin-James) and 'Cadrawd (T. C. Evans), *Hen Gwndidau, Carolau, a Chywyddau* (Bangor, 1910).
Howell, John, *Blodau Dyfed;. . . o gynnulliad John Howell (Ioan ab Hywel)* (Caerfyrddin, 1824).
Hughes, Jonathan, *Bardd a byrddau:. . . o waith Jonathan Hughes* (Amwythig, 1778)
Jones, Dafydd, *Blodeu-gerdd Cymry*, y Trydydd Argraphiad (Treffynnon, 1823). First published in 1759, but running to later editions.
Jones, Emrys (gol.), *Odlau Moliant: carolau a cherddi Sion Ebrill o Ardudwy, 1745–1836* (Caernarfon, 1987).
Jones, Ffion Mair (gol.), *Y Rhyfel Cartrefol, Huw Morus* (Bangor, 2008).
Jones, Hefin, *Dic Dywyll y Baledwr* (Llanrwst, 1995)
Jones, Hugh, *Dewisol ganiadau yr oes hon:. . . a gasglwyd ac a gyfansoddwyd gan Hugh Jones* (Amwythig, 1759).
Jones, Tegwyn, *Abel Jones, Bardd Crwst* (Capel Garmon, 1989).
Jones, Tegwyn, *Baledi Ywain Meirion* (Y Bala, 1980).
Millward, E. G. (gol.), *Cerddi Jac Glan-y-Gors* (Llandybïe, 2003).
Morris, Edward, *Barddoniaeth Edward Morris, Perthi Llwydion, wedi eu casglu gan Hugh Hughes* (Lerpwl, 1902).
Morus, Huw, *Eos Ceiriog: sef casgliad o bêr ganiadau Huw Morus; o gynulliad W. D.* [i.e. Walter Davies], Llyfr 1 a 2 (Wrecsam, 1820 a 1823).

Parry-Williams, T. H., *Canu Rhydd Cynnar* (Caerdydd, 1932).
Parry-Williams, T. H., *Hen Benillion* (Llandysul, 1940).
Parry-Williams, T. H. (gol.), *Llawysgrif Richard Morris o Gerddi, &c [BL Add. MS 14992]* (Caerdydd, 1931).
Prichard, Rees, *Canwyll y Cymry/The Welshman's Candle* (Llundain, 1646). A great many further editions were published.
Telyn Seion: wedi eu dethol gan [Richard?] Parry a Dorkins (Caernarfon, c.1860).
Thomas, David, *Corph y Gaingc, neu ddifyrwch teuluaidd ... a gasglwyd gan Ddafydd Thomas ... neu Dafydd Ddu o Eryri* (Caernarfon, 1834).

Books and articles

ap Gwilym, Ifor, *Y Traddodiad Cerddorol yng Nghymru* (Abertawe, 1978).
Burney, Charles, *A General History of Music from the Earliest Ages to the Present Period, to which is prefixed a Dissertation on the Music of the Ancients*, vol. II (London, 1782).
Crossley-Holland, Peter, 'Secular homophonic music in Wales in the middle ages', *Music & Letters*, 23 (1942), 135–62.
Crossley-Holland, Peter, *The Composers of the Robert ap Huw Manuscript: The Evidence for Identity, Dating and Locality* (Bangor, 1998).
Davies, Aled Lloyd, *Cerdd Dant: Llawlyfr Gosod* (Caernarfon, 1983).
Davies, Aled Lloyd, *Canrif o Gân: Datblygiad cerdd dant ym Meirionnydd, Dinbych a Fflint, 1881–1998* (Llanrwst, 1999).
Davies, Aled Lloyd, *Canrif o Gân: Datblygiad cerdd dant ym Môn, Arfon, Llŷn ac Eifionydd, Maldwyn, y de-orllewin, Cwm Tawe a'r de-ddwyrain* (Llanrwst, 2000).
Davies, J. H., *A Bibliography of Welsh Ballads printed in the 18th Century* (London, 1911).
Davies, John, *A History of Wales* (London, 1993).
Edwards, Hywel Teifi, *Yr Eisteddfod* (Llandysul, 1976).
Edwards, Owain T., *Matins, Lauds and Vespers for St David's Day* (Cambridge, 1990).
Ellis, Osian, 'Welsh music: history and fancy', *Transactions of the Honourable Society of Cymmrodorion*, 1972–3 (1974), 73–94
Ellis, Osian, *Hanes y Delyn yng Nghymru/The Story of the Harp in Wales* (Cardiff, 1980).
Ellis, Osian, *The Story of the Harp in Wales* (Cardiff, 1991).
Ellis, Osian, *Allwedd y Tannau*, 51 (1992), 48–63.
Ellis, Tecwyn, *Edward Jones 'Bardd y Brenin' 1752–1824* (Caerdydd, 1957).
Ellis, Tecwyn, 'Welsh music in Georgian times', *Welsh Music/Cerddoriaeth Cymru*, 3, 10 (1971), 11–19.
Evans, Meredydd, 'Cipdrem ar rai o alawon Richard Morris', *Welsh Music/Cerddoriaeth Cymru*, 4, 6 (1974), 20–6.
Evans, Meredydd, 'Hel achau', *Welsh Music/Cerddoriaeth Cymru*, 4, 10 (1975), 34–50.

Evans, Meredydd, 'Contest Singing', *Welsh Music History/Hanes Cerddoriaeth Cymru*, 1 (1996), 84–91.

Evans, Meredydd, 'Canu Cymru yn yr unfed ganrif ar Bymtheg', *Cof Cenedl* XIII, (1998), pp. 33–68.

Evans, Meredydd, 'Who was "Orpheus"? of the 1858 Llangollen Eisteddfod', *Welsh Music History/Hanes Cerddoriaeth Cymru*, 5 (2002), 65–71.

Evans, Meredydd, *Hela'r Hen Ganeuon* (Talybont, 2009).

Gerald of Wales, *Journey through Wales/The Description of Wales: translated with an introduction by Lewis Thorpe* (London, 1978).

Griffith, R. D., *Hanes Canu Cynulleidfaol Cymru* (Caerdydd, 1948).

Griffith, Robert, *Llyfr Cerdd Dannau* (Caernarfon, 1913).

Gwilym, Arfon, *Cerddoriaeth y Cymry: cyflwyniad i draddodiad cerddorol Cymru* (Talybont, 2007).

Harper, Sally, 'The Robert ap Huw manuscript and the canon of sixteenth-century Welsh harp music', in *Welsh Music History/Hanes Cerddoriaeth Cymru*, 3 (1999), 130.

Harper, Sally, *Music in Welsh Culture before 1650: a Study of the Principal Sources* (Aldershot, 2007).

Harper, S. and W. Thomas (eds), *Cynheiliaid y Gân/Bearers of Song: Ysgrifau i Anrhydeddu/Essays in Honour of Phyllis Kinney and Meredydd Evans* (Caerdydd/Cardiff, 2007).

Hopkins, Delyth M., 'Eisteddfod Genedlaethol Caerdydd, 1883', *Welsh Music/Cerddoriaeth Cymru*, 5, 8 (1978), 25–31.

Huws, Daniel, 'Tair o Lawysgrifau Telynorion' (Three Harpers' Manuscripts) *Welsh Music/Cerddoriaeth Cymru*, 4, 9 (1975), 24–32.

Huws, Daniel: 'Melus-seiniau Cymru', *CG*, 8 (1985), 32–50, and 9 (1986), 47–57.

Huws, Daniel, 'Caneuon llafar gwlad ac Iolo a'i fath', *Darlith Goffa Amy Parry-Williams*, 1993 (Aberystwyth, Cymdeithas Alawon Gwerin Cymru).

Ifans, Rhiannon, *Sêrs a rybana: astudiaeth o'r canu gwasael* (Llandysul, 1983).

Jarman, Eldra and A. O. H. Jarman, *The Welsh Gypsies* (Cardiff, 1991 and 1998).

Jarman, A. O. H. and G. Rees Hughes (eds), *A Guide to Welsh Literature*, vol. 1 (Swansea, 1976).

Jarvis, Branwen (ed.), *A Guide to Welsh Literature*, vol. IV, c.1700–1800 (Cardiff, 2000).

Jenkins, Geraint H., *The Foundations of Modern Wales 1642–1780* (Oxford, 1987).

Jenkins, Geraint H. (ed.), *A Rattleskull Genius: the Many Faces of Iolo Morganwg* (Cardiff, 2005).

Jones, John Gwynfor, 'Cerdd a bonedd yng Nghymru: Rhai argraffiadau (rhan 1)', *Welsh Music/Cerddoriaeth Cymru*, 6, 9 (1981–2), 22-33.

Jones, John Gwynfor, 'Cerdd a bonedd yng Nghymru, 1540–1640: Rhai argraffiadau pellach', *Welsh Music/Cerddoriaeth Cymru*, 7, 1 (1982), 25–40.

Jones, John Gwynfor, 'Cerdd a bonedd yng Nghymru ca. 1540-1640: Rhai argraffiadau terfynol', *Welsh Music/Cerddoriaeth Cymru*, 7, 3 (1983), 30–47.

Jones, Tegwyn, *Llyfryddiaeth Baledi'r Bedwaredd Ganrif ar Bymtheg. A bibliography of nineteenth-century ballads in the National Library of Wales.*

Jones, Tegwyn, *Hen Faledi Ffair* (Talybont, 1971).

Jones, Tegwyn, *Tribannau Morgannwg* (Llandysul, 1976).

Jones, T. Gwynn, H. Idris Bell and W. S. Gwynn Williams, *Hen Faledi Cymreig/Old Welsh Ballads* (Llangollen, 1946).

Keen, Elen Wyn, 'The musician's art and scientific prowess: J. Lloyd Williams and his Journal', *Welsh Music History/Hanes Cerddoriaeth Cymru*, 5 (2002), 150–61.

Kennedy, Peter (ed.), *Folksongs of Britain and Ireland* (London, 1975).

Kinney, Phyllis, 'An Irish-Welsh tune Family', *Welsh Music History/Hanes Cerddoriaeth Cymru*, 1 (1996), 114–19.

Kinney, Phyllis, 'Hunting the wren', *Welsh Music History/Hanes Cerddoriaeth Cymru*, 6 (2004), 104–11.

Kinney, Phyllis and Meredydd Evans, 'The history and development of canu gyda'r tannau', *Welsh Music History/Hanes Cerddoriaeth Cymru*, 6 (2004), 174–92.

Ley, Rachel, 'Lady Llanover and the triple harp', *Welsh Music History/Hanes Cerddoriaeth Cymru*, 1 (1996), 136–43.

Löffler, Marion, *The Literary and Historical Legacy of Iolo Morganwg 1826–1926* (Cardiff, 2007).

McVeigh, Simon, *Concert Life in London from Mozart to Haydn* (Cambridge, 1993).

Meurig, Cass, 'The fiddler in eighteenth-century Wales/Y ffidler yng Nghymru'r ddeunawfed ganrif', *Welsh Music History/Hanes Cerddoriaeth Cymru*, 5 (2002), 22–58.

Miles, Bethan Ellis, 'Swyddogaeth a Chelfyddyd y Crythor' (Traethawd M.A., Prifysgol Cymru, Aberystwyth/M.A. thesis, University of Wales, Aberystwyth, 1983).

Morgan, Prys, *Iolo Morganwg* (Cardiff, 1975)

Morgan, Prys, *The Eighteenth Century Renaissance* (Llandybïe, 1982).

Owen, Hugh (ed.), *Additional Letters of the Morrises of Anglesey (1735–1786)*, 2 vols (London, 1947–9).

Owen, Trefor M., *Welsh Folk Customs* (Cardiff, 1959).

Owen, Trefor M., 'The Celebration of Candlemas in Wales', *Folklore*, 84 (1973), 238–51.

Parry, John, 'Welsh Music – No. VII', *The Cambro-Briton*, vol. I, 1820, 415–16.

Pennant, Thomas, *The Journey to Snowdon*, vol. I (London, 1781).

Powell, Nia, 'Robert ap Huw: A wanton minstrel of Anglesey', *Welsh Music History/Hanes Cerddoriaeth Cymru*, 3 (1999), 5–29.

Rees, A. J. Heward, 'Henry Brinley Richards (1817–1885): A nineteenth century propagandist for Welsh music', *Welsh Music History/Hanes Cerddoriaeth Cymru*, 2 (1997), 173–92.

Rimmer, Joan, 'Edward Jones's musical and poetical relicks of the Welsh bards, 1784', *CG*, 10 (1987), 26–42.

Roberts, Gwyneth Tyson, *The language of the Blue Books: the perfect instrument of Empire* (Cardiff, 1998).

Rosser, Ann, *Telyn a Thelynor: Hanes y delyn yng Nghymru, 1700–1900* (Cardiff, 1981).

Saer, D. Roy, 'Cymdeithas Alawon Gwerin Cymru (1908–1983)', *Welsh Music/Cerddoriaeth Cymru*, 7, 6 (1984), 21–32.

Saer, D. Roy, 'A midnight Plygain at Llanymawddwy Church', *Folk Life*, 22 (1983–4), 99–106.

Saer, D. Roy, *Cymdeithas Alawon Gwerin Cymru: Canrif Gron/The Welsh Folk-Song Society: A Whole Century 1908–1983* (Cardiff, 2006).

Saer, D. Roy (ed.), 'Carolau Plygain/Plygain Carols', a booklet to accompany the LP record of carols from the sound archives of St Fagans: National History Museum.

Simpson, Claude M., *The British Broadside Ballad and its Music* (New Brunswick, 1966).

Thomas, Ben Bowen: *The Old Order: based on the Diary of Elizabeth Baker (Dolgelley, 1778–1786)* (Cardiff, 1945).

Thomas, Wyn, 'John Roberts (Telynor Cymru), 1816–1894', *Welsh Music History/Hanes Cerddoriaeth Cymru*, 1 (1996), 172–9.

Vychan, Idris, *Hanes ac Henafiaeth Canu gyda'r Tannau: Traethawd ar ganu penillion* (London, 1885).

Weller, Philip, 'Gerald of Wales's view of music', *Welsh Music History/Hanes Cerddoriaeth Cymru*, 2 (1997), 1–32.

Williams, G. J., *Iolo Morganwg: Y Gyfrol Gyntaf* (Cardiff, 1956).

Williams, G. J. and E. J. Jones, *Gramadegau'r Penceirddiaid* (Cardiff, 1934).

Williams, Gareth, *Valleys of song: music and society in Wales, 1840–1914* (Cardiff, 1998).

Williams, John, *Cyfaill mewn llogell: neu ddifyrwch i'r pererinion. Yn dair rhan, etc* (Caerfyrddin, 1797).

Williams, J. Lloyd, 'Welsh National Melodies and Folk-song', *The Transactions of the Honourable Society of Cymmrodorion*, 1907–8, (1909), pp. 1–46.

Williams, J. Lloyd, 'Antient British Music, *JWFSS* II/1 (1914), 15–28.

Williams, J. Lloyd, *Atgofion Tri Chwarter Canrif* (four autobiographical volumes published in Denbigh 1941, 1942, 1944, and London 1945).

Williams, J. Lloyd, *Y Tri Thelynor* (Llundain, 1945).

Journals

Y Cerddor Cymreig, J. Roberts ('Ieuan Gwyllt') (Merthyr Tydfil, 1861–73).

The Red Dragon (1882–7).

Cerddor y Cymry, W. T. Rees (Alaw Ddu) (Llanelli, 1883–94).

Y Cerddor, first series (Wrexham, 1889–1921), second series (Wrexham, 1930–9).

Cylchgrawn Cymdeithas Alawon Gwerin Cymru/Journal of the Welsh Folk-Song Society, 5 vols (1909–77).

Allwedd y Tannau: Cylchgrawn Cymdeithas Cerdd Dant Cymru (1936–).

Welsh Music/Cerddoriaeth Cymru: The Journal of the Guild for the Promotion of Welsh Music/Cylchgrawn yr Urdd er Hyrwyddo Cerddoriaeth Cymru (1959–)

Folk Life: Journal of the Society for Folk Life Studies (1963–).

Canu Gwerin/Folk Song (1978–).

Welsh Music History/Hanes Cerddoriaeth Cymru (Cardiff, 1996–).

Index

24 Country Dances for the Year 1711 45
24 New Country Dances for the year 1716 38

'A Phrŷnn Sy' Ar' 50, 51
Aberdare National Eisteddfod (1861) 192
'Aberdare Railway Polka' 184
Aberdeenshire 217
Abergavenny (*Y Fenni*) see Cymreigyddion y Fenni
Abergwesyn 177
Aberpergwm 166
Aberystwyth
    Arts Centre 245
    Castle tower 219
    Morfa 219
    Musical Union 219
    Penmaes-glas 219
    Penparcau 219
    Van driver of 212
    see also 'Ffarwel i Aberystwyth'; National Library of Wales
'About the Banks of Helicon' 22, 33, 39
    see also 'Fedle Fawr, Y'
Accidentals 129, 236
Accordion see Button accordion
Acts of Union of England and Wales (1536 and 1543) 6, 7, 17, 39
'Adar Mân y Mynydd' 146, 205, 237
Aeolian/la mode 141, 201, 236
'Agoriad y Cwrw' 68
'Agoriad y Cywair' 68
Agriculture 71, 199, 202, 207
    see also Cows; Oxen
'A'i Di Perot Purion Per' 182
'Alaw Salmon' 62, 68
    see also 'Ela Salmon'

'Alawon Fy Ngwlad' 197
    see also 'Hobed o Hilion'
Alawon Fy Ngwlad – The Lays of My Land (1896) 199–202
All Saints, feast of 29
Allwedd y Tannau 245–6
Almain (dance) 48, 62
    see also 'Monsieur's Almain'
Almanac eisteddfod 163
Almanacs 35–6, 39, 58, 119, 121, 163
America 23, 30, 173, 207, 223
    American tunes 199
    War of Independence 118
    see also Boston
Anacrusis 165
Ancient National Airs of Gwent and Morganwg (1844) 75, 94, 132, 133, 166, 170–1, 193
'Aneurin' see Owen, Aneurin
Anglesey 23, 42, 87-9, 93, 96, 109-13, 120, 214, 223
    see also Bodorgan; Bodwigan; Christmas carol service; Dwyran; Edwards, Maurice/Morris, *fiddler*; 'Llanerch-y-medd'; Morris, Lewis; Morris, Richard; Morris, William; 'Mwynen Môn'; Parry, Owen, *farmer, of Dwyran*; Prichard, Morris, *father of the Morris brothers*; 'Talaith Aberffraw'
Anglican Church see Church of England
'Anglo-Italian farces' see Concerts
'Anhawdd Ymadael' 144, 232
Animal guising 93, 100
'Annerch i'r Derin Du' 140
Anterliwt 25, 58, 64, 103, 121–6, 135
    see also Brenin Llur, Y; Cwymp Dyn; Dywysoges Genefetha, Y; Ffrewyll y Methodistiaid; Jeils; Llur

Anthems 175, 183
Antient British Music (1742) 38, 41–52, 55, 67, 135, 137, 156, 158–9, 162, 242, 247
    Facsimile of title-page 46
Antiphonal singing 108
'Ar Fore Dydd Nadolig' 106
'Ar Hyd y Nos' 58, 124
'Ar Lan y Môr' 217–18
'Ar y Bryn Mae Caseg Felen' 224–5
Argentina
    Welsh colony in 107, 207
'Arglwydd Llywelyn' 36, 38
'Anhawdd Ymadel' 52, 115
    see also 'Loath to Depart'
'Arglwyddes Druan' 44
Aria di Camera 25, 39, 45, 48, 49, 52, 147, 231, 247
'Armeinda' 31
Arne, Thomas 64
Arpeggios 66
Arthur (king) 11
As You Like It 64
Australia 207
Autumn equinox 71
Avebury 42
Awdl 11
Awdl-gywydd metre 26, 35, 36, 88, 116, 119, 128, 132, 134, 137, 142
'Awn Heddyw er Mwyn Haeddiant i Ganu Gogoniant' 108
'Awn i Fethlem' 28, 107, 175–6

Bach (family of German composers) 175
'Bachgen Main, Y' 119–20, 184
Bagpipe 25
Baker, Elizabeth, *of Dolgellau* 105, 122
Bala, Bardic meeting at (1663) 163
'Balaclafa' 201–2
Baldwin, Archbishop 3
Ballads 22–3, 24, 31, 36, 37, 39, 68, 71, 73, 112, 114–21, 122, 141, 143, 145, 147, 149, 151, 153, 166, 169, 170, 174–5, 181, 183, 184, 188, 199, 206
    Ballad airs/tunes 52, 54, 55, 64, 65, 87, 110, 114–15, 125, 143, 144, 147, 149, 154, 158, 165, 181, 184, 188, 189, 199, 200, 206, 207, 235
    Ballad-mongers 114, 122
    Ballad sheets 35, 37, 144, 199
    Ballad singers 114–15, 137, 181, 199, 213, 223
    Ballad singing 101, 147
    Ballad style 221
    Ballad words 31, 132, 185
    Drawing-room ballads 58
    English ballad operas 242
    Erotic ballad 185
    Folk ballads 153
    Foreign balladry 115
    Murder ballads 115
    see also *Last Leaves of traditional Ballads and Ballad Airs*; Williams, Richard, 'Dic Dywyll' (fl. 1822–62), *blind ballad-singer*
Bands (instrumental) 162, 170, 205
Bangor, co. Caernarfon 181, 205, 220, 226
    Normal College 203
    UCNW 204–5, 208, 227
    University 12, 227
    see also Edwards, Morris; Hartley, Lewis
Bangor MS 2255 136–7
Bangor Pontifical 6
'Banks of Ireland, The' 115
    see also 'Bryniau Iwerddon'
Baptists 173
'Bardd Alaw' *see* Parry, John (1776–1851)
'Bardd Nantglyn' *see* Davies, Robert (1769–1835)
Bardd teulu 2
'Bardd y Brenin' *see* Jones, Edward (1752–1824)
Bardic Museum, The (1802) 12, 22, 57, 58, 63, 64, 66, 68, 157, 247
Bards 1, 6, 7, 17, 18, 19, 38, 61, 68, 77, 87, 115, 141, 163, 164
    Bardic contention 162
    Bardic declamation 31
    Bardic descent from druids 42
    Bardic exemplar 136
    Bardic examinations 7
    Bardic grammar 7
    Bardic musical terminology 22
    Bardic order 7, 8, 17, 22, 29
    Bardic past 68
    Bardic poetry 22, 30
    Bardic religious poetry 231
    Bardic schools 7
    Bardic system 6, 230
    Bardic training 2, 6
    Classical bardic tradition 163
    'Historical account … of the Welsh Bards' 63
    Household bard 17

'Inferior bards' 115
    Meeting at Bala (1663) of 163
    New bardic metres 163
    Regulating bardic tradition 163
    Strict-metre bardic poetry 242
    Ynys Prydain, history of bards of 135
    see also Eisteddfod; Poets
Barlines 128, 130, 165, 200, 230
Barthélemon, François Hippolyte, *French violinist* 12, 64
Bath 164
Bawdy entertainment 64, 121, 122, 185
Bedwen haf 101
Bedwen Ifan 101
Beer 163, 206
Beethoven, Ludwig van 163, 203
'Belle-Isle March, The' 87, 114, 121, 240
Bells 106, 205
Bennett, Nicholas (*c*.1628) 199
Bennett, Nicholas (1823–99) 199–200, 202
'Beth Su Mor Feinion' 90
Bethan Bryn 244–6
Bethesda
    Cymdeithas y Cantorion Crefyddol 174
'Betty Brown' 91
'Betty o Lan Sant Ffraid' 185–6
Bible 26, 107
Bibliography of Welsh Traditional Music (1982 and 2006) 227
'Bid ale' 71
Billings, William, *American composer* 175
Binary tunes 62
Bingley, William 157, 158, 190
Bishop, Henry, *composer* 164
'Black-Eyed Susan' 121, 126
    see also 'Susan Lygad-ddu'
'Black Friar' 153–4
    see also 'Mynach Dû, Y'
Blackbirds 163, 217, 219
Blaenau Ffestiniog 203
Blind harpists *see* Parry, John, *Ruabon*; Roberts, Richard
'Blind Parry's School', *school of harpers* 41
    see also Parry, John, *Ruabon*
'Blodau Ffestiniog' 66
'Blodau Gwynwydd' 67
'Blodeu Gwynedd' 66
Blodeu-gerdd Cymry (1759) 12, 22, 48, 58, 107, 138, 141, 143, 144, 147, 148, 149, 152
'Blodeu'r Dyffryn' 43–4, 48
'Blotyn Du, Y' 115–16, 184, 188

Blwch o Bleser... (1822) 147, 149
'Blwyddyn Newydd Dda i Chi' 85–6
'Bod ac yn un' 81
Bodorgan, *co. Anglesey*
    Estate 65
    Library 8
Bodwigan, *co. Anglesey* 8
'Bohemia of the Queen' 39
'Boni Dawn Di' *see* 'Bonny Dundee'
'Bonny Dundee' ('Boni Dawn Di') 37
'Bonny Jockey' 37–8
'Bonny Laddy' 64
'Bore Glas, Y' 166
Boston 226
Botany 203–4
Bowen, *Rev*. John, *of Bath* 164
Boyce, William 64, 140
Bragod gywair 11
Brecon 3, 6
    see also Powell, Philip, *of Brecon*
'Bredi Ban' 91
Brenin Llur, Y 235
'Breuddwyd' 169–70
'Breuddwyd Dafydd Rhys' 45, 156
'Breuddwyd y Frenhines' 52, 61, 125, 151, 232
    see also 'Queen's Dream'
Bridal-contest song 97
'Bright For-Evermore, The' 86
British Harmony (1781) 13, 24, 52, 53, 55, 65, 67, 69, 152, 156, 157, 162, 184, 200, 247
British music 41
'Bro Gwalia/Bro Galia/Fro Golier' 43
Broadwood, Lucy 208
Brut y Tywysogion (Chronicle of the Princes) 163
'Bryniau Iwerddon' 115, 125, 144, 153, 184, 201
    see also 'Banks of Ireland, The'
'Buffons' 23
'Bugeilio'r Gwenith Gwyn' 132–3, 166
Burden (instrumental) 190
Burgess, Thomas, *bishop of St Davids* 164, 173
Burney, Charles 11, 41, 57
Burney, Fanny 57
Burns, Robert 160, 199
'Burstoy' 45
'Buttered Pease' 122
Button accordion 228
'Bwrn o Wellt Haidd' 37

'Bwrw Gofal Ymaith' 232
Bye-Gones (1885) 82
Byrd, William, *composer* 7
Byron, John, *1st Baron Byron of Rochdale* 43
'Bywyd y Milwr' 52
    see also 'Soldier's Life'

Cadence (musical) 182
Cadi 100
'Cadi Ha' 99–100, 210–11
Caernarfon, *county* 40, 44, 96, 155, 223
Caernarfon, *town* 94, 116, 227–8
    Castle 43
    Galeri 227
    Eisteddfod (1880) 192
Caerwys
    Eisteddfod (1523 and 1567) 7, 163
Cainc (harp melody) 241
'Cainc ar y Cyhydedd Hir' 128
'Cainc Stwffwl' 38
'Cainc y Cathreiwr' 129
'Cainc y Wraig o Faes-y-Neuadd' 45
'Cainc yr Arglwydd Llywelyn' 22
'Cainc yr Odryddes' 129–30
Caine, Ruth *see* Lewis, *Lady* Ruth Herbert
'Caingc Dafydd Brophwyd' 12, 63, 64, 67, 158
'Caingc Llandyfaelog' 146
'Caingc Llywelyn' 22, 63, 64
'Caingc y Crythor Garw' 165
'Caingc y Fflemynes' 144–5
Caledonian Country Dances (1733) 48, (1735) 64
Calendar festivals 71–114
'Calenig' 52–3, 156
'Calennig' 52, 68, 83–7
Calennig (decoration) 83
Calennig songs 84, 135, 200
'Calon Drom' 31, 32–3, 50, 51, 115, 144
    Illustration of 51
    see also 'Galon, Drom, Y'; 'Heavy Heart'; 'Trwm Galon'
Cambrian Harmony (1829) 162, 184, 247
Cambrian Minstrel, The (1845) 170–3, 193, 221
    see also *Caniedydd Cymreig, Y* (1845)
'Cambrian Minstrels, The' 178
Cambrian Society of Gwent 164
Cambridge 35, 41
    St John's College 22
Cambro-Briton, The (1820) 62
'Cân Aberhonddu' 169

'Can ar Owain Cordolen – Y Siacced Fral' 149–50
'Cân Gloi'r Pwnco' 73
'Can i ddosbarthwr y Llythurau ar Nutmeg and Ginger' 151
'Can Love Be Controul'd By Advice' 52
'Cân Merthyr' 213
'Cân Twm y Sane' 213
'Cân y Berllan' 80
'Cân y Cardi' 224
'Cân y Gaethes Ddu' 149
Candlemas 29, 87–97, 223
Candles 97, 102–3, 105
Caneuon Llafar Gwlad (Songs from Oral Tradition) 222
Caneuon Traddodiadol y Cymry 222
Cangen haf 99
Caniad(-au) 1, 10, 11
Caniad Beuno 11, 13
'Caniad Gwyl Fair iw Ganu ar Bum Mesur' 91
'Caniad Hun Wen Llian' 64
    see also 'Hun Gwenllian'; 'Erddigan Hun Gwenllian'
'Caniad Pibau Morfydd' 63, 64
'Caniad San Silin' 10
'Caniad y Twrch Trwyth' 11
Caniadau Seion (1840) 175
Caniadau y Cyssegr (1839) 174
Caniedydd Cymreig, Y (1845) 170–3, 193, 248
    see also *Cambrian Minstrel, The* (1845)
Canorion, Y 205, 219
'Canu Cwnsela' 75
Canu Gwerin (Folk-Song) 223, 224
Canu gyda'r tannau 49, 128, 133, 241–6
Canu halsingod 29
Canu llofft stabal 228
    see also Stable-loft songs
Canu penillion *see* Penillion
Canu yn drws 87
'Canu yn iâch i Dwm Bâch' 14
    see also 'Ffarwel Dwm Bach'
'Canu'r Bugail' 94
Canwyll y Cymry (1658–1730) 28, 121
'Captain Kid's Farewel to the Seas' 112
'Captain Wedderburn's Courtship' 36
Cardiff 176, 211
    see also National Museum of Wales
Cardigan, *county* 77, 86, 106, 113, 137, 146, 149, 177, 181, 212, 224
    see also Aberystwyth; Gogerddan;

Gwynionydd; Hafod; Llandysul; Nant-y-moch; Pontarfynach; Pont-rhyd-y-groes; Strata Florida, *abbey*
Cardigan, *town* 78
    Castle 3, 163
'Cariad Cyntaf, Y' 212
'Carmagnole' 114
Carmarthen, *county* 80, 145–6, 151, 170, 181
    see also 'Carmarthenshire Hornpipe'; Llandyfaelog; Llangyndeyrn; Pibwr-lwyd
Carmarthen, *town* 170, 176, 192
    Eisteddfod (15th cent.) 163
    Eisteddfod (1819) 164
'Carmarthenshire Hornpipe' 184
'Carnhuanawc' *see* Price, Thomas (1787–1848)
Carol gwirod yn drws 88
'Carol Gwirod yn Drws ar Fesur Triban Morg' 88
Carolau a Dyriau Duwiol (1696) 35, 36, 107
Carolau haf 119
    see also May carols
Carole 25
'Carolau Plygain/Plygain carols' (LP booklet) 234
Carolion (*halsingod*) 29
Carols 19, 22, 25, 30, 68, 77, 87, 98, 105–14, 118, 121, 138, 141–2, 144, 189, 234
    Airs/tunes 52, 99, 110, 155, 178, 200, 207, 209
    Christmas 20, 39, 98, 107, 118, 130, 175, 200, 209, 222, 231
    Easter 98
    May 53, 98–9, 107, 119, 131, 142, 231, 232
    Plygain 55, 105–14, 122, 141, 189, 223, 227
    Singers 137
    Summer 33
    Wassail 36, 87–8, 91, 130
    Writers of 114
Carters 122
'Carwr Gwirion, Y' 186
'Carwriaeth' 187
'Castell Moreton; or Moreton Castle in Shropshire' 67
'Castell Towyn' 67
Catches (musical) 18, 23
'Cawn Fynd Adref Fory' 86

CD recordings 223, 228
'Ceiriog' *see* Hughes, John Ceiriog (1832–87)
Celtic airs 58
Celtic Church 6
Celtic society 1, 2
Celtic traditions 6
Centre for Advanced Welsh Music Studies, Bangor 12
'Cerais Ferch' 166–7
Cerdd(-i) 1, 61
Cerdd dafod 7, 42
Cerdd dant 7–8, 42, 241–6
    see also Penillion
Cerdd Lyfr (1683) 35
Cerddor (Welsh Laws) 2
Cerddor, Y (1889) 198, 200
Cerddor Cymreig, Y (1861) 198, 200
Cerddor y Cymry (1883) 198
Ceredigion *see* Cardigan, *county*
Ceri (Kerry), co. Montgomery 137
Chair (eisteddfod) 163–4
Chapel culture 170, 175–6, 183
'Charity Mistress' 31, 126, 184, 239
    see also 'Gerard's Mistress'
Charlemagne 11
Charles I, *king of England* 29
Charles II, *king of England* 30, 31, 231
Charles, Thomas, *of Bala* 177
Chester 19, 194
'Chestnut or Dore's Vagary' 24
Choir-master 194
Choirs 170, 173, 192, 202, 203, 204, 223, 244
    see also Aberystwyth Musical Union; *Canorion, Y*; Llanidloes Choral Society
Chopin, Frédéric 193
Chorea 25
'Chow Bente' 23, 47
Christianity
    Calendar 98
    Celebrations 105
    Praise 1
Christmas 17, 79, 91, 105–14, 227, 233
    Anglesey carol service 112–13
    Carols 20, 39, 98, 107, 118, 130, 175, 200, 209, 222, 231
    Day 71
    Eve 105
    Mass 106
    Masque 152

Wassailing festivities 91
  see also Plygain
Chromaticism 202
Church of England 102, 154, 173, 176, 203
  National Schools 203
Chwilog 93
'Cil y Fwyalch' 31, 67, 232
Cistercian order 6
Civil War (1642–9) *see* English Civil War
Clanricarde, Marquis de 2
Clera 227–8
'Clod Gwen' 141
  see also 'Lliw'r Gwinwydd'
Club dinners 183
'Clychau Rhiwabon' 28
Clymau cytgerdd 42
'Cobler Coch o Hengoed' 128
Cock-fighting 25
'Codais Heddiw'n Fore' 85
'Codiad yr Ehedydd' 61, 241–2
'Codiad yr Haul' 63, 66
Coety, *co. Glamorgan* 14
Collection of Welch Airs, A (1810) 162, 247
Collection of Welsh, English and Scotch Airs, A (1752 or 1761) 50, 52, 147
'Colliers Daughter' 88
Communal songs 133
Complaynt of Scotland, The (1549) 11
Concertina 100
Concert Life in London from Mozart to Haydn 49
Concerto 65
Concerts 41, 58, 142, 164, 165, 170, 172, 178, 183, 191, 199, 205, 208
Congregational singing 26, 173–4, 192
Conjurers 18
'Conseat y Ddafad Ddu' 36
'Conset Abram Evan' 68
  see also 'Hoffedd Abram ab Ifan'
'Consêt Arglwydd Strain' 44
'Consêt Gruffydd ap Cynan' 24, 232
  see also 'Vienna'
'Consêt Gwŷr Aberffraw' 91
'Consêt Syr Watkin' 48
'Contar dreinsiwr' 126
Contest singing 72, 87, 97, 234
'Contraboncin' *see* 'Country Bumpkin'
Coopers 39, 122
Corelli, Arcangelo, *composer* 65
Corph y Gaingc (1834) 142
'Corporal' (*Mari Lwyd*) 72

Counterpoint 11, 65, 207, 241
'Country Bumpkin' ('Contraboncin') 37
'Cow Heel' 45
  see also 'Sawdl y Fuwch'
Cows, songs to summon 129–30
'Cowper Mwyn, Y' 126, 165
Craig Ddinan, *Llandrillo* 22
Cras gywair 11
Creation, The (Haydn) 175
'Crimson Velvet' 12, 22, 24, 31, 33, 35, 38, 107, 115, 232
  see also 'Ffion Felfed, Y'
Crismond, William 36
'Croeso Gwraig y Ty' 68
Crossley–Holland, Peter 10, 11, 223
Crotch, William 40, 157–60
Crowthers 3, 17, 22
Crusades 3
Crwth/Crowd/Crotta 1, 3, 4, 10, 12, 17, 18, 22, 165, 241
  see also Crowthers; Rowland, Dafydd, *crwth*-player
Cuckoo 214
'Cuckoo, The' 64
'Cudyn Gwyn' 62, 152
'Cudyn Gwyn Ffrainc' 152
  see also 'Whitelock's Coranto'
Cumulative songs 88, 91, 93, 94, 207, 222
Cutty Wran (Hunting the Wren) 77
'Cutty Wren' 81–2
'Cwbwl i gyd' 81
Cwlwm 10
Cwlwm mawr 13
Cwrt-mawr, *co. Cardigan* 212
Cwrw bach 71
Cwymp Dyn (anterliwt) 122
'Cwympiad y Dail' 52, 156, 237
'Cwyn Mam yng Nghyfraith' 215
'Cwyn y Prentis' 139
'Cwynfan Brydain' 232
Cydweli *see* Kidwelly
Cyfaill mewn Llogell (1797) 173
Cyfalaw 241
'Cyfri'r Geifr' 93, 96
Cylchgrawn Cymdeithas Alawon Gwerin Cymru 206
  see also Journal of the Welsh Folk-Song Society
Cymanfa ganu 192, 204
Cymdeithas Alawon Gwerin Cymru 228
  see also Welsh Folk-Song Society
Cymdeithas Cerdd Dant Cymru 245–6

Cymdeithas Gymroaidd Dyfed 164
Cymdeithas Gymroaidd Gwynedd 164
Cymdeithas Offerynnau traddodiadol Cymru 227
Cymdeithas y Cantorion Crefyddol, Bethesda 174
Cymdeithas yr Eisteddfod Genedlaethol 192
Cymmrodorion, Honourable Society of 165, 204, 206
Cymreigyddion y Fenni, 165, 179
'Cymru Lân, Gwlad y Gân' 195
Cynghanedd 22, 32, 48, 142, 151, 220, 230
'Cynghansail Cymru' (Welsh ground) 62
   see also 'Welsh Ground, The'
'Cynsêt Gwŷr Penn Morfa' 65
'Cyntaf Dydd o'r Gwyliau, Y' 91–3
Cyweirdant 10
Cywydd deuair fyrion 20–1, 36, 79, 82, 84, 128, 135, 230
Cywydd [deuair hirion] 11
'Cywydd deuair: Morganwg' 20, 128, 230

'Dacw 'Nghariad' 211
'Dadl Dau' 24, 63, 123–4, 232
   see also 'Flaunting Two'
'Daeth Mari Lwyd Lawen' 77
Dafydd ap Gwilym 6, 138
'Dafydd Ddu Eryri' see Thomas, David (1759–1822)
Dafydd Ifan, *veteran of Waterloo* 120–1
'Dafydd y Garreg Wen' see Owen, David (1709–39)
'Dal Atto or Buckle To' 38
Dan y Wenallt 244–5
Dances 24–5, 62, 110, 114, 184
   Country dance books 37, 38, 39, 64, 65, 66
   Country dance tunes 48, 62, 64, 66
   Country dances 183
   Dance patterns 110
   Dance tunes 37, 48, 59, 66, 122, 125, 153, 184, 197, 200
   Folk dances 68
   Welsh dance tunes 184
   Welsh dances 228
Dancing 58, 73, 93, 100, 102, 103, 105, 114, 122, 131, 132, 147, 177, 189, 218, 228
   Grand balls 183
   'Half dancing' 93
   Harp music for 65
   In Wales 24–5, 59, 71

Dancing Master, The (c.1726–8) 38, 40, 67
Danes 5
'Dargason'/'Dargeson' 22, 23
Darowen, *co. Montgomery* 141, 144, 165
Dart, Thurston 11, 12
'Dashing White Sergeant, The' 184
'Datgeiniad Pen Pastwn' 18, 115
Datgeiniaid 7, 18, 62, 241, 246
Davies, Grace Gwyneddon 96, 208, 216
Davies, J. Ffos 222
Davies, Mary (1855–1930) 181, 208, 209, 211, 214, 222
Davies, Richard, 'Mynyddog' (1833–77) 199
Davies, Robert, 'Bardd Nantglyn' (1769–1835) 200
Davies, Robert, *of Llanerch, St Asaph* 8
Davies, William Cadwaladr, *first Registrar of UCNW, Bangor* 208
'Dawns Triban Deublyg' 131–2
Dawnsio haf 99–100
'Ddafad Gyrnig, Y' 168
De Excidio et Conquestu Britanniae 1
'Ddau Farch, Y' 212
Declaimers see Datgeiniaid
Declamatory style 1, 11, 149, 197, 206, 216, 217, 218, 221, 226
'Deffrwch Ben Teulu' 84, 135
Deloney, Thomas, *ballad-writer* 125
Denbigh, *town* 162
'Deryn Du Pigfelyn, Y', 168–9
'Deryn Du Sy'n Rhodio'r Gwledydd' 219
'Deryn Pur, Y' 166
Descriptio Kambriae 3–4
Devil's Bridge see Pontarfynach
Devonshire, 3rd Duke of (William Cavendish, 1698–1755) 49
'Dewch i'r Frwydr' 236
'Dewch Ymlaen' ('Haf etti'r Glocsen') 140
'Dewis Howel' 67
'Dewis Meinwen' 43–4
'Dewisol Gân Dafydd o'r Garreg-Wen' 67
   see also 'Dafydd y Garreg Wen'
Dewisol Ganiadau yr Oes Hon (1759) 141
Dialogue songs 206, 209
Diatonic scale 158
'Dic Dywyll' see Williams, Richard (fl. 1822–62), *blind ballad-singer*
'Diddanwch Arglwyddes Puleston' 66
   see also 'Lady Puleston's Delight'
'Diddanwch Madam Edwards' 67

Difficulties of the journey (*Mari Lwyd*) 72, 88
'Difyrrwch Gwŷr Dyfi' 63
'Difyrrwch Madam Eyton' 67
'Difyrrwch yr Arglwyddes Owen' 45, 52, 55
'Difyrwch Gwyr Caernarfon' 178–9
'Digan Philip Ystwyth' 47
'Digan Wil Bifan Bennoeth' 47
'Digby's Farewell' 31, 35
  see also 'Lord Sandwich's Farewell'
Diliau Barddas (1827) 200
Dinas Mawddwy 77
'Dinevor Waltz' 184
'Diniweidrwydd' 36, 126, 171, 174–5, 184
'Diniweidrwydd y Golomen' 156
Discords 245
'Dissertation on the Musical Instruments of the Welsh' 62–3
'Distyll y Don' 158, 232
Diversions 127, 153
'Dives and Lazarus' 188
Diwedd (refrain sections) 11
Dolgellau 105–6, 122
  see also Dolserau; 'Malldod Dolgellau'; Shon Robert, *shoemaker*
Dolmetsch, Arnold 12
Dolserau 105
Dolwyddelan 47
'Dôn Fechan, Y' 20, 90, 116–17, 172
Dorian/re mode 113, 129, 141, 166, 171, 174, 182, 201, 220, 236
Dovaston, John Freeman Milward 164
Dowland, John 43
Drinking songs 188, 224
'Dros yr Afon' 171
Drovers 40
Druids 41–2, 66, 78, 195, 242
  'Druidical Song, A' 58
  Druidism ('Iolo Morganwg') 164
Drums 18, 218
Drunkenness 174, 176, 177, 206
'Dryw Bach Ydi'r Gŵr' 79
Dublin 41
'Dugan y Crythor Du' 38–9
'Duke of Gloucester's March, The' 151–2
  see also 'Hoffedd Glandyfroedd'
'Duke of York's March, The' 152
Duple time 116, 149
D'Urfey, Thomas 24, 31, 37, 50
  see also *Pills to Purge Melancholy*
'Duw Gadwo'r Brenin' 118
  see also 'God Save the King'

Dwyran, *co.* Anglesey 214
'Dydd Llun y Bore' 121, 165
  see also 'Monday Morning'
Dydd Mawrth Crempog/Ynyd 98
'Dydd Trwy'r Ffenestr', 165
'Dyferiad y Gerwyn' 55
'Dyma Wyliau Hyfryd Llawen' 21
Dyn hysbys 178
Dynamics 244–5
'Dynwared yr Eos' 45, 55
Dyriau 36
Dywysoges Genefetha, Y 123–4, 235

'E Fu Ers Doe' 45
Easter 17, 22 35, 98
Ebillon (mulled) 105
Eden, Garden of 28
Edinburgh 160
'Edinburgh town' 37
Education 176–7, 203, 204
Education Act (1870) 202
Edwards, Maurice/Morris, *Anglesey fiddler* 14, 58, 64, 65, 67–8, 110, 125, 152, 162
Edwards, Morris, *Bangor* 65
Edwards, Thomas, 'Twm o'r Nant' (1739–1810) 122, 135–6, 137, 141
'Eira, Yr' 181–2
'Eira Mynydd' 36
Eisteddfod 7, 75, 136, 137, 157, 163–5, 170, 172, 173, 177, 179, 184, 194, 195, 199, 202, 204, 216, 244
  Almanac 163
  Bala (1663) 163
  Caernarfon (1880) 192
  Caerwys (1523 and 1567) 7, 163
  Caerwys (1789) 164
  Cardigan Castle (1176) 3, 163
  Carmarthen (15th cent.) 163
  Carmarthen (1819) 164
  Chancellor of Llandaf Cathedral (*c.*1600) 163
  Chapel 176
  Cymreigyddion y Fenni (1834–53) 165, 170, 179
  Gwyneddigion (1789–95) 164
  Llangollen (1858) 75, 181, 192, 194, 238
  Merthyr Tydfil 170
  Provincial 164, 165
  Rural 195
  Tavern 183

Temperance 176
Welsh eisteddfodic culture 195
Welshpool (1824) 136, 164, 236
see also National Eisteddfod
'Ela Salmon' 68
see also 'Alaw Salmon'
Elegies 30, 138, 141–2, 144
Elijah 192
Elizabeth I, *queen of England* 22–3, 26, 39, 67, 138
Elizabethan dance tunes 48, 122
Ellis, John
Mawl yr Arglwydd (1816) by 174
Ellis, Osian 12, 49, 242
England 6 and *passim*
 English airs/tunes 17, 22, 23, 24, 30, 31, 32, 35, 36, 37, 38, 118, 121, 184
 English ballads 31, 35, 183
 English conquest of Wales (1282) 2, 6
 English dances/dance tunes 12–13, 24, 37, 38, 158
 English language 7, 17, 164
 English lyrics 157, 162
 English music 37, 158
 English-medium education 202
 English middle class 162
 English songs/singing 4–5, 199, 202
English Civil War (1642-9) 29, 30, 39, 43, 143
English Dancing Master, The (1651) 22
English Folk-Song Society 204, 206, 208
Englyn(-ion) 11, 19, 163, 199, 230
'Englynion y misoedd' 36
'Eos-Lais, Yr' 67
'Eos y Gogledd' *see* Jones, W. O. (1868–1928)
'Erddigan Caer Waun' 61–2
'Erddigan Hun Gwenllian' 47, 137, 232
 see also 'Hun Gwenllian'; 'Caniad Hun Wen Llian';
'Erddigan Tro'r Tant' 13–14, 61, 158
'Erddigan William Befan Benouth' 64
Erotic symbols 224
'Evan's Jig' 39
Evangelising songs 199
Evans, —., *harper to Charles II* 231
Evans, D. Emlyn 198, 200, 201
Evans, E., *Llanfair Talhaearn* 8
Evans, Evan, 'Ieuan Brydydd Hir'/'Ieuan Fardd' (1731–88) 8
Evans, Evan, 'Ieuan Glan Geirionydd' (1795–1855) 237

Evans, John, *of Bala* 102
Evans, Margaret, 'Margaret Fwyn ach Evan' 44
Evans, Meredydd 29–30, 87, 226, 234
Expressiveness 245

Fairs 18, 103, 114, 115, 119, 199
Fall of Man, The 28
'Fall of the Leaf, The' 237
'Fanny Blooming Fair' 64
'Farewell Frances' 160
Farewell songs 193–4, 218–19
'Fe Hwyliwyd Llestr Egwan' 226
Feat songs 91
'Fedle Fawr, Y' 24, 39, 54–5, 68, 91, 144, 158
 see also 'About the Banks of Helicon'
'Ferch o'r Scer, Y' 134, 167, 187
Fertility customs 77, 82
Festival of Britain (1951) 233
Festival of Light 87
'Ffani Blodau'r Ffair' 140
'Ffarwel Abel Salmon' 45
'Ffarwel Dai Llwyd' 45, 115, 119, 144
'Ffarwel Dwm Bach' 14–15
'Ffarwel Dwm Bach or Coeti' 14
 see also 'Canu yn iâch i Dwm Bâch'
'Ffarwel Ednyfed Fychan' 63, 67
'Ffarwel Gŵyr Aberffraw' 65, 111–12, 219–20
'Ffarwel i Aberystwyth' 219
 see also 'Grim King of the Ghosts'
'Ffarwel i Blwy Llangywer' 218
'Ffarwel Ieuan Glyn Teifi' 18
'Ffarwel Ned Puw' 24, 35, 54, 62, 65, 107, 108–10, 119, 126, 158, 159, 184, 232
'Ffarwel Philip Ystwyth' 47, 64
'Ffarwel Prydain' 154
'Ffarwel Trefaldwyn' 36, 37, 88
Ffestiniog 219
'Ffion Felfed, Y' 115, 144
 see also 'Crimson Velvet'
'Fflamgwr gwrgan' 10
'Ffylan Tin Tw' (and variant forms) 123–4
 see also 'Dadl Dau – Flaunting Two'
Ffrewyll y Methodistiaid 124
Fiddle 18, 25, 37, 50, 72, 73, 99, 100, 101, 122, 145, 204
 Manuscripts 64–5, 99, 110
 Tunes 58
 see also Violin

269

Fiddlers 23, 24, 25, 37, 64, 101, 112, 125, 126, 177, 210
    see also Edwards, Maurice/Morris; Thomas, John (c.1730–60); 'Wil Ffidler'
Figure Four (Llanfarian) 219
'First Day' 45
First World War 222, 244
Fishing 64
Fitzwilliam Virginal Book 237
'Flaunting Two' 123–4
    see also 'Dadl Dau'; 'Ffylan Tin Tw'
Flight into Egypt 106
Flint, *county* 115, 118, 208, 209, 210
    see also Caerwys; Holywell; Mostyn
Flute 62, 66
    see also German flute
Folk
    Airs/tunes 149, 157, 207
    Culture 206
    Customs 68, 127, 200, 207
    Dancing 68, 77
    Groups 223
    Modes 153, 156
    Music 205, 220, 228
    Orchestra 228
    Singing/song 3 and *passim*
    Tales/legends 122, 127
    Verses/words 149, 151, 153
Folk-Song (journal) see *Canu Gwerin*
Folk-song movement in Wales 208
Fool (*anterliwt* character) 122–3
Fool (Morris dancing) 100
Football contests 25
Forgery (literary) 127
Fornication 174
'Fortune My Foe' 115
Foster, Stephen Collins 199
France 31, 214
    French Revolution 114
    French songs 30
    War with French (18th cent.) 118
'France Air' 51
Frazer, James 82–3
'Frog Galliard' 43
    see also 'Bro Gwalia'
'Frwynen Las, Y' 236
Funerals 29
'Fwyalchen, Y' 217
'Fwyalchen Ddu Bigfelen, Y' 183
'Fwyna'n Fyw, Y' 63
'Fy Mrodyr a Chwiorydd' 99
'Fy Ngwen Mae'r Eira ar y Bannau' 191

'Gadael Tir' 31, 32, 35, 36, 50, 58, 59, 61, 115, 142, 232
    see also 'Leave Land'
Gaelic hymn-singers 5
'Galar Gwraig y Milwr' 195–6
'Galar Gwŷr Ffrainc' 114
Galliard 47, 48, 62
    see also 'Frog Galliard'; 'Grymanders Galliard'
'Galon Drom, Y' 32–3, 61, 232
Galops 184
    see also 'Hungarian Gallopade'
Game songs 133
Gamut (music) 173
'Garddinen' see 'Gerddinen, Y'
Garndolbenmaen 155, 203, 220
Gaul 2
'Gavot in Otho' 52
Gavottes 65
'Gelynen, Y' 132, 214
Gems of Welsh Melody (1873) 194–8
George, David Lloyd 208
'Gentle maid in secret sigh'd, A' 137
George II, *king of England* 231
George III, *king of England* 52
George IV, *king of England* 58
'Gerard's Mistress' 31, 115, 184
    see also 'Charity Mistress'; 'Gwledd Angharad'
'Gerddinen, Y' 47, 63
German flute 49
Gewgaws 114
Gilchrist, A. G. 217
Gildas 1
'Gilderoy' 188
'Gin Thou Wert Mine Ain Thing' 52
Giraldus Cambrensis/Gerald of Wales/ Giraldus de Barri 2, 3–6, 25, 41, 69, 129
Glamorgan, *county* 3, 14, 25, 75, 76–7, 83, 101, 127–37, 143, 167
    see also Coety; 'Cywydd deuair: Morganwg'; Gwenfô (Wenvoe); 'Hen Erddigan Morganwg'; 'Hen Gainc Washaela Morganwg'; Llangynwyd; Merthyr Tydfil; 'Morganwg. Morris Dance Tune'; 'Morganwg cyhydedd 8 a 7'; Nantgarw; Oxen; Swansea; 'Treban Morganough'; 'Triban Morgannwg'
'Glan Meddwdod Mwyn' 52, 158, 195, 232

'Glan Rhondda' (Welsh National Anthem) 183
Glanyrafon, co. Montgomery 199
Glees 164
'Glomen, Y' 220
Glyn Ceiriog 153
Go gywair 11
Goat songs 93–6
'God Save the King' 118
    see also 'Duw Gadwo'r Brenin'
'Gog Lwydlas, Y' 89–90
Gogerddan 177
    see also Wood, Jeremiah, *'Jerry Bach Gogerddan'*
Gogwyddor i ddysgu y prikiad 10
Golden Bough, The 82
'Gorddinam' see 'Gerddinen, Y'
'Goreuman Drws Galia' 38, 47
'Gorhoffedd Gwŷr Harlech' 63
'Gorhoffedd Owain Cyfeiliog' 63
Gorse 99
Gospel hymns 86
Gosteg(-ion) 10, 11, 12
'Gosteg yr Halen' 11
Grace notes 5, 186
Gravedigger 155, 220
Graves, A. P., *of Harlech* 204
'Gramwndws Galia' 47
Gray, Thomas, *poet* (1716–71) 41
'Gray Mundus' 47
'Greece and Troy' 36, 38
Greenly, *Lady* Elizabeth Coffin (1771–1839) 165–6, 170
'Greensleeves' 12, 17, 23, 31, 65, 115
Griffith, Robert, (author of *Llyfr Cerdd Dannau*) 241
Griffith, Tal 222, 226
'Grim King of the Ghosts' 219
    see also 'Ffarwel i Aberystwyth'
Ground basses 22
Grounds (musical) see 'Cynghansail Cymru' (Welsh ground); Italian grounds; Tudor Ground; 'Wales Ground'; 'Welsh Ground, The'
Gruffudd ap Cynan, Statute of 7
'Grymanders Galliard' 38, 47
Guitar 52, 228
'Gun, The' (tune) 24, 232
Gwaith y Bardd Bach 151
'Gwatwariad yr Eos' 45
'Gwêl yr Adeilad' 39, 68, 110–11, 112, 115, 125, 144
    see also 'See the Building'

'Gwên Dando' 50, 51
    see also 'Queen Dido'
Gwenfô (Wenvoe) 101
Gwir er Gwaethed Yw, Y (1684) 35, 36
'Gwledd Angharad' 31, 115, 144
    see also 'Gerard's Mistress'
'Gwn Dafydd Ifan' 120–1
'Gwrandewch ar Ferch sy'n Serchog' 184–5
'Gwydr Glas, Y' 223–4
Gŵyl Fair [y Canhwyllau] 87–97
Gŵyl Ifan 101
Gwyliau, Y 71–2, 77
Gŵyl mabsant 25, 102–3
Gwyneddigion Society 162, 163, 164
    see also Eisteddfod
Gwynionydd 234
Gwynne, John, *of Darowen, 'Philomusus'* 136, 165, 221, 236
'Gwŷr Harlech' 87, 114
Gwŷr wrth gerdd 17
Gypsies 177–8

'Haf etti'r Glocsen' 140
Hafod, co. Cardigan 135
'Hafod y Wraig Lawen' 63
'Hafren' 67
Halifax, 2nd earl of (George Montagu-Dunk, 1716–71) 49
Hall, Augusta, *Lady Llanover* 165
'Halsing y Dryw' 78, 79
Halsingod 29, 30
Handefull of pleasant delites, A (1584) 17, 31, 39
Handel, George Frideric 52, 64, 65, 175, 202, 203
    see also Judas Maccabeus
Hanes Cerddoriaeth Cymru/Welsh Music History 227
Hanes y Byd a'r Amseroedd (1721) 102–3
Harlech 204
    Castle 159
Harmonics 66
Harmony 11, 41, 65-6, 148, 166, 174, 204, 244
Harper, Sally 8
Harpers/Harpists 10, 12, 14, 17, 18, 22, 23, 24, 37, 38, 40, 41, 42, 49, 52, 57, 58, 61, 64, 67, 68, 94, 99, 128, 137, 138, 141, 142, 162, 164, 165, 166, 170, 177–8, 181, 183, 185, 200, 231, 241, 242

see also 'Blind Parry's School'; Ellis, Osian; Evans, —., *harper to Charles II*; Ifan y Gorlan; Jones, Edward, *'Bardd y Brenin'*; Parry, John, *'Bardd Alaw'*; Parry, John, *Ruabon*; Powel, —. (father and son, *temp.* George II), *London*; Robert ap Huw; Roberts, John, *'Telynor Cymru'*; Roberts, Richard

Harps 1, 2, 3–4, 6, 11, 12, 18, 19, 20, 25, 31, 36, 37, 40, 47, 48, 49, 50, 51, 52, 55, 59, 62, 66, 68, 69, 71, 73, 99, 100, 101, 105, 128, 134, 142, 145, 147, 151, 153, 157, 158, 162, 163, 165, 166, 167, 170, 175, 177, 178, 183, 192, 195, 201, 205, 207, 218, 228, 239, 241, 246
    Airs/music 12, 38, 55, 137, 148, 151, 157, 183, 246
    Contests 164
    Manuscripts 65, 162

Harpsichord 49, 62

Harpsichord or Spinet Miscellany, The (1761) 23

Harris, Howel 173

Harvest celebrations 71

Hartley, Lewis, *of Bangor* 181

'Hast i'r Briodas' 184

'Haste to the Wedding' 184

Have With You to Saffron-Walden (1596) 17

Hawkers 199

Haydn, Franz Joseph 160, 175, 237
    see also *Creation, The*

Hazel (wood) 96

'Heavy Heart' 31–3, 36, 50, 51, 115, 119, 125
    Illustration of 51
    see also 'Calon Drom'; 'Galon Drom, Y'; 'Trwm Galon'

'Heb Dduw, heb ddim' 17

Hebrides 5

Hela'r Dryw, 72, 77–83

'Hela'r Ysgyfarnog' 232

Helston Furry Dance 25, 131

'Hemp Dresser, The' 24

Hen Alawon (Carolau a Cherddi) 223

Hen benillion see Penillion

'Hen Cwmpeiniwr Mwyn, Yr' 151

'Hen Dôn Llyfr Ficer' 90–1

'Hen Erddigan Morganwg' 130, 236

'Hên Fesur' 107–8

'Hen Fyharen, Yr' 217

'Hen Gainc Washaela Morganwg' 76–7

'Hen Ganfed, Yr' 30

Hen Ganiadau Cymru (1820 and 1825) 14, 58, 66, 67, 68

'Hen Syr Salmon, Yr' 38

'Hen Wlad Fy Nhadau' 183, 195

'Hen Ŵr Mwyn, Yr' 206

'Hên Ŵr o'r Coed' 116

'Hen Wr o'r Coed Yn ol Dull Dyfed' 172

Henry VII, *king of England* 40

Henry VIII, *king of England*, 173

'Henwau Mesurau Cerdd Dafod a Thant...' 38

Herod 106

Heterophony 5

Hibberd, Lloyd 5

'Hey Boys, Up Go We' 35

High Arcal, *co. Salop* 24

'Highland Laddie' 52

'Hir Oes i Fair' 117
    see also 'Let Mary Live Long'

'Hiraeth' 216

'Historical Account of the Welsh Bards and Their Music and Poetry' 63, 69

'Hob y Deri Dando' 63, 190–1, 232
    see also 'Hwp i Diri Dando Arwest Salmau'; 'Hwp y Diri Dando'

'Hobi horse'/'Hobby Horse' 91

'Hobed o Hilion' 197
    see also 'Alawon Fy Ngwlad'

'Hoffedd Abram ab Ifan' 68
    see also 'Conset Abram Evan'

'Hoffedd Duwc William' 146–7

'Hoffedd Glandyfroedd' 152
    see also 'Duke of Gloucester's March, The'

'Hoffedd Hywel ab Owen Gwynedd' 63

'Hoffedd y Prins Rupert ney Tyb y Tywysog' 143–4
    see also 'Prince Rupert's Delight or the Prince's Fancy'

Holland, Peter Crossley- *see* Crossley-Holland, Peter

Holly 19, 83, 96

Holy Spirit, The 25

Holywell, *co. Flint* 100, 209
    'Cadi' at, illustration of 100
    Workhouse at 209

'Home Sweet Home' 87

Homophony 10

Hopping 25

Hornpipes 66, 122, 184
    see also 'Carmarthenshire Hornpipe'

Horse 72–7
'Hosanna Mwy' 155
Howells, J. 143
Howells, John, 'Eos Glandyfroedd' (1774–1830) 151–2
'Hûd Tynghedven' 67
'Hûd y Bibell' 68
Hughes, John Ceiriog, 'Ceiriog' (1832–87) 137, 199
Hughes, Jonathan (1721–1805) 118, 122, 141
Humber 4
Humorous songs 200, 222
'Hun Gwenllian' 31, 47, 135–7, 232
 see also 'Caniad Hun Wen Llian'; 'Erddigan Hun Gwenllian'
'Hungarian gallopade' 184
'Hunt's Up, The' 18, 23, 47
Hunting the hare 206
 see also 'Hela'r Ysgyfarnog'
Hunting the wren see Wren
Hutton, Ronald 82–3
'Hwp i Diri Dando Arwest Salmau' 191
'Hwp y Diri Dando' 128
'Hyd y Frwynen' 24
'Hyd y Frwynen Las' 167, 187–8
'Hyd Yma Bu'n Cerdded' 75
Hymns 86, 138, 154, 173–4, 175, 176, 192, 203, 209
 Hymn-singing festivals 192, 204
 Hymn tunes 141, 146, 153, 173, 174, 189
Hywel Dda/Hywel the Good 2, 163

'I Ysgafnhau ein Gwaith' 225–6
'Idris Fychan' see Jones, John (1825–87)
'Ieuan Brydydd Hir' see Evans, Evan (1731–88)
'Ieuan Ddu' see Thomas, John (1795–1871)
'Ieuan Glan Geirionydd' see Evans, Evan (1795–1855)
'Ieuan Gwyllt' see Roberts, John (1822–77)
Ifan y Gorlan, harpist 14
'Ifor Ceri' see Jenkins, John (1770–1829)
Ifor Hael 138
Immoral/frivolous songs 207
Improvisitore 59
Incarnation, doctrine of 28
Independents 173
Industry 157, 170, 176, 202, 224, 225–6
Instrumental music 192, 194, 195, 227, 228

Instrumentalists 209, 228
Interlude (rustic drama) see Anterliwt
'Ioan Ceri' see Jenkins, John (1770–1829)
'Ioan Siencyn' see Jenkins, John (1716–96)
'Iolo Morganwg' see Williams, Edward (1747–1826)
'Iolo Morganwg: Morris Dance Tune' 26, 101–2
Iorwerth 22
Ireland 1, 2, 3, 7, 41, 160, 162, 188, 199
 Music of 4, 158
 Terms of Irish origin 10
'Irish Bataroo' 39
Irish Folk-Song Society 204, 206
'Irish Tune, The' 38
Irish wren song 82
Is gywair (*is gower*) 11, 12, 19, 230
 see also 'Tro Tant or Is gower'
'Is gywair Sidanen' 18
Italy 31, 214
 Italian grounds 23
Itinerarium Kambriae 3
'I've Got Sixpence' 226
 see also 'Mae Gen i Swllt'

'Jac Glan-y-Gors' see Jones, John (1766–1821)
'Jack Latin' 64, 122
James I, *king of England* 18, 231
James, Evan, 'Ieuan ap Iago' (1809–78) 183
James, James, 'Iago ap Ieuan' (1833–1902) 181–3, 195, 233, 238
 see also 'Orpheus'
Jeils (anterliwt) 123, 235
Jenkins, David, *musician* (1848–1915) 198
Jenkins, Geraint H. 29
Jenkins, John, 'Ifor Ceri' (1770–1829) 68, 78, 79, 99, 137–56, 163, 164, 165, 173, 183, 192, 193, 221, 236, 238
Jenkins, John, 'Ioan Siencyn' (1716–96) 237
'Jenny Dang the Weaver' 64
'Jenny Making Hay' ('Gini Making Hea') 37
Jerry, *Twm y Sane's mule* 213
'Jerry Bach Gogerddan' see Wood, Jeremiah
Jesus Christ 28, 29
Jigs 59, 62, 66, 122, 138, 149, 150, 193
 see also 'Evan's Jig'
'Joanna' 175
Join-in songs 153, 193, 196
John a Kent and John a Cumber 23

'John Come Kiss Me Now' 23, 36
John of Affligem 5
Jones, D., *of Llanidloes* (*c.*1913) 212
Jones, Edward, 'Bardd y Brenin' (1752–1824) 22, 23, 24, 38, 49–50, 57–69, 87, 93–4, 107, 110, 128, 134, 141, 142, 144, 157, 162, 163, 165, 166, 171, 178, 183, 190, 193, 194
    Facsimile of part of letter to 60
Jones, Geraint Vaughan, *rector of Mallwyd* 227
Jones, Hugh (1700?–82), *anterliwt writer* 122
Jones, John, 'Idris Fychan' (1825–87) 199
Jones, John, 'Jac Glan-y-Gors' (1766–1821) 185
Jones, John, 'Talhaiarn' (1810–70) 199
Jones, Lewis David, 'Llew Tegid' (1851–1928) 205
Jones, Rhys, 'o'r Blaenau' (1713–1801) 8
Jones, Richard (*c.*1584) 17
Jones, Richard, *gravedigger of Garndolbenmaen* 155, 220
Jones, T. James 244–6
Jones, Thomas, *of Shrewsbury* (1648?–1713) 35–6
Jones, W. O., 'Eos y Gogledd' (1868–1928) 237
Jones, William, *of Llangadfan* (1726–95) 8, 24, 25, 59, 60, 62, 68, 107, 127, 134, 231, 232
    Facsimile of part of letter from 60
Journal of the Welsh Folk-Song Society 94–5, 206, 207, 208, 216, 220, 221, 222, 223
    see also *Cylchgrawn Cymdeithas Alawon Gwerin Cymru*
Journey to Snowdon (1781) 59
'Joy, Health, Love and Peace' 79
Judas Maccabeus (Handel) 192
Julius Caesar 2

'Karoli' 25
Kefn ewin 10
Kerry, *co. Montgomery* 137
Key signatures 128, 129
Kidson, Frank 208
Kidwelly 80, 82
'King Solomon' 181
'King's Farewell' 36, 45
'King's Health, The' 31
'King's Round' 31

Knitting evenings 71
Knox Psalter 26
'Korffiniwr' 10
Kynaston, Nathaniel 38

'La-da Li, a La-da Lo' 100–1
'Labandala Shot' 31
Lady Huntingdon's Chapel 194
'Lady Owen's Delight' 45
'Lady Puleston's Delight' 66
Lampeter 77
'Landlord Fill the Flowing Bowl' 188
Landlords 115
Lark 205
'Lass of Patie's Mill, The' 52
Last Leaves of traditional Ballads and Ballad Airs 217
'Last Rose of Summer, The' 199
Latin language 26, 39, 41, 105
Lays of My Land, The (1896) see *Alawon Fy Ngwlad*
'Leave Land' 31, 32, 36, 115
    see also 'Gadael Tir'
Leeds 41
Lent 98
'Let Mary Live Long' 117
    see also 'Hir Oes i Fair'
Lewes, Dr —., *of co. Pembroke* 150
Lewis, David, *adjudicator and music teacher* 198
Lewis, *Sir* John Herbert, *M.P. for co. Flint* 208
Lewis, Kitty (*later* Mrs Kitty Idwal Jones) 208, 211
Lewis, Mostyn 208
Lewis, *Lady* Ruth Herbert (*née* Caine) 115, 208, 209, 210, 211, 222, 225
Lhuyd, Edward 22, 77, 82, 230, 233
'Lilliburlero' 24
Literary societies 170
Liverpool, 214
Llanbryn-mair 178
Llandaf Cathedral 163
Llandderfel 57
'Llandovery' 193
Llandrillo 22
Llandyfaelog 146
Llandysul 86
Llanegryn 87
'Llanerch-y-medd' 89, 90
Llangadfan see Jones, William, *Llangadfan*
Llangamarch 177

Llangollen
   Eisteddfod (1858) 75, 181, 192, 194, 238
'Llangollen Market' 181
Llangyndeyrn 145
Llangynwyd 73, 77, 83, 233
   Illustration of 'calennig' at 83
Llanidloes 175, 197, 212
   Choral Society 175
Llanover, Lady see Hall, Lady Augusta
Llanrhaeadr-ym-Mochnant 80
Llanrhystud 219
Llanrwst 203
Llansilin 30
'Llantrisant' 175–6
Llatai (bird messenger) 40, 146, 153, 168, 181, 182, 205, 217, 237
Llawr-y-glyn 202
Lleddf gywair 11
'Llef Caerwent' 184
'Llew Tegid' see Jones, Lewis David (1851–1928)
Llewelyn, Thomas David, 'Llewelyn Alaw' (1828–79) 23, 167, 170, 181, 183-93, 194, 199, 201, 221, 239, 240
'Llewelyn Alaw' see Llewelyn, Thomas David (1828–79)
Lleweni 17, 23, 24, 25, 37, 39
'Lliw'r Gwinwydd' 141
   see also 'Clod Gwen'
'Lliw Gwyn Rhosyn yr Haf' 209–10
'Lloer Dirion Lliw'r Dydd' 197–8
Llur (anterliwt) 122
'Llwyn Onn' 61, 63, 87
Llyfr Cerdd Dannau (1913) 241
Llyfr Coch Hergest 77
'Llyfr George Tudur Y Salmwr' 236
Llywelyn, Thomas, 'o Regoes' 236
Llywelyn ap Gruffudd, Prince of Wales 23
   see also 'Arglwydd Llywelyn'
'Loath to Depart' 52, 115
   see also 'Anhawdd Ymadel'
London 17, 24, 35, 39, 40–1, 42, 49, 50, 51, 52, 57, 58, 61, 68, 71, 107, 134, 142, 158, 162, 163, 165, 176, 192–3, 204, 206, 208, 231
   London Welsh Society (Gwyneddigion) 163
   Nassau Street Welsh chapel 208
   National Eisteddfod (1909) at 208
   'Polly Perkins of Paddington Green' 199

Powel, —. (father and son, temp. George II), harpers 231
Royal Academy of Music 192–3
Royal College of Music 49
Royal College of Science 204
Vauxhall Gardens 162
'London Apprentice' 31
'Lord Sandwich's Farewell' 31
   see also 'Digby's Farewell'
'Lord Strain's Fancy' 44
Love 146, 217
Love messenger see Llatai
Love songs 30, 73, 153, 166, 167, 200, 214, 216, 217, 220, 222
'Love's a Sweet Passion' 35, 36
Low Countries 31
LP recordings 223
Luck 83–4, 86, 98
Ludlow 22
Lullaby 58
'Lusty Gallant' 17, 31
Lute 8, 11, 18, 125
'Lycidas' 42
Lyre 1, 2

'Mab Addfwyn, Y' 221
Mabinogion, The 245
MacDonald, Sara, Gaiman, Patagonia 107
McVeigh, Simon 49
Macaronic songs 183, 213
Madrigals 18
'Mae Gen i Swllt' 226–7
   see also 'I've Got Sixpence'
'Mae Gennyf Fi Fwthyn a Gardd' 221–2
'Mae Gwyr Ifanc' 189
Maelgwn Gwynedd 1, 163
Maid of Cefn Ydfa, The 73
Maid of Sker, The 73
Major mode 11, 66, 129, 149, 153, 156, 166, 171, 174, 188, 195, 201, 221, 245
'Mak y delgi' 10
'Mak y mwn hir' 10
Malchair, Jean-Baptiste, violinist 158, 159–60
'Mall Sims'/'Male Sums'/'Mael Syms'/ 'Mael Swm' 12, 37, 48, 62
   see also 'Symlen Ben Bys'
'Malldod Dolgellau' 50, 232
'Malltraeth' 66, 67
Mallwyd 227
'Mantell Siani' 242–3

275

Index

Manuscripts 65, 135, 150, 159, 150, 160, 162, 178, 181, 183–4, 185, 190, 191, 199, 200, 220, 222, 236
   see also Bangor MS 2255; Bangor Pontifical; Bennett, Nicholas; Edwards, Maurice/Morris; Jenkins, John, 'Ifor Ceri' (1770–1829); Llewelyn, Thomas David, 'Llewelyn Alaw' (1828–79); 'Llyfr George Tudur Y Salmwr'; 'Melus-geingciau Deheubarth Cymru'; 'Melus-seiniau Cymru'; 'Orpheus' manuscript; Peate, William, *cobbler of Llanbrynmair*; Penpont Antiphonal; 'Philomusus'; Robert ap Huw
Marches 65, 114, 135, 151, 184, 200
   see also 'Marts'; 'Monk's March'; 'Napoleon's Retreat March'
Marching songs 140, 146, 153
'Margaret Fwyn ach Evan' 44
Mari Lwyd 72–7, 87, 91, 97, 100, 167, 181, 233
   Tunes 86
'Mari Lwyd Farewell' 74
Marloes 78
Markets 199
'Marts' 91
Marwnadau see Elegies
Mary, *mother of Jesus* 87, 96–7, 103
Mary of Poulton's Chapel 19
Mary Tudor, *queen of England* 26
Masques 62
Matins, lauds and vespers 6
Mawl yr Arglwydd (1816) 173
May carols 53, 98–9, 107, 119, 130, 131, 142, 200, 231, 232
May carol tune 131
Maypole 99, 101
Measures *see Mesurau*
Medieval ecclesiastical music 6, 230, 231
'Megan a Gollodd ei Gardas' 39, 52, 62
   see also 'Pegi Hath Lost Hur Garter'
'Meillionen' 48, 52, 66, 131
'Meillionen o Feirionydd' 39
'Mel Wefus Deheubarth' 144
Melismas 50, 99, 113
Melody 220
   Melodic style 149, 207
'Melus-geinciau Deheubarth Cymru' 138, 139, 141, 151, 156
'Melus-seiniau Cymru' 139–56, 193, 200
Mendelssohn, Felix 202

'Mentra Gwen' 54, 63, 112–13, 144, 153, 156, 160–1, 232, 236
   see also 'Venture Gwen'
'Merch Ifanc o'n Ben Boreu' 120
'Merch Megan' 159, 165, 184
'Merch y Melinydd' 166
Merioneth, *county* 79, 178
   see also Dolgellau; Dolserau; Harlech; Llandderfel; Llanegryn; Mallwyd; 'Mwynder Meirionydd'; 'Mwynen Meirionydd'; 'Palé Hall
Merlin 22
'Merryman' 72
Merthyr Tydfil 170, 171, 184, 192, 213
   'Cân Merthyr' 213
   Merthyr Tydfil Volunteers, The 146
   National Eisteddfod (1881) at 192
   'Trigolion Plwyf Merthyr' 184
'Mesur Carol Haf' 131
Mesur Salm 26
Mesurau (measures) 10, 142, 143
Metamorphoses (Ovid) 11
'Methinks the Poor Town Has Been Troubled Too Long' 45
Methodist Revival (1735—) 29, 157, 173, 174, 175, 177
   Anti-Methodist *anterliwt* 124
Metrical psalms 26, 30
   Facsimile of *Llyfr y Psalmau* (1621) 27
'Mi Fuais yn Medi'r Cynhaea'' 225
'Mi Godais yn Fore' 87
'Mi Welais Rhyfeddod' 150–1
Mills, *family, of Llanidloes* 175
   Henry 175
   James 175
   Richard 175, 238
Milton, John 42
Milkmaid's song 129
'Milder to Melder' 81–2
Military songs 146, 151
Minor mode 129, 149, 153, 156, 166, 171, 174, 188, 201, 245
Minstrels 7, 87, 199
'Minuet in Ariadne' 52
Minuets 48, 52, 62, 64, 65, 66, 67
Miser (*anterliwt* character) 122–3
Miserliness 144
'Miss Corbett of Shawbury Park's Minuet' 67
'Mock Nightingale' 45
Modal airs/tunes 141, 201, 208–9
Modes 11, 188, 220

see also Aeolian/la mode; Dorian/
    re mode; Major mode; Minor mode
Modulating vocal line 142
'Moes Hen Salmon' 45
'Monday Morning' 121
    see also 'Dydd Llun y Bore'
'Monk's March' 232
    see also 'Ymdaith Mwngc'
'Monsieur's Almain' 38, 45
    see also 'Hen Syr Salmon, Yr'; 'Moes
    Hen Salmon'; 'Moses Solomon';
    'Mounsier Salmon'
Montgomery, *county* 108, 178, 199, 202,
    231, 232
    see also Ceri/Kerry; Darowen; Gwynne,
    John, *of Darowen*; Llanbryn-mair;
    Llanidloes; Llawr-y-glyn
Moral maxims 121
Moral songs 142, 144, 199
Moore, Thomas 199
Moreton Castle, *co. Salop* 67
'Morfa Rhuddlan' 24, 37, 39–40, 48, 62,
    147–9, 232
    see also 'Rhuddlan Marsh'
Morgan, *Sir* Charles, *of Tredegar Park* 164
Morgan, Dafydd Siencyn 146
Morgan, David, *of Llanidloes* 197
'Morgan Jones o'r Dolau Gwyrddion' 116–17
'Morgan's Thoughts' 39
'Morganwg. Morris Dance Tune' 25
'Morganwg cyhydedd 8 a 7' 128
Morley, Thomas 7
Morris, John, *Y Canorion* 205, 206, 219
Morris, Lewis, *of Anglesey* 8, 11, 30, 39, 41,
    127, 229, 242
Morris, Richard, *of Anglesey* 23, 36–9, 41,
    48–9, 51, 58, 68, 87, 88–9, 91, 110,
    112, 123, 127, 147
Morris, William, *of Anglesey* 39
Morris dancing 25, 100, 101, 131
    Tunes 25–6, 101–2, 131
    see also 'North Welch Morris'; 'Staines
    Morris'; 'Welsh Morris Dance'
Morys, Huw (1622–1709) 30–3, 35, 40,
    115, 122, 141, 184, 239
'Moses Solomon' 45
Mostyn, *co. Flint* 210
Motival tunes 20, 67
'Mounsier Salmon' 45
Mozart, Wolfgang Amadeus 175, 203
Munday, Anthony 23
Murder ballads 115

Music hall 199
Musical and Poetical Relicks of the Welsh Bards
    (1784 and 1794) 13, 23, 24, 49–50,
    57–9, 61–3, 66–7, 124, 134, 142, 144,
    152, 156, 157, 160–1, 184, 190
Musical education 176, 198
Musical instruments, prejudice against 175
Musical intervals 186
Musical literacy 228
Musical periodicals 198–9
Musical Union *see* Aberystwyth
Musicians 2 and *passim*
'Mwynder Meirionydd' 44, 158
'Mwynen Cynwyd' 23
'Mwynen Gwynedd' 22, 63
'Mwynen Llangyndeyrn' 145
'Mwynen Mai' 53, 68, 99
'Mwynen Meirionydd' 66, 67
'Mwynen Merch' 220–1
'Mwynen Môn' 45, 52, 62
'My Lady Byram/Biron/Bryan' 43–4
'Myfyrdod neu Ddeusyfiad Cantores'
    12–13, 25, 37
'Mynach Dû, Y' 153–4
    see also 'Black Friar'
'Mynyddog' *see* Davies, Richard (1833–77)
Myvyrian Archaiology 8

Nantgarw 73
Nantglyn 165
Nant-y-moch, *co. Cardigan* 224
'Napoleon's Retreat March' 184
Nashe, Thomas (1567–c.1601) 17
Nassau Street Welsh Chapel, *London* 208
National Anthem ('Glan Rhondda') 103,
    183
'National' songs 194, 195, 198
National Eisteddfod 192, 195, 204, 244,
    246
    Cymdeithas yr Eisteddfod Genedlaethol
    192
    London (1909) 208
    Merthyr Tydfil (1881) 192
National History Museum (*formerly* the
    Welsh Folk Museum), *St Fagans* 79, 84,
    100, 127, 211, 222–3, 225, 234
National Library of Wales, *Aberystwyth* 61,
    181, 183, 204, 208, 211, 215
National Melodies of England, Ireland,
    Scotland and Wales (1810) 162
National Museum of Wales, *Cardiff* 204
Nationalism, use of folk airs in 208

Index

'Naw Gafr gorniog' 94
'Nefar Beyond' 81
Neath, Vale of 166
'Neithiwr ac Echnos' 24, 31, 115
New Citharen Lessons (1609–29) 18
New Year 83–7
    New Year's Day 98
    New Year's Eve 54
    see also Calennig
New Zealand 207
'Newcastle' (tune) 24
Newcastle, Duchess of 49
Night-visit song 187
Nightingale 205
'Nightingale, The' 67
Nonconformists 97, 130, 173, 176, 203
    British schools 203
Nonsense Songs 190, 217
Normans 6
North Wales wren song, collected in 1976 81
'North Welch Morris' 25, 39
Norwegians 5
'Nos Galan' 52, 54, 58, 59, 190
Noson lawen 149, 196, 228
Noson Lawen (1949 Welsh-language film) 223
Noswyl Fair 94
'Not for Joe' 199
Notation, unconventional 129
Nursery songs 222
'Nutmeg a Ginger Deheubarth' 237
'Nutmeg and Ginger' 151
'Nutmegs and Ginger' 125, 151

'O Deued Pob Cristion' 209
'O Gwcw, O Gwcw' 214
'O Wela Ni'n Dyfod' 75–6
Odington, Walter 5
Odikle 41, 231
'Oes Gafr eto?' 93, 95
'Of Noble Race Was Shenkin' 50, 52
Offa's Dyke 33, 155
'Old Darby' 189–90
'Old Hundredth' 30
    see also 'Hen Ganfed, Yr'
'Old Tune Room, The' 198–9
Operas 176
Operettas 204
Oratorio 208
    see also Creation, The; *Elijah*; *Judas Maccabeus*

Orchestras 176
Orchestration 204
'Orddigan Hun Gwenllian' 63, 64
    see also 'Caniad Hun Wen Llian'; 'Erddigan Hun Gwenllian'; 'Hun Gwenllian'
Organist 194
'Orpheus' *see* James, James, 'Iago ap Ieuan' (1833–1902)
'Orpheus' manuscript (NLW Minor Deposit 150) 208, 233, 238
'Os Gwelwch yn Dda Ga'i Grempog?' 98
'Os Wyt Richard' 45
'Ostler' 72
Ovid 11
'Owain Alaw' *see* Owen, John (1821–83)
Owen, Aneurin (1792–1851), *of Nantglyn* 165, 190
Owen, David, 'Dafydd y Garreg Wen' (1709–39) 67
    see also 'Dewisol Gân Dafydd o'r Garreg-Wen'
Owen, Humphrey, *of Dolgellau* 105
Owen, John, *nephew of Lewis Morris* 8
Owen, John, 'Owain Alaw' (1821–83) 194–8
Owen, Trefor M. 223
Owens, Ffoulke 35
Oxen 22
    'Cainc y Cathreiwr' 129
    Glamorgan oxen or plough chant 128
    Songs, 3, 129, 151, 153
    Ychen Bannog, Yr 11, 22
Oxford 35, 41, 137, 158
'Oxford Scholar and his Penny Cow-Heel, An' 45

'Pa Bryd y Deui Etto?' 171–2
Packington's Pound' 115
Palé Hall, *co. Merioneth* 178
'Pan O'wn y Gwanwyn' 166
'Pant Corlan yr Wyn' 63
'Pantycelyn' *see* Williams, William (1717–91)
Paris 193
'Parlement, The' 125
Parlour songs 64, 183, 191, 199
Parrots 182
Parry, David, *son of John Parry, Ruabon* 52
Parry, J. 145
Parry, John, 'Bardd Alaw' (1776–1851) 52, 62, 68, 142, 162–3, 164, 165, 175, 183, 190, 193

278

Parry, John, Ruabon, (1710?–82) 38, 40–1, 48, 49, 50, 52, 57, 58, 59, 63, 65, 68, 99, 110, 127–8, 141, 157, 162, 166, 171, 178, 183, 194
   'Blind Parry's School' 41
Parry, Owen, *farmer, of Dwyran* 214
Parry, S. 145
'Parson of the Parish, The' 22
Part-songs 172, 244
Patagonia (Welsh Colony) 107, 207
'Pebyll Penon' 132–3
'Pe Cawn i Hon' 172
Peate, Iorwerth Cyfeiliog 233
Peate, William, *cobbler of Llanbryn-mair* 178, 190–1, 200
'Peg a Ramsey' 17, 88
'Pegi Hath Lost Hur Garter' 39
   see also 'Megan a Gollodd ei Gardais'
Pembroke, *county* 71, 77, 78, 79, 81, 82, 84, 142, 145, 150
   see also Marloes; St David's Cathedral
'Pen Rhaw' 23, 36, 61
Pencerdd 2–3, 7, 10, 42
'Pencerdd Gwalia' see Thomas, John (1826–1913)
'Pencraig' 50, 52
Pennill (pl. *Penillion*) 28, 49, 50, 59, 62, 69, 115, 116, 128, 153, 167, 170, 178, 207
   Hen benillion 69
   Penillion telyn 20
   Penillion singing (*canu penillion*) 23, 31, 49, 50, 57, 59–61, 71, 128, 164, 165, 170, 194–5, 200, 241–6
   Penillion tunes 54, 58, 59, 68
Pennant, Thomas 59–61
Penpont Antiphonal 6
Pentatonic (music) 11, 74, 217
'Pepper is Black' 17, 122
Pepys collection 45
'Per Alaw' 45
'Per Oslef' 45, 67
   see also 'Sweet Richard'
Per-seiniau Cymru 139, 153–6
Perllan 80, 82
Persia 119
Peru 119
Phallic dances 122, 126
Phillips, Ben 222, 223
Phillips, Dorothy 79
Phillips, Elizabeth 79
'Philomusus' (*pseud.*) see Gwynne, John, *of Darowen*

Phiol 80
Phonograph 209, 211, 212
Piano (Pianoforte) 66, 69, 142, 157, 160, 166, 192, 193, 195, 200, 201, 204
Pibwr-lwyd, *co. Carmarthen* 170
Picton, *Sir* Thomas 142, 146
'Pigau'r Dur' 52
Pills to Purge Melancholy (1719–20) 37, 67, 231
Pipes/Pipers 3, 4, 7, 18, 25
Pitch pipe 106
Playford, John 37
Playing cards 105
Plays 176
   see also Anterliwt
Plethiad y pedwarbys (four-finger plait) 10
Plough 72
   Ox-ploughing songs 128–9
Plygain 39, 122, 178, 227
   Airs/tunes 178, 200
   Carols 55, 105–14, 122, 141, 189, 223, 227
'Plygain Carols' (recordings) 223
'Plygeingan' 196
'Plygiad y Bedol' 47
'Plygiad y Bedol Fach' 23
PMP devices 228
'Pob Peth' 64
Poetry 137, 138, 141, 142, 143, 146, 164, 165, 195
Poets 2, 50, 63, 66, 69, 77, 98, 107, 118, 134, 135, 137, 141, 151, 153, 154, 157, 163, 186, 187, 195, 199
   'Poets of the dung-hill' 18
   'Poets who sing at fairs' 18
   see also Bards
'Poginili Pigynelo' 39
Polkas 184
'Polly Perkins of Paddington Green' 199
Polyphonic music 5, 10
Pontarfynach 212
Pont-rhyd-y-groes 212
Porthmadog 203
Postmaster 151
Poulton vigil 19, 103
Powel, —. (father and son, *temp.* George II), *harpers, London* 231
Powell, Phillip (*c.*1635), *of Brecon* 18
Powell, Tom, *of Pwllheli* 148
Powis, Earl of (William Herbert, 1665–1745) 40

Powys 64
Powys Cymmrodorion Society 164
'Pretty Peggy' 65
Presbyterians 173
Price, *family, of Gogerddan* 177
Price, Thomas, 'Carnhuanawc' (1787–1848) 165
Prichard, Morris, *of Anglesey, father of the Morris brothers* 39
Prichard, Rhys, *vicar of Llandovery* (1579?–1644) 26, 28, 29, 107, 121
Prichard, Thomas ('Twm bach'), *of Coety* 14
Prince Rupert of the Rhine (1619–82) 36, 39, 143–4
'Prince Rupert's Conceit' 36, 39
'Prince Rupert's Delight' 143–4
'Prince's Fancy' 143–4
'Princess Royal' 121
Printing presses 39, 199
Profiad 10, 12
Prophecies 35
Prophets 2
Prose settings (of *cerdd dant*) 245
Protestantism 26, 28, 29, 106, 173
Prys, Edmwnd 22, 26–8, 30
    Facsimile of *Llyfr y Psalmau* (1621) by 27
Psalms 6, 26–8, 174, 191
Psaltery 18
Pughe, William Owen 68, 135, 236
Pulli cantus 105
Punch (drink) 10
'Punch and Judy' 72, 100
Punning verse 19
Purcell, Henry, *composer* (1659–95) 23
Puritans 173
Puzzles 88
Pwllheli 148
Pwnco 72–3, 97, 167
'Pwyo Pen y Gofid' 133

Quadrilles 184
Quakers 173
'Queen Dido' 51
    see also 'Gwên Dando'
'Queen Fancy' 65
'Queen of Prussia's Waltz' 184
'Queen's Dream' 52, 125, 151
    see also 'Breuddwyd y Frenhines'
'Queen's Dream ffordd fyrraf' 151
Queen's Scholarship 203
'Queenes Goeing to the Parliament, The' 125, 235

Question-and-answer songs 207
Quicksteps 184

Radnor, *county* 181
'Ragad or Reged' 67
Railways
    'Aberdare Railway Polka' 184
    Cheap excursions 181
Ranz des Vaches 129
'Ravish'd Lover, The' 64, 140
Red Book of Hergest, The 77, 233
Red Dragon 200
Reels 184
Reichel, *Lady* Charity Mary 205
Reichel, *Sir* Harry, *Principal of UCNW, Bangor* 204, 205
'Rejoice and be Merry' 108
Relicks see Musical and Poetical Relicks of the Welsh Bards
Religion 157
Religious revivals 203, 206, 207, 209
Religious prejudice and folk-songs 207
Religious songs 130
Renaissance 42
'Respectable' words 199
Restoration of the Monarchy (1660) 173
'Rhaid Sirio' 38, 45
'Rhuddlan Marsh' 52, 147
    see also 'Morfa Rhuddlan'
'Rhyfelgan ap Ifan Bennaeth' 47
Rhymes 148
Rhys, Siôn Dafydd 18
Rhys ap Gruffydd, *Lord of Deheubarth* (1132–97) 3, 163
Rhythm/rhythmic 128, 129, 130, 132, 133, 134, 142, 143, 156, 165, 175, 189, 207, 216, 220, 244
Richards, *family, of Darowen* 141
Richards, Henry Brinley (1817–85) 157, 192–3
Richmond Heiress, The (1693) 50
Riddles 36, 71, 88, 90
Rituals 130
Robert ap Huw, *harper* (1580–1665) 8–12, 17, 18, 23, 39, 41, 47, 51, 61, 63, 64, 67, 135, 229, 231
    Illustration from manuscript of 9
Roberts, Bob, *Tai'r Felin* 222, 223
Roberts, David, 'Telynor Mawddwy' (1875–1956) 242
Roberts, Elis (d. 1789) 122
Roberts, Grace, *of Liverpool* 214

Roberts, John, *of Henllan* 174
Roberts, John, 'Ieuan Gwyllt' (1822–77) 5, 86, 198
Roberts, John, 'Telynor Cymru' (1816–94) 177–8
Roberts, John, 'Y Cynjer' 178
Roberts, Richard, *blind harper* 162, 178
Robin Clidro 115
Rock groups 223
'Roedd yn y Wlad Honno' 118–19
'Rogero'/'Rhaid Sirio'/'Yr Hen Rogero Bengoch' 18, 22, 23, 38, 45
Roman Catholicism 26, 97, 102–3, 106, 173
    Anti-Papist verses 35
    Cistercian order 6
    Pre-Reformation carol 106
    Recusant printing presses, 39
Romans 1, 2, 41, 83
Rondellus 5–6
Rounds 18
Rowland, Dafydd, *crwth*-player 22
Rowland, Daniel, *Methodist reformer* (1713–90) 173
Ruabon 52
    see also 'Clychau Rhiwabon'; Parry, John, *Ruabon*
Running notes 186
Rŵm ford 72
Royal Academy of Music *see* London
Royal College of Music *see* London
Royal College of Science *see* London
Rupert, Prince *see* Prince Rupert of the Rhine

Sacred music 174, 175
Sacred poetry 121
Saer, D. Roy 222–3, 234
St David, *patron saint* 6
St David's Cathedral 6
St David's Day 6
'St David's Day' (tune) 39, 195
St Eluned 3, 25
St Fagans (National History Museum *formerly* Welsh Folk Museum) 79, 84, 100, 127, 152, 211, 222–3, 225, 233–4
St John's birch 101
St John the Baptist, Feast of (24 June) 101
St Patrick 2
'St Patrick's Day in the Morning' 183
'Saith Rhyfeddod, Y' 144–5
Salisbury 7
    see also Sarum Use

Salon songs 136, 157, 187
Sanders, Ernest 5
Sankey and Moody 199
Sarum Use 6
Satire/satyrical 50, 59
Saunders, Erasmus (1670–1724) 29
'Sawdl y Fuwch' 45
'Sbonc bogel' 122–3, 126
Scordatura 11
'Scotch haymakers' 37–8
Scotland 11, 37, 81, 112, 160, 162, 199, 217
    Airs/tunes 22, 39, 52, 160
    'Scotch music' 158
    'Scottish Manner' 128
    Western Isles psalm-singing 6
Scott, *Sir* Walter 59, 67
Seasons
    Seasonal festivities 71–103
    Seasonal games 127
    Seasonal songs 222
'Sedany, or Dargason' 22, 23, 42
'See the Building' 39, 110, 115
    see also 'Gwêl yr Adeilad'
'Sel Imi Ffo' 38
Selection of Welsh melodies, A (1809) 162
Sequences (musical) 135, 137
'Serch Hudol' 67
'Seren Ddydd, Y' 174–5
'Sergeant' (*Mari Lwyd*) 72
Sextons 122
Sexual promiscuity 176
Shanty 226
Sharp, Cecil 208
Sheep-shearing 71
'Shenkin' 62
Shipwrecks 115
'Shoe bend' 23, 47
Shon Robert, *shoemaker, of Dolgellau* 105
Shrewsbury 35
Shropshire 164
    see also High Arcal; 'Miss Corbett of Shawbury Park's Minuet'; Moreton Castle; Shrewsbury; Strange, *Lord, of Knockin*
Shrove Tuesday 98
'Siani Aeth am Serch' 138–9
'Sidanen' 17, 22–3, 37, 42–3
    'Skower Sidanen' 18
    'Welsh Sydanen' 23
Sidney, *Sir* Philip 18
'Sigl Din ar y Drain' 132

Sill am dant 241
'Since Celia's My Foe' 31, 38
　see also 'Irish Tune, The'; 'Sel Imi Ffo'; 'Sunseila'
Singing schools 174
Singing festivals 176, 183
Siôn Dafydd Rhys see Rhys, Siôn Dafydd
'Siôn Singer' see Williams, John
Sixty of the most admired Welsh airs (1803) 157
Slurs (musical) 51, 137, 142
Skipping 189
'Skower Sydanen' see 'Is gywair Sidanen'; 'Sidanen'
'Snapping' (musical) 189
'So Early in the Morning' 87
Soap 215
'Soldier's Life' 24, 52
　see also 'Bywyd y Milwr'
Soldiers 146
　'Galar Gwraig y Milwr' 195–6
　Soldier's farewell ballad 169
'Solo-and-chorus' songs 207
Songs from Oral Tradition 222
Songs of Wales, The (1873) 68, 136, 137, 157, 166, 192–3, 194, 195
'Spanish Gipsy' 24
'Spanish Pavan' 31, 35
Specimens of Various Styles of Music (1806–7) 40, 157–60
Sports 25, 103
Spring carols 130
Spring celebrations 98–103, 131
Stable-loft songs (*canu llofft stabal*) 196, 207, 214, 223, 228
'Staines Morris' 25
'Star of the County Down, The' 188
Statute of Gruffudd ap Cynan 7
Stephens, Bertie 222
Stonehenge 42
Story of the Harp in Wales, The 12
Story-tellers/story-telling 2, 71, 101
Stradling, Sir John 18
Strange, Lord, of Knockin, co. Salop 44
Strata Florida, *abbey* 6
Strasburg Psalter 26
Stukeley, William 42
'Stwffwl, Y' 67
'Sumer is icumen in' 5
Summer 98
Summer Solstice 101
Sunday 102

'Sunseila' 31
'Susan Lygad-ddu' 121
　see also 'Black-Eyed Susan'
'Susannah' 54, 68
Swansea 164, 176
'Sweet Richard' 39–40, 45, 52, 67, 158–9, 184, 232
　see also 'Os Wyt Richard'; 'Per Alaw'; 'Per Oslef'; 'Welch Richard'
Switzerland
　Swiss mountain songs 129
Sydanen see 'Sidanen'
'Symlen Ben Bys' 48, 62
Symphonies 50, 51, 53, 59, 134, 143, 146, 203, 234, 236
　Symphonic music for orchestra 193
Syncopation 201, 221
'Syr Harri Ddu' 50, 66

Tablature 8–10, 11–12
Takiad y fawd (thumb stop) 10
Tailor 211
'Talaith Aberffraw' 67
Tales 68, 127, 225
'Talhaiarn' see Jones, John (1810–70)
Taliesin 22
Talygarth Isa 25
Tannau 99, 107
Tant Aur, Y (1911) 242
'Tap the barrel' 72
Tape-rcordings 222
Taverns 114, 115, 149, 157, 163, 170, 174, 176, 192, 207
　Eisteddfod in 183
　Taproom songs 183
　Tunes 29
Tea-drinking 118
Teifi valley 29, 78
'Telynor Cymru' see Roberts, John (1816–94)
'Telynor Mawddwy' see Roberts, David (1875–1956)
Temperance
　Choirs 170
　Eisteddfod 176
　Festival (1836) 176
　Marches 176
　Meetings 199
　Movement 176
　Singing festivals 183
　Societies 176
　Songs 176

Tempo 129
Tenby 78
Tessitura 152
Teulu Abram Wood 177
Theatres 176
    Lack of 122
    Music 64
Third Book of the Compleat Country Dancing-Master (1735) 25
Thirty New and Choice Country Dances (1731) 134
Thomas, David, 'Dafydd Ddu Eryri' (1759–1822) 68, 93–4, 142
Thomas, Dylan 244–6
Thomas, John, *fiddler* (c.1730–60) 23, 58, 64, 65, 67, 99, 110, 112, 123–4, 125, 126, 152
Thomas, John, 'Ieuan Ddu' (1795–1871) 170–3, 193, 207, 221, 238
Thomas, John, *Maes-y-fedw* 222, 223
Thomas, John, 'Pencerdd Gwalia' (1826–1913) 10, 12
Thomas, Margaretta 73
Thomas, Simon, author of *Hanes y Byd a'r Amseroedd* (1721) 102
Thomas, T. Soley 202
Thomas, Wyn, *Bangor University* 227
Thomson, George 67, 141, 160–2, 190, 237
'Three Ravens, The' 199
Time signatures 128, 130, 189
Tiompán 2
'Tit for Tat' 64
'Titrwm Tatrwm' 214–15
'Tomorrow Shall be My Dancing Day' 108
'Ton Carol ar Gyffiniau Clawdd Offa' 155
'Ton Deuair' 88, 135
'Tôn y Ceiliog Du' 232
'Tôn y Fammaeth' 63
'Tôn y Melinydd' 184, 196
Tonality 129, 223
Tongue twisters 36, 88, 96
Tonic Sol-Fa 192, 216
Topographica Hibernica 3, 4
'Toriad y Dydd' 67, 158
'Tra Bo Dau' 216
Traditional music 1 and *passim*
Trawsfynydd 219
Treacle toffee 105
'Treban Morganough' 134
'Tri Chwarter Tôn' 88
'Tri Tharawiad Deheubarth, Y' (neu 'Gadael Tir y Ffordd Hwyaf') 142

'Tri Tharawiad Gwynedd' 32, 142
'Tri Tharawiad Trichwmwd' 146
Tri-thrawiad (metre) 31–2, 35, 36, 88, 90–1, 107, 116, 119, 142, 153
Triads (*Trioedd*) 218
Triban 36, 45, 88, 97, 115, 116, 119, 128, 131, 132, 133, 134, 137, 143
    Airs/tunes 131, 132, 236
'Triban deublyg' 128, 131
    see also 'Dawns Triban Deublyg'
'Triban Lewis Llwyd' 45
'Triban Morganwg' 36, 59, 88, 134, 143, 167, 168
    Facsimile of music of 60
'Triban Morganwg' (with symphonies) 143, 236
    (omitting symphonies) 234
Tribannau Morgannwg 133
Trichwmwd 146
'Trigolion Plwyf Merthyr' 184
Trios 223
Triple Harp 62–3, 165, 177
    see also Harp
Triple time 116, 148, 149, 195
'Tro Tant or Is gower' 10–11, 12–13
    see also 'Is gywair (is gower)'
'Tro'r Tant' 13
    see also 'Erddigan Tro'r Tant'
Trochaic tetrameter 21
Trochaic quatrain 115, 116
'Troiad y Droell' 66
'Tros y Garreg' 24, 161–2, 232
Trumpet 18
'Trwm Galon' 35
    see also 'Calon Drom'; 'Galon Drom, Y'; 'Heavy Heart'
'Trwsgwl mawr' 10
'Trymder' 154–5, 200–1
Tudors 6
    Tudor England 36
    Tudor Ground 47
    Tudor Period 39
    see also Elizabeth I, *queen of England*; Henry VII, *king of England*; Henry VIII, *king of England*; Mary Tudor, *queen of England*
Tumblers 18
Twelfth Night (6 January) 77, 78
    Twelfth Day 78
    Twelfth-tide 79-80
'Twelve Days of Christmas, The' 91
'Twll yn ei Boch' 45

'Twm bach', *of Coety, see* Prichard, Thomas
'Twm o'r Nant' *see* Edwards, Thomas (1739–1810)
'Twm y Sane' *alias* 'Twm y Weaver' *alias* 'Twm y Dafedd' 212–13
'Tyb y Tywysog' 143–4
  see also 'Hoffedd y Prins Rupert'
Tyniad 10

Uchelwyr 6
'Un o Fy Mrodyr I' 93
Under Milk Wood 244–6
United States of America *see* America
Univesity of Bangor *see* Bangor, *co.* Caernarfon
University of North Wales, Bangor *see* Bangor, *co.* Caernarfon
University of Wales 204
Use of Sarum 6

Variety, The (17th cent. theatre piece) 23
Vaughan, *Sir* Robert (early 19th cent.) 164
Vaughan Williams, Ralph 208
Vauxhall Gardens *see* London
Venantius Fortunatus 1
'Venture Gwen' 160
  see also 'Mentra Gwen'
Victoria, *queen of England* 177, 178
Victorian mores 195
'Vienna' (dance) 24
  see also 'Consêt Gruffydd ap Cynan'
Vienna, Siege of (1683) 24
View of the State of Religion in the Diocese of St David's, A 29
Vigils 19, 21, 103
Viol 37, 123, 147, 205
Violin 49, 62, 66
  Notation 123, 124
  see also Fiddle
Violinist 158
  see also Barthélemon, François Hippolyte; Malchair, Jean-Baptiste
Virgin Mary 87, 96–7, 103
Vivaldi, Antonio Lucio, *composer* 65
Voice-and-harp principle 134

Wakes 25, 29
Wales 1 and *passim*
  East 155
  Mid 137, 141, 149, 164, 175, 198, 209, 224
  North 17, 77, 80–1, 87–8, 93, 95, 99, 100, 115, 121, 126, 127, 128, 133, 135, 137, 139, 141, 142, 160, 164, 166, 170, 173, 192, 194, 198, 204, 207, 208, 232, 241, 246
    see also 'North Welch Morris' 25, 39
  North-east 209
  South 77, 87, 99, 100, 101, 128, 132, 137, 138, 140, 141, 144, 145, 149, 166, 170, 176, 181, 187, 191, 192, 209, 224, 246
  South-west 225
'Wales Ground' 23
Walsh, John 48, 64, 134
'Walsingham' 22
Waltzes 184
  see also 'Dinevor Waltz'; 'Queen of Prussia's Waltz'
Ward, John 25, 31
Warfare 146
Wassail 72, 83, 93
  Airs/songs 54, 76, 91, 167
  Carols 36, 87–8, 91, 130
  Cup and drink 87
  Customs 83, 87
  Procession 93
  Verses 87
'Wassail song variant 1, air "Llanerch-y-medd"' 89
'Wassail song variant 2, air "Y Gog Lwydlas"' 89
'Wassail song variant 3, air "Y Dôn Fechan"' 90
'Wassail song variant 4, air "Llanerch-y-medd"' 90
Wassailers 88–9, 91, 96, 97, 105, 167
Waterloo, battle of (1815) 120, 142
Wedding *pwnco* 97
'Wel Dyma Ni'n Dwad' 73–5
'Welch Morgan' 39
'Welch Richard' 39
  see also 'Sweet Richard'
'Welch Whim, The' 39
'Welsh Air' (Mesur Nos Galan) 190
Welsh Folk Museum *see* National History Museum, St Fagans
Welsh folk music 1 and *passim*
Welsh Folk-Song Society 181, 203–28, 239, 245
'Welsh Ground, The' 23
  see also 'Cynghansail Cymru (Welsh ground); 'Wales Ground'
Welsh Harper, The (1839 and 1848) 68, 163

Welsh language 6–7, 17, 26, 160, 165, 173, 176, 177, 206, 208, 211, 223, 245
Welsh Laws (Hywel Dda) 1, 2, 3, 4, 42, 163
'Welsh melodies' 68
'Welsh Morris Dance' 25
Welsh Music History/Hanes Cerddoriaeth Cymru 227
Welsh musicology 195
'Welsh National Melodies and Folk-Song' (lecture) 207
Welsh National Music and Dance (1932) 222
Welsh poets and poetry *see* Bards; Poetry; Poets
Welsh publishing 35
'Welsh Sydanen' 23
  see also 'Sidanen'
Welshpool
  Eisteddfod (1824) 136, 236
Wenvoe 101
Wesley, John 173
Whitelocke, Bulstrode 152
'Whitelocke's Coranto' 62, 152, 159
  see also 'Cudyn Gwyn Ffrainc'
Whitsun 17
'Whoop! Do me no Harm, Good Man' 22
'Wil Ffidler' 210
William and Mary, *king and queen of England* 117
Williams, E. Ylltyr 136, 196
Williams, Edward, 'Iolo Morganwg' (1747–1826) 8, 20, 25, 76–7, 94, 101–2, 127–37, 142, 153, 164, 167, 170, 172, 190, 191, 235–6
  Facsimile of music in hand of 20
Williams, Evan 38, 41, 50, 51, 52, 59
Williams, *Sir* Ifor 233
Williams, *Mrs* Jane, *of Holywell Workhouse* 209
Williams, John, 'Siôn Singer' 173
Williams, John Lloyd (1854–1945) 94–5, 203–22, 228
  Photograph of 204
Williams, Maria Jane (1795–1873), *of Aberpergwm* 166–70, 171, 172, 187, 194, 207, 221
Williams, Richard, 'Dic Dywyll' (*fl.* 1822–62), *blind ballad-singer* 116
Williams, Robert, *Bethesda* 174
Williams, W. S. Gwynn, *Llangollen* 222

Williams, William, *Llandygái* 96–7
Williams, William, *Pantycelyn* 121, 173
Williams, William, 'Wil Penmorfa' (1759–1828) 40
Williams–Wynn, Sir Watkin *3rd baronet, of Wynnstay* 38, 40, 41, 48
  see also 'Consêt Syr Watkin'
Williams-Wynn, Sir Watkin, *4th baronet, of Wynnstay* 40
Williams-Wynn, Sir Watkin, *5th baronet, of Wynnstay* 164
Wind instruments 162
Winter solstice 71, 77, 83
Wise Men 106
Wood, Abram, *gypsy* 177
Wood, Jeremiah, 'Jerry Bach Gogerddan' 177
'Woodycock' 232
Work songs 222, 226
Wren
  Hunting the wren 23, 72, 77–83, 140, 233
  'King of the Birds' 78
  Wren party 97
  Wren-house 78–9
  Wren songs/tunes 77–83, 86, 200
  see also Cutty Wran; 'Cutty Wren'
Wrexham 19
'Wood Waltham Green' 39
Wynn, *of Wynnstay see* Williams-Wynn
Wynne, *family, of Maesyneuadd* 45
'Wyres Megan' 61

Ychen Bannog, Yr (The Horned Oxen) 11, 22
'Ymadawiad y Brenin' 232
'Ymdaith Mwngc' 232
  see also 'Monk's March'
'Yn Iach i Ti Gymru' 193–4
'Yn Mhontypridd Mae Mwriad' 182
'Yn Nhloty'r Sir yr Wyf yn Byw' 188
Yorkshire 4
'Ymadawiad y Brenin' 45, 184
'Ymddiddan rhwng yr Wtreswr a'r Dylluan' 18–19
'Ystafell yr Hen Alawon' ('The Old Tune Room') 198–9
'Ystafell yr Hen Alawon – Moesol a Chysegredig' 198
Ystwffl 13

Index of Music

'Adar Mân y Mynydd' 205
'A'i Di Perot Purion Per' 182
'Alawon Fy Ngwlad' 197
'Annerch i'r Derin Du' 140
'Ar Fore Dydd Nadolig' 106
'Ar Hyd y Nos' 124
'Ar Lan y Môr' 218
'Ar y Bryn Mae Caseg Felen' 225
'Awn Heddyw er Mwyn Haeddiant i Ganu Gogoniant' 108
'Awn i Fethlem' 28, 107

'Bachgen Main, Y' 119–20, 184
'Balaclafa' 201–2
'Beth Su Mor Feinion' 90–1
'Betty o Lan Sant Ffraid' 186
'Black Friar' 153–4
'Blodeu'r Dyffryn' 43–4, 48
'Blotyn Du, Y' 116, 188
'Blwyddyn Newydd Dda i Chi' 86
'Breuddwyd' 169–70
'Breuddwyd y Frenhines' 125
Bridal-contest song 97

'Cadi Ha' 99–100, 210–11
'Cainc y Cathreiwr' 129
'Cainc yr Odryddes' 130
'Caingc Llandyfaelog' 146
'Caingc y Fflemynes' 145
'Calenig' 53
Calennig Song 84
'Calon Drom' 32–3
'Cân Aberhonddu' 169
'Can ar Owain Cordolen – Y Siacced Fral' 150
'Cân Gloi'r Pwnco' 73
'Can i ddosbarthwr y Llythurau ar Nutmeg and Ginger' 151

'Cân Merthyr' 213
'Cân Twm y Sane' 213
'Cân y Berllan' 80
'Cân y Cardi' 224
'Cân y Gaethes Ddu' 149
'Canu Cwnsela' 75
'Canu'r Bugail' 94
'Cariad Cyntaf, Y' 212
'Carol Gwirod yn Drws ar Fesur Triban Morg' 88
'Carwr Gwirion, Y' 186
'Carwriaeth' 187
'Cawn Fynd Adref Fory' 86
'Cerais Ferch' 167
'Charity Mistress' 185
'Clychau Rhiwabon' 28
'Codais Heddiw'n Fore' 85
'Codiad yr Ehedydd' 241–2
'Cutty Wren' 81–2
'Cwyn Mam yng Nghyfraith' 215
'Cwyn y Prentis' 139
'Cyfri'r Geifr' 96
'Cyntaf Dydd o'r Gwyliau, Y' 92
'Cywydd deuair fyrion' 20–1

'Dacw 'Nghariad' 211
'Dadl Dau' 123
'Daeth Mari Lwyd Lawen' 77
Dan y Wenallt 244–5
'Dawns Triban Deublyg' 131–2
'Ddafad Gyrnig, Y' 168
'Ddau Farch, Y' 212
'Deffrwch Ben Teulu' 84, 135
'Deryn Du Pigfelyn, Y' 168–9
'Deryn Du Sy'n Rhodio'r Gwledydd, Y' 219
'Dewch Ymlaen' ('Haf etti'r Glocsen') 140
'Dewis Meinwen' 43–4
'Difyrwch Gwyr Caernarfon' 178–9

Index of Music

'Digan Wil Bifan Bennoeth' 47
'Diniweidrwydd' 171, 174–5
'Dôn Fechan, Y' 20, 90, 116, 117, 172
'Dros yr Afon' 171
'Dryw Bach Ydi'r Gŵr' 79
'Duke of Gloucester's March, The' 152
'Duw Gadwo'r Brenin' 118
'Dyma Wyliau Hyfryd Llawen' 21

'Eira, Yr' 182
'Erddigan Caer Waun' 61–2
'Erddigan Hun Gwenllian' 47, 137
'Erddigan Tro'r Tant' 13–14

'Fe Hwyliwyd Llestr Egwan' 226
'Fedle Fawr, Y' 54–5
'Ferch o'r Scer, Y' 167
'Ffarwel Dwm Bach' 14–15
'Ffarwel Gwŷr Aberffraw' 111–12
'Ffarwel i Aberystwyth' 219
'Ffarwel i Blwy Llangywer' 218
'Ffarwel Ned Puw' 108–10
'Ffylan Tin Tw' 124
'Flaunting Two' 123
'Fwyalchen, Y' 217
'Fwyalchen Ddu Bigfelen, Y' 183
'Fy Mrodyr a Chwiorydd' 99
'Fy Ngwen Mae'r Eira ar y Bannau' 191

'Gadael Tir y Ffordd Hwyaf' 142
'Galar Gwraig y Milwr' 195–6
'Galar Gwŷr Ffrainc' 114
'Galon Drom, Y' 32–3
'Gelynen, Y' 132 (metre), 214
'Gentle maid in secret sigh'd, A' 137
'Gerard's Mistress' 185
'Glomen, Y' 220
'Gog Lwydlas, Y' 89–90
'Gwêl yr Adeilad' 110–11
'Gwn Dafydd Ifan' 121
'Gwrandewch ar Ferch sy'n Serchog' 185
'Gwydr Glas, Y' 223–4

'Haf etti'r Glocsen' 140
'Halsing y Dryw' 78
'Heavy Heart' 32–3
'Hen Dôn Llyfr Ficer' 90–1
'Hen Erddigan Morganwg' 130
'Hên Fesur' 108
'Hen Fyharen, Yr' 217
'Hen Gainc Washaela Morganwg' 76
'Hen Ganfed, Yr' 30
'Hen Ŵr Mwyn, Yr' 206
'Hên Ŵr o'r Coed' 116
'Hen Wr o'r Coed Yn ol Dull Dyfed' 172
'Hir Oes i Fair' 117
'Hiraeth' 216
'Hob y Deri Dando' 191
'Hobed o Hilion' 197
'Hoffedd Duwc William' 146–7
'Hoffedd Glandyfroedd' 152
'Hoffedd y Prins Rupert ney Tyb y Tywysog' 143–4
'Hosanna Mwy' 155
'Hun Gwenllian' 136–7
'Hyd y Frwynen Las' 187–8
'Hyd Yma Bu'n Cerdded' 75

'I Ysgafnhau ein Gwaith' 225–6
'Iolo Morganwg: Morris Dance Tune' 26, 101–2

'Joanna' 175
'Joy, Health, Love and Peace' 79

'La-da Li, a La-da Lo' 101
'Let Mary Live Long' 117
'Llanerch-y-medd' 89, 90
'Llantrisant' 176
'Lliw Gwyn Rhosyn yr Haf' 210
'Lloer Dirion Lliw'r Dydd' 197–8

'Mab Addfwyn, Y' 221
'Mae Gen i Swllt' 227
'Mae Gennyf Fi Fwthyn a Gardd' 221–2
'Mae Gwyr Ifanc' 189
'Malchair Example' 159–60
'Mantell Siani' 243
'Margaret Fwyn ach Evan' 44
'Mari Lwyd Farewell' 74
May carol tune 131
'Mel Wefus Deheubarth' 144
'Mentra Gwen' 112–13, 161
'Merch Ifanc o'n Ben Boreu' 120
'Mesur Carol Haf' 131
'Mi Fuais yn Medi'r Cynhaea'' 225
'Mi Godais yn Fore' 87
'Mi Welais Rhyfeddod' 150–1
'Milder to Melder' 81–2
'Morfa Rhuddlan' 147–9
'Morgan Jones o'r Dolau Gwyrddion' 117
'Mwynder Meirionydd' 44
'Mwynen Mai' 53

'Mwynen Merch' 220–1
'My Lady Byram/Biron/Bryan' 43–4
'Mynach Dû, Y' 153–4

North Wales wren song, collected in 1976 81
'Nos Galan' 54, 190
'Nutmeg and Ginger' 151

'O Deued Pob Cristion' 209
'O Gwcw, O Gwcw' 214
'O Wela Ni'n Dyfod' 76
'Oes Gafr eto?' 95
'Old Darby' 189–90
'Os Gwelwch yn Dda Ga'i Grempog?' 98

'Pa Bryd y Deui Etto?' 171–2
'Pan O'wn y Gwanwyn' 166
'Pebyll Penon' 132–3
'Pe Cawn i Hon' 172
'Plygeingan' 196
'Pwyo Pen y Gofid' 133

'Queen's Dream' 125

'Rhyfelgan ap Ifan Bennaeth' 47
'Roedd yn y Wlad Honno' 118–19

'Saith Rhyfeddod, Y' 145
'Sbonc bogel' 123
'Seren Ddydd, Y' 174–5
'Siacced Fral, Y' 150
'Siani Aeth am Serch' 139
'Sidanen' 42–3

'Sigl Din ar y Drain' 132
'Sweet Richard' 158–9

'Titrwm Tatrwm' 215
'Ton Carol ar Gyffiniau Clawdd Offa' 155
'Ton Deuair' 135
'Tôn y Melinydd' 196
'Tra Bo Dau' 216
'Tri Tharawiad Deheubarth, Y' (neu 'Gadael Tir y Ffordd Hwyaf') 142
'Tri Tharawiad Gwynedd' 32, 142
'Triban Morganwg' 134, 168
'Triban Morganwg' (with symphonies) 143
'Trigolion Plwyf Merthyr' 184
'Tros y Garreg' 161–2
'Trymder' 155, 200–1
'Tyb y Tywysog' 143–4

'Un o Fy Mrodyr I' 93

'Wassail song variant 1, air "Llanerch-y-medd"' 89
'Wassail song variant 2, air "Y Gog Lwydlas"' 89–90
'Wassail song variant 3, air "Y Dôn Fechan"' 90
'Wassail song variant 4, air "Llanerch-y-medd"' 90
'Wel Dyma Ni'n Dwad' 73, 74
'Welsh Air' (Mesur Nos Galan) 190

'Yn Iach i Ti Gymru' 193–4
'Yn Mhontypridd Mae Mwriad', 182
'Yn Nhloty'r Sir yr Wyf yn Byw' 188